The New American Middle School

Third Edition

The New American Middle School

Educating Preadolescents in an Era of Change

Jon Wiles
University of North Florida
Joseph Bondi
University of South Florida

Merrill
Prentice Hall

Upper Saddle River, New Jersey,
Columbus, Ohio

Library of Congress Cataloging-in-Publication Data

Wiles, Jon.
    The new American middle school: educating preadolescents in an era of change / Jon
Wiles, Joseph Bondi.—3rd ed.
      p. cm.
    Rev. ed. of: The essential middle school. c1993.
    Includes bibliographical references and index.
    ISBN 0-13-014493-2
      1. Middle schools—United States. 2. Computer and children. I. Bondi, Joseph. II.
Wiles, Jon. Essential middle school. III. Title.
LB1623.5 .W48 2001
373.2'36—dc21
                                               00-020675

Vice President and Publisher: Jeffery W. Johnston
Editor: Debra A. Stollenwerk
Editorial Assistant: Penny S. Burleson
Production Editor: Linda Hillis Bayma
Production Coordination: WordCrafters Editorial Services, Inc.
Photo Coordinator: Lori Whitley
Design Coordinator: Diane C. Lorenzo
Cover Designer: Jeff Vanik
Cover art: © SuperStock
Production Manager: Pamela D. Bennett
Director of Marketing: Kevin Flanagan
Marketing Manager: Amy June
Marketing Services Manager: Krista Groshong

This book was set in Palatino by Carlisle Communications, Ltd. It was printed and bound by R.R. Donnelley & Sons Company. The cover was printed by Phoenix Color Corp.

Earlier editions, titled *The Essential Middle School,* © 1993 by Macmillan Publishing Company and © 1986 by Merrill Publishing Company.

Photo Credits: Pages 1, 59, 99, 183: Scott Cunningham/Merrill; pages 27, 161: Anne Vega/Merrill; pages 125, 215, 245, 265: Anthony Magnacca/Merrill.

Merrill
Prentice Hall

10 9 8 7 6 5 4 3 2 1
ISBN: 0-13-014493-2

*This book is dedicated to
William M. Alexander,
the true "father of the American middle school,"
and to the faculty of the College of Education
at the University of Florida,
whose guidance and encouragement
enhanced our professional development
as educators.*

Preface

Exactly twenty years ago we produced *The Essential Middle School,* a text that served as a guide to thousands of schools as they developed programs for preadolescents. Early middle schools featured a variety of innovations such as team teaching, block scheduling, and interdisciplinary units, and our book served as a guide to schools trying to implement such ideas.

Today the middle school organization is the dominant form of intermediate education in America, and there is more sophistication in communication among educators in the middle grades. The organizational tasks called for twenty years ago have essentially been completed in most schools. Not yet completed, however, is the promise of early middle schools to serve each preadolescent learner as an individual and to recognize his or her specialness as a person in transition.

The New American Middle School has been written because something dramatic and wonderful has occurred in the area of teaching and learning. The Internet and other interactive learning technologies now present middle school educators with the opportunity to complete the mission of the American middle school. Educators now have the tools to reach and teach each child as an individual.

Intermediate education in the United States is about to take its third step (junior high, middle school, new middle school), and this book is designed to help middle school leaders make that transition. We believe that middle schools in the 21st century will be distinctively and qualitatively different from those of the late 20th century. Additionally, we believe that teachers will emerge as the critical change agents in making this "sea change" from a traditional to a more distributive form of learning.

NEW TO THIS EDITION

This edition introduces many new ideas and techniques for approaching the change to a technological middle school. Indeed, the book itself introduces a novel format that starts to bridge the "book-to-Internet" chasm. Throughout the text, you will find websites that enhance or expand on the print messages. There is a strong attempt to put you in touch with active and technological middle school models around the nation. Discussions of the changing role of the teacher in middle schools is pervasive in this text. Specific areas in which you will find new ideas include

- Significant treatment of how middle schools must act to respond to the standards-based expectations found in so many states

- Goals for 21st century middle school students
- A major research-based rationale that supports middle grades learning and middle school organization
- Identification and discussion of new instructional learning resources for teachers and students in terms of classroom applications
- A greater emphasis on how middle schools must act to respond to the complexities of 21st century life in the United States
- A primary focus throughout the text on new technologies and how their application can change the face of learning in today's middle schools
- A complete definition of *full-service schools* and the necessary response to IDEA legislation for children with special needs
- Extensive and practical appendixes to lead you to resources
- Websites in both the text and appendixes to assist you in utilizing web-based resources relevant to middle school education
- Completely updated bibliographic references and suggested learning activities to reflect the real world of the modern middle school

In summary, *The New American Middle School* seeks to arm teachers and other leaders with practical suggestions as they make the transition to the new technological era. Practical and relevant ideas characterize the new topics.

ACKNOWLEDGMENTS

The authors deeply appreciate the editorial guidance of Debbie Stollenwork of Prentice Hall as well as the editorial services of Linda Zuk at WordCrafters. We also have received important review comments from the following persons: Carolyn Cartwright, Texas A&M University; Mohammed Kahn, Albany State University; William E. Klingele, The University of Akron; Allen Larson, Indiana Wesleyan University; and Beth Row, Southeastern College.

Discover the Companion Website
Accompanying This Book

The Prentice Hall Companion Website:
A Virtual Learning Environment

Technology is a constantly growing and changing aspect of our field that is creating a need for content and resources. To address this emerging need, Prentice Hall has developed an online learning environment for students and professors alike—Companion Websites—to support our textbooks.

In creating a Companion Website, our goal is to build on and enhance what the textbook already offers. For this reason, the content for each user-friendly website is organized by topic and provides the professor and student with a variety of meaningful resources. Common features of a Companion Website include:

For the Professor

Every Companion Website integrates **Syllabus Manager**™ an online syllabus creation and management utility.

- **Syllabus Manager**™ provides you, the instructor, with an easy, step-by-step process to create and revise syllabi, with direct links into Companion Website and other online content without having to learn HTML.

- Students may logon to your syllabus during any study session. All they need to know is the web address for the Companion Website and the password you've assigned to your syllabus.

- After you have created a syllabus using **Syllabus Manager**™**,** students may enter the syllabus for their course section from any point in the Companion Website.

- Clicking on a date, the student is shown the list of activities for the assignment. The activities for each assignment are linked directly to actual content, saving time for students.

- Adding assignments consists of clicking on the desired due date, then filling in the details of the assignment—name of the assignment, instructions, and whether or not it is a one-time or repeating assignment.

- In addition, links to other activities can be created easily. If the activity is online, a URL can be entered in the space provided, and it will be linked automatically in the final syllabus.

• Your completed syllabus is hosted on our servers, allowing convenient updates from any computer on the Internet. Changes you make to your syllabus are immediately available to your students at their next logon.

For the Student

- **Topic Overviews**—outline key concepts in topic areas
- **Electronic Bluebook**—send homework or essays directly to your instructor's email with this paperless form
- **Message Board**—serves as a virtual bulletin board to post—or respond to—questions or comments to/from a national audience
- **Chat**—real-time chat with anyone who is using the text anywhere in the country—ideal for discussion and study groups, class projects, etc.
- **Web Destinations**—links to www sites that relate to each topic area
- **Professional Organizations**—links to organizations that relate to topic areas
- **Additional Resources**—access to topic-specific content that enhances material found in the text

To take advantage of these and other resources, please visit *The New American Middle School: Educating Preadolescents in an Era of Change,* Third Edition, Companion Website at

www.prenhall.com/wiles

Contents

Chapter 5 ORGANIZING THE MIDDLE SCHOOL CURRICULUM 125

Chapter 6 DEVELOPING INSTRUCTIONAL MATERIALS 161

NOTE: Every effort has been made to provide accurate and current Internet information in this book. However, the Internet and information posted on it are constantly changing, so it is inevitable that some of the Internet addresses listed in this textbook will change.

CHAPTER 1

Rationale for a New School in the Middle

A successful middle school depends more on faculties than facilities, more on people than on the purse.

The American intermediate school is nearly ninety years old as we enter the twenty-first century. Beginning as a reaction to a six-year high school, the first "junior" high schools emerged around 1910 and continued until the early 1960s. A second wave of activity in intermediate education in America, known as the "middle school movement," continued for nearly the next forty years. The authors believe that a third evolutionary step in intermediate education in the United States, the New American Middle School, is now beginning to unfold. This third evolutionary step will bring the form of schooling even closer to the hopes and dreams of those who have championed "schooling in the middle." The new school will have a clearer philosophy and will be able to deliver, for the first time, a promised pattern of individualized instruction to its client, the preadolescent.

This chapter begins with a cursory look at the new American middle school. This school uses new communication technologies to tailor instructional delivery in schools and classrooms. As this new school rapidly unfolds, many important curriculum and instructional questions are emerging. What is the purpose of intermediate education? What organizational and programmatic designs are most effective in educating preadolescent learners? How can new technologies allow educators to provide a better educational experience?

Because these questions are largely unanswered at the time of this writing, the authors have chosen to review the historical development of intermediate education in the United States so that the reader can understand the basic issues that have shaped our intermediate programs and that will influence future middle schools. Using a historical reconstruction, we seek to identify the critical elements of the intermediate school, and to paint a portrait of the challenges ahead in designing and implementing the new American middle school. But before we begin, let us look at the emergence of this new school at the turn of the 21st century.

REFORM, THE THIRD PHASE

Reform of middle school programs has been a constant theme of curriculum work for ninety years. Most recently, in the 1990s, stimulation from outside agencies including the National Science Foundation, the Clark Foundation, the Anneberg Grants, the New American Schools Grants, the Kellogg Foundation, and the Champion Middle School Partnerships, to name a few, have fostered creative new forms of instruction. For the first time, technology is allowing the dissemination of these new exciting ideas without books, conferences, or consultants. Any teacher and any school in the United States has instant access to these new and creative programs. Samples of some of the changes that are occurring as this book is written are described below:

Information Is Becoming More Accessible

Students in Union Hill School (Alabama) can access resources over the Internet from their classrooms including the Library of Congress, the University of

Alabama Library, the Birmingham Public Library, the News Channel 19 in Huntsville, the History Channel Online and the Smithsonian Institution Online, The Why Files: Science Behind the News, and the Research-It Search Engine. (mindspring.com/~unionhil/)

Students at the Albert Ford Middle School in Acushnet, Massachusetts, a school of 375 students, can take electronic field trips to the Library of Congress, Yosemite National Park, the Great Wall of China, and the Palaeolithic Painted Caves at Vallon, France. They can also access La Louvre in Paris, the Luxembourg Art Museum, museums in New Zealand and Singapore, and thirty art galleries and museums in the United States. (ultranet.com/~fordms/our_school.html)

Parent-Teacher Communication Is Improving

- Irmo Middle School, near Columbia South Carolina, has a web-based VIP program for parents that allows them to interact with the school in a number of new ways. (www.lex5.k12sc.us/ims/default.htm)
- The Bridge School in Hillsborough, California, is using assistive technology and innovative instructional strategies to assure parents of students with speech and physical impairments that their children are included in all school activities. (Yahoo! Regional:US:States:California:Cities:Hillsborough. Education)
- The Harbor Lights Middle School in Bandon, Oregon, is filtering out unwanted Internet material through its subscription to N2H2's Bess Internet Proxy Service, thus calming parental fears of undesirable contacts. (www.coos.k12.or.us/~hlms4415/filter.html)
- Manatee Middle School in Naples, Florida, describes many of its practices on the Web for parents and other visitors. Now parents know the meaning of "looping," "ESOL," and "blocking." (http://manateemiddle.org/manateemiddle/looping.htm)
- The Meads Mill Middle School in Northville, Michigan, lists its after school program on the Internet, and parents can schedule a class and ride home for their student by clicking on "sponsor." (http://mm.www.northville.k12.mi.us/Mini.htm)
- Florence, Kentucky's R. A. Jones Middle School has its own "Parent Power" page where parents can find advice on parenting, academics, promoting study habits, or even where to take an educational summer vacation. (http://www.ashland.com/education/ppower/fall_97/special feature.html)
- Parents at the Centennial Middle School in Boulder, Colorado, can actually watch their children being educated via live webcams in science rooms 224 and 300. (http://bvsd.k12.co.us/schools/cent/Centennial Home.html)

Teachers Are Becoming Empowered

Teachers can access the Virtual Schoolhouse to promote their own professional growth. At this site they will find a Teacher's Lounge where they can gain updates on subjects, a place to retrieve free software, a guide to networking with other teachers, and an essential reference site where everything from Bartlett's Familiar Quotations to the Old Farmer's Almanac is available. Teachers can create their own virtual reference desk, and they can even invite their principal to find suggestions for "administration in the information age." (http://metalab.unc.edu/cisco/schoolhouse.html)

Florida teachers have discovered a wonderful new compilation of teacher resources and curriculum. (http://www.learnweb.org)

Teachers at the Wayland Middle School in Massachusetts have their own Faculty Discussion Group where they discuss items such as block scheduling and the new building renovations. (http://www.wayland.k12.ma.us/middle_school/teachers/fac_ discussion.htm)

Teachers who have questions about students with emotional disabilities can visit the teacher training site at George Washington University to ask a question, secure resources, find out about formal study, or link to other teachers and resources. (http://www.gwu.edu/~ebdweb/index.html)

The Curriculum for Students Is More Relevant

Beginning with the Global Schoolhouse Project, sponsored by the National Science Foundation in 1994 to 1995, schools have been in touch with each other, and the actual school curriculum has become expansive (http://k12.cnidr.org/gsh/gshwelcome.html). For example, students at the Mt. Garfield Middle School in Colorado have their own Amateur Radio Club that connects "ham" operators in six countries and 26 schools. (http://mgms.mesa.k12.co.us/scrtext.html)

Students in Miami and Fort Lauderdale schools, in collaboration with the University of Miami, are creating a web page "organ donation curriculum" to raise awareness among middle and secondary students. (http://www.life 101.org)

Students at Hellgate Middle School in Missoula, Montana, are involved in a statewide curriculum project to trace the path of the Lewis and Clark expedition. The governors of both Montana and Idaho have served as guides to students as they build long houses, visit salt works, and camp at the historic Glade Creek campsite. (http://www.hellgate.k12.mt.us/middle/clark/index.htm) Other examples of the new world of the middle school curricula include: students creating their own webpages through online instruction at Northeast Middle School in Minneapolis (http://www.mpls.k12.mn.us/northeast/creating webpages.htm); the Warner Robbins Middle School in Georgia providing Internet Tutorials and other hands-on instruction for students (http://www.hom.net/~wrmstech/wrmshome/htm); students at the Desert Mountain Middle School in Phoenix, Arizona, applying their learning each day during the "marketplace period" (http://wwwdvusd.k12.az.us/DVUSD/ SCHOOLS/dmms.html); students learning "civility" through a special curriculum at the

Andalusia Middle School in Alabama (http://199,88.17.100/kyle/New%20Folder%20 (2)/amssafe.html); students adopting a grandparent and visiting a nursing home every Wednesday to do community service at Mattacheese Middle School, Massachusetts (http://www.capecod.net/mamiddle/adopt.html); and the students at Freeport Middle School in Maine checking the weather or even shopping at L. L. Bean on its web page.

Perhaps the ultimate in student learning in the new middle school, from the students' perspective, is the Kidspage on the website of Ford Middle School in Massachusetts. Here, as a reward, students can visit the Disney Experience, the Crayola Factory, a link to the comics, the Barbie Page, Dinosaur World, the Endless Star Trek Episode, NASA's Volcano World, Sports Illustrated Online, the Apollo II Mission to the moon, or 20 equally enticing sites.

From this very brief overview, the reader can note that a dramatic change has occurred in middle schools because of the new communication technologies. The development of programs offered, the nature of instructional learning, the ability to individualize curricula, and the role of teachers in the new school have all changed as we enter this third period of middle school development. The new American Middle School is, and will continue to be, a very interesting place to work.

As we transition into the twenty-first century in intermediate education, it is extremely important to know what has shaped this unique form of schooling in the past. By gaining this insight, we may be able to shape, improve, and preserve the new middle school as it unfolds in the early years of the twenty-first century. In the next section the authors offer a review of the foundations of early intermediate schools in America, including the identification of its prevailing philosophy and critical elements.

ORIGINS OF INTERMEDIATE EDUCATION

When the junior high school was first conceptualized at the turn of the twentieth century, there was an awareness of the preadolescent period of development that is surprisingly contemporary. That conception of a special learner and a special approach to teaching was quickly lost in the popular expansion of public education during the 1910–1930 period. When the middle school movement began in America during the 1960s, educators spoke of a program to serve the uniqueness of the preadolescent learner. That conception, also, was diluted by the rapid growth of middle schools. If the new middle school of the 21st century is to succeed in developing an appropriate and effective learning experience for the preadolescent, administrators and teachers must understand and internalize a set of beliefs that will guide decision making on a day-to-day basis.

Ideas about education in the United States at the beginning of the last century fell into two groups. The old model, a time-worn design, was mechanistic in its orientation. Public education was seen as a system, a governmental program, where literacy was taught and foundational knowledge was inculcated.

Public education was a mass production event with a mechanistic psychology (behaviorism), having taken into account no real sociology. The program lacked aesthetics, it lacked a philosophy of educating, and it certainly didn't differentiate among various learner groups.

As the last century began, a second set of ideas about education began to surface based on the humanistic (person-centered) writings of Europeans. Challenging conventional thinking about children and schooling, Rousseau observed that the mental development of humans was organic or natural, and that learning was a process of individual development.

Another European, Pestalozzi, spoke of education as an individual process based on drawing out, rather than filling up. He called for a holistic model of teaching focusing on not only the head, but also the heart and the hand of the student.

A third European writer, Froebels, suggested that learning for children should be built around the interests and the experiences of students. He saw the education process as basically a social phenomenon since ideas were tested in trial interactions with the environment.

Charles Darwin, famous for his theory of evolution, influenced the thinking of educators of the late nineteenth century. If evolution occurred by adaptation, he reasoned, why would human growth be any different? Children were not empty containers, fixed in their properties and capacities, but rather dynamic organisms with many growth possibilities. Student learning was a self-activity springing from one's own interests and motivated by one's own desires.

These vague notions of a different definition of education were first formally introduced into the United States during the centennial celebration held in Philadelphia in 1876, then they floated in abstraction until the mid-1890s when they were operationalized by America's most famous educator, John Dewey. Between 1894–1904, Dewey combined the philosophy, psychology, and pedagogy (teaching) of these ideas at his Laboratory School at the University of Chicago.

In contrast to the old mechanistic school, Dewey proposed a natural school centered on the development of the child (child-centered). He proposed that the school was actually a community, where a climate of positivism should prevail. According to Dewey, subject matter was for living and should be integrated into everyday experiences. Lessons were to be based on experience, on first-hand observations by the learner. Competence in education would be based on skills for application, as well as on the act of knowing. There would be room for differences, for creative expression.

Dewey held that there were certain conditions necessary for growth in children, and these conditions included (1) a freedom to investigate, (2) choice in school experiences, and (3) the ability to meet and solve problems that would be confronted later in life. He called this process the development of a "growing consciousness" on the part of the child.

Because the philosophical influence of John Dewey has been so great in America, the reader may wonder what the assumptions of the older and more traditional programs of school had been. The roots of that program were strongly based in a fear of human nature, often tied to religious beliefs (Martin

Luther) that man was constantly tempted by evil. Traditional educators believed that "beating the devil out of children" was sometimes necessary. Children were perceived as imperfect adults, and needed to be filled with those ideals and behaviors thought desirable. Measurement of these common learnings, and a progression through a fixed and tiered curriculum (the grade levels) defined mastery and being "educated." (Table 1.1)

The followers of John Dewey came to be called "progressives" because they had these new beliefs about children, schooling, and learning. The original junior high school, and the early middle schools of this country possessed a very progressive notion about schooling, including recognition of the uniqueness of individual students and the need to individualize the educational process whenever possible. Over time, both the junior high and the middle schools of the late twentieth century seemed to lose this philosophical emphasis in the curriculum.

In his Laboratory School at the University of Chicago, Dewey experimented with teaching methods. Over time, what emerged in the curriculum of the school was a kind of "action learning" format where students investigated, reflected, and developed generalizations that would guide future decision making. Dewey spent much time trying to decide on the role of subject matter in this new way of learning. In contrast to the traditional approach of linear mastery of knowledge, Dewey proposed finding "roots" in the direct and present experiences of learners "from which the elaborate technical and organized knowledge might grow." A very basic part of this new pedagogy was

TABLE 1.1 *Models for Educating Contrasted*

Traditional Model	*Progressive Model*
Human nature is suspect and imperfect.	Humans, particularly children, are good.
Children are really incomplete adults.	Children represent a unique period of human growth.
Students must be controlled and corrected by teachers.	Students grow naturally and need guidance by teachers.
Common and minimal learnings are desirable.	Learning is an individual experience.
Common outcomes are desired and measured.	Outcomes must be flexible and reflect diversity of student experience and capacity.
A fixed, standardized curriculum is needed.	The curriculum should be individualized and developmentally appropriate to the degree possible.
Teachers are knowers and should direct learning in the classroom.	Teachers are learners and should provide instructional guidance to students.
School should be a knowledge-based endeavor.	School should be an experienced-based endeavor.

the concept of "apperception," a belief that new knowledge was perceived or comprehended in terms of old or previously experienced understandings.

During the 1890s a famous committee of university presidents, the Committee of Ten, had proposed a common curriculum in the many states and had enforced their desire for uniformity by developing college entrance requirements. Learning was defined in terms of subjects studied for predetermined periods of time for students to earn credits for high school graduation. Part of the difficulty for the Committee of Ten was that there was already too much to know. A subcommittee on Economy and Time suggested that two years be taken from the elementary grades, thus creating a 6–6 plan, to solve the need for additional study time in the high school. This program was implemented, unsuccessfully, between the mid-1890s and 1910. Eventually, the problems encountered by having 12- and 13-year olds studying a high school curriculum led to the establishment of a "junior high school."

Paralleling this attempt to enforce a mechanical and mass education system on older children, were the first studies of a special group of learners who were older children or early adolescents. The now classic early study of 4,000 youth in New York City in 1904 by G. Stanley Hall symbolizes many studies that documented a unique and dramatic stage of development, the preadolescent period. Statements about the "individual differences of students" and "meeting the needs of early adolescents" began to show up in educational literature. As the problems of the six-year high school grew, and the awareness of the preadolescent emerged, progressive educators called for a new and different form of schooling in America. By 1909, the first "junior high school" in name was established in Columbus, Ohio, and in 1910 Superintendent Frank Bunker of Berkeley, California, established an introductory high school or junior high school "to relieve overcrowding and reduce the high dropout rate" in his district. By 1920, there were over 400 of these prehigh schools or junior high schools defined as schools in which seventh, eighth, and ninth grades were placed in a building of their own with their own teaching staff and administrators. By the mid-1950s, there were approximately 6,500 junior high schools in America.

THE JUNIOR HIGH SCHOOL 1910–1965

There is a myth among middle school educators that the junior high school was simply a bisected high school. In reality, by the 1915–1920 period there was extensive literature on the junior high school that spoke of the specialness of preadolescent learners and the need to individualize their educational experience. Educational theorists knew of the uniqueness of the early adolescent period of development, and sought to program a broad and flexible learning experience for those students. Unfortunately, the growth of the American high school from 1890 to 1920 (from 200,000 students to five million students) resulted in attention being detracted from the development of the junior high school curriculum to focus on providing buildings, books, and teachers.

By the 1930s, the junior high school curriculum came to parallel the high school curriculum, actually becoming a "junior" version of it. The absence of a body of teachers trained to work with preadolescents meant that the secondary-trained staff emphasized subject matter much as in the high school. Departmentalization of teachers and a bureaucratic administrative orientation reduced flexibility and retarded any meaningful innovation in instruction. By the 1940s, junior high had also adopted traditional high school activities such as varsity athletics, cap-and-gown graduation, and even marching bands. The junior high school had really become a "junior" high school.

In the beginning, however, junior high schools sought to deal with the same problems that interfere with middle school instruction such as discipline problems, motivation problems, and a high dropout rate. Leaders in junior high education, such as Leonard Koos, Calvin Davis, and Thomas Briggs were knowledgeable about the theories of progressive education and the ideas of John Dewey. They fully understood the need to tie together the personal life of the student with the educational program being delivered.

The high point for such theory in the junior high school was the list of six basic functions for the junior high school developed by William Gruhn and Harl Douglas in the mid-1940s.

> Function One—Integration. To help students use the skills, attitudes, and understandings previously acquired and integrate them into an effective and wholesome behavior.
>
> Function Two—Exploration. To allow students the opportunity to explore particular interests so that they can make better choices, both vocational and academic. To help students develop a wide range of cultural, civic, social, recreational, and avocational interests.
>
> Function Three—Guidance. To help students make better decisions about vocational and recreational activities and help students make satisfactory social, emotional, and academic adjustments toward mature personalities.
>
> Function Four—Differentiation. To provide differential educational opportunities and facilities in accord with varying backgrounds, personalities, and other individual differences so that each pupil can achieve economically and completely the ultimate aims of education.
>
> Function Five—Socialization. To furnish learning experiences intended to prepare students for effective and satisfying participation in a complex social order as well as for future changes in the social order.
>
> Function Six—Articulation. To provide for the gradual transition from preadolescent education to an education program suited to the needs of adolescent girls and boys.

These six functions—to integrate learning, to encourage exploration, to guide development, to individualize the learning experience, to promote healthy social development, and to bridge learning from the elementary years to the high school years—would all become part of the middle school rationale.

Besides the rapid growth of the high school, which in so many ways robbed the new junior high school of teachers, facilities, and leadership, other events acted to sabotage this first intermediate school in America. The Great Depression era of the 1930s detracted from all new efforts in education. The six-year period of the Second World War was equally distracting to program development in American schools. Finally, the recovery period after the war found an America drifting and without conviction in the development of educational programs.

Perhaps more than anything else, however, the inclusion of the ninth grade in the junior high organization kept the school from developing a curriculum to truly serve the preadolescent. The ninth graders were tied to the graduation requirements established in the 1890s and were required to have fixed courses with fixed time requirements (units). Once the ninth graders were scheduled, little flexibility remained for the eighth and seventh graders in the school.

Finally, the fact that ninth graders are no longer preadolescents detracted from the development of a real junior high school program. The junior high attempted to meet the needs of two very different developmental stages during its fifty-year existence.

THE EARLY MIDDLE SCHOOL 1965–2000

Although there was considerable criticism of the junior high school during its final decade, there was no specific alternative until several junior-high-school advocates suggested a reform model under the label *middle school.* Dr. William M. Alexander is given official credit for proposing the middle school, although in reality John Lounsbury, Gordon Vars, and William Van Til were involved in planning to reestablish the school for preadolescents in America. Alexander revived the term *middle school,* long used in some private schools and in Europe, and gave the term a new set of educational attributes.

Those who gave birth to the American middle school were of the progressive school of thought in education. William Alexander, for example, had worked closely in his graduate work with Harold Caswell, who in turn had been a student of John Dewey. Alexander was a "humanist" because he believed the new middle school should focus on the student, the preadolescent, rather than on the subject matter content like the high school. While seeing the junior high school as an organization focused and structured around subject matter and the emerging middle school as a school using the development of the student as its rationale is simplistic, the distinction may aid in the reader's understanding. This philosophic watershed would be important in the basic organizational decisions such as the curriculum offerings, schedules, hiring teachers, and even building construction.

As a student-centered educator, Alexander chose to extend the years within the middle school downward from a 7-8-9 pattern to a 6-7-8 pattern (or even 5-8). This allowed the middle school to teach only older children and preadolescents who had in common the fact that they were experiencing puberty.

Alexander also followed the original literature of the junior high school to define the middle school as a broadly based general education, standing on three points: education for social competence, mastery of basic learning skills, and personal development. The curriculum was to be wide, not narrow, and to be focused on exploration, not mastery. Middle school would be a "bridging" school. It would educate students at a unique stage of development. It would not be a "junior" high school.

The timing of Alexander's proposal to start the middle school in America was facilitated by a number of factors, four of which we shall mention. First, in 1965 there was a general unhappiness with all schooling in the United States at this time and in particular with the poor academic performance of the junior high school. In 1957 the Russians had launched the first orbiting satellite, Sputnik, a technological feat that shocked America. Soon, schools were blamed for a low performance in math and science, and the junior high bore the brunt of such criticism.

A second factor leading to the establishment of the middle school form of intermediate education in this country was the effort to eliminate de facto segregation. The 1954 U.S. Supreme Court decision, *Brown* v. *Topeka* had struck down the old separate-but-equal orientation, and racial integration in schools was perceived as the best hope for uniting the populations of the United States. Schools, particularly in the South, were challenged by the wide range of achievement in these newly integrated schools. The middle school seemed to provide the flexibility to address this range of student development.

Third, and perhaps as powerful a force as any, was the increased enrollment in the school population in the 1960s. Children conceived in the peaceful aftermath of World War II swelled the population in many school districts, causing building and resource shortages reminiscent of the 1890–1920 era when the junior high was launched. Elementary schools could become less crowded by moving the sixth grade up into a middle school. Junior high schools could alleviate crowding by moving the ninth grade into the high school where new buildings were first constructed.

A final factor, very important to the rapid growth of the early American middle school, was a readiness for change. It was widely accepted that the junior high school was largely dysfunctional by 1960, and school districts jumped on the "middle school bandwagon" just to eliminate the junior high school.

These four factors, and others, may have been wrong reasons for starting the middle school in the United States, but they provided the right opportunity for launching what has been termed America's longest running curriculum innovation. The school for preadolescents was underway!

The authors believe that a major error was made in beginning the middle school that should not be made again as the new middle school evolves in the early 21st century. As graduate students of William Alexander, the authors were aware of a choice of strategy selected by the former junior high school leaders to deemphasize the humanistic or child-centeredness of the prescribed curriculum.

These leaders felt that such an emphasis would be misunderstood to mean that focusing on the student would detract from the academic mission of the school. They believed that the two wings of American education, traditional and progressive could be united at that time only if the child-centeredness of the middle school were deemphasized. Because of these assumptions, Alexander chose to emphasize the grade levels in the middle school (6, 7, and 8) and used a survey technique asking about grade levels, not programs, to call attention to this new form.

The result of this strategy, during the next thirty-five years was to make numerous middle schools but to leave the curriculum ill-defined and incapable of sound evaluation. Such a quantitative orientation to middle school development also bisected the middle school program from applications in the classroom; there was no clear learning theory because the criteria for being a middle school was organizational rather than instructional.

There are today about 13,000 intermediate schools in the United States that incorporate some combination of grades five through nine. In his first survey of new middle schools in the United States (1967), Alexander identified 300 schools that were moving toward a reformed curriculum and housing grades five through eight or six through eight. These innovative junior high schools or middle schools in name had some distinctive characteristics but few common organizational structures. The early literature described them as innovative, and the features most often cited were flexible schedules and teaching teams.

By 1973, the middle school movement was well under way. The *Digest of Education Statistics* noted some 2300 so-called middle schools. In some states, such as Florida, New York, Ohio, and Michigan, early state-level middle school associations were formed linking these new middle schools. A fledgling National Middle School Association was formed. Numerous journal articles described various innovative schools.

Twenty years later, the middle school was established as the basic form of intermediate education. For every existing junior high school (3970) there were nearly three middle schools (9500). Of these middle schools, two-thirds included grades five through eight or six through eight. Various grade combinations made up the final one-third of the schools, and most of these were in rural areas. By 1995, only 13 percent of all intermediate schools were still grade seven through nine junior high schools.

The successful growth of the middle school in the United States, numerically, masked fundamental growing pains for this uniquely American school form. The purposefully nebulous curriculum and the absence of clear learning theory kept many principals uncertain about how to operationalize the concept.

The philosophy of the middle school, and the junior high school for that matter, was easy enough to define. Writing in 1966, for example, Donald Eichhorn wrote:

A special program is needed for the 10–14 year old child going through the unique "transescent" period in his growth and development. The widest range of differences in terms of physical, social, and intellectual growth is found in the middle school youngster. Such a wide range of differences calls for an individualized program that is lacking in most junior high schools. The middle school provides for individual differences with a program tailored to fit each child.[1]

While individualization was desirable, in reality the concept was largely undefined and certainly not operational in most early middle schools. In the late 1960s and early 1970s, recognition of individual differences in the preadolescent period led to a prescription for "a well-balanced program focusing on personal development, emphasizing skills for continued learning, and utilizing knowledge to foster social competence."[2]

Early model intermediate schools that intuitively promoted organizational flexibility became the trend leaders that most other middle schools followed. Early middle schools often announced that their program featured block schedules, team teaching, common planning periods, advisory guidance, interdisciplinary instruction, and a host of other "organizational means" to developing programs in the middle school. While many middle schools developed programs that featured diverse curricula, many did not. The standardization that so characterized the junior high school was found in too many middle schools. The early commitment to focusing on the grade levels, not the instructional program, was taking its toll.

There were, of course, numerous efforts to help schools make the inferential leap (if–then) from a school focused on the most diverse group of learners in the school ladder to a program in which each student is treated according to their individual needs. A 1975 A.S.C.D. Working Group on the Emerging Adolescent Learner, chaired by co-author Joseph Bondi, identified 14 points that should guide program development:[3]

1. Learning experiences for transescents should be at their own intellectual levels, relating to intermediate rather than remote academic goals.

2. A wide variety of cognitive learning experiences should be used to account for the full range of students who are at many different levels of concrete and formal operations.

3. The curriculum should be diversified and exploratory resulting in daily success that will nurture intellectual development.

4. Opportunities should be provided to develop problem solving, reflective thinking, and an awareness of the order in the student's environment.

5. Cognitive learning experiences should be structured so that each student can progress in an individualized manner.

6. The program should develop and extend basic learning skills, show real-life applications, and allow each student to appraise his or her own interests and talents.

7. The curriculum should emphasize concept development with appropriate attention to the development of values.

8. Previous learnings taught in departmentalized format should be broken down and taught around integrative themes and experiences.

9. Personal curiosity in the learning experience should be encouraged.

10. The role of the teacher should be one of a guide to learning instead of a purveyor of knowledge. Traditional lecture–recitation methods should be minimized.

11. Grouping of students should be according to physical, social and emotional criteria, as well as by the traditional intellectual criteria.

12. Development of the student's self concept, attitudes toward school, and general happiness are as important as how much and what the student knows.

13. Experiences in the arts should be provided for all transescents to foster aesthetic appreciation and to stimulate creative expression.

14. Curriculum offerings should reflect cultural, ethnic, and socio-economic subgroups within the middle school population.

Another such list that attempted to define the emerging program of the middle school was provided by Neil Atkins in his article "Rethinking Education in the Middle:"[4]

1. Absence of the "little high school" approach.

2. Absence of the "star system" in which a few special students dominate most performance areas, so that success experiences occur for greater numbers of students.

3. Attempt to use instructional methods more appropriate to this age group: individualized instruction, variable grouping size, multimedia approaches, independent study, inquiry-oriented instruction.

4. Increased opportunity for teacher–student guidance.

5. Increased flexibility in scheduling with variable length periods.

6. Some cooperative planning and team teaching is present.

7. Teachers using interdisciplinary teaching to show students how the subjects fit together in the real world.

8. Provision for a wide variety of exploratory opportunities.

9. Increased opportunity for participation in physical activity at school, including more frequent physical education.

10. Earlier introduction of organized academic knowledge.

11. Attention given to the skills of continued learning, allowing students to learn independently at higher levels.

12. Accenting the student's ability to be independent, responsible, and self-disciplined.

13. Providing more flexible physical facilities and environments for students.

14. Attention to personal development in the student, including, developing group skills, values, and directed orientations to family, health, and career.

15. Teachers who are trained for and committed to the education of emerging adolescents.

The reader will note from these two lists that early middle school educators, like their junior high school predecessors, held high aspirations for the school programs. But, in many ways, the junior-high-school and the middle-school experiences were similar in their inability to deliver on the philosophic conceptions of educating. The junior high school was sidetracked by the growth of the American high school, while the middle school floundered for lack of a vision of how to meet the individual needs of its students. Said simply, the philosophy of the middle school from 1965 through 2000 was not translated, in most schools, into an operational instructional design. Standardization, not individualization, was the most common format. The promise exceeded the performance.

EARLY WARNING SIGNS OF FAILURE

In a 1977 publication by the National Middle School Association, *The Middle School: A Look Ahead,* leading writers assessed the progress of the middle school after a decade of operation. The observations were remarkably similar, and they all contained a warning that the middle school could become sidetracked:[5]

Thomas Gatewood   "There is a significant gap between the main tenets of the theoretical middle school proposed by leading authorities and the actual practices in most middle schools. It appears that many of these schools have adopted practices of the long-condemned junior high. . . . [T]he first ten years of the middle school movement in the United States were primarily a growth phenomenon more than the development of significant, identifiable, authentic middle school programs."

James Fox   "The danger to middle schools stems from the age old pressure to cut out the so-called frills. Programs could lose the flavor of a student-focused curriculum that help the student become a well-integrated human being."

Joseph Bondi   "The diverse needs of the transescent youngster dictate a diverse program. The basics must mean programs designed to help youngsters understand the physical changes and social and emotional traumas of transescence. We just simply cannot ignore the psycho-social changes occurring in the middle years."

William Alexander   "Even if the middle schools do differ from their predecessor institutions, the standardized middle school can result from the same forces that produced the standardized junior high school . . . differing relatively little from the school of a quarter-century earlier."

Jon Wiles   "In moving from a conceptual toward a programmatic orientation, the middle school movement is threatened by three unresolved issues:

communicating the philosophy to those developing programs, overcoming the theory–practice gap, and establishing evaluation criteria. Failure to accomplish these ends will result in the middle school being a cliche."

Donald Eichhorn   "If middle school educators are going to break the junior high–middle school cycle (rationale, partially appropriate program, inappropriate program, rationale . . .) a fundamental change must occur. In my opinion, the grade–age model must be abandoned."

Conrad Toepfer   "The greatest threat to its [the middle school's] survival will be if the school becomes institutionalized as a singular pattern of schooling. Such regression to a linear, conceptual organization would render the middle school just as unresponsive to the educational needs of the emerging adolescents as the junior high eventually became. To avoid this fate, the middle school must become a "multiple school," consisting of a wide range of optional learning environments which match learning styles with teaching styles."

John Lounsbury   "The middle school must guard against becoming a victim of its apparent success; pleased with its good press, its numerical status, and its firm position aboard the [educational] bandwagon. The more it becomes institutionalized, the greater the danger of it becoming petrified."

The middle schools of the 1965–2000 era were, in many cases, exciting instructional centers. With time, most sixth-through-eight programs adopted a block-of-time schedule, used teaching teams, integrated subject areas some of the time, provided a kind of group guidance, offered more numerous electives, and increased participation in physical activity and intramural sports. The fact that the innovativeness of the middle schools stretched over a 35-year period is significant. However, what these schools did not do was adjust instruction to the individual needs of students. This shortcoming was, unfortunately, magnified in a time when public education was documenting the needs of children in many new ways.

One of the first tests for the middle school concept came in adjusting to the integration of public schools in the late 1960s and early 1970s. In many parts of the United States, minority children had attended "separate" schools and school systems. The historic "separate but equal" clause of the 1890s Supreme Court case (*Plessey* v. *Ferguson*) was struck down in 1954 by *Brown* v. *Topeka*. Following court tests and delaying actions, public schools began to combine previously separate school systems into unitary systems. The middle school, with its new grade arrangement (6–7–8) seemed a logical place to target such change. The result of such integration was a much wider range of development and achievement among students.

The flexibility of the middle school organization, such as its schedules and electives, was not easily matched at the classroom level. Teachers, without special training and the use of standardized delivery mediums, such as a text, uniform exams and grading criteria, were unable to make individualization work. Early techniques like learning activity packages and "skill drill" computer programs simply could not manage the many differences found in the preadolescent learner. Like the junior high school before it, the middle school was soon plagued by overaged students and a soaring dropout rate.

Another challenge to the middle school's ability to "meet the individual needs of students" came in the form of Public Law 94–142, a federal mandate detailing the rights of handicapped children. Such children, being "mainstreamed" into middle school programs, presented the teachers with an even wider range of needs to be met. Again, teachers with mostly traditional secondary teaching skills were unable to design instruction to meet these needs. Still later in the 1990s, the Individuals with Disabilities Education Act (IDEA) forced middle schools to adopt an "inclusion" strategy in which students would be in the regular classroom, regardless of handicap, unless they could be better served in a different educational environment. Middle schools valiantly tried various strategies to meet the needs of those students and continue to do so as this book is being written.

The changing social face of America from 1965 through 2000 also meant many new variables for educators at the middle school level. Trends in the national economy increased the percentage of children living in homes below the poverty level to approximately 30 percent. The general breakdown of the family meant that all school children had a 50 percent chance of living in a single-parent home sometime during their school years. Personal mobility of children and their families, due to work location and opportunities, often meant that students would not complete a full year in any one school building.

On the high end of the same continuum, gifted programs dating from 1972 (the year the federal government first recognized giftedness) documented the incredible potential of middle school students to become educated. Research documented the many talents of middle schoolers and the "window of opportunity" for learning that so characterizes the pubescent period of development.

Perhaps one of the greatest problems for the middle school movement was its inability to document successes due to the nonstandard programming and lack of evaluative know-how. Writing as early as 1972, co-author Wiles warned that a lack of data to support middle school programming would constitute the "Achilles heel" of the middle school.[6] By the late 1980s, this prophecy was substantiated as various traditional groups began to question the efficacy of middle school programs. In particular, there were assertions that the middle school did not promote achievement in basic skills as well as the traditional junior high school had. Evidence for either position was simply not available.

By the mid-1990s, school boards in various districts across the United States were beginning to challenge the format of the middle school, in many cases for non-educational reasons. Regardless of such motivations, critics were accurate in that the middle school had not achieved its avowed goals of serving the uniqueness of the preadolescent learner. The early model of middle school education was running out of gas.

THE MIDDLE SCHOOL PROMISE

The early promises of the American middle school were strong on philosophy and weak on details. Theorists advocated a unique school, not an extension of the elementary grades and certainly not a "junior" high school. The new school would serve a special population of learners—preadolescents, whose common denominator was a period of development in which passage from childhood to adolescence occurred. In Chapter Two, the reader will learn about the complexity of these learners. It can be observed that there is more diversity among students at this level than at either the elementary or the secondary level.

If this is true, and if a special school for preadolescents is to be maintained, any planning for organization or instruction in the new school, must focus on the student. The preadolescent period is unique and contains many social and emotional dimensions that affect learning. To continue as a viable school form, the American middle school must make this student the focal point of instructional decision making.

The early middle school promised in its literature to develop a school that could serve each learner according to his or her uniqueness. While most middle school curricula pay lip service to serving the physical, social, intellectual, and emotional dimensions of student growth, few schools have operationalized this aspiration. The traditional practices of grouping students by ability and serving students by label fall woefully short of meeting the needs of each unique learner. To accomplish this goal of individualizing instruction, the middle school must have a way of seeing each student and monitoring the progress of each student on a daily basis. To date this has not been done in many middle schools.

The early middle school literature spoke of providing a balanced curriculum for the preadolescent in which knowledge, learning skills, and personal development would be equally promoted. With the "back to basics" movement of the 1980s and the "testing and accountability" emphasis of the 1990s, many middle schools have abandoned such balance. This is unfortunate, indeed, for it illuminates the absence of learning theory in middle-grade education. As John Dewey and other progressive educators observed at the turn of the last century, a failure to base learning on the background and knowledge of the learner will make the curriculum sterile. Further, the progressives stated, "the application of formal learnings in real life make the various instructions come to life."[7]

Many middle schools in the 1990s unbalanced their curriculum to emphasize basic skills so that their schools could score well on standardized tests. While the authors sympathize with educational leaders under pressure from political activists to make school a place of test scores and work readiness, such an unidimensional emphasis is the antithesis of what a middle school should be. As the new middle school emerges in the beginning of the twenty-first century, perhaps less attention should be paid to the number of schools bearing the label and more attention to the kind of program being offered to the student.

One of the major themes of the early middle school was that it would promote exploration and help the learners to determine their interests so that they might make wiser educational choices in high school and beyond. To some extent, early middle schools were very successful in having "exploratory wheels" that replaced the old either-or electives of the junior high school. But true individualized exploration would mean that each student in growing up would come to understand himself or herself and his or her place in the world. Middle schoolers are, by nature, curious, and school should represent a place where they can seek and think in a controlled and caring environment. Unfortunately, the social statistics addressing sexual behavior, juvenile delinquency, and a somewhat antisocial youth culture in many schools suggest these needs are not being met fully. (See Chapter 2.) The connection between learning and livelihood, in particular, is not well established in most middle schools.

The early middle school literature promised to provide a caring and accepting climate in which the competitive rigors of academia would be de-emphasized. This promise was an extension of the beliefs of early humanistic educators that learning occurred best when students felt comfortable and confident. To de-emphasize the "star system" in schools and encourage teacher receptiveness of students' natural behaviors during preadolescence was an important concept in the middle school philosophy. Unfortunately, daily practices in many middle schools do not adhere to this goal.

Perhaps the most dramatic promise of the early middle school literature was to provide personal guidance to the student in the middle. The transition from childhood to adolescence is difficult, a pathway with many pitfalls, and students need a caring adult to guide them along. While most middle schools adopted an "advisory guidance" approach, in which a teacher met with a group of students on a regular basis to discuss concerns, this innovation has withered badly in the 1990s. The pressures of testing and "time on task" have made rationalizing a 25-minute guidance group each day difficult for those leaders who do not understand the basic function of this innovation. The average middle school has only one school counselor for every 400 students, and the social–psychological–emotional needs of middle schoolers are primary in relation to academic learnings.

In conclusion, the early middle school held lofty aspirations for serving the preadolescent learner. The survival and growth of the middle school concept over the past 35 years is testimony to the acceptance of those original ideas by school personnel throughout the United States. However, it must be recognized as we enter the 21st century that the middle school did not fully meet the goals of: (1) a school that is designed for the preadolescent period, (2) a school that would serve each learner in an individual manner, (3) a school with a comprehensive and balanced learning program, (4) a school that would allow the learner to explore and understand himself or herself, (5) a school with a caring and accepting climate, and (6) a school providing a personal guidance program.

After 35 years of refinement of the organizational structures, the middle school must step up and develop an instructional component that meets the above specifications. The time has arrived when these target goals can be accomplished, and the middle school can move to a new level of service to the preadolescent.

THE NEW MIDDLE SCHOOL IN TRANSITION

The beginning of a new century provides a good opportunity to look at the status of the American middle school and to project where it seems to be headed. The authors are quite optimistic that the middle school is entering a new stage of development that will be characterized by teacher-developed instruction and high technology delivery systems. Whether this transition can successfully occur depends on the awareness of teachers in the field to the possibilities at hand and upon the ability of administrators to embrace change. Ultimately, for the middle school to accomplish what was envisioned at the beginning of the 20th century by sincere and supportive educators, many things must change.

In the 1965–2000 period, the middle school was highly successful in focusing attention on this level of education. Early studies of physiology and human development illuminated the special nature of the preadolescent period. A virtual "cottage industry" of associations, leagues of schools, and orientation experiences emerged in the late 1960s and the label "middle school" became part of the educational vocabulary. As has been observed, in the beginning the middle school movement was organizational and concerned with growth. False dichotomies were drawn between the new middle school advocates and the old junior high proponents, and middle school educators were delighted to provide a running tally of the number of schools converting from the old to the new.

Most new middle schools, however, were less successful in placing this new knowledge of preadolescence in an instructional context. As will be seen in the next chapter, the sixth, seventh, and eighth grades (or even fifth through eighth) fit the years spanning puberty like a glove. Teachers were workshopped on the actual sequences of physical, intellectual, social, and emotional development during this period of growth. While some of these training experiences were serious, a disturbing trend of entertainment emerged early in the movement with consultants characterizing intermediate children as "wild and crazy," "moody," or simply "unpredictable." This entertainment perspective, shown in popular magazines, reached its zenith with the television show *The Wonder Years.*

The basic facts were that within the sixth, seventh, and eighth grades, teachers faced the most diverse group of learners in the school ladder. Puberty, hardly wild and crazy, was a predictable sequence of unfolding beginning as early as the fifth grade and ending in the early ninth grade for 95 percent of American school children. Girls preceded boys by about nine months in this process. The difficult thing for teachers was that each child had his or her own unique timetable for this unfolding. Once started, the process took about 18 months.

While middle-grade educators knew this, and talked incessantly about this process, they did not make significant instructional adjustments to accommodate the knowledge. A natural adjustment successful in some elementary schools, multi-age grouping, placed children together by their growth stage instead of their chronological age. This concept never caught on in the middle schools. Neither did the concept of continuous progress curricula, in which a student progressed through material at his or her own rate and without artificial grade level markers. Some middle schools, of course, did recognize these techniques as appropriate and built them into the program to better serve preadolescents. Where possible in this text, such schools will be highlighted. However, most middle schools did not make this connection and continued to educate older girls with younger boys, overaged students with young children, and even nonreaders with superior students—the traditional pattern.

Following leads by consultants, most middle schools did promote some form of flexible grouping within grade levels to address this problem of student diversity. It was recognized that ability grouping is inappropriate for a population changing so rapidly in cognitive capacity. Likewise, there was some differentiation of materials so that students could have a more grade appropriate resource for learning. Later, in the 1980s, most middle schools provided special programs, such as Title I and Gifted Education, for the far range of abilities in the middle school. Otherwise, the program remained as standardized as the junior high school at the classroom level. The middle schools could not see each child as unique, nor accommodate for student differences.

In the first 20 years of existence, middle schools did a much better job of providing a balanced curriculum for preadolescents. The old junior high school had adopted the academic program of the high school, and students studied mostly required courses and maybe a single selection elective, such as band or shop. Middle schools quickly took the theme of "three legs" (knowledge, skills, and personal growth) and developed a more complex curriculum using integrated learnings (interdisciplinary instruction) and elective wheels (short courses). Basic skills were addressed both within the curriculum and as special short courses.

By the late 1980s, the back-to-basics movement was eroding any sort of balance in the middle school curriculum. Accountability legislation in 38 states, and competency-based testing meant that middle schools were scrutinized as never before and their outcomes and even philosophy were questioned. Since there was no definitive evaluation data, many middle schools refocused on basic skills and seriously unbalanced the instructional program. Unfortunately, this trend continues as we enter the new century.

Early middle school did do a good job of promoting exploration during the first 35 years. The "exploratory wheels" (short duration electives) enabled student in grades six, seven, and eight to have as many as 18 separate experiences while in the middle school. Many of these activities were nonmastery academics, such as introduction to German or astronomy, some promoted student interests, such as ham radio, and some developed leisure activities for adult life, such as quilting or photography. Certainly, academic skills were integrated into these exploration courses, such as using math to measure quilts, and many of the courses provided quality time for adults and young people to communicate informally.

Of course, not all so-called middle schools offered exciting explorations. In some cases the sports programs at the schools captured the period, offering weight-lifting, or the schools utilized the shops inherited from old junior high buildings to offer metal work. But after 35 years, these exploratories represent a true achievement for the school that took over from the junior high school.

The promise of the American middle school to create a caring and compassionate learning environment, an accommodating climate, just never happened in many schools. As an individual's home is different from a dentist's office, schools have traditionally been institutional and even overbearing for many students. While many teachers developed enticing learning spaces in their classrooms, more did not. John Goodlad's review of the junior high school classrooms in his classic book, *Behind Classroom Doors,* unfortunately remains the norm in many schools.[8] Take a walk and look in the rooms. In so many schools, standardization is still the norm. Teachers are talking, or students are reading, or there is silence.

This inability to create a place for preadolescents did not indicate bad intent on the part of educators, but was more the result of old inflexible buildings, too many overaged students in the middle school, a very legalistic period in schools in terms of safety, and without a doubt a lack of understanding and imagination by middle school faculties about what a middle school should look like.

If the middle school is to personalize instruction and individualize to meet the learning needs of pupils, each student must have space, some privacy, and some choice in creating where he or she lives and works. Administrators and teachers in the middle school can do this, within existing buildings, but a commitment to this goal would be called for.

Finally, the middle school literature spoke of a need to deliver relevant and personal guidance to middle school students. The advisory program, described in Chapter Three, made an excellent start in this direction. Teacher-led guidance can be successful to the extent that it is understood and carefully planned. Unfortunately, there has been very serious erosion in this commitment in middle schools of the 1990s, and in this book we will attempt to describe those schools that we know of which are doing this approach correctly.

The other observation to be made about the guidance programs of middle schools is that the curriculum has become seriously outdated in many cases. As the reader will learn in the following chapter, the middle schooler of today is quite a bit different from the children of the 1960s, 1970s, 1980s, and even the 1990s. While the act of becoming preadolescent is the same, the environment in which students mature today is quite different and unique. A new curriculum is called for in this area, and the authors offer their best thinking on this subject for the consideration of middle school educators.

In summary, then, the early American middle school made a number of promises in replacing the first intermediate school, the junior high. It promised a new school that would truly be for preadolescents and have its own unique identity. It promised that the middle school would focus on the development of the preadolescent and make administrative, organizational, and instructional decisions based on this criterion. It promised to serve each student as a person, recognizing his or her uniqueness. It promised a broad and balanced curriculum that would facilitate a comprehensive pattern of development rather than only a narrow academic band or growth. It promised a program of exploration and personal development. It promised a caring and responsive learning environment. Finally, the early middle school promised a guidance component in which every child would be aided in his or her passage to preadolescence, adolescence, and adulthood.

The American middle school during its 35-year existence has shown many models and forms of schooling in an attempt to satisfy these promises. While some of these goals have been partially achieved, many remain elusive. In all probability, many middle schools will never attain these ends under the present definition and organization.

THE CHALLENGE OF CHANGE

Things have occurred in the 1990s that will revolutionize American education, and middle school education in particular, during the next 25 to 50 years. Three trends recognized by the authors as most significant are the decentralization and privatization of schooling, the revolution in communication technology, and the changing role and meaning of teaching and learning. Each of these areas spell change for public and private schooling, and each of these areas suggest an opportunity for the new American middle school of the 21st century to finally meet the lofty goals set forth a century ago.

During the 1990s a major trend toward decentralization of authority and teacher involvement in governance occurred. Under labels such as Decentralized Decision-Making (DDM) and School-Based Management (SBM), these efforts included more teacher and community input into curriculum development, staff development, and fiscal decision making. Borrowing know-how from industry, middle school conferences spoke of Demming's 14 Points, Theory Z leadership, and Quality Circles (TQM). As a whole, these activities signaled that the traditional bureaucratic structure of school governance was declining.

Further evidence of increased local and teacher involvement came in the form of school advisory committees (SAC), school instructional teams (SIT), school councils, and school study teams. Finally, the advent of magnet schools, charter schools, the voucher movement, and even home schooling indicated a shift away from a single institutional form for schooling in America. For middle school educators, all of these subtle changes in education meant greater flexibility in program planning.

A second major wave of influence on school programming came in the form of new communication technology. It is nothing short of phenomenal to realize that the commercial Internet that is so much a part of our lives today was established in 1993. The 1990s was a decade of cell phones, scanners, interactive TV, e-mail, and other combinations of ISDN (integrated services digital networks). At the school level a rapid evolution of change occurred through electronic bulletin boards, server groups, integrated learning systems, and world nets.

The accessibility of communication technology and its declining costs has presented schools with a major dilemma of too many choices. Today, even the most rural schools can "tune in and turn on" to learning, but in most schools the lack of clarity in philosophy and instructional strategy make choosing technology a discouraging exercise. The positive side of this massive change is that schools do have choices, and technology promises to set school free from a century of increasing control by government and industry.

Finally, and ever so slowly, school leaders are recognizing that the most basic relationship between the teacher and the student is changing. For thousands of years, the teacher has been the knower who possessed knowledge, and the student has been the one who needed knowledge. Although other media, such as the television, hinted at a breakdown of this relationship, it is now a fact that the 21st century will demand a different teacher–pupil relationship. Every pupil in any school can have an army of scholars (knowers) at their fingertips inside a small laptop computer. The role of the teacher must soon transition from that of a purveyor of knowledge to a guide to learning. The whole structure of education as we understand it, including buildings, books, grades, and teachers, will be questioned in response to this change.

Listen to a seventh grader at Union Hill School in Alabama, Lacey Howard, speak of the future: "My name is Lacey Howard, and I am the web mistress of my school homepage. In our school, learning is turning toward computers and the Internet. We use computers in any research we have to do, and I use them all the time for papers and projects. It allows parents and children to see what is happening at our school and it is very lively. There is something there for everyone."

Students like Lacey Howard know, intuitively, that the learning medium of the twenty-first century cannot continue to be a classroom coverage of preexisting knowledge. Fortunately for middle school educators, these changes in roles, technology, and the teacher–student relationship fit well with our conception of education. As we move to develop a personal, balanced, relevant, and developmentally appropriate curriculum, change is on our side. From the existing middle school with its 35-five year history of innovation, can come the new American middle school; a school designed for living in the twenty-first century.

In the chapters that follow, the authors will lead the reader toward that new conception. Our experience with middle schools dates from the beginning, and as senior educators in this movement we can empathize with the leaders of the old junior high school who launched middle schools in America. The task is large, but the journey will be exciting. This time, however, the new middle school must advocate its philosophy and not worry about numbers or movements. Middle schools are an established fact in American education, but the true middle school program has yet to find form at the classroom level. Our theory of educating, of learning, must be clear and our tolerance for diversity must grow. We will have to let go of old structures and adopt new delivery technologies. We must climb into the new boat!

Most important, the authors believe, middle schools in the twenty-first century must be characterized by teachers who are guides and students and parents who are active partners in the learning process. The world is truly a web in terms of learning, and our students will live in that world. Teachers can lead us to that future, and we believe they will!

As it was in 1910, and again in 1960, the redesign of the middle school will begin with a study of the client, the preadolescent. Unlike a generation ago, today's middle school student is more adolescent than child. Chapter 2 introduces the reader to those things that we know to be true about the preadolescent that can help us develop a meaningful program of study.

SUMMARY

Intermediate education in America is 90 years old and its lasting objective is to provide an appropriate educational program for older children and young adolescents. The early attempt, the junior high school, was replaced by the American middle school in the 1960s, and as we enter the twenty-first century, a new type of middle school is evolving.

The ideas that undergird middle school education are consistently progressive. Taking ideas from humanistic educators like Rousseau, Frobels, Pestolozzi, and John Dewey, the middle school literature clearly addresses human development as its instructional focus. The preadolescent period, transitioning childhood to adolescence, is the rationale, basis of organization, and criterion for curricular decision making in the middle school. The challenges to develop such a developmentally appropriate school in America always have revolved around the reduction of standardization and the expansion of the curriculum beyond knowledge acquisition.

Due largely to the deteriorating condition of the junior high school, the American middle school grew rapidly during a 20-year period to become the dominant form of intermediate education. Early advocates of the middle school warned of the dangers of becoming preoccupied with growth and with focusing on organization rather than instruction. Imperceptibly, during the past 20 years, the middle school has become preoccupied with test scores and practices of standardization. It has come, in many instances, to be indistinguishable from the school it replaced.

As we enter the twenty-first century, three trends act to promote renewal of the middle school model. Decentralization of control, new interactive communication technologies, and the rapidly changing relationship of the teacher and the student all support efforts to redirect the middle school program. The authors believe that teacher-led change efforts can revolutionize instruction in middle schools and a new form of middle school education will evolve. The prerequisite for a successful transition to this new form will be emphasizing our beliefs about children and learning, rather than masking them as a strategy of growth.

Selected Learning Activities

1. Using any search engine on the Internet go to Yahoo.com, and enter "middle schools." Select the Ford Middle School webpage in Achushnet, Massachusetts, and then pro-ceed to your state. Browse the webpages and find at least five ideas that excite you.

2. The authors have stated that the junior high school and the middle school have similar

goals. If this is true, what was unique about the American middle school 1965–2000?

3. The authors are calling for a reformed middle school to meet the needs of students in the twenty-first century. In 500 words or less, write a rationale for this new American middle school.

Notes

1. Donald Eichhorn, "Middle School Learner Characteristics," in *The Middle School: A Look Ahead* (Fairborn, OH: National Middle School Association, 1977), pp. 88–105.
2. Jon Wiles and Joseph Bondi, *The Essential Middle School* (Columbus, OH: Charles Merrill, 1980), pp. 16–17.
3. Joseph Bondi, "Programs for Emerging Adolescent Learners," in *Middle School in the Making* (Alexandria, VA: Association for Supervision and Curriculum Development, 1974), pp. 17–19.
4. Neil Atkins, "Rethinking Education in the Middle," *Theory into Practice,* June 1968, pp. 118–119. Columbus, OH: Ohio State Univ.
5. Paul George, ed., *The Middle School: A Look Ahead* (Fairborn, OH: The National Middle School Association, 1977).
6. Jon Wiles and Julia Thomason, "Middle School Research: A Review of Substantial Studies 1968–1974," in *Middle School in the Making* (Alexandria, VA: ASCD, 1974), pp. 124–127.
7. John Dewey, *The Child and the Curriculum* (New York: Macmillan, 1902), pp. 20–26.
8. John Goodlad and Francis Klein, *Behind Classroom Doors* (Worthington, OH: Charles A. Jones Publishing Company, 1970) .

Selected References

Association for Supervision and Curriculum Development. 1975 Joseph Bondi, ed. *The Middle School We Need.* Washington, DC: ASCD.

ASCD. 1974. *Middle School in the Making.* Alexandria, VA: ASCD.

Beane, James. 1993. *The Middle School Curriculum: From Rhetoric to Reality.* Westerville, Ohio: National Middle School Association.

Bondi, Joseph. 1972. *Developing Middle Schools: A Guidebook.* Wheeling, WV: Whitehall Publishing.

George, Paul, and Alexander, William. 1997. *The Exemplary Middle School.* New York: Holt Rinehart Winston.

Gerrick, Gregory. 1999. *Affirming Middle Grades Education.* Boston: Allyn and Bacon.

Kellough, Richard, and Kellough, Noreen. 1998. *Middle School Teaching: A Guide to Methods and Resources.* Upper Saddle River, NJ: Prentice-Hall.

McEwin, Kenneth. 1996. *America's Middle Schools: Practices and Programs-A 25 Year Perspective.* Westerville, OH: National Middle School Association.

National Middle School Association. 1977. *The Middle School: A Look Ahead.* Fairborn, OH.

Queen, J. Allen. 1999. *Curriculum Practice in the Elementary and Middle Schools.* Columbus, OH: Charles Merrill Publishing.

Van Til, William, Vars, Gordon, and Lounsbury, John. 1961. *Modern Education in the Junior High School Years.* New York: Bobbs-Merrill.

Wiles, Jon. 1976. *Planning Guidelines for Middle Grades Education,* Dubuque, IA: Kendall-Hunt.

CHAPTER 2

Today's Preadolescent Learner

Nothing is so unequal as the equal treatment of unequals.

An early adolescent is . . .

a canvas to be filled.
a field to be tilled.
clay to be molded.
a bulb to develop.
a diamond to be cut.
a challenge to be met.
a poem to be written.
a song to be sung.
a fragrance to be released.
a life to be saved.
a friend to be made.
a gift to the future.
a bridge to the stars.
a pain in the heart.
a tear in the eye.
energy to be channeled.
a riddle to be solved.
a birdsong in December.
a candle to be lit.
a rain for the sod.
the right hand of God.

—Georgia Ensminger, Oldham
Middle School, LaGrange Kentucky.
Used with permission.

The most important pupils in today's schools is that diverse group caught in the middle years—the years between childhood and adolescence. A growing body of knowledge shows that what happens to students between the ages of 10 and 14 determines not only their future success in school, but success in life as well.

Writings on the subject are filled with short, sometimes clever, descriptions of young adolescents—"awkward and clumsy," "filled with turbulent emotions," "displays emerging independence," "trying." Yet, who *are* these young adolescents in our schools' middle grades?

This chapter is designed to give the reader a better understanding of the characteristics of emerging adolescent learners and resultant implications for school programs. It also provides a study of the problems that affect a modern society, problems that exert a profound influence on an impressionable age group.

The poem in Figure 2.1 reflects the uncertainty of the emerging adolescent who is neither boy nor man, neither girl nor woman. Because we often do not understand the behavior of others, we are likely to attribute negative motives to them. This especially holds true for young adolescents. When confronted with normal behaviors of young adolescents, such as loud talking or wearing out-

FIGURE 2.1   Understanding the Emerging Adolescent Learner

> How high is the sky?
> Who invented the tie?
> Why was I born?
> Who am I?
> What is the reason?
> When is a season?
> Where am I going ——
> This I really have to know.

Source: Fred Buckman, Fitzgerald's Middle School, Largo, Florida. Used with permission.

landish clothes, we attribute them to a purposeful attempt to frustrate or infuriate us. David Elkind,[1] a child psychologist, has, through the interpretation of his studies and those of Piaget (see Table 2.1), provided us with insights into the troubling behaviors of emerging adolescents[2].

A common problem of young adolescents is their tendency to interpret situations more complexly than is warranted. For instance, simple decisions about what slacks or dress to wear are complicated when they consider extraneous concerns about how and why the clothes were bought in the first place. In school, young adolescents often approach their subjects at a much too complex level and thereby fail in them—not because the studies are too hard, but because they are too simple.

Elkind attributes such behaviors to newly attained thinking capacities made possible through what Piaget calls *formal operations*. Formal operations allow a pupil to consider many variables at the same time, to conceive ideals and contrary-to-fact propositions. But in the young adolescent, these newly attained formal operations often are not under full control. The capacity to think of many alternatives is not coupled immediately with the ability to assign priorities and to decide which choice is best. That is why young adolescents sometimes appear backward, when in fact they are bright.

Formal operations also allow young adolescents to think about other people's thinking. This ability is not always coupled with the ability to distinguish between what is of interest to others and what is of interest to self. Because the emerging adolescent is concerned with the physical and social changes going on in his life, he believes everyone else to be equally preoccupied with his appearance and behavior. Young adolescents, then, surround themselves with an imaginary audience.

The imaginary audience makes this age group extremely self-conscious; they believe themselves to be the center of everyone's attention. Fantasies of making a touchdown or singing before a large audience are common imaginary audience fantasies in which the youth is the center of everyone's attention.

TABLE 2.1 Stages of Intellectual Development as Described by Piaget

Stages of Development–Middle Years	*7–15 Age Range*
Concrete Operations Thinks out problems previously worked out. Logical thought as evidenced by genuine classification, learning to organize objects into a series; reversing operations (as in arithmetic). a. Masters logical operations using material with a concrete content b. Unable to think abstractly about a problem c. Understands the principle of conservation leading directly to an awareness of reversibility d. Uses various approaches to the solution of a problem e. Concerned with the relationship of the parts to the whole f. Performs the operation of serializing g. Uses primarily sociocentric language while egocentric speech decreases h. Can comprehend the following four concrete operational groupings; combinativity, reversibility, associativity, and identity or nullifability.	7–11 years
Formal Operations Comprehends abstract concepts as evidenced by ability to form ideas and reason about the future, ability to handle contrary-to-fact propositions, and ability to develop and test hypotheses.	11–15 years
Substage A Appears to be a preparatory stage in which adolescents may make correct discoveries and handle certain formal operations, but the approach is cumbersome and they are not yet able to provide systematic and rigorous proof.	11–12 years
Substage B Capable of formulating more elegant generalizations and advancing more inclusive laws. Most of all they are able to provide spontaneously more systematic proof since they can use methods of control. Higher degree of mastery of the formal operations; they have the ability to make logical combinations in the following four ways: by conjunction, by disjunction, by implication, by incompatibility.	13–15 years onward

Source: Table form adapted from Ernest R. Hilgard and Richard C. Atkinson, *Introduction to Psychology,* 4th ed. (New York: Harcourt Brace Jovanovich Inc. 1968). The information presented here represents a synthesis of descriptions of Piaget's theory of intellectual development cited in Robert F. Biehler, *Psychology Applied to Teaching* (Boston: Houghton Mifflin, 1971), p. 81; and Herbert Ginsburg and Sylvia Oper, Piaget's *Theory of Intellectual Development* (Upper Saddle River, NJ: Prentice Hall; 1969), pp. 26–206.

Groups of young people sometimes contrive to create an audience by their loud and provocative behavior. This behavior often annoys adults within listening range. The pervasive imaginary audience of young adolescents accounts for both their self-consciousness and their distasteful public behavior.

Vandalism in schools, which seems irrational, becomes less so when one understands that it is often done with audience reaction in mind. While committing the act, the young vandal speculates about how outraged the audience will be.

The center-stage, I–me world of emerging adolescents leads them to believe that they are special and not subject to the natural laws that pertain to others. The young girl who becomes pregnant, or the young boy who experiments with drugs, believes others will get caught, "not me."

The *self* is an all-important preoccupation of young people, and they assume that what is common to everyone is unique to them. One example is the son who says, "Dad, you just don't know how it feels to be in love," or the daughter who says, "Mom, you just don't know how much I need extra allowance."

The reverse preoccupation also occurs; that is, young adolescents may feel that everyone is concerned with the freckles on their nose. Any argument to the contrary carries little impact because it is arguing with another person's reality.

As young people grow and mature, they begin to share their concerns with others and develop friendships in which intimacies are shared. The tragic, self-destructive behavior of many young adolescents often occurs because they have a sense of loneliness brought on by the belief that their problems are uniquely theirs.

The emerging adolescent often displays hypocritical behavior. For instance, he will refuse to allow a brother or sister in his room to borrow things, but will go into his father's or mother's study, borrow a laptop, calculator, or CD player, and not return it. Hypocrisy is but another by-product of formal operations that has not been fully elaborated. The young adolescent is able to conceptualize fairly abstract rules of behavior but lacks the experience to see their relevance to concrete behavior. The youth who believes roles are for everyone else but him or her upsets adults who regard such behavior as self-serving. Again, it must be remembered that this behavior results from intellectual immaturity, not from lack of moral character.

Adolescent idealism often results in the ability to conceive and express high moral principles but not the ability to find concrete ways to attain them. As adolescents mature and begin to engage in meaningful activities, they learn the need to work toward ideals. The middle school can be a place where young people become pragmatic without becoming cynical about ideals and moral principles.

Piaget and Elkind have helped middle school educators shift a whole set of behaviors attributed to emerging adolescents from the realm of "bad" to the realm of "behavior typical for the age." By recognizing that behaviors of middle school students reflect intellectual immaturity, middle school educators can themselves become more rational in their reactions to those students.

CHARACTERISTICS OF EMERGING ADOLESCENTS AND IMPLICATIONS FOR THE MIDDLE SCHOOL

Preadolescents and early adolescents experience dramatic physical, social, emotional, and intellectual changes that result from maturational changes. More biological changes occur in the bodies of 10- to 14-year olds than any other age group, with the exception of children in their first three years of life. The middle school has benefited from recent research relating to children going through the major transition from late childhood to adolescence. Those research data have provided additional validated facts about the physiological and psychological dynamics acting in and on emerging adolescent learners.

When junior high schools were first developed more than 90 years ago, only generalized data regarding growth and development of students were available. Although important longitudinal studies featuring the growth and development of boys and girls were conducted between 1930 and 1960, the results of those studies had little impact on the educational program of young adolescents.

The middle school has attempted to use data pertinent to growth and development of 10- to 14-year olds to justify certain organizational patterns. Unfortunately, some of the data are incorrect, such as data relating to the earlier maturation of girls than boys. Middle school literature is filled with statements purporting to show that American girls are reaching sexual maturity at a younger and younger age. Such statements often were used to justify moving sixth-grade and, in some cases, fifth-grade students into the middle school. In reality, no comparative studies indicate that the average age at which girls first menstruate has changed. The most conclusive study was conducted in 1976 by the National Institutes of Health, which reported that no significant age difference existed in the first menstrual period (menarche) between girls in the study and their mothers. Seven hundred eighty-one girls participated in this study conducted at the Massachusetts Institute of Technology and Massachusetts General Hospital. (Girls in the study were of similar background and about the same height and weight of girls about the same age studied in 1943, 1954, and 1973.) These results also did not support the belief that each generation is taller and healthier than the last.

Because the transitional years between childhood and adolescence are marked by distinct changes in the bodies and minds of boys and girls, the success of the middle school depends on teachers and administrators understanding each learner and his or her unique developmental pattern. Table 2.2 details characteristics of emerging adolescent learners, together with implications for the middle school.

The extreme differences in the rate and scale of growth and development among preadolescents is dramatized in Figure 2.2. Most of these conditions might be found in a typical eighth-grade middle school classroom. Figure 2.3 examines the shaky bridge linking childhood to adolescence.

TABLE 2.2 Development of Emerging Adolescents and Its Implications for the Middle School

Characteristics of Emerging Adolescents	*Implications for the Middle School*
Physical Development	
Accelerated physical development begins in transescence, marked by increase in weight, height, heart size, lung capacity, and muscular strength. Boys and girls grow at varying rates. Girls tend to be taller for the first two years and tend to be more physically advanced. Bone growth is faster than muscle development, and the uneven muscle/bone development results in lack of coordination and awkwardness. Bones may lack protection of covering muscles and supporting tendons.	Provide a health and science curriculum that emphasizes self-understanding about body change. Guidance counselors and community resource persons (e.g., pediatricians) can help students understand what is happening to their bodies. Schedule adaptive physical education classes to build physical coordination. Equipment design should help students develop small and large muscles.
In pubescent girls, secondary sex characteristics continue to develop, with breasts enlarging and menstruation beginning.	Limit intense sports competition; avoid contact sports. Schedule sex education classes; health and hygiene seminars.
A wide range of individual differences among students begins to appear. Although the sequential order of development is relatively consistent in each sex, boys tend to lag a year or two behind girls. There are marked individual differences in physical development of boys and girls. The age of greatest variability in physiological development and physical size is about age 13.	Provide opportunities for interaction among students of different ages, but avoid situations in which physical development can be compared (e.g., communal showers). Emphasize intramural programs rather than interscholastic athletics so that each student may participate regardless of physical development. Where interscholastic sports programs exist, number of games should be limited, with games played in afternoon rather than evening.
Glandular imbalances occur, resulting in acne, allergies, dental and eye defects—some health disturbances are real and some are imaginary.	Provide regular physical examinations for all middle school students.
Boys and girls display changes in body contour—large nose, protruding ears, long arms—have posture problems, and are self-conscious about their bodies.	Health classes should emphasize exercises for good posture. Students should understand through self-analysis that growth is an individual process and occurs unevenly.
A girdle of fat often appears around the hips and thighs of boys in early puberty. Slight development of tissue under the skin around the nipple occurs briefly, causing anxiety in boys who fear they are developing feminine characteristics.	Films and talks by doctors and counselors can help students understand the changes the body goes through during this period. A carefully planned program of sex education developed in collaboration with parents, medical doctors, and community agencies should be developed.
Students are likely to be disturbed by body changes. Girls especially are likely to be disturbed about the physical changes that accompany sexual maturation.	

TABLE 2.2 Continued

Physical Development	
Receding chins, cowlicks, dimples, and changes in voice result in possible embarrassment to boys.	Teacher and parental reassurance and understanding are necessary to help students understand that many body changes are temporary.
Boys and girls tend to tire easily but won't admit it.	Advise parents to insist that students get proper rest; overexertion should be discouraged.
Fluctuations in basal metabolism may cause students to be extremely restless at times and listless at others.	Provide an opportunity for daily exercise and a place where students can be children by playing and being noisy for short periods.
	Encourage activities such as special-interest classes and hands-on exercises. Students should be allowed to move around physically in classes and avoid long periods of passive work.
Boys and girls show ravenous appetites and peculiar tastes; may overtax digestive system with large quantities of improper foods.	Provide snacks to satisfy between-meal hunger as well as nutritional guidance specific to this age group.

Social Development	
Affiliation base broadens from family to peer group. Conflict sometimes results due to splitting of allegiance between peer group and family.	Teachers should work closely with the family to help adults realize that peer pressure is a normal part of the maturation process. Parents should be encouraged to continue to provide love and comfort even though they may feel rejected.
	Teachers should be counselors. Homebase, teacher-adviser house-plan arrangements should be encouraged.
Peers become sources for standards and models of behavior. Child's occasional rebellion does not diminish importance of parents for development of values. Emerging adolescents want to make their own choices, but authority still remains primarily with family.	Sponsor school activities that permit students to interact socially with many school personnel. Family studies can help ease parental conflicts. Parental involvement at school should be encouraged, but parents should not be too conspicuous by their presence.
	Encourage co-curricular activities. For example, an active student government will help students develop guidelines for interpersonal relations and behavior standards.
Society's mobility has broken ties to peer groups and created anxieties in emerging adolescents.	Promote family-like grouping of students and teachers to provide stability for new students. Interdisciplinary units can be structured to provide interaction among various groups of students. Clubs and special-interest classes should be an integral part of the school day.
Students are confused and frightened by new school settings.	Orientation programs and buddy systems can reduce the trauma of moving from an elementary school to a middle school. Family teams can encourage a sense of belonging.

Social Development

Students show unusual or drastic behavior at times—aggressive, daring, boisterous, argumentative.	Schedule debates, plays, play days, and other activities to allow students to show off in a productive way.
"Puppy love" emerges, with a show of extreme devotion to a particular boy or girl. However, allegiance may be transferred to a new friend overnight.	Role-playing and guidance exercises can provide the opportunity to act out feelings. Provide opportunities for social interaction between the sexes—parties and games, but not dances in the early grades of the middle school.
Youth feel that the will of the group must prevail and sometimes can be almost cruel to those not in their group. They copy and display fads of extremes in clothes, speech, mannerisms, and handwriting; very susceptible to media advertising.	Set up an active student government so students can develop their own guidelines for dress and behavior. Adults should be encouraged not to react with outrage when extreme dress or mannerisms are displayed.
Boys and girls show strong concern for what is right and for social justice; also show concern for less-fortunate others.	Foster plans that allow students to engage in service activities, such as peer teaching, which allows students to help other students. Community projects (e.g., assisting in a senior citizens club or helping in a child care center) can be planned by students and teachers.
They are influenced by adults—attempt to identify with adults other than their parents.	Flexible teaching patterns should prevail so students can interact with a variety of adults with whom they can identify.
Despite a trend toward heterosexual interests, same-sex affiliation tends to dominate.	Plan large group activities rather than boy–girl events. Intramurals can be scheduled so students can interact with friends of the same or opposite sex.
Students desire direction and regulation but reserve the right to question or reject suggestions of adults.	Provide opportunities for students to accept more responsibility in setting standards for behavior. Students should be helped to establish realistic goals and be assisted in realizing those goals.

Emotional Development

Erratic and inconsistent behavior is prevalent. Anxiety and fear contrast with reassuring bravado. Feelings tend to shift between superiority and inferiority. Coping with physical changes, striving for independence from family, becoming a person in her own right, and learning a new mode of intellectual functioning are all emotion-laden problems for an emerging adolescent. Students have many fears, real and imagined. At no other time in development is he or she likely to encounter such a diverse number of problems simultaneously.	Encourage self-evaluation among students. Design activities that help students play out their emotions. Activity programs should provide opportunities for shy students to be drawn out and loud students to engage in calming activities. Counseling must operate as a part of, rather than an adjunct to, the learning program. Students should be helped to interpret superiority and inferiority feelings. Mature value systems should be encouraged by allowing students to examine options of behavior and to study consequences of various actions.

TABLE 2.2 Continued

Intellectual Development	
Middle school learners prefer active over passive learning activities and prefer interaction with peers during learning activities.	Encourage physical movement with small-group discussions, learning centers, and creative dramatics suggested as good activity projects. Provide a program of learning that is exciting and meaningful.
Students are usually very curious and exhibit a strong willingness to learn things they consider useful. They enjoy using skills to solve real-life problems.	Organize curricula around real-life concepts (e.g., conflict, competition, peer-group influence). Provide activities in formal and informal situations to improve reasoning powers. Studies of the community and the environment are particularly relevant to the age group.
Student often display heightened egocentrism and will argue to convince others or to clarify their own thinking. Independent, critical thinking emerges.	Organized discussions of ideas and feelings in peer groups can facilitate self-understanding. Provide experiences for individuals to express themselves by writing and participating in dramatic productions.
Studies show that brain growth in transescents slows between the ages of 12 and 14.	Learners' cognitive skills should be refined; continued growth during ages 12 to 14 may not be expected. Provide opportunities for enjoyable studies in the arts. Encourage self-expression in all subjects.

FIGURE 2.2   Portrait of a Thirteen-Year Old

6 feet 2 inches tall	*or*	4 feet 7 inches tall
Trips going up the stairs	*or*	Wins an Olympic gold medal with a perfect 10.0 in parallel bar competition
An alcoholic or drug addict	*or*	A Sunday school leader and Little Leaguer
Wears dental braces	*or*	Competes in Miss Teenage America
Looking forward to quitting school	*or*	Curious and enthusiastic about learning
Unable to read the comic page	*or*	Reads the *Wall Street Journal*
Has trouble with whole numbers	*or*	Solves geometry problems easily
A "regular" in juvenile court	*or*	An Eagle Scout
Already a mother of two	*or*	Still plays with dolls

Source: Beth Jana Bondi.

FIGURE 2.3   *The Shaky Transition from Childhood to Adolescence*

Stability →	N A L Y	→	Stability
	I T I T		
	S B I		
☐ Security of childhood is a world in which everything is O.K.	PHYSICALLY		☐ Restored faith in self-concept
☐ Things are either good or bad, with few shades of gray	SOCIALLY		☐ Ability to look at the world realistically
	EMOTIONALLY		
☐ The future is of little concern	INTELLECTUALLY		☐ Ability to reason abstractly
☐ Physically equal to peers	→	→	☐ Physically equal to age group
☐ Academic demands are primarily concrete		→	☐ Academic demands are more complex
☐ The preadolescent period entails perhaps the most radical transformation of self-concept since the so-called terrible twos.			
☐ This age group undergoes the greatest degree of change since infancy, the likes of which will not be experienced perhaps until senility.			
☐ Puberty is a traumatic experience.			
☐ No other age group encompasses such a wide range of developmental diversity—and this is the group with which we work.			

Source: Joseph Bondi, *Developing Middle Schools: A Guidebook.* Whitehall Publishing, Wheeling, WV, 1972, p. 28.

NEEDS SUGGESTED BY GROWTH AND DEVELOPMENT CHARACTERISTICS

The foregoing table of physical, emotional, social, and intellectual characteristics of students and the implications for the middle school suggests two terms: *transition* and *difference.* We must develop a school to encompass the transitional nature of the group as a whole and to consider the vast differences within the group.

Middle graders need security on one hand and freedom to experience and explore on the other. They need an environment that protects them from themselves without smothering the "self."

Although variations among individuals are marked, certain basic needs appear to be common among this age group.

- To be safe and free of threat
- To be recognized
- To be loved
- To be independent
- To be part of a group with identification and acceptance

Preadolescence is a restless age for girls and boys. The torture of trying to sit still in school is obvious, and some pupils learn to perform remarkable feats of contortion without falling out of their chairs. Therefore, a school atmosphere in which physical movement is integral to the educative process is of high priority for the preadolescent. Activity-related learning, such as drawing, designing, constructing, and making displays, as well as moving from classroom to library or from classroom to play center, is vital to the preadolescent. In other words, a steady grind at the school desk is undesirable at this restless age.

Personal development begins to undergo significant and perplexing alterations and frequently children commence a self-searching quest on which they seek to locate themselves in a shifting social complex—a journey some adults never complete satisfactorily. Despite a commitment to fair play, these youth nonetheless must struggle to establish a relationship between their own sense of values and the value inconsistencies of others, especially adults.

Transescents are curious, explorative, and interested in many things. They are in the early stages of the conflict between their desire to be independent and the necessity to depend on others. They live in a world of shifting sands—unsure of themselves, unsure of their environment, and puzzled by the relationship between the two.

Pupils need guidance in the middle years to help them grow and develop into fully functioning individuals. The middle school has been suggested as a school for producing such individuals. Perhaps the message found in the following letter from a junior high school student will help illustrate the needs of young adults at this critical turning point.

Who Am I?

I have many things I want
            to say but—
No one will listen.

I have many things I want
            to do but—
No one will let me.

There are so many places
            I want to go but—
No one will take me.

And the things I write
            are corrected but—
No one reads them.

Who am I?

—A sixth grader

EMERGING ADOLESCENTS IN A CHANGING SOCIETY

Normal developmental or maturational changes that occur in 10- to 14-year olds create a set of problems unlike those experienced by any other age group. Middle school students of the 2000s are also faced with another set of problems, not of their own making: They have become victims of a changing society that no longer has the time or inclination to provide the nurturing environment that emerging adolescents need to grow and to develop into fully functioning adults. Even though a considerable body of knowledge proves that success in school, and indeed success in life, depends on what happens to preadolescent and early adolescent students, this group is the least understood, the least cared for, and the most fragile in our society.

Misunderstood and Neglected

Today's social institutions operate on the premise that all students between the ages of 10 and 14 are difficult, disruptive, obstreperous, and almost impossible to deal with. Parents and educators alike know that early adolescent bodies begin to mature sometime in the middle school years, but they do not understand why some students grow up early while others are slow to reach physical maturity. Even though physical growth is often traumatic and unpredictable, some parents and educators are unaware to what extent transescents can be affected by the changes occurring in their bodies. Although the onset of menstruation, acne, and development of secondary sex characteristics, for example, may create tensions that affect their school performance, girls still are expected to display the same behavioral patterns every day. Consider how emerging adolescent girls begin to compete with their mothers in ways mothers do not understand and which may create conflicts at home.

Boys are also affected by a society that leads them to believe men should be tall, broad-shouldered, and narrow-hipped—the so-called all-American look. Long before puberty, boys believe that being tall is equated with being masculine. Tall, early-maturing boys get picked as team captains, date the prettiest girls, and are chosen as class leaders whether they exhibit leadership qualities or not. Often, early maturers are thrust into situations in which they are expected to behave like adults socially when they are still mere children.

On the other hand, life is often difficult for the late maturer, but when he does catch up, he may have gained in the long run from his painful experiences. Because they have had to live with and overcome a delicate problem of their own, late maturers are often more sensitive, more thoughtful, and more understanding in dealing with other people than are early maturers.

Adults often treat emerging adolescents as small children. Because students are grouped by chronological age, a 13-year-old, sexually active girl is expected to possess the same basic interests as a 13-year-old boy who may still be two years away from puberty. Too many schools maintain age segregation and grade structures based on chronological age rather than on maturation.

In addition to physical growth, social changes occur in the middle school years. As indicated earlier in the chapter, emerging adolescents begin to pull away from adults and gravitate toward peers, as evidenced by dress, habits, and language. Without understanding the dynamics of this transformation from dependent, obedient, sweet child to independent, disobedient, ill-tempered young adolescent, adults misread signals and become impatient and short-tempered. Worst of all, they may abdicate their responsibility as adults and parents by no longer going to PTA meetings when their sons or daughters reach grade seven, ceasing to visit the school, and hesitating to show approval or disapproval of their children's behavior. Consider parents who have called the middle school teacher or principal and said, "I don't know what to do with my daughter; *you* do something."

Society has created a myth about boys and girls in transescence, the myth that they will somehow grow up by themselves and that adults should leave them alone until they are full adolescents.

The survey in Figure 2.4 has been administered to over fifty-five thousand middle school students from all socioeconomic levels. Students were asked to rank the eleven values (all important values to emerging adolescents), from most to least important. Their teachers were also asked to rank the values and to indicate how they thought students would rank the values. Results of the survey are listed in Table 2.3.

Overwhelmingly, students and teachers chose family security as their most important value. The results clearly indicate that middle school students do not want their parents to abdicate their parental responsibility.

The middle school years for 10- to 14-year olds are characterized by emotional instability. It is difficult for some adults to understand why students are happy one moment and sad the next, why chemical changes in the body trigger certain emotions, or how chemical and hormonal imbalances affect their personalities.

A final area in which understanding is lacking lies in achievement. The widest range of achievement occurs in the middle grades. Students falling a half year behind grade level in elementary school reading find themselves two to three years behind by the time they reach middle school. Parents do not understand why middle school educators do not eliminate affective programs (those that help pupils understand themselves) and simply concentrate on basic skills. Parents need help in understanding that there should be a balance in the curriculum among personal development activities, basic skills programs, and content studies.

As for our society's negligence in caring for emerging adolescents, it is possible to quantify some of that neglect. Middle schools cannot fulfill all the needs of emerging adolescents; yet some would hold the schools solely responsible for the health and well-being of this age group. Only five percent of the generalists who practice pediatrics or family medicine have received training in adolescent health care. Although millions of dollars are spent on juvenile delinquency in the United States, less than one percent of grants and research funded by the National Institute for Child Health and Human Development places a primary emphasis on preadolescents and early adolescents.

Most national voluntary organizations and clubs have experienced declining memberships among young adolescents. Furthermore, too little national research has been conducted on middle school learners. As a result, there seems to be little relationship between what many schools do and what is actually known about young adolescents. The major tasks of adolescence include sepa-

FIGURE 2.4 *Values Survey: Teacher–Student*

Rank 1 (*most* important) to 11 (*least* important)	I am a: ____ Student ____ Parent
Self	**Other**
____ A comfortable life (nice house, plenty of money)	____
____ Equality (brotherhood; equal chance for all, rich or poor, black or white, man or woman)	____
____ Family security (family getting along together, all living together, all caring for each other)	____
____ Self-respect (liking yourself, feeling good about what you do)	____
____ Sense of accomplishment (doing something worthwhile for society; making a lasting contribution)	____
____ Freedom (being independent, having free choice)	____
____ Happiness (personal contentment)	____
____ True friendship (having friends who are close and loyal)	____
____ Exciting life (fun-filled, active, enjoyable)	____
____ World at peace (no wars, riots, less crime and violence)	____
____ Good education (opportunity to finish high school—go on to college or further training)	____

TABLE 2.3 *Results of Values Survey*

Ranked by Students	*Ranked by Teachers*	*As Teachers Believed Students Would Rank*
Family	Family	World at peace
Freedom	Self-respect	True friendship
Happiness	Equality	Family
Self-respect	Freedom	Exciting life
Comfortable life	World at peace	Happiness
True friendship	Sense of accomplishment	Comfortable life
Good education	Happiness	Self-respect
World at peace	True friendship	Freedom
Exciting life	Good education	Sense of accomplishment
Equality	Comfortable life	Equality
Sense of accomplishment	Exciting life	Good education

ration, individualization, and commitment; yet, few aspects of schooling have accommodated those tasks. The middle school must do so in the midst of a society that is often too busy to care. Middle school leadership must help parents and the community understand that only through their combined efforts will middle graders receive the care and nurture they need to make a successful transition from childhood to adolescence.

The American Family—Fractured and Fragile

Entering the twenty-first century, it seems Americans see the same sorry trajectory of moral decline and long for earlier and better times (see Figure 2.5).

If there is any outrage among the citizenry, it is directed at Hollywood. Many blame violence and sex on television and in the movies. Others blame the materialistic culture of the '90s, which saw a worship of $100 Nike sneakers and a culture that crowds out relaxed family time.

The impressionable group of youngsters found in the middle grades are direct targets of many of the preceding changes in society. As this group surfs the Internet, it becomes even more vulnerable.

In the 1989 document, *Turning Points: Preparing American Education for the 21st Century,* the Carnegie Council on Adolescent Development stated: "Freed from the dependency of childhood, but not yet able to find their own path to adulthood, many young people feel a desperate sense of isolation. Surrounded by their equally confused peers, too many make poor decisions with harmful or lethal consequences. Middle grade schools are potentially society's most powerful force to recapture millions of youth."[3]

Today, many children are growing up in conditions that do not provide the moral or ethical framework to develop good character. Even when families try hard to provide a strong foundation, they often find efforts undermined by the media, the child's peers and, increasingly, the Internet.[4]

The American Family—A Profile

The United States Census Report in 2000 revealed about 45 million Americans moved in 1999 and 2000—about 18 percent of the population.

Children represent 40 percent of the poor although they make up only 26 percent of the population.

The dropout rate remained about 5.4 percent of students in grades 10, 11, and 12 during the last year of the twentieth century.

The number of single parents tripled between 1980 and 2000. The divorce rate exceeds 50 percent—the highest in the world. Consequently, one in four children in public schools comes from a nontraditional home. Half of all children spend all or part of their childhood with one parent (see Figure 2.6).

Men and women are marrying later than before, with the average age at first marriage of 27.1 for men and 24.8 for women.

Because fewer people are being born and more dying as the population ages, the rate of increase in population is less than it has been since the 1990 census. Still the population of the United States will grow to 394 million by 2050, about 50 percent more than in 2000.

Eighty percent of new workers are minorities, including women. More Americans moonlight than at any other time in history.

Drug risks for middle school students continue to rise at the beginning of the new century. This confirms what researchers have long known: that cigarettes, alcohol (primarily beer) and inhalants are used by children more than

FIGURE 2.5

American Families: The Lives They Live...

Percentage in each group who say description applies to them

		GENDER		AGE				EDUCATION			RACE	
	ALL	MEN	WOMEN	18-34	35-49	50-64	65 AND OLDER	HIGH SCHOOL	SOME COLLEGE	COLLEGE GRADUATE	WHITE	AFRICAN AMERICAN
Two-working-parent household	23	22	23	30	39	8	1	21	25	23	22	31
Attend religious service at least weekly	39	34	44	29	39	45	55	36	43	42	39	47
Someone in household has tattoo	21	22	21	35	21	16	9	27	24	13	21	24
Watch shows like Jerry Springer or Jenny Jones	20	21	18	29	20	16	9	28	19	11	16	42

And the Problems They Face

Percentage who feel that each problem facing American families is very serious

Societal problems

- Peer pressure on children to use drugs — 63%
- Media sex or violence influencing children — 67%
- Movie and television violence — 51%
- Declining role of religion — 49%
- Declining sense of community — 47%
- Poor role models in sports and entertainment — 42%
- Young people feeling rejected by peers — 42%

Family problems

- Parents' inattention to their children's lives — 83%
- High divorce rate and family breakups — 63%
- Lack of discipline in schools — 56%
- Pressure to make ends meet — 50%
- More single-parent households — 46%
- Emphasizing career ahead of family — 42%
- More two-working-parent households — 31%

Source: Wall Street Journal/NBC News Poll, 6/24/99.

FIGURE 2.6   A Changing America

Of 100 children born today:

- 12 are born out of wedlock
- 41 are born to parents who divorce before the child reaches 18
- 5 are born to parents who separate
- 2 will experience the death of a parent before reaching 18
- 40 will reach 18 without experiencing any of the above

Source: US Dept of Commerce, Census Bureau, 1998.

marijuana or harder drugs. In spite of an all-out attack on tobacco use, the misperception on the part of students that "everybody is doing it," can be a powerful motivator behind much drug use.

Teenage pregnancy fell in the 1990s to the lowest level since 1973. Abortion rates were also down. Reasons are mixed, including more reliable contraceptions, fear of AIDS, a new focus on abstinence and even the strong economy.[5]

As we enter a new century, more and more schools teach values—some sensibly and some in unintended ways. The question is, "Where are the parents?" Character Education in some form has been mandated in all fifty states and the federal government (both Congress and the President) proposed funding in 1999 for character education. Remembering the early middle school and programs like Values Clarification and Self-Esteem Development, educators are cautious about what form character education will take. Even the best character education programs, though, can be seen as the culmination of a long process for which schools have assumed more and more responsibilities traditionally handled at home. The typical middle/secondary school now teaches students how to schedule a balanced day, drive, balance a checkbook, have sex (in sex education), not have sex (in abstinence programs), identify sexual abuse, and avoid HIV.[6] Parents at every opportunity will tell you how busy they are. Of course, they have time to worry aloud about the quality of their local schools, but character education is evidence that our schools worry about the quality of local parents. Figure 2.6 is illustrative of what is happening to children in America.

Segregation on the Rise

A study released in 1999 by the Harvard University Civil Rights Project, "Resegregation in American School," reported that Resegregation in the 1990s reversed a decades-long trend of the South leading the nation in integrated schools.[7] The report also pointed out facts that American schools were continuously increasing segregation among Hispanics, especially in the Northeast and among African-American and Hispanic children in suburban schools. According to the study, all racial groups except whites experience considerable diversity in their schools, but whites remain in overwhelmingly white schools even in areas of significant nonwhite enrollment. The study, based on data from the United States Bureau of the Census and the federal government's National Center for Educational Statistics said the shift to resegregation continues to occur into 2000 as the Hispanic share of the school population has risen 218 percent, the African-American share has grown by a fifth, and the white share has decreased by a sixth. Finally, the study found a close correlation between school districts with few whites and those with high rates of poverty, which is linked to lower educational achievement.

The middle school is the first break many youngsters have from schools of one dominant race or ethnic group. As the urgent crises of higher student achievement and preparing students for a high-tech and global society continue to face middle school educators, parents and educators are concerned about whether their children are going to good schools, whether they are safe, and whether they will learn to read. If this nation is to float back to an educational pattern that in the nation's history has never produced equal and successful schools, the lofty goals stated in Goals 2000 (developed in 1994) will not be realized by a substantial number of students. National political leaders largely ignored the growth of segregation in the 1990s, and that, coupled with court decisions freeing school districts from desegregation orders plus public indifference, will pose new challenges for educators well into the twenty-first century.

Improving Achievement of African-American Students in the Modern Middle School

The National Task Force on Minority High Achievement, founded by the College Board in 1997, studied dozens of middle-class, racially integrated communities across the country attempting to determine reasons for which black students' achievement lagged behind that of whites of comparable socioeconomic status. Reported findings in 1999 were disturbing and puzzling (see Figure 2.7). On some tests, black students from middle class or wealthier families did no better than white students who lived in poverty. And some especially puzzling data suggested that at higher achievement levels, the gap between black and white performance was even wider. More than a dozen of the communities studied networked to learn more about this disparity and to try to do something about it.

No one has claimed to have answers about the problem of underachievement, but there are some factors that have been discussed including: (1) black students in a recent study were found to watch twice as much TV as white students, (2) middle-class, college-educated black parents were often the first generation of their families to have such success, so the roots of their academic and economic accomplishments are less established than those of white families, (3) peer pressure from other African-American students is not conducive to academic achievement, (4) on their upwardly mobile trajectory, black families move frequently, switching children from school to school, not usually an educational plus, (5) teachers have lower expectations, curricula, and access to information for black students, and (6) lingering racism exists in schools.

As the American middle school serves as the foundation for achievement in high school and beyond, those schools must develop programs to overcome the above factors. High on the list is getting more involvement of African-American

FIGURE 2.7

The Gap in Test Scores

Gaps between black and white
students on achievement tests
persist across different levels of
parent income and education.

Black students
White students

INCOME Average combined S.A.T.
scores by college-bound high
school seniors in 1990.

Parental income below $10,000

683
866

Parental income above $70,000
854
998

EDUCATION Average combined
S.A.T. scores by college-bound
high school seniors in 1995.

No parent has high-school degree

655
792

At least one parent with
graduate degree

844
1035

Source: College Entrance Examination
Board, Princeton, NJ, 1999.

parents in their children's education. Not only schools, but African-American
parents are going to have to step up to the plate and do more in the new century.
Parent involvement programs (discussed in a later section) will be one of the keys
to getting all children to achieve to their potential.

Responding to Religious and Sexual Diversity in the Middle Grades

During the twenty-first century, children of traditionally under-represented
groups, often called minorities, will constitute a new majority within the United
States. For schools to be successful, teachers must:

1. Raise awareness about the needs of children and their parents who are not members of the mainstream culture.
2. Support students who are members of diverse religious and cultural groups.
3. Enhance sensitivity to cultural differences in classroom instruction.
4. Raise awareness about the dilemmas that parents of diverse groups face within the mainstream system.
5. Adopt a policy of no tolerance of student-to-student sexual harassment.

Professional educators, regardless of their moral or political convictions are duty-bound to protect and promote the human and civil rights of all people in a classroom. This implies enforcing responsible standards of professional and student conduct in terms of verbal and physical harassment of gay and lesbian students.[8]

The Influence of Television

A national organization, TV-Free America, sponsors a national TV-turnoff week for youngsters and adults annually with tips on how to find replacement activities such as going for a walk, talking to a friend or reading a book. It may be about time for such an activity. The average American spends about three hours and 43 minutes watching television each day (the equivalent of some 56 days a year).

The influence of television on the lives of Americans, particularly middle school students can be seen in the following statistics summarized in Figure 2.8, compiled by TV-Free America.

School Violence

As students leave neighborhood schools to enter middle schools, parents often worry about their safety. The school shootings in the late '90s increased that concern. The shooting, a new kind of violence seems different because it is more heartless, more senseless, and more random. Guns have been brought into schools each day. Student-to-student violent behavior is being played out in our schools, and it mirrors the violent culture that is part of American society.

A number of factors have been identified that are roots of violence in our schools:

- Poverty—The high rate of child poverty in the United States
- Disintegrating home environments
- Child abuse—Children are more likely to be the victims than the perpetrators of violence and many become attackers themselves
- Our violent culture—Adults romanticize violence in our culture
- Our materialistic culture—Even as advertisers target children as an economic resource to be exploited

FIGURE 2.8   *TV Statistics*

- Hours per day that TV is on in an average U.S. home: seven hours and 12 minutes
- Percentage of Americans that regularly watch TV while eating dinner: 66
- Number of videos rented daily in the United States: six million
- Number of public library items checked out daily: three million
- Chance that an American falls asleep with the TV on at least three nights a week: 25%
- Percentage of Americans who say they watch too much TV: 49
- Number of minutes per week that the average American child ages two through 11 watches television: 1,197
- Number of minutes per week that parents spend in meaningful conversation with their children: 38.5
- Percentage of four- to six-year-olds, who, when asked to choose between watching TV and spending time with their fathers, preferred television: 54
- Hours per week of TV viewing shown to negatively affect academic achievement: 10 or more
- Percentage of fourth graders who watch more than 14 hours of television per week: 81
- Chance that an American parent requires that children do their homework before watching TV: 1 in 12
- Percentage of teenagers who can name the city where the U.S. Constitution was written (Philadelphia): 25
- Percentage of teenagers who know where you find the ZIP code 90210 (Beverly Hills): 75
- Number of medical studies since 1985 linking excessive TV watching to increasing rates of obesity: 12
- Percentage of American children ages six to 11 who were seriously overweight in 1963: 4.5
  In 1993: 14
- Number of ads aired for junk food during four hours of Saturday morning cartoons: 202
- Percentage of local TV news broadcast time devoted to advertising: 30
- Percentage devoted to stories about crime, disaster, and war: 53.8
- Percentage devoted to public service announcements: 0.7
- Percentage of Americans who can name the Three Stooges: 59
- Percentage of Americans who can name three Supreme Court justices: 17

—Compiled by TV-Free America, Washington, DC

- Pressure to achieve—Many young people respond to devaluation and pressure with antisocial behavior. Cliques that include labeling with names such as geeks, jocks, and cool people lead to outcasts who often strike back violently (such as in the 1999 school shootings).

In the American middle school, lasting attitudes toward self and others are often formed. The middle school then must become a living laboratory for helping pre- and early adolescents deal with fears, anger and rejection. Four major keys in this process include parent involvement, peer mediation, conflict resolution, and fostering youth leadership.

Parent Involvement

Although studies over the past thirty years identify a strong link between parent involvement in school and increased student achievement, enhanced self-esteem, improved behavior, and better school attendance, family involvement in American schools remains minimal.

Several barriers exist that lead to lack of parent participation in schools. They include cultural, racial, and economic differences between the school staff and parents which lead to stereotyping and incorrect assumptions on both sides.

There are factors, too, that lead to increased parent participation. Included are making sure everyone in the school from teacher to custodian to front office personnel connect with parents to make them aware of how to help students. Parents can help with clean-up and beautification programs organized by the custodian, volunteer at the front desk, man phone banks to call parents, or help mail or deliver school brochures to help the secretaries. Joining with families helps the parents connect with the school. It is important that the school also recognize families validating their contributions to their child's welfare whether it be donating time or materials, being active in the school's governance, or even helping their child with homework in the evening.

Peer Mediation

Understanding what conflict is, how it is a necessary and normal part of life, and why not all conflicts can be resolved using the mediation process is the first skill taught in peer mediation for students. Schools using peer mediation believe they can and do help solve many student conflicts, however. Students who participate in the process either as peer mediators or who seek resolution of a conflict, learn that conflicts over misunderstandings and material items are easier to resolve than conflicts over beliefs and values.

Implementing a Peer-Mediation Program. How do middle school staffs implement a program for peer mediation and conflict resolution?

1. *Support of the administration.* The principal, staff, and community must be involved in the planning, implementation, and assessment of this project. Without this triangle of support the program will have little chance of success.
2. *Selection of students and staff.* Students should be selected to form a cross-section of the school community. Qualities associated with success as peer mediators are willingness to learn, good verbal skills, and having the respect of peers. One staff member should be assigned to oversee and lead the program, as well as to provide ongoing training and feedback for peer mediators.
3. *Peer mediators assigned in pairs to work with each mediation.* This gives each mediator a degree of support needed to build confidence in his or her mediation skills.

4. *Staff in-service programs.* The staff needs to know how the program can benefit the school community. Peer mediators themselves can become the best source of positive publicity for the program.
5. *Ongoing maintenance.* Training must be built into the program. Each participant should fill out an evaluation before leaving a mediation session. Data on the number of mediations held, types of conflicts, and outcomes of mediations should be kept for program evaluation.
6. *Contingencies.* Not all teachers will buy into this program. This is not a teacher-centered style of management, and many teachers may find it an encroachment on instructional time. Much in-service training is needed, as well as support from the parents and the community.

Benefits for the school staff, peer mediators themselves, student body, families, and society are too great to dismiss this idea. Schools that teach students positive ways to resolve conflicts aid in the reduction of violence in society today. Youths who learn to resolve conflicts positively today are likely to do the same when they grow up!

Conflict Resolution

There is some confusion about the difference between conflict-resolution and violence-prevention programs. Johnson and Johnson describe six key ways to help staff and students better understand the difference between the two.

1. Schools should go beyond violence-prevention programs to conflict-resolution training. Violence-prevention programs do not decrease violent behavior or the risk of victimization.
2. The program should not attempt to eliminate all conflicts. Some conflicts can have a positive outcome. Schools need to teach students how to manage conflicts constructively.
3. One program goal should be to create a cooperative context. The best programs transform the total school community. A cooperative effort is a key principle of conflict resolution.
4. The program should identify and decrease school at-risk factors. Academic failure, alienation from school, psychological pathology, and low self-esteem make students less able to handle conflict.
5. Teachers should use academic controversy to increase learning. The teacher can help guide students with diverse opinions by role-playing all sides of the conflict. Students then drop all advocacy and come to the best-reasoned judgments based on a synthesis of positions and options.
6. The program should encourage all students to learn how to resolve conflicts constructively. This is the most effective approach. Students learn how to negotiate agreements and mediate their school mates' conflicts.

Fostering Student Leadership

Conflict resolution programs in schools are empowering for the students who participate as mediators and as disputing parties. The process of mediation is self-empowering in that it enables students to make decisions about issues and conflicts that affect their own lives.

All teenagers have been touched by abuse and violence. If we define abuse as restricting, controlling, humiliating or hurting another, it's clear that abuse is a daily experience for most.

A term often used in ignoring student voices is "adultism." Adultism occurs when adults hold special meetings and organize committees to discuss issues related to young people and then decide what is best for them without consulting the young people themselves.

If young voices are heard, they are often selected from young people with the best grades or those who belong to sanctioned organizations and say what adults want to hear. Other pre- and early adolescents often are labeled troublemakers, irresponsible, immature, lazy or apathetic. Young people often internalize their oppression and blame themselves for failure. With a total sense of frustration a student might bring a gun to school and kill people.

Providing a forum for students to be heard, encouraging student leadership in making school decisions and policies, and using students as trainers for peer mediation all will help schools increase student leadership, self-discipline, and the ability to make decisions and resolve conflicts. In turn, a conflict resolution program may help win the battle against violent environments in middle schools.

Health Care

The physical health status of America's children is still inferior to that in other countries.[9] Despite massive government investments in health care services, about 20 percent of children in the United States, age 7 to eleven, have serious health problems; many do not receive proper health care. So-called full-service schools now include on-site health services for students and their parents, along with other social services that are located on-site.

Between 1990 and 2000, the average age of beginning smokers dropped from 14 to 10. The number of girls age 13 through 17 who began smoking rose five percent during the same decade.

The mental health status of youth is a major concern in the United States as well as in other countries.[10] This nation's mental health sources (as reported by HEW) show the second leading cause of death among teenagers—after accidents—to be suicide, which doubled between 1980 and 1990. Whereas in Germany and Japan the reason most often cited for teen suicide is stress, in the United States apathy and rejection are singled out as the major contributing factors among adolescents and postadolescents. More specifically, insecurity in family life is cited.

Figure 2.9 provides a checklist for identifying potential teen suicide.

FIGURE 2.9 *Adolescent Suicide Checklist*

Indicators	Yes	No
1. A social isolate, a loner	___	___
2. Has deformity or chronic disease	___	___
3. Home life unstable over long period of time	___	___
4. Has history of regular student–parent conflict	___	___
5. Recently lost parent or other significant person	___	___
6. Family experiencing financial troubles	___	___
7. Lives in unstable, transitional neighborhood	___	___
8. Married at early age (15–20 years old)	___	___
9. Evidences sexual identity crisis	___	___
10. Displays sexual promiscuity unchecked by actions of parents	___	___
11. Voices feelings of pessimism, worthlessness	___	___
12. Appears fatigued, reports insomnia	___	___
13. Acts despondent or is unusually quiet	___	___
14. Shows accelerating neglect of appearance	___	___
15. Reports pressure from parents concerning ability to meet school or social expectations	___	___
16. Develops pattern of varied sicknesses during school hours	___	___
17. Displays irregular emotional outbursts, anger	___	___
18. Displays unusual social anxiety in school	___	___
19. Suddenly becomes promiscuous or flirtatious	___	___
20. Writes or speaks of suicidal thoughts	___	___
21. Becomes unusually aggressive, boastful	___	___
22. Begins heavy use of drugs	___	___
23. Evidences neglect of school work	___	___
24. Unable to concentrate on school work	___	___
25. Develops record of excessive absenteeism or unexpectedly drops out of school	___	___

SOCIAL CHANGES: IMPLICATIONS FOR MIDDLE SCHOOL YOUTH

Early adolescence is characterized by numerous developmental changes, among them cognitive and social changes that produce dramatic results. All of the changes are normal and occur at differing rates; however, coping with these changes is a major task for transescents and for the adults who serve them. Nowhere are those changes more evident than during the middle school years.

Other sociological changes, such as altered family structures and different working patterns of adults, have left a substantial number of American youth vulnerable to reaching adulthood unable to adequately handle requirements of the workplace, commitments to relationships with families and friends, and responsibilities of participating in a democratic society.

Compounding normal changes in preadolescents and early adolescents—as dramatic as they are—have been changes in the surrounding society that nurtures those youth. In addition to the changes in family structure described earlier, U.S. demographics have undergone startling variations. For example, by the year 2010, 38 percent of all Americans under age 18 will be African-American, Hispanic, Asian, or other minority. (Hispanics will be the largest minority group in the United States by 2009.) In the biggest states—California, New York, Texas, and Florida—minority children will be a majority by 2010.[11] For many youth, the first real assimilation with children from other cultures will come in the middle school years. (It is not unusual in middle schools in Los Angeles, New York, and Miami to hear fifty different languages spoken.)

As parents wrestle with divorce, dual careers, and an uncertain economy, they often look to their children to carry part of the load, thrusting them into the hard world of adulthood before they are ready. Child psychologists point to evidence of a growing problem: declining academic achievement; crime in the schools; growing number of cases of depression, suicide, runaways, drug and alcohol abuse, and psychosomatic illnesses (see statistics in previous subsections).

As the number of mothers in the workforce increases, millions of children are being cared for by outsiders—sitters, centers, neighbors, and before-school and after-school programs. High-quality day care is scarce, and many children are shuffled to three or four settings within a day. More than five million children under age 13 spend a large amount of time unsupervised. Many youth are charged with adult responsibilities—caring for younger siblings and cooking dinner, for example.

Single parents often turn to their children as confidants, discussing with them personal problems and family finances. At the time, young children may not resent the hurried pace, but in early adolescence they pay parents back for all the real and imagined slights committed against them during childhood. Only one child in five is able to maintain a good relationship with both divorced parents. Thus, divorce is perhaps the greatest factor affecting early adolescents in the past 20 years.

Mobility has affected middle school youth more than any other school-age group. For example, parents tend to move, split, and find other jobs when their children complete elementary school. The move to the Sunbelt brought on by job opportunities, grandparents living nearby, and the desire to start a new life, also contributes to the mobility scenario.

FIGURE 2.10   *The New Preadolescent*

Self-fulfillment	Individual growth
	Increased responsibility
	Achievement
Self-esteem	Recognition
	Status
Sense of belonging	Interpersonal relationships
External expectations	Work performance
	Rules, regulations
Security	Classroom conditions
	School conditions
	Home conditions

A. H. Maslow, *Personality and Motivation*, adapted from Davis, K. *Human Relations at Work*, New York: McGraw Hill, 1967, p. 37.

The fragile nature of the middle schooler is reflected in many ways. The search for acceptance can lead to alcohol and drug use, pregnancy, and gang affiliation. Students "wear their feelings on their sleeves"; that is, they worry about fairness. That sense of fairness is often seen on the playground where middle school students spend half their recreation time making up rules to games they play.

Teachers need to be especially sensitive to the physical and social needs of these students. Many of the programs (advisory, guidance, family teams) discussed later in the text are responses to these needs. The impressions on students made by a middle school teacher are lasting. Interviews with high school students demonstrate that the personal needs met by middle school teachers are much more important than cognitive knowledge attained.

Students, like all persons, have needs. Those needs are not equal but rather are ordered. A hierarchy of needs can be identified, allowing teachers to view student motivation in an analytic fashion. Needs of middle school students are ordered into a hierarchy, as demonstrated in Figure 2.10.

ESSENTIAL GOALS FOR NEW MIDDLE SCHOOL STUDENTS

If lasting attitudes toward self, others, school, and life itself are formed during the middle school years, we must identify those goals that are essential to adult success. Figure 2.11 outlines goals and indicators the authors suggest. They are by no means all inclusive, but reflect the attitudes and skills employers often cite as critical to job success.

The authors encourage middle school teachers and administrators to utilize the guidelines in Chapter 1 and this chapter to conduct a thorough study of the students they will serve. A focus on individualization should follow.

FIGURE 2.11   Wiles-Bondi Essential Goals for Middle School Students

Thirst for Knowledge

- ❑ Reads key books
- ❑ Joins academic clubs
- ❑ Corridor curriculum (out-of-classroom)
- ❑ Significant adult–tutor interaction
- ❑ Has own library
- ❑ Reads newspapers, watches news

Positive Attitude

- ❑ Enthused about learning
- ❑ Participates in activities; Total involvement
- ❑ Completes tasks
- ❑ Volunteers
- ❑ Joins service organizations
- ❑ Does community service

Courteous

- ❑ Dresses properly
- ❑ Practices etiquette
- ❑ Introduces self; eye contact
- ❑ Less aggressive, less aggressive language
- ❑ Carries on family conversations
- ❑ Can serve as host or hostess at gatherings

Achievement

- ❑ Maintains and improves test scores
- ❑ Reduced failures; fewer failure notices
- ❑ Less retention
- ❑ Better average grades
- ❑ More students on the honor roll
- ❑ Lower high school dropout rate
- ❑ Meets needs of high achievers as well as low
- ❑ Honors–For spelling, mathematics, music, science, and such

Organization

- ❑ Brings materials to school and class
- ❑ Does homework more frequently
- ❑ Keeps a calendar
- ❑ Brings gym clothes
- ❑ Uses time wisely
- ❑ Asks questions to determine clarity

Problem Solving

- ❑ Uses subject matter information
- ❑ Solves word problems
- ❑ Applies knowledge to "real world"
- ❑ Engages in hands-on activities
- ❑ Uses analysis skills and critical thinking skills
- ❑ Thinks creatively

Responsibility

- ❑ Cares about self, others, environment
- ❑ On time, prompt
- ❑ Less vandalism
- ❑ Cares about wrongdoing
- ❑ Lowered level of discipline problems
- ❑ Ability to change behavior
- ❑ Serves as peer tutor
- ❑ Helps keep school clean

Respect for Others

- ❑ Sensitivity to others; sensitivity for disabled
- ❑ Uses proper language; sarcasm reduced
- ❑ Helps others, engages in peer learning
- ❑ Respects different races and cultures

Health

- ❑ Exercises
- ❑ Proper diet
- ❑ Deals with stress
- ❑ Practices safe health habits with opposite sex
- ❑ Identifies and avoids activities that lead to AIDS
- ❑ Participates in lifelong sports

FIGURE 2.12   *What is a Middle Schooler?*

What is a middle schooler?
I was asked one day.
I knew what he was,
But what should I say?

He is noise and confusion.
He is silence that is deep.
He is sunshine and laughter,
Or a cloud that will weep.

He is swift as an arrow.
He is a waster of time.
He wants to be rich,
But he cannot save a dime.

He is rude and nasty.
He is polite as can be.
He wants parental guidance,
But fights to be free.

He is aggressive and bossy.
He is timid and shy.
He knows all the answers,
But still will ask "why."

He is awkward and clumsy.
He is graceful and poised.
He is ever changing.
But do not be annoyed.

What is a middle schooler?
I was asked one day.
He is the future unfolding,
So do not stand in his way.

—Pamela Bondi,
An eighth grader

SUMMARY

Emergent adolescent learners are characterized by their diversity and unique patterns of development. They are curious, physical creatures who are full of energy and imagination and interested in many things.

The physical, social, intellectual, and emotional changes that take hold during these transitional years between childhood and adolescence necessitates a school atmosphere in which middle graders age 10 to 14 can grow and develop into fully functioning, mature adolescents.

Along with normal (but sometimes traumatic) maturational changes, this age group must also contend with social problems that typify the 2000s. These problems, due primarily to the breakdown of the U.S. family structure, include increased rates of teen suicide, teen pregnancy, alcoholism, drug abuse, higher crime among youth, and job and family mobility. Although these social ills do not affect this age group exclusively, they do affect them at their most impressionable stage of development.

The more knowledgeable middle school staff and administrators are about this age group, the better equipped they are to plan and design a facility tailored to meet their unique learning needs. This chapter provided a detailed profile of today's middle schoolers. The following chapter will focus on the kind of teacher best suited to instruct them.

Suggested Learning Activities

1. Conduct a values survey like the one in Figure 2.4. How do your results compare with those found in Table 2.3?

2. Develop procedures for studying the lives of students in your middle school. What processes and instruments would you use to gather information about students?

3. Prepare a list of characteristics of emerging adolescents with implications for your middle school program.

4. Develop a position paper on the need for sex education in the middle school.

5. Prepare a visual presentation illustrating various physical, social, intellectual, and emotional characteristics of transescent youth.

6. Prepare an oral presentation for parents that would make them more aware of the social problems affecting middle school students.

Notes

1. David Elkind, *A Sympathic Understanding of the Child: Birth to Sixteen* (Boston: Allyn and Bacon, 1974). Elkind continues his theme of "behavior typical for the age" in numerous other publications. The authors are grateful to Dr. Elkind for furnishing background information for this section from talks delivered to professional groups and other notes he has generously shared with us.

2. Leona Zacharias, William Rand, and Richard Wurtman, "A Prospective Study of Sexual Development and Growth in American Girls: The Statistics of Menarche," *Obstetrical and Gynecological Survey*, 31 April 1976: 325–327.

3. Carnegie Council on Adolescent Development, *Turning Points: Preparing American Youth for the 21st Century* (New York: Carnegie Corporation, 1989).

4. Ester Schaeffer, "Character Education in the Curriculum and Beyond," *The Education Digest*, 63 March 1998: 15–17.

5. U.S. Department of Health and Human Services Statistics 2000. Washington, D.C.

6. Andrew Ferguson, "Character Education Goes Back to School," *Time Magazine*, 24 May 1999, pp. 68–70.

7. Harvard Civil Rights Project, "Resegregation in American School," June, 1999, Boston, MA.

8. Norma Gaily and Tracey Phariss, *Gay Students in the Middle School* (Columbus, OH: National Middle School Association, 1996).

9. U.S. Department of Health and Human Services Statistics 2000.

10. U.S. Department of Health and Human Services Statistics 2000.

11. U.S. Department of Health and Human Services Statistics 2000.

Selected References

Association for Supervision and Curriculum Development, Working Group on the Emerging Adolescent Learner. Joseph Bondi, chairman, 1975. *The Middle School We Need*. Washington, DC: ASCD.

Carnegie Council on Adolescent Development. 1989. *Turning Points: Preparing American Youth for the 21st Century*. New York: Carnegie Corporation.

Elkind, David. 1974. *A Sympathic Understanding of the Child: Birth to Sixteen*. Boston: Allyn and Bacon.

Wiles, Jon, and Bondi, Joseph. 1999. *Working with At-Risk Middle School Students*. Tampa: Wiles, Bondi and Associates.

CHAPTER 3

Effective Organizational Structures

You can either knock down the walls or you can go around them.

As discussed in Chapter 1, the regimented (corrective) approach to instruction used formerly in the junior high setting has been replaced with student-centered teaching techniques in the middle school setting. This change is the result of research findings on early childhood development—particularly the unique physical, emotional, social, and intellectual needs of 10- to 14-year olds. Consequently, middle school teachers, administrators, and support staff are applying new strategies tailored specifically for emerging adolescents.

Efforts are under way to structure broader and more relevant programs for the diverse student population found in the middle grades. To ensure continued movement in this direction, middle schools are becoming more flexible in terms of how they teach and where they teach.

All middle schools consist of five variables—students, teachers, time, space, and media/curriculum[1]—and skillful manipulation of these variables allows staff to provide flexible curricula and organizational structures. The result is more individualized (student-centered) instruction, which leaves room for each student to exercise his or her growing independence *while at the same time* satisfying state mandates regarding core subjects to be learned.

Prior to this change, traditional intermediate schools operated on a principle of uniformity, a principle based on certain assumptions about how all students learn. For example:

- *Uniformity of students:* Once a group was formed, that same group remained unchanged for a wide range of learning activities.

- *Uniformity of teachers:* The same teacher was qualified to teach all aspects of a subject during the same school year. All students received the same kind and level of supervision.

- *Uniformity of time:* Appropriate time for learning a subject was always 40 to 60 minutes per day, six or seven periods per day, or 36 weeks out of the school year. All learners were capable of mastering the same subject matter in the same length of time—for example, everyone was given the same test on the same material on the same day, or everyone was passed from level one to level two in June.

- *Uniformity of space:* The same classroom was equally suitable for a spectrum of learning activities—no conference rooms for teacher–student conferences, no large group facilities for mass dissemination of materials. A group of 30 to 35 students was most appropriate for a wide variety of learning experiences.

- *Uniformity of media/curriculum:* The same learning media were appropriate for all members of a group—for example, the same assignment from the same workbook was given to the entire group.

However, research has shown there to be nothing magical about rigid class size, fixed classroom space, or repetitive schedules. Therefore, current emphasis has shifted to designing facilities and schedules that allow for a variety of group sizes based on individual learning needs and the activities to be performed. The effect is that a child's learning progress is defined by his or her unique mastery of skill levels or competencies at the child's own pace.

Ideal school buildings do not guarantee flexibility. For example, a number of good middle schools operate effectively in buildings originally designed for conventional high school or junior high programs. They do so either by knocking down walls—symbolically and literally—or going around them. Conversely, some highly rigid structures remain in place despite new, open-space classrooms designed specifically for middle graders. All of which is to say that flexibility of physical space does not guarantee flexibility (or effectiveness) of instruction. This chapter discusses four innovations geared toward breaking down this organizational lockstep: team teaching, interdisciplinary teaming, flexible modular scheduling, and nongraded structure.

TEAM TEACHING

What Teaming Is

Team teaching (or teaming) is a type of instructional organization in which two or more teachers pool their resources, interests, expertise, and knowledge of students and take joint responsibility for meeting a significant part of the instructional needs of the same group of students.

In terms of organization and facilities, many middle schools have accommodated team teaching by clustering teachers and students in designated sections of the building and by providing a common instructional block of time and common teacher planning time. Newly constructed facilities have been built with open-space areas and movable walls, whereas older buildings have been renovated for this purpose.

Teaming makes maximum use of teacher strengths and allows teachers to work flexibly with individuals, small groups, and large groups. In the middle school this strategy involves two types of skills: ability to facilitate student academic and social growth, and ability to work cooperatively and collaboratively with other adults. For example, in terms of promoting academic and social growth, teaming offers support and aid in attempts to provide better instruction and classroom management; gives students and teachers the feeling of belonging to a small group that has common goals and whose members are supportive of each other; permits correlation of subject-matter content and concepts through planned repetition and reinforcement; and provides teachers with opportunities to share ideas, plans, student information, and classroom observations. In terms of students learning to work with other adults, team teaching requires a common group of students to be assigned to a common group of teachers who share a common planning time, which results in a more productive classroom and school environment. Consequently, this student-teacher interaction fosters students' sense of human interdependence, responsibility, and citizenship. These areas have particular import at this stage of child development.

Aside from contributing to the overall quality of education, team teaching is intended to serve a number of organizational purposes in the middle school. Among these are improving staff utilization, serving diverse student populations, presenting more sophisticated instructional media as a result of scientific and technological advances, providing more varied educational experiences, and treating students as individuals.

In fulfilling these purposes, many middle schools have clustered teachers and students in certain sections of the building and provided for a common instructional block of time and teacher planning time. Whereas new middle schools are constructed with open-space areas and movable walls, older buildings may be renovated to accommodate this instructional approach.

Some Advantages of Team Teaching

Students benefit from team teaching in a number of ways:

- Superior teachers are shared by all students.
- The effect of the poor teacher is neutralized.
- Students receive more individualized attention.
- Pupils can be grouped based on shared interests.
- Students can enjoy independence and broaden their boundaries while retaining security and nurturing as they learn responsibility.
- Students can work across grade lines with subject-matter specialists.
- Pupils have access to more than one image or role model.

Teachers benefit from the team approach in the following ways:

- Their professional talents and interests are used more effectively.
- They can share information and ideas that help solve problems and improve their professional backgrounds.
- Team teaching provides inservice education opportunities.

Generally speaking, both students and teachers benefit from the flexible scheduling, which makes for better correlation of school work, homework, and field experiences. The wider range of grouping possibilities (e.g., small groups, large groups, independent study teams) also facilitates a wider resource of talent, knowledge, skills, and experience from which students *and* teachers derive new educational opportunities. Finally, the fact that the *whole* of the participants working together will be more productive than the *sum* of individuals working in isolation can only further the primary goal—improved quality of education.

Some Disadvantages of Team Teaching

This discussion would not be complete without also looking at certain problems that can arise with the team approach. For example:

- Teachers may not always agree on how to evaluate or discipline individual students.
- Unless a facility has provided blocks of common time, teachers may find it difficult to plan lessons, activities, and study during the day.
- Conflicts may arise as a result of differing teaching styles.
- Unless teachers are trained specifically for the middle school environment, they may lack confidence in this unique setting.
- The need for a designated leader, the danger of pupil detachment in a large group (if this is the case), or the tendency toward restriction of a teacher's freedom of action can create further conflict.
- Sometimes teams tend to gang up on certain students.
- Unhealthy competition may emerge among teams.

What Teaming Is Not

Teaming is not "turn" teaching; that is, it is not a large group situation in which teachers take turns conducting classes. Nor does teaming imply homogenization of teaching styles, which probably is not desirable in any case.

Teaming is not comprised of daily coordination of interdisciplinary subject matter, but it does permit opportunity for teachers to coordinate and reinforce subject matter when doing so is convenient, desirable, or advantageous to the students. This coordination need not involve all of the usual subject areas—language arts, math, science, and social studies—every time. Occasional interdisciplinary units are a very desirable aspect of teaming and will be discussed later in this chapter. Teaming does not mean "anything goes," because it does give students enrichment experiences, such as independent study or exploration opportunities while keeping sight of subject content as the primary goal. Whereas the clustering of rooms is desirable, it is not essential. Finally, team teaching is not a panacea but a strategy for identifying problems and working for improvement in a combined, supportive setting rather than in an isolated one.

INTERDISCIPLINARY TEAMING

As its name suggests, an interdisciplinary team is made up of teachers from different subject areas who plan and conduct instruction for particular groups of pupils.

Designing Interdisciplinary Units

Over the past 40 years, middle schools in the United States have attempted to integrate subject matter for students through the interdisciplinary unit. As an outgrowth of the core curriculum in the 1940s and 1950s (and earlier), in "unified studies" and "common learnings," the interdisciplinary unit attempts to interrelate subject matter from various disciplines through a central topic or theme. Rather than fuse disciplines together, such as core subjects did with language arts, social studies, math, or science, the interdisciplinary unit is conceptually flexible. Rather than a central body of knowledge to be communicated, the interdisciplinary unit allows teachers to weave together many subjects into a creative pattern.

In schools that have highly developed units, the vertical curriculum is first mapped and then unit topics are identified. Topics or themes are broad enough to encompass teachings in the four basic subjects commonly found in the middle school—language arts, social studies, science, and mathematics. The topics are also broad enough to include other areas such as guidance, music, art, vocational areas, and physical education. Figure 3.1 illustrates themes by nine-week grading periods (6–1 is first nine weeks of sixth grade, 6–2 is the second nine weeks, and so on).

The interdisciplinary approach is based on at least five premises:

1. This approach is a way of organizing the school in terms of curriculum, instruction, and human and material resources.

2. Disciplines do not lose their integrity because of a team approach; rather, each discipline's unique contribution to problem solving is demonstrated.

FIGURE 3.1 *Interdisciplinary or Thematic Unit Titles*

6–1	7–1	8–1
Ancient Civilizations	Plants of the Earth	Decision Making
People and Environment	Dependence	Problem Solving
World Cultures	Population	Class/Cultures
Family	Disease Prevention	Exploration
	Around the World	
	Contraptions	
6–2	**7–2**	**8–2**
Our Physical World	Structures of World	Safety
Weather	People's Habits/Customs	Atomic World
Personal Health	Microscopic World	Change
6–3	**7–3**	**8–3**
Ecology	Life Cycles	People and Machines
Communication	Our Neighbors	Exploration
Endangered Species	Metrics	Milestones in Human History
	Changes	
6–4	**7–4**	**8–4**
Consumerism	Pollution	Recycling
Values and Self	Money	Life-styles
Water and People	Exotic Cultures	Technology
People and Laws	Leisure	
	Conservation	

3. The interdisciplinary approach is compatible with team teaching; in addition, it is compatible with flexible scheduling and nongrading.

4. The approach is ideally suited to the middle school student because it provides many and varied opportunities for success, exploration, and growth.

5. All disciplines need not combine for all interdisciplinary teaming; only teachers of complementary skills may combine. Moreover, some areas of instruction may be isolated best in the discipline to which they belong.

Factors that are essential to interdisciplinary team teaching are a staff committed to this particular approach as a means of serving students' needs, positive interpersonal and professional relationships among all staff members, and a sufficient amount of common team planning time.

The aim of interdisciplinary teaming is to promote communication, coordination, and cooperation among subject-matter specialists (guidance counselor, art teacher, music teacher, and such) so that students benefit from instruction planned by specialists while escaping the fragmentation that characterizes many departmentalized plans. Working together, interdisciplinary team teachers deal with individual student problems, consult with specialists, integrate subject areas, and consider other school-related topics.

The Wiles-Bondi Curriculum Mapping Model

Because interdisciplinary (thematic) units of instruction interrelate what is taught in each subject area of an interdisciplinary team, the authors, in their consulting work with middle schools, have developed a vertical mapping model of the middle school curriculum. The Wiles-Bondi model includes a sequenced set of middle school content or topics in a subject area, a list of major concepts or generalizations taught in that subject, and a list of intended outcomes and specific skills to be mastered.[2] Logical connectors from either content or concepts are identified, and they form the theme for an interdisciplinary unit. (Remember, not all disciplines need to combine during an interdisciplinary unit.) Units may vary in length from two days to two weeks.

Too many middle school teams pick topics randomly. Those topics may be interesting to students and teachers but may not fit the material being taught during the grading period. (Either nine-week or six-week grading periods are most common in middle schools.) Teaching an interdisciplinary unit that fails to take into consideration what is being taught during a grading period further disjoints an already unrelated curriculum. There must be continuity and cohesion within a program.

Team teachers are also content-focused and, in most school districts, each delivers his or her curriculum 180 days a year. If comfortable with delivery of their content, teachers will be more willing to find connectors that reinforce learning from one discipline to another and to reduce isolation of one subject area from another.

The mapping process (usually a grading period is mapped on one sheet for ease of communication among teachers on an interdisciplinary team) is a simple way to provide instant communication about what each team member is teaching in his or her own discipline.

Much emphasis has been on affective (e.g., arousing feelings, emotions) education in middle schools, and rightfully so. This sense of concern with student feelings is present in the concept of family teams that address student needs, discipline, parent conferences, and reward activities—and this is what should be happening. What was missing, before schools adopted the Wiles–Bondi process, was daily or weekly teacher discussions about material being taught in the subject areas. Upon visiting team meetings, we found teachers heavily engaged in discussions about student rewards or discipline problems—except that teachers often returned to their classrooms to teach their subject matter in isolation. Once every few months, a team would teach an interdisciplinary unit (often borrowed from another school and unrelated to content being taught) and then return to affective discussions. With a mapped curriculum, teams can discuss student needs *and* content, concepts *and* skills that are being taught to the same students that the team shares. Interdisciplinary units have become natural outgrowths of those discussions, and students find teachers often relating their course topics to information that was taught in the students' previous class period. For instance, students are more attentive when the language arts teacher uses vocabulary from social studies and science and the science teacher talks about the climate of the Egyptian desert along with the social studies teacher's teaching unit about Egypt.

It must be pointed out here that the authors are not minimizing the affective approach of middle school teams but are attempting to make teams more functional and eliminate the conflict of middle school teachers being either student-centered *or* subject-centered; they must be both. In addition, interdisciplinary units of instruction include many affective activities, and when combined with cognitive activities they present a holistic approach to learning. Table 3.1 is an example of a curriculum map for a subject area for one grading period.

Distinct from team teaching, interdisciplinary team organization is a way of structuring teachers, students, resources, and facilities. Even if a middle school does not utilize a team approach, interdisciplinary team organization, when used to its fullest extent, will provide benefits tantamount to teamed instruction.

Three Functions of Interdisciplinary Teams

In its commitment to promote communication, coordination, and cooperation among specialists, interdisciplinary team teaching has three major functions: instruction, organization, and establishment of team identity and climate.

Instruction. A team of teachers with common students and common planning time can provide many innovative instructional opportunities. On a practical level it is the classroom teachers who best assess the academic needs of their students. Agreement among team members allow teachers to move students about in the most appropriate groupings for instruction. A new

TABLE 3.1 Curriculum Mapping

Curriculum Area/Subject: Middle School/Jr. High General Science Grade Level: 6 Grading Period: Weeks 5 and 6

Major Topics	Generalizations/Concepts	Intended Outcomes (Specific Skills/Standards)	CAT**	SE**	MSPS**
1. Earth's Resources Living Renewable Resources Nonliving Renewable Resources Recycling Fossil Fuel Resources Ocean Resources Cycles: Oxygen Carbon Water	1. Natural resources are valuable materials found in nature and are used by people to meet their needs. 2. Because the earth's population is increasing faster than some resources are being replaced, knowledge of resource use, recycling, and conservation is important to our survival.	1. Recognize the interactions among science, technology, and society. The student will: 7.01 describe specific ways by which an individual can conserve energy. 7.02 describe how one is a consumer of the various natural resources. 7.03 identify those factors that contribute to or harm environmental quality. 7.04 explain how population growth affects Florida's environment. 7.05 explain how water quality and quantity affect Florida's environment. 7.06 describe how heat influences our everyday lives (i.e., food, cooking and refrigeration, heat, air conditioning, and weather).			G211 K280 K281 K285 K284 F183
2. Changes in the Earth's Crust: Floating Crust Earthquakes Plate Tectonics Volcanoes Mountain Building Fossil Records	1. The earth's surface is experiencing dynamic changes. Studying the two forces acting on the earth help us to understand how and why violent change occurs (earthquakes, volcanoes). 2. This understanding can help us prepare for future change, predict future events, and explain our past.	2. Describe major earth/space science concepts and facts from the following topics: meteorology, astronomy, geology, oceanography. The student will: 5.21 identify the natural resources found in the ocean. 3. Describe the major earth science concepts from the following topics: meteorology, astronomy, geology, oceanography. The student will: 5.01 name the most common gases that make up the earth's atmosphere.			G221

**CAT—California Achievement Test
SE—Standards of Excellence
MSPS—Michigan Student Progress Standards

student may then be assigned a schedule based on teacher recommendation rather than on class size.

Common planning time provides an opportunity for teachers to meet to correlate subject matter into integrated messages for students. For example, instead of *assuming* that every seventh-grade student should become proficient in the use of metrics, teachers introduce metrics in mathematics, reinforce its vocabulary in language arts, and practice its use in science and social studies activities.

Finally, if students are the focus of common team meetings, constant checks may be kept on their educational progress. Teachers may compare notes on frequency of homework completions, rising or falling test scores, absenteeism, and excessive tardiness. Student learning problems can be identified earlier and addressed with consistent effort from all team teachers.

A team teacher's instructional responsibilities fall into three categories:

1. *Subject area:* A teacher has been given an assignment in his or her area of certification, along with a course description as mandated by state regulations. Most of the instruction in this area will be done independently of what the other team members are doing.

2. *Interdisciplinary activities:* Many concepts and skills taught in the assigned subject area can be coordinated with or reinforced in other subject areas. When teachers share their course content and lesson planning with other team members, interdisciplinary activities can be developed as feasibility allows. This may involve anywhere from two teachers to all members of the team.

3. *Thematic units:* These units of study are carefully planned around a central theme. Research indicates that thematic units are especially important to the middle school age group in that they can foster an understanding of the interrelationship of all subjects. Consequently, thematic units must involve the entire team and therefore require a great deal of advance planning. It is recommended that two or three projects that involve thematic units be undertaken during the school year.

Organization. In addition to improving instruction delivery, team teachers may agree to set team rules, grading and homework policies, headings for assignments, and the like. Such organizational planning provides students with the guidelines and consistency they need at this stage of their development.

Teachers are able to work together to ensure the most appropriate uses of resources. For example, a guest speaker can appear once at a team assembly rather than five different times; media skills can be reinforced through subject content along with the language arts curriculum; lessons can be scheduled so that students do not have an overabundance of homework assignments and major tests.

Parent conferencing can become more effective if a team of teachers meets with parents to discuss the educational and social progress of each child. This structured approach makes it easier to pinpoint patterns of learning difficulties and behavioral problems.

Teachers working cooperatively often leads to discovery of new insights into school policies and procedures that may help administrators improve schools.

Team Building. When organizing a team, a number of factors must be taken into consideration. Because each team is comprised of different personalities, personality scales may be used to identify personality types. Other instruments give indications of teaching styles or ability to function in small group planning. Additional factors to be considered include balancing teachers according to their strengths and weaknesses and achieving a racial and gender balance on each team. Not all teachers are team players, and those who are not should be counseled into other school organizations. Figure 3.2 shows some guidelines for team building.

Team components include a team leader, a team leader council, team principal, other team members, and support personnel. Working together is a foreign

FIGURE 3.2   *Team Building: A Worksheet*

1. What do we expect from each other as team members? _____
2. How will the team make decisions?
   Subgroups?
   Majority?
   Consensus?
   Other?
3. What kind of attendance is expected?
   Regularity?
   Lateness?
   Leaving early?
   Absenteeism?
4. How frequently will we meet? _____
5. How long will meetings last? _____
   Will we start and end on time? Yes   Not necessarily
6. How will the team communicate with absentee members? _____
7. How are members expected to participate in meetings?
   Active listening?
   Paraphrasing?
   Identifying similarities and differences?
   Asking questions?
   Saying the same thing in meetings as are said between meetings?
   Other?
8. How will the team assess itself? _____When? _____
9. How will a team leader be chosen? _____
10. What is expected of the chairperson? _____
11. How will team exchange feedback? _____
12. What functions or activities does the team need to plan in order to accomplish its purpose? _____
13. What format will be used to record and report upon team meetings? _____
14. What is the team reporting protocol (e.g., when, to whom)? _____
15. What specific information will be reported? _____
16. What work schedule will enable the team to accomplish its functions and activities? _____
    (Include meetings, topics for each meeting, person responsible for planning each meeting, and resources needed such as people, materials, and the like).

notion for many teachers who are used to working in their own classrooms with their own group of students. Once a team is in place, questions may arise as to who is responsible for what with regard to team activities. Thus, most administrators either appoint or allow teams to elect a *team leader*. Whereas some principals select team leaders in consultation with teachers or allow teachers to select their own leaders, other schools rotate leaders each year. No matter how he or she is chosen, the team leader is in a unique position to ensure that the information, ideas, and concerns of the team are channeled to the appropriate groups. Following are some key responsibilities of the team leader.

- *Coordination:* Call, conduct, and preplan meetings (curriculum, student scheduling, discipline, parent conferences, and so forth).
- *Administration:* Prepare reports, assist in inventory control (requisition and distribute supplies and equipment), disseminate information to team members, evaluate team program and recommend changes, and the like.
- *Leadership:* Orient and assist new teachers; assist substitute teachers; energize and mobilize other team members; communicate effectively and tactfully with parents, faculty, and administration; sample letter to parents.

A team meeting agenda might include the following:

- Making announcements
- Establishing and evaluating team goals and expectations
- Solving educational and behavioral problems cooperatively
- Discussing student grouping and scheduling
- Discussing school progress reports
- Planning interdisciplinary units and sharing information
- Coordinating parent–team and student–team conferences
- Coordinating field trips and speakers
- Delegating responsibilities

Finally, the team leader acts as liaison between team and administration and serves as a member on the grade-level steering committee. Team leaders should be compensated for all extra time spent on team business.

The *team leader council* consists of building administrators, team leaders, and other staff members as needed. The council meets weekly to coordinate building activities, provide consistency in building policy and programs, help resolve conflicts among teams, evaluate team performance, organize task forces as needed, and facilitate communication. Team leader council minutes are distributed to all staff members and district supervisors.

Principals ensure that the team building model (Figure 3.2) is implemented in a manner that is consistent with district guidelines. They support teams by providing common time for teams to meet, screening new teachers (with the help of team members if possible), and preparing a weekly agenda for the team leader council. In addition, a principal chairs a weekly meeting at which, among a multitude of other functions, he or she provides opportunity for staff input; facilitates building goals; assesses and monitors for continuous improvement of staff, students, and curriculum; and troubleshoots problems.

Whereas the team leader is responsible for communicating with the administrative staff, *team members* must work together to keep the group operational. Toward this end, members should share in all decisions, be on time for scheduled meetings, bear equal responsibility for the team's well-being, be open to innovation, and ask for help when needed.

Support personnel are often overlooked in the team's effort to provide optimal instruction to middle graders. Team leaders should invite occupational specialists, guidance counselors, and media specialists, for example, to attend team meetings on a regular basis. These visitors can save hours of work and can be or provide valuable resources. For example, an occupational specialist can plan field trips, correlate career opportunities with current unit theme, facilitate a career day, or help set up a career resource center. A guidance counselor can work with the team to identify students with special emotional needs, provide individual or group counseling, or provide peer tutors and peer counselors. A media specialist might provide bibliographies of print and nonprint materials, conduct workshops for teachers and students on better use of library materials, or videotape projects and presentations related to a current theme.

Team Goal Setting. The team must agree on a common set of goals and actions. Although individual teacher requirements still will exist, addressing common areas of concern will benefit students and teachers alike. Possible goal-setting areas include courtesy and respect, preparedness, punctuality, classroom discussion, and quality of work.

Students will also benefit from procedural goals set by the team, such as devising a grading scale, exam schedule, homework schedule, special projects, field trips, guest speakers, and audiovisual coordination.

Team Planning Activities. As noted earlier, common planning time should be provided daily so that team members can review, plan, and evaluate operations. Specific issues might include:

- Student behavior and emotional problems
- Individual progress (e.g., parent–teacher conferences)
- Compatibility of team schedule and student needs
- Curriculum changes throughout the school and within the team
- Advisement activities and home–school communication
- Space utilization
- Specific information to be kept in student folders
- How to translate student needs into course designs
- How to get feedback from students

- Enrichment activities (e.g., career days, speakers)
- Consultation with specialists (e.g., guidance counselor, speech teacher, psychologist)
- Correlation of subject areas
- Other school-related issues (e.g., student council, field trips, assemblies, cafeteria)

One very important team activity is the parent–teacher conference. Whether initiated by parents or teachers, whether to inform or inquire, conferences result in better understanding and improved home–school relationships. Also, parents see that their children are being instructed by an organized group of teachers driven by specific goals and strategies.

Prior to the conference the team should agree on specific objectives to be accomplished, discuss the student, and establish a conference time limit. During the conference teachers should encourage parent responses and suggestions, be clear about areas of a child's progress that need improvement, and end on a note of hope.

At no time during a conference should a teacher label a child's character traits, focus on past misdeeds, urge or cajole or moralize, discuss himself or herself or his or her children, play psychologist, or gang up with other teachers.

Grouping. Flexible organization in the middle school means that different student grouping patterns are used in instruction. Some of these patterns include the following:

- Large group: Consists of up to 120–150 students in a team (or house); used to present introductory material, speakers, or to administer standardized tests
- Medium or class-size group: Consists of 20 to 35 students; the most common class grouping
- Small group: Operates within a class-size group; can be very effective when students have common interests or skill levels
- One-to-one group: May be teacher-to-student or student-to-student
- Independent study group: May be a part of classwork, homework, or community study

Figure 3.3 illustrates various student groupings commonly found in the middle school.

One question that often arises is whether there should be homogeneous or heterogeneous grouping in the middle school. The answer is both. Skills groups should be homogeneous but not static; that is, students should be able to move from group to group as they progress along a skills continuum. Students grouped heterogeneously in teams may be grouped and regrouped according to interests, tasks to be accomplished, and skill levels.

The middle school, with its team approach, is a perfect vehicle for shared decision making, a model for which is shown in Figure 3.4. In this model, di-

FIGURE 3.3   *Sample Student Groupings*

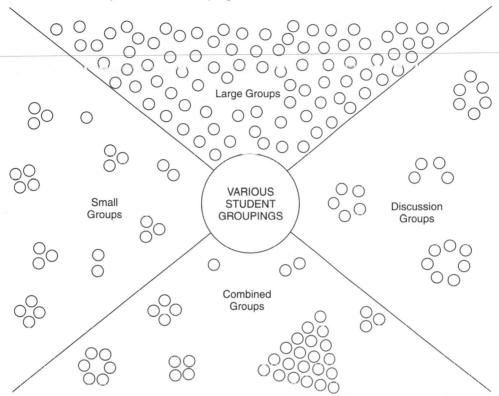

rective management and facilitative management work in harmony to meet the needs of those who provide and receive services in the organization.

The norms of the organization are stated in the goals, characteristics, and expectations. The basic structure of the organization calls for an instructional team formation with a representative on the facilitative management team, which directs the school's resources in response to program change and development within the organization.

Team Identity and Team Climate. Interdisciplinary team organization promotes within students a healthy sense of belonging. It is generally agreed that students who enjoy school perform better academically. Furthermore, building team identity and team pride will endow students with ownership— a stake—in their school, improve attendance, have a positive effect on behavior, and further nurture their commitment to study.

Some activities a team might undertake to create group identity are discussed below.

1. *Bring team members together.* Share time as a large group to present team goals and expectations and to discuss concerns of the total team

FIGURE 3.4 *Shared Decision Management Model*

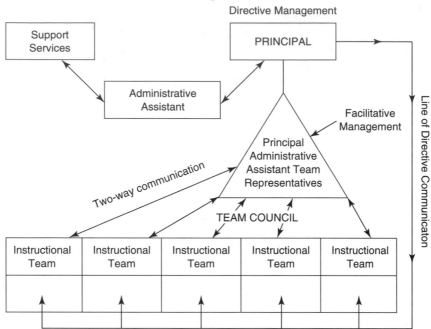

community. Assemblies are especially effective for speakers, demonstrations, entertainment, or team awards.

2. *Discuss team responsibilities.* Some teams involve their students in creating the team's list of expectations. Allow students to take some ownership in identifying team rules and responsibilities. The fewer rules needed to achieve the desired results, the better.

3. *Involve teams in the total school.* Help student groups function as a catalyst for positive school involvement. For example, one team might provide the principal with its own list of fact and opinion questions to be read over the intercom to help prepare for the eighth-grade assessment test. Another school might allow for team involvement in activities such as student councils and special teacher–student committees such as library or energy committees.

4. *Acknowledge academic achievement.* Display lists of honor-roll students by team in prominent areas. A little interteam competition—not too much—may be fruitful. Promote academic recognition, such as for "student of the month," as well as athletic recognition.

5. *Explore new worlds.* Field trips can become more meaningful when four teachers pool their resources to provide activities that reinforce the purpose of the field trip. For example, during a trip to Cape Canaveral, students might be given a booklet that requires them to calculate the average miles per gallon the bus gets on the trip (math); rank in

chronological order the historical events that led to the flights of the space shuttles (history); complete a crossword puzzle based on a vocabulary list prepared for the trip (science/English); or write a paragraph, that begins "if I could take the space shuttle anywhere in the universe, I would . . . " (writing). Pages of this booklet could be taken apart easily and graded by the assigning teacher.

6. *Expand community awareness.* Thanksgiving and Christmas baskets for needy families from team members can promote social responsibility. Some teams might adopt a community service organization to support. Still others might become ecologically aware, helping to fight pollution by collecting and recycling aluminum cans. Each of these projects reminds the student of the larger world beyond his or her own.

7. *Spread the word.* Many teams publish their own team newsletters highlighting team activities and individual members (hobbies, interests, pets, and awards). Puzzles or contests can incorporate names of students or teachers, vocabulary, or common math problems. A section entitled "from teachers to parents" can facilitate home–school communication.

8. *Celebrate birthdays.* Announcements, displays, or cupcake giveaways can make one day very special for each student in the group. Student behavior can be improved if the child feels valued.

9. *Locate a team bulletin board.* Make students responsible for decorating a bulletin board (preferably in a hallway) to celebrate holidays, interdisciplinary and thematic projects, and special activities.

10. *Choose a logo.* Choose a symbol to represent team spirit and incorporate it onto bulletin boards, wall murals, clothing, and reproducible materials.

11. *Design a t-shirt or team banner.* Use logo and school colors to create team identity for special occasions. Some schools have graphic arts departments that can produce t-shirts at minimal cost.

Note: Although team spirit is desirable and important, students must maintain a sense of grade-level and schoolwide identity. Teams should be encouraged to share successful experiences and work together toward improving the total school climate.

The team should not be isolated from other school programs and may be a vehicle through which special-area teachers can lend support, communicate program goals, and monitor student progress.

Planning Cycle for an Interdisciplinary Unit. The following outline is suggested for developing an interdisciplinary unit.[4,5]

1. Select a theme.
   • Brainstorm possible themes for your unit. Look for a theme that relates to a district, school, or team goal and fits the curriculum map.

Possibly survey students' interests before you begin brainstorming. Or, you might want to suggest several possible themes and have your students vote for the one that appeals to them.

- Define (expand or narrow) the theme so that it justifies the time you will put into it, fits within the time you will allot to it, and can be mastered by your students in the time you will schedule for it.

- Perhaps appoint one teacher on your team to be the leader for the development and implementation of the unit.

2. Work independently.

- Develop *topics* that can be addressed within your individual subjects that relate to the theme you have agreed on.

- Develop one or two *objectives* for your subject-area topic.

- Identify *skills* that your subject can address within the topic.

- Think of specific *activities* that you might like to use. However, do not set these in concrete; the activities for the unit should ultimately be planned jointly with your team.

3. Meet together to define objectives for the unit. Do not think of this as a step as for four separate subject units but as one combined unit that must be perceived by your students as something they can accomplish.

- Discuss each of your topics, objectives, and skill areas.

- Combine each of these into a manageable package for your unit.

- Generally develop a maximum of four objectives and six to eight skill areas.

4. Meet together to select activities.

- Match activities to your goals.

- Match activities to your *subjects.* Be flexible here! If you are devoting time to a unit your team has developed, several activities may not match your course description. Try not to think of this as detracting from your content teaching. Consider it as expanding your stated curriculum.

- Consider providing students with options within the unit. You may have a certain number of required activities combined with optional ones from which the students select an established number. Think about including some open-ended, exploratory activities.

5. Brainstorm resources.

Media specialists	Field trips
Electives teachers	Reference books
Physical education teachers	Commercial kits
Occupational specialists	Learning center ideas
Guidance counselors	Guest speakers
Films/filmstrips/tapes	Community service agencies
Parents	

6. Develop your activities (individually and collectively).
   - Order materials if necessary.
   - Prepare materials.
   - Contact resource people.
   - Divide Tasks. Determine who is responsible for what. No one person could possibly do all of this. If each person is responsible for one area, the process becomes manageable. The process will fall apart at this point if everything is put on the shoulders of one person.

7. Schedule your unit.
   - Put the activities and events on a calendar.
   - Reserve the library, stage, gymnasium, or other sites if needed.
   - Schedule guest speakers.
   - Schedule field trips.
   - Schedule large group and individual classroom activities.

8. Advertise your unit.
   - Distribute teasers! Make your students eager for the unit.
   - Decorate your bulletin boards with "Coming Attractions."
   - Send a letter home to parents explaining the theme and objectives of your unit. This would be a good vehicle to get parent permission for field trips or to solicit financial support, for example.
   - Wear slogans on your lapel or collar that relate to the upcoming unit.
   - Advertise over the public address system.
   - Announce it in the PTA or team newsletter.

9. Implement your unit.
   - Do not expect everything to go perfectly.
   - Have fun with it!

10. Evaluate your unit.
    - Posttest your students if desired.
    - Survey your students' attitudes about the unit.
    - Analyze the experience from your perspective.
    - Maintain a resource file. Decide which activities, speakers, and events were beneficial. Which ones would you want to use again? Keep this evaluation on file; it can save time should you decide to repeat the unit next year. You can also share this information with other teachers.

The inspiration for an interdisciplinary unit can come from a current event, a school or team goal, a current curriculum focus, a passage from a textbook, an understanding for the characteristics and the needs of early adolescents, or any number of ideas or comments expressed by a teacher or a student. The realm of possibilities is endless, limited only by your imagination.

FLEXIBLE MODULAR SCHEDULING

A *module* in a school schedule simply refers to a period of time. Many middle schools have adopted flexible modular (block) scheduling, which means that the school day is arranged in modules of varying length. Modules may be 15, 20, 25, or 30 minutes, or longer. The smaller the module, the more flexibility in grouping patterns. For example, operating under a 15-minute module plan, an hour can be broken into one, two, three, or four time periods. A 30-minute module plan can allow for two.

Most middle schools operate blocks of time during the school day during which the core academic disciplines (science, mathematics, language arts, and social studies) can be taught in longer time periods than those afforded by a single class period. Such blocks consist of a number of modules grouped together, for instance, seven modules, each of which is thirty minutes, where four-member teams teach a group of 120 to 135 students. Blocks of time allow for correlation among the participating disciplines and permit teachers to utilize instruction for small or large groups with varying lengths of time depending on the needs of students. An example of flexible modular scheduling appears in Figure 3.5, and ideas on how to develop flexible scheduling appear in Figure 3.6 and 3.7.

Variables That Affect Scheduling

A number of variables affect attempts to develop a block schedule, any one of which will cause deviation in the traditional rotating pattern in which the same students move as a group during the school day. Among these variables are:

1. *Size of school:* Schools with populations of 800 to 1,200 students have enough teachers who do not teach core subjects to take up the student slack while core teachers are otherwise engaged (planning, at lunch). Smaller schools with fewer than 600 students occasionally will need to have core teachers serve in multiple roles so that a rotation works. Regardless of school size, the objective is to create blocks of students who share common teachers, common blocks of time, and, hopefully, common spaces.

2. *Number of teachers:* Each middle school needs a certain number of teachers in order to offer a broad curriculum, including physical education, fine arts, related arts, and guidance services, for example. Without a sufficient number of specialists, the school must rely on regular teachers to assume more diverse responsibilities.

3. *Teacher sharing:* If located in a high school, a middle school might have to share teachers with the high school (or junior high). One scheduling

FIGURE 3.5   *Parts of a Block Schedule*

Sixth Grade	Seventh Grade	Eighth Grade		
ADVISORY	ADVISORY	ADVISORY	8:30	①
			8:50	
BASICS	EXPLORATORY/ PHYSICAL EDUCATION	BASICS English Math Reading Science Social Studies		②
90*	90			
EXPLORATORY/ PHYSICAL EDUCATION	BASICS 60			
	LUNCH 30			
90				
LUNCH 30		210	12:20	
		LUNCH 30	12:50	③
BASICS	BASICS	EXPLORATORY/ PHYSICAL EDUCATION		④
120	150	90	2:20	
ENRICHMENT AND REMEDIATION 40	ENRICHMENT AND REMEDIATION 40	ENRICHMENT AND REMEDIATION 40	3:00	⑤

*Indicates number of minutes

task is to break the practice in which the middle school gets its share of teachers only after the high school (or junior high) is staffed.

4. *Student–teacher ratio:* Efforts to maintain a uniform student–teacher ratio in all classes during all periods complicate scheduling efforts. With team and other cooperative teaching, students can be grouped appropriately for the scheduled activity (for example, sixty for a field trip, ten for reading review). Being able to break standardized patterns will make scheduling easier.

5. *Nonspecialist teachers:* Teachers who do not teach core subjects (or who do not have special credentials) need to be more diverse in their instructional duties. Few departments of education have objected to a

FIGURE 3.6   *Scheduling: A Step-by-Step Process*

1. Determine total number of students.
2. Identify total number of teaching and support staff.
3. Identify all teaching, planning, guidance, administrative spaces.
4. Examine bus schedule.
5. Identify school day for students and teachers.
6. Identify all shared or itinerant staff.
7. Identify all special-needs students.
8. Schedule lunches.
9. Determine team planning periods—during student day or before or after school.
10. Schedule electives and physical education classes to cover planning periods for core teachers.
11. Block core courses together in as large a block of time as possible. (Consider common students, common teachers, common planning time.)
12. Schedule teachers in common areas of the building, such as four rooms side-by-side for English, math, science and social studies. Science facilities sometimes must be moved to accommodate clustering of rooms.
13. Keep grade levels in one wing or area of the building, if possible.
14. Determine traffic patterns for students exiting core areas to lunch, electives, and physical education. Find the shortest straight line for students to travel when moving between or during classes.

FIGURE 3.7   *Some Hints on Flexible Scheduling*

- Manipulate time. Shorten school days for intramurals, advisement programs, field days, and so on.
- Create a six-day schedule if desired.
- Schedule music three days a week and art two days a week during fifth period to fit in more electives.
- Try a 45-minute period. Must bells ring every 55 minutes? Must there be periods at all?
- Vary period length. A period can be 30, 40, or 90 minutes if desired.
- Manipulate grade terms. Why not split a grade term?
- Avoid letting the tail wag the dog. Neither high school, band director, nor coach should dictate scheduling (although their input should be welcome).
- Barter. Talk the superintendent into changing the bus schedule if you'll take on more students.
- Barter some more. Do not hesitate to trade teaching positions if doing so means achieving a balanced program and schedule. Will one more English teacher and one less art teacher make the schedule work?
- Look into certification areas. Are there staff who are fully certified to teach in areas other than those they cover currently?

teacher's being "out of field" for a period—particularly when the school occasionally uses an interdisciplinary curricular design.

6. *Number of rooms:* Teachers who feel ownership of their classrooms and are indignant if their space is used while they are otherwise engaged create major scheduling headaches. Use of team spaces, coupled with use of community spaces, such as lunchroom, auditorium, or library,

scheduled by the team leader council helps remedy space shortage and makes more efficient use of available space.

7. *Lunchroom capacity:* Due to multiple lunch shifts, middle school principals (or other schedulers) are concerned about lunchroom capacity. But because it is deemed community space, the lunchroom should be put to other use when meals are not being served.

8. *Daily time requirements:* Usually middle schools follow a state-mandated requirement or a districtwide schedule that defers to bus schedules. Requesting extra minutes in the school day should not be overlooked as an option if this will facilitate scheduling.

9. *Pull-out programs:* Special programs such as ESE and ESOL may present unique problems. A joint effort between special teachers and team teachers can alleviate scheduling crunches.

10. *Grouping prerequisites:* Middle schools group heterogeneously when forming groups and homogeneously within teams as conditions dictate. A schedule that begins with all the special groups in a traditional setting will surely end up being a traditional—and ineffective—schedule.

11. *Length of periods:* Periods do not have to be a certain length, and there is no Carnegie requirement as for high schools.

Scheduling Priorities

Principals, teachers, and counselors should draw on a carefully defined school philosophy in determining scheduling priorities, which should be program-driven. Priorities include:

- Extended time blocks for selected core curriculum classes
- Differentiated assignments of instructional time based on the nature of the subject (e.g., laboratory versus expository instruction)
- Alternated time to allow a broader range of learning experiences within fixed time constraints (e.g., classes that meet every day, alternate days, alternate weeks, alternate semesters, or other variations, as appropriate)
- Elective or exploratory course options
- Shared planning time for teachers who team or collaborate; scheduled planning time for all teachers; allocated time for counseling and guidance programs; options to be accommodated within a common alternating time block include advisory programs, group guidance activities, tutorials and mentoring sessions for special groups of students (e.g., underrepresented minorities, gifted, basic skills deficient; limited English proficient); shortened or otherwise modified activity schedules to allow for assemblies or other special events without canceling regularly scheduled classes

Principals, teachers, and counselors should view the schedule as dynamic and always subordinate to changing program requirements.

All middle school schedules contain five essential sections:

1. Advisory guidance or homeroom
2. Basics or core instruction
3. Lunch
4. Exploratory or physical education
5. Enrichment or remediation

Figure 3.5 illustrates those five sections in a typical middle school schedule.

GRADED VERSUS NONGRADED ORGANIZATION

If educators want to do more than give lip service to the idea of individualized instruction in the middle school, then *nongraded organization*—that is, dropping grade-level barriers—must be considered.

Although for accounting purposes many middle schools retain grade levels, they nevertheless devise a curriculum that allows pupils to work at school levels in subject areas. In other words, there is a continuum of learning objectives to be mastered in each academic area and some students, although classified as seventh graders, for example, are actually doing work that should have been mastered in the third or fourth grade. Other middle schools may cut across grade lines in grouping students, whereas still others have progressed to nongraded organization after being developed initially in a graded format. Table 3.2 summarizes the respective features of graded versus nongraded structures.

Benefits of Smaller Class Size

In a landmark study of Tennessee students (1999) who attended smaller classes in their first years of school, those students performed significantly better than students who began in larger classes. Even though students returned to larger classrooms after the third grade, high school students who attended smaller classes beginning as early as kindergarten were less likely to drop out, more likely to graduate from high school on time, more likely to take advanced-level courses, and more likely to earn superior grades than students who began their education in larger classes, researchers reported. A similar study of California's experience in reducing class size was also undertaken in 1999.[6]

Although some educators argue that the quality of teaching is more important than class size, clearly the results of this study and others to follow must be reviewed carefully.

Middle grades schools have always suffered from funding inequities as they received normal funding while early childhood and specialized high school courses received additional funding. With the importance of a good academical, social and physical foundation established for students in the middle

TABLE 3.2 SOME CHARACTERISTICS OF GRADED VERSUS NONGRADED STRUCTURE

Graded Organization	*Nongraded Organization*
Each year's progress in subject matter is deemed roughly comparable to each year student spends in school.	Each year's school life is valued in direct proportion to each year's progress in subject matter.
Each current year's progress is deemed comparable to each past or each successive year.	Progress is deemed dynamic so that students may advance rapidly one year and slowly the next.
Progress is deemed unified, advancing in lock-step with all areas of development, and probably close to grade level in most subjects.	Progress is deemed dynamic across studies so that a student may leap ahead in one area yet lag in another.
Certain content is deemed appropriate and so labeled for successive grade levels; in other words, subject matter is packaged by grade.	Certain content is deemed appropriate over a span of years; learning is viewed vertically or longitudinally rather than horizontally.
Student's progress is measured based on coverage deemed appropriate to the grade.	Adequacy of progress is measured by comparing a student's attainment to ability and both to long-term accomplishment desired.
Progress deemed inadequate is penalized by grade failure; progress deemed satisfactory or better is rewarded through enrichment; horizontal expansion is encouraged over vertical advancement in work.	Slower progress is accommodated by longer time for given blocks of work without grade repetition; rapid progress is accommodated vertically and horizontally, with encouragement to move ahead regardless of grade level of work.
Inflexible grade-to-grade advancement usually occurs at end of year.	Flexible pupil movement occurs whenever indicated resulting in innovative semester systems.

grades, middle grades school can and should make a strong argument for reduced class size as well as increased funding programs.

THE MIDDLE SCHOOL AND MULTIAGE GROUPING

Multiage classrooms utilize an organizational structure in which children of different ages (at least a two-year span) and ability levels are grouped together, without dividing them or the curriculum into steps labeled by grade organization.

One of the challenges facing educators in the twenty-first century is how to nurture the developmental needs of all children. One viable means is the use of multiage grouping. In multiage grouping an integrated program is provided that spans several grade levels. The rationale behind multiage grouping is the realization that children develop at different rates. Because the grade-level system cannot meet the varying needs of all students, multiage grouping is offered as an alternative.

Some of the attributes of multiage grouping include:

- Multiage and mixed-ability grouping
- Developmentally appropriate practices

- Flexible grouping patterns for learning (individuals, pairs, triads, small groups, large groups, whole class)
- Continuous progress (learn in a continuum from easier to more difficult and from simple to complex)
- Professional teamwork (team teaching, collaborative teaching, peer coaching)
- Authentic assessment (children demonstrate skills and competencies, and use portfolios, presentations, exhibits, demonstrations)
- Qualitative reporting
- Parent involvement
- Sample groupings see Internet site:

http://www.ncrel.org/sdrs/areas/issues/methods/instructn/in500.htm

Lincoln School in Mundelein, Illinois, is an example of a successful multiage program in a kindergarten through fifth grade multiage school that uses technology, multiple intelligences, problem-based learning, and a year-round calendar in multiage education.

http://www.ncrel.org/sdrs/areas/issues/methods/instruction/in500.htm

Children's International School in Palo Alto, California is located in the Cubberley Community Center with access to sports facilities. It contains grades kindergarten through eight, divided into four groups. It is open year round. As part of the science curriculum students participate in annual camping experiences and other outdoor activities to acquire understandings of the environment and ecology.

In the lower (kindergarten through second grade) and middle (third through fifth grade) schools, enrichment activities include weekly trips to the Mitchell Park library, and field trips which include whale watching on the Monterey Bay, theater excursions, concerts, bird watching, and lunch in Chinatown. Children's International School is committed to instilling the habits and rewards of service to others in its students. All students are involved in an on-going outreach program which includes intergenerational activities with a senior home in Palo Alto, such as planting flowers and sharing gardening tips and participating in an intergenerational reading program beneficial to both groups.

In the upper school (sixth through eighth grade), the curriculum extends the same developmental sequence, disciplines, and learning activities on which the lower and middle school programs are based. The upper school social studies curriculum includes a trip to the east coast to study the history and government of the United States, and an international trip to Japan or Europe to culminate foreign language and international studies.

http://www.cis.pvt.k12.ca.us/overview/brochue-no pix.html

At Chinook Charter School in Fairbanks, Alaska, multiage groupings allow for several grade levels to work together to encourage leadership and to provide individualized learning opportunities. The school has a working relationship with the University of Alaska, Fairbanks and is a development site which values innovation, teacher research, and excellence in teaching. Students work in small learning groups within the learning lab and studio. Students participate in the Mentors Project which places them with professionals in fields such as engineering, geological services, law, a locksmith company, a local TV station, a local veterinary office, and a charter flying service where they learn about the world of work from experts in each field.

http://www4.northstar.k12.ak.us/schools.../mentors_project.ht

Alternative Middle Years (AMY) at James Martin School in Philadelphia, Pennsylvania features cross-grade and mixed-ability grouping in almost all classes. AMY uses a trimester system that allows students to choose their own schedules and to take many courses in areas that are of interest to them. Teachers design their own courses which address both student interest and teacher interest. The classes are taught with an interdisciplinary team-taught approach, and integrate a variety of subjects around a specific theme. Students take responsibility for learning by developing their own academic programs.

Apart from some math courses and state- or district-required courses, students may choose seven courses from over 120 course offerings each 60-day trimester. Students from sixth to eighth grades with similar interests may choose from the teacher-designed courses called "mods."

Students take interdisciplinary courses such as the Team Europe mod in which 40 students are divided between two teachers—a language arts and a social studies teacher in learning groups that can change each day. Writing, research, geography, earth science, social events, architecture, and zoology are integrated into the course. Teachers team teach and circulate among students to assist where needed.

At AMY groups are mixed ages, sometimes ranging from ages 11 to 15 in the same class. Teachers group during cooperative learning activities and spread leadership responsibilities to members of all ages to encourage cross-age learning.

An interesting note regarding teachers is that they teach more courses (six versus the district's five per day) and have fewer preparation periods in exchange for smaller classes (average of 18 students) than other teachers in the district. They are involved in meetings and course development during lunch periods and outside the paid weekday. Part of the success of the program is the teachers' investment of unpaid, personal time as a contribution to the program.

http://inet.ed.gov/pubs/Raising/raise2/profl.html

At Seeley Elementary School in Seeley Lake, Montana, a multiage class of third, fourth, and fifth graders was piloted with plans to create a multiage class for sixth, seventh, and eighth graders within two years. The small class of 18 students is a key to the success of the multiage class. The teacher is able to work personally with all 18 students. At Seeley, multiage classrooms encourage students to work at their own pace on projects of their own choosing. They can progress when they are ready, with no fear of failure. Individual learning styles are addressed. The focus is on learning rather than on grades. Older children develop leadership skills as they work with and help the younger students. Younger students learn class routines and imitate appropriate behavior as they see older students modeling such. In multiage classrooms, cooperation is encouraged and competition is reduced.

http://www.seeleysanpathfinder.com/pfnews/1rmscl.html

Lilian Katz describes advantages of using mixed-age groupings in education. She lists the benefits as:

- opportunity to nurture—children become more tolerant of each other when they are placed in multiage learning situations
- addressing various ways of learning—children learn at varying rates and in different ways
- social participation—allows for younger children to participate and contribute to more complex activities than they could initiate if in a same-age group and older children are able to remain "unsophisticated" longer than same-age peers would allow
- intellectual benefits—learning from one another

http://ericae.net/ericdb/ED382411.htm

4 × 4 Block Scheduling in the Middle School

In a traditional school schedule, students take six classes and teachers teach five classes. Each class meets daily, usually for a semester or year. Class time ranges from 45 to 55 minutes.

A 4×4 plan consists of:

- Four 90 minute classes
- Language arts—annual course
- Mathematics—annual course
- Social studies—annual course taught in one semester
- Science—annual course taught in one semester
- Physical education and elective—A and B schedule

A number of middle school educators believe the 4×4 block scheduling plan provides for more efficient and innovative use of instructional time, more individualized instruction, and personalized attention for students. They also believe it provides an ambience which promotes teamwork, improves student performance, and thereby creates happier and more productive students. Figure 3.8 illustrates the team structure in a 4 × 4 schedule. Figure 3.9 shows the semester schedules, and Figure 3.10 a student day.

Advantages of 4 × 4 Block Scheduling

For Students:

1. Decrease in the number of students a teacher must know at a given time.
2. Increased personal attention given to students.
3. Standardized test scores improve.
4. Student morale improves.
5. Decrease in number of courses a student must prepare.
6. Focus on comprehension rather than coverage of materials.
7. Less stress and better relationships within the school community.
8. Improved attendance.

FIGURE 3.8   Team Structure—4 × 4

TEAM STRUCTURE

4 × 4

GRADE 6

Teacher 1	Teacher 2
Reading Language Arts Social Studies	Mathematics Science

60 STUDENTS

GRADE 7/8

Teacher 1	Teacher 2
Language Arts Science	Mathematics Social Studies

TEACHER 3   TEACHER 4

150 STUDENTS

Teacher 1	Teacher 2
Reading Language Arts Social Studies	Mathematics Science

60 STUDENTS

Teacher 1	Teacher 2
Language Arts	Mathematics
Social Studies	

TEACHER 3
(90 STUDENTS)

Teacher 1	Teacher 2
Language Arts	Mathematics
	Science

TEACHER 3
(90 STUDENTS)

180 STUDENTS

FIGURE 3.9   *4 × 4 Semester Middle School, Grades Six, Seven, and Eight*

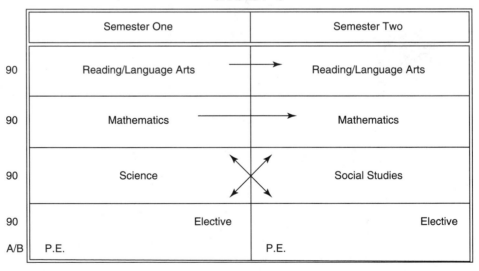

4 × 4 SEMESTER MIDDLE SCHOOL
GRADE SIX

	Semester One	Semester Two
90	Reading/Language Arts →	Reading/Language Arts
90	Mathematics →	Mathematics
90	Science	Social Studies
45	Elective	Elective
45	P.E.	P.E.

4 × 4 SEMESTER MIDDLE SCHOOL
GRADES 7 - 8

	Semester One	Semester Two
90	Reading/Language Arts →	Reading/Language Arts
90	Mathematics →	Mathematics
90	Science	Social Studies
90	Elective	Elective
A/B	P.E.	P.E.

FIGURE 3.10 4 × 4 Block Scheduling

STUDENT DAY

15 minutes	Teacher Planning
20 minutes	TA Program
5 minutes	Passing Time
90 minutes	Block 1
5 minutes	Passing Time
90 minutes	Block 2
5 minutes	Passing Time
30 minutes	Lunch
5 minutes	Passing Time
90 minutes	Block 3
5 minutes	Passing Time
90 minutes	Block 4
5 minutes	Planning Time

435 MINUTE STUDENT DAY

9. More individualized attention from teachers.

10. Focus on three core subjects at a time rather than four.

11. More interesting courses.

12. Less stress from four classes rather than six.

13. Facilitates in-depth learning and instructional strategies (simulations, group project work, lab work) that work better in longer time blocks.

14. Fewer school discipline problems.

15. Schedules fewer classes and fewer students per teacher per grading period.

For Teachers:

1. Less start-up and shut-down time.

2. Increased teacher planning and training time.

3. Increase in staff morale.

4. Faculty attendance improves.

5. Less time spent on attendance and other paperwork, more time on teaching.

6. Allows for varied assessment strategies such as exhibitions.

7. Reduces school discipline problems because students are in the hallways less often.

8. Fewer students per day.

9. More interaction with students.

10. Increase in opportunities to use cooperative learning.

11. Facilitates in-depth learning and instructional strategies, such as simulations, group project work, and lab work, that work better in longer time blocks.

12. Decreases frustrations of students (especially at-risk students) while they learn as well.

FACILITIES

When the time comes to build a new school or to refurbish an existing one, great planning is involved. This is one of the challenges facing educators, administrators and communities today. By planning properly, the process can be less painful and reduce delays. Here are a few things to keep in mind when it is time to put the hard hat on.

1. Seek an early consensus on what the community needs. This is basically a shopping list. Think short term and long term.

2. Use the architect/engineer (A/E) as a resource. The A/E should give you a good idea on costs.

3. Establish clear priorities before work begins. Know what is going to be urgent.

4. Do not expect taxpayers to agree with all rehabilitation plans.[7]

Many educators feel that students graduating from the small environments of elementary schools are intimidated by the larger, more open environments of middle schools. As elementary school students, they are protected, spending most of their time in single classrooms and escorted by their teachers to special classes and programs. When they become high school students, they move independently from class to class, managing their own programs and time. But in between, when they enter middle school, preadolescent students often are awkward and insecure as they emerge from childhood, moving from small to large, from protection to independence.

A middle school provides transition, and when it is segmented into smaller units—often called clusters or houses—students spend much of their time in their own classroom clusters and build valuable relationships as they and their teachers get to know each other better. Smaller units foster greater sensitivity to the problems and successes of each student.

While segmenting is not the traditional way of organizing our schools, the idea of schools within schools has ample precedent. The ecclesiastical quadrangle campuses at Oxford and Cambridge universities provide fine historical examples. These large universities are divided into separate residential colleges, each with its own facilities and personality. Each includes classrooms, a library, rooms for teachers, residence-hall rooms for students, a dining hall and a chapel. A student at Oxford or Cambridge has a small-college experience, but in a large university.

Protection and Outreach

For the architect or planner of a middle school based on the cluster concept, the challenge is to design units of comfortable scale, intimate and protected, yet with ample opportunities for students to reach out into the larger school environment for various functions and activities. The design must provide facilities that are more varied and complex than an elementary school, yet not on the daunting scale of a junior high or high school.

Because outreach is an important objective of the middle-school experience, it is vital that the clusters not be isolated from one another, or from the facilities they share. Convenient and inviting passages should connect each cluster to other parts of the school. Entries, corridors, and walkways should be direct, logical, easy-to-read paths that allow students to move easily about the buildings and the campus.

When a middle school has multiple buildings, or is one of the buildings in a larger school complex, the courtyard, or quadrangle, also is a key element in how students perceive their academic world. The quad becomes a window through which they observe many of the possibilities of the larger school. It is a space where they meet students from all grades. And if it is surrounded by the buildings, it offers a sense of protection from the world outside the school. The design of a school's outdoor space should be an integral part of the overall scheme, not an afterthought.[7]

YEAR-ROUND SCHOOLING

Year-round schooling in many school districts nationwide is a result of increased enrollments and budget problems. Year-round school schedules allow districts to serve more students without constructing more buildings. As in traditional nine-month schools, students in year-round schools attend classes about 180 days a year. In the 45–15 plan, students attend school for 45 days and then have 15 days off. The Concept 6 plan divides the calendar year into six two-month blocks. Students have classes for four consecutive months and then a vacation for two months. One year-round schedule divides the school year into five 45-day terms, or quinmesters. Another year-round schedule has students attend school for three 60-day periods, separated by three-week breaks.

When administrators, teachers, parents, and the community consider year-round schooling, they must take into account the cost of the year-round school effort and the attitudes of people directly affected by the idea.

School planners must look at the advantages and disadvantages of year-round schooling. This will serve as a guide for planners as they decide on whether or not to push for year-round schooling.

Advantages of Year-Round Schooling

- Review time is reduced.
- Can reduce overcrowding.
- Reduced burnout for both teachers and students.
- Fewer discipline problems and better morale among teachers.
- Better use of facilities.
- Increase in student attendance.
- Dropout rate decreases.
- Achievement scores have improved.

Disadvantages of Year-Round Schooling

- The need to adjust teaching materials to the year-round schedule.
- Operating costs increase.
- Courses available to students could be limited.
- The opportunity for students to attend specialty camps could be eliminated.
- Childcare is not as readily available during the vacation times offered by year-round schools.

- Coping with students who need summer school to make up a failed or missed course could present problems.
- Possible loss of family income.
- Disruption of traditional family vacations.

Questions to Consider About Year-Round Schooling

Before forming a firm opinion on year-round schooling the community should answer the following questions:

1. Would year-round schools actually and significantly increase the quality of education provided in the community?
2. What exactly are the additional costs in terms of staff, busing, air conditioning improvements, maintenance, and utilities?
3. Would year-round schools increase absenteeism?
4. Would year-round schools realistically inhibit teachers from additional professional development?
5. Do year-round calendars help to significantly increase SAT or other standardized achievement scores?
6. How would year-round school affect community businesses, especially those which are seasonal or tourist oriented?
7. Do year-round-school students enroll in college at a higher or lower rate than students in traditional schools?
8. Does the year-round calendar really provide the greatest good for the greatest number of people at a comparable price?

COMPUTER-BASED MANAGEMENT TOOLS

Management and Administration

Middle school teachers, administrators, and professional staff use their computers to make record keeping easy and increase productivity. An unexpected, but powerful, outcome has been increased collaboration.

Why Use Computer-Based Management Tools?

Principals and other school administrators have enormous responsibilities to communicate with teachers, students, and parents; find and analyze information; manage people; and administer discipline. Technology helps school leaders accomplish these tasks with greater efficiency and productivity.

Computer networks, electronic mail, presentation software, desktop publishing, and a computer database are all components of technology that make a school administrator more effective in accomplishing his or her everyday tasks. For instance, local telephone lines allow meetings, workshops, and conferences to be held over a network, eliminating the need for travel and time away from school. Electronic mail allows for communicating with staff and parents by removing the boundaries of time and place, and powerful desktop publishing capabilities permit school administrators to make professional presentations to parents and colleagues.

What the Research Says

- Providing computers and printers (and training) to all teachers and school administrators for at home or in school use increases both administrative productivity and feelings of professionalism.

- Principals using technology for administrative purposes in their schools report an increase in autonomy from district office control and the ability to be more personally productive using word processing.

- Principals who learn about both administrative and educational applications of technology feel more confident in dealing with staff requests and purchase decisions.

- Establishing a "homework hotline" using telecommunications increased homework time by two hours per student per week—and students continued getting schoolwork from the system during the summer.

- Elementary teachers provided with laptop computers tend to increase their use of the computers for administrative applications, especially record keeping and grading.[8]

- Teachers with laptop computers report significant pedagogical changes, including increases in the amount of inquiry-oriented instruction and project-based activities, increased collaboration with teachers, and more communications with students.[9]

ISSUES IN MIDDLE SCHOOL ORGANIZATION

Where Does Sixth Grade Belong?

Issues

- Does placing sixth grade with middle school force children to grow up too fast?

- Do sixth grade students have more in common with seventh and eighth grade students than with first grade students?

Considerations. There is no one right answer. Communities need to take into consideration the following factors in deciding whether to use the junior high school, middle school, or separate sixth grade center strategy:

- Number of students
- Transportation costs
- Socioeconomic backgrounds of their students

- School district's goals for student achievement
- Effects on other schools
- Number of transitions for students
- School building design
- Effects on parent involvement

Much depends on how the transition is implemented. Differences between middle school and elementary school include tougher academic demands, larger size, different teachers for each subject, leaving behind friends when elementary schools feed into several middle schools, transition from oldest to youngest in school, and different behavioral standards—all this and puberty too.

Begin transitions in the spring prior to the move. Teachers and staff from middle school meet with students in elementary school. Then students go to middle school to visit. In fall, an orientation day gives students time to find classes, lockers, and meet teachers. Parent involvement is very important to successful transition.

How Can the Quality of Time Students Spend in School Be Improved?

Issues

- Fragmented instructional time caused by attending different periods in a day that are unconnected results in little in-depth study.
- Transitional times result in increased referrals.

Considerations. Several strategies that could allow students who need more learning time that opportunity follow:

- Four-block schedule—90 minutes in language, math, either social studies or science, and one in PE or exploratory.
- 75-75-30 Plan—two 75-day units of academic block scheduling followed by 30 days of exploratory, mastering grade level expectations, or enrichment activities.
- Concept-Progress Model—Spend time teaching concepts in larger classroom settings two days a week and then break up into smaller groups based upon understanding of the material presented (progress). This time may be used for remediation or enrichment.
- 35–5–35–15–35–5–35–15—35 days of instruction followed by five days of reteaching or enrichment, followed by 35 days of teaching and 15 days of reteaching or enrichment to end the semester. The cycle repeats.

SUMMARY

Flexibility enhances the instructional program of middle schools, which have used a number of organizational patterns to break the regimentation found in traditional school programs.

This chapter highlighted five such innovations: team teaching, interdisciplinary teaming, flexible scheduling, nongraded structure, and block scheduling. Team teaching involves multiple teachers who pool their respective resources, interests, and professional expertise to instruct the same group of students. Interdisciplinary teaming correlates different subject-matter areas so as to complement and reinforce instruction within the same group across disciplinary lines. Flexible scheduling breaks the traditional mold of a set arrangement in terms of classroom period length by creating 15-, 20-, and 30-minute modules. Nongraded organization has to do with dropping grade-level barriers so that each student can move from group to group on the basis of his or her unique mastery of skill levels. Block scheduling offers other advantages.

Accompanying factors that contribute to organizational flexibility include team building (components of which are a team leader, team leader council, team principals, other team members, and support personnel); team goal setting (there must be consensus of objectives and actions); team planning (a common block of time must be made available for the team to plan, review, and evaluate its activities); grouping (creating large, medium-size, small, one-to-one, or independent study groups); and, finally, shared decision making (a move from top-down management of the past to teacher-participative/partnership management).

Organizational patterns, schedules, and staff usage of selected middle schools illustrate the many creative ways in which time, space, and instructional media have been structured to provide diverse experiences for middle graders.

Suggested Learning Activities

1. Prepare an organizational plan for your school that would include block scheduling and team teaching.

2. Discuss the advantages and disadvantages of team teaching in the middle school.

3. Prepare a talk to a parent group about flexible scheduling in the middle school.

4. Interdisciplinary instruction has been proposed for your school. What subject areas would you include in interdisciplinary teams? Why?

5. What is the role of fine-arts and practical-arts teachers in interdisciplinary instruction? Suggest ways they could work with other academic teams in preparing an interdisciplinary unit of instruction.

6. Discuss the pros and cons of block scheduling in the middle school.

Notes

1. Jon Wiles and Joseph Bondi, *Teaming in the Middle School* (Tampa: Wiles, Bondi and Associates, Inc., 1990).

2. ———, *Subject Area Curriculum Maps for the Middle Grades 6, 7, 8* (Tampa: Wiles, Bondi and Associates, Inc., 1991).

3. See *Focus,* Board Reports of the Dade County (Miami, Florida) middle school conversion project, 1989, 1990, 1991, for positive results of the school-based management/shared decision-making process. Each of the 52 middle schools involved in the conversion process (the largest

middle school conversion in the history of the middle school) used the school-based/shared decision-making model. The reader is also referred to the Dade County evaluation document of the middle school program, the first longitudinal-comparative study of progress of middle school students compared with junior high students.

4. ———— , *Designing Interdisciplinary Units* (Tampa: Wiles, Bondi and Associates, Inc., 1990).

5. ———— , *The Interdisciplinary Unit Sampler* (Tampa: Wiles, Bondi and Associates, Inc., 1990).
6. Melzno, Foster, 1998.
7. Peter Gisolfi, "A Sum of Its Parts," *American School and University, 71*, 5 (January 1999): 29–30.
8. Apple K–12 Effectiveness Reports, 1999.
9. James Doud and Edward Keller, "A Ten Year Study of K–8 Principals," Alexandria, VA: NAESP, 1998.

Selected References

Association for Supervision and Curriculum Development, Commission on Secondary Curriculum. 1961.*The Junior High We Need.* Washington, DC: ASCD.

———— , Working Group on the Emerging Adolescent Learner. Joseph Bondi, chairman, 1975. *The Middle School We Need.* Washington, DC: ASCD.

Dade County School Board, Joseph Gomez, principal evaluator, and Jon Wiles and Joseph Bondi, chief consultants, 1991, 1992. *Evaluation of the Middle School Project.* Miami: Dade County School Board.

Wiles, Jon, and Bondi, Joseph. 1986. *Making Middle Schools Work.* Alexandria, VA: ASCD.

CHAPTER 4

Teachers for the New Middle School

More the guide on the side than the sage on the stage.

Finding and training teachers for the middle school of the twenty-first century will call for a clear understanding of the mission and the client to be served. School curricula are, in reality, designs for learning, and teachers are the delivery media for such a plan. In developing middle schools, what is needed is a consistency in the design and delivery of the school program. Needed also are teachers who are competent to perform as instructional leaders in the middle school.

In Chapter One, it was noted that middle schools now have the ability to respond to the diversity of the middle school learner. Using a kind of if–then logic, it is possible to spell out the kind of learning experiences that are desirable for preadolescents, and the kind of teachers needed to deliver those experiences. A major organizer for such a school plan is the concept of "developmentally appropriate" curriculum.

David Elkind, a humanistic educator who writes of childhood, describes the developmentally appropriate curriculum as "one that includes some conception of the learner, of the learning process, and the goals to be accomplished. The learner is viewed as having developmental abilities, not measurable abilities. The learning process is seen as a creative activity, not as the acquisition of content and skills. The goal of education from the developmentally appropriate perspective is the construction of knowing by the learner, not to quantify knowledge acquisition by tests."[1]

We have seen in Chapter Two that the one thing preadolescent learners have in common is their differences. While all of the learners in a middle school go through a predictable unfolding as they mature, such development does not begin and end for all students at the same time and such development is often uneven. The various domains of growth—social, physical, intellectual, emotional—are often not synchronized as the student matures. And, if this is the case, the curriculum will have to be responsive and appropriate to the development of each student. High degrees of individualization are called for in this program.

The National Middle School Association has produced a position paper, "The Middle Level Curriculum: A Work in Progress," that sketches the kind of learning experiences one would project for the preadolescent.[2] The association sees a broad program addressing all of the developmental domains. It speaks of relevance as the application of learnings in the real world, and it sees the curriculum built around the developmental needs of the students. It is hoped that such a curriculum would encourage curiosity, provide challenges, and develop caring, responsible students.

The NMSA statement continues to promote a success-oriented learning experience, where staff members serve as role models, and where the family and the community are partners in assisting the preadolescent student in his or her growth. The position paper calls for instructional flexibility, varied learning media, and an active involvement of the students in planning for learning. By contrast, the statement of the NMSA suggests the phasing out of such practices as separate subjects, labeling and tracking, lecture, rote drill, textbook approaches, and departmentalization.

We might gain some insight into the goals of this new middle school by reviewing a statement of beliefs by one school, the Darnell-Cookman Middle School in Jacksonville, Florida:

We believe that learning should take place in a safe environment conducive to learning.

We believe that individual students should be treated with value, respect, and dignity.

We believe that learning should be a challenging, enjoyable, and positive experience for all students.

We believe that school should help each individual student realize his or her own potential.

We believe that for students to succeed there must be a real partnership between the home, the school, and the community.

Another statement by a middle school faculty addresses the characteristics of such a curriculum when it is operational as:

1. A unique program adapted to the needs of the preadolescent learner.
2. A wide range of intellectual, social and physical experiences.
3. A respect for individual differences.
4. A sensitivity to the stresses, fears, and frustrations of this period of development.
5. A climate that encourages an openness to new ideas and experiences.
6. A program that allows success by all students.
7. A program that teaches competencies for successful citizenship and group participation.
8. A program staffed by competent adults who understand the school mission.[3]

The reader may be wondering what such a school would look like, and how the teacher would act in such a school. It is the purpose of this chapter to project such an instructional environment and the teacher who would work successfully in such a school. As the chapter progresses, you may wish to conduct an informal self-assessment of your suitability for such a teaching assignment.

PARAMETERS OF PRACTICE

Writing in 1976, author Wiles contrasted what he believed the middle school would do in comparison with the traditional intermediate school. This vision is still of assistance in focusing the middle school curriculum:[4]

Middle Schools	Traditional Intermediate Schools
Recognize and respond to the uniqueness of each learner.	Treat learners in a uniform manner.
Involve students in the learning process as active partners.	Give the teacher full responsibility for the learning process.
Provide for instructional balance among the domains of growth.	Possess an overriding concern for only intellectual development.
Integrate the knowledge bases in classroom instruction.	Emphasize the distinctiveness of each subject or discipline of study.
Present learning through many curriculum forms and media.	Present learning through standard didactic learning format (drill and respond).
Emphasize the application of information and skill acquisition.	Provide little opportunity to assess the meaning of information.
Teach through student interests and needs.	Teach according to the predetermined subject matter organization.
Define progress in terms of the growth of each student.	Define progress in terms of mastery of administrative criteria such as standardized tests.
View teachers as guides or facilitators of learning.	View teachers as subject matter specialists.
Use individualized approach to student evaluation.	Use a standardized approach to student evaluation.

From this 25-year-old list, the reader can readily see that the teacher in a modern middle school does not teach in a traditional, secondary-school kind of way. A middle school teacher recognizes the mission of the middle school in teaching the preadolescent and, like the curriculum, the teacher must exhibit flexibility. Many of those things listed in the middle school column suggest specific teaching skills that must be mastered in order to be successful in the classroom.

CRITICAL TEACHING SKILLS

Teachers in middle schools possess more highly developed instructional skills than teachers in traditional intermediate programs because the curriculum is more complex. Some of these skills are obtained before entering teaching (presage skills) and some are learned in college preparation programs. By far, most of the skills needed to be a successful middle school teacher are learned on the job.

All things considered, middle school teachers need to be "people people." The teacher who has experience in working with youth, as a parent, a little league coach, or a girl scout leader, will enter the classroom with a broader understanding of the many roles of a teacher. It is especially important for the middle school teacher to understand the developmental stage of preadolescence, and see herself or himself as a guide through this most difficult passage. The middle school student will transition from a calm and respectful older child to a turbulent character experiencing puberty, and then back to a more stable form of early adolescent. Teachers in the middle school must be, above all else, calm and patient.

It is also helpful if the middle school teacher can see the world as a preadolescent does. For the preadolescent, the average day is too full, and each new event is somewhat traumatic. Middle school students are characterized by their belief that everything that happens to them is personal and unique. The emotions of a preadolescent can ebb and flow like the tide. Teachers need to understand that the needs of the preadolescent are usually low on Maslow's Hierarchy (physical needs, safety, belonging) while the teacher's needs are quite high (achievement). The time orientation of the preadolescent is present and future, while often the teacher dwells on past and present.

Having made these observations, the authors believe that a friendly, positive, and cheerful person has more of a chance of succeeding as a middle school teacher than a tense and overly serious type. A flexible personality—outgoing, accepting, encouraging, trustworthy—these are the things that preadolescents consistently identify in a favorite teacher. If the reader is thinking, "I'm not like that," don't be disheartened. These are human relations skills that can be learned. The basic lesson is "you get back what you send" in communicating with preadolescents.

A second preteaching skill is to understand the great importance of the environment in which you will teach these students. Middle school classrooms should reflect the students; they should be interesting, exploring, and comfortable places. In the traditional room, distractions are held to a minimum since learning is "all business." Middle school rooms often look slightly congested since there is an effort to provide something for many kinds of learners.

The reader might ask, "Should my room resemble a dentist's office or my home?" If you want the students' attention, you will have to decorate your learning place in the things that are of interest to preadolescents. You will also need to be sure that there are some things, such as pictures and possessions, that reveal information about you. The students at this age are always curious about adults, and they watch them carefully. See your learning space as they see it.

Basic learning theory for the preadolescent learner is fairly simple. Middle schoolers learn about those things that interest them. They also learn about new things in terms of what they already know. If the teacher enters the room and begins talking about something abstract and never before experienced by the students, the attention span will be depressingly short. Before teaching anything, take the time to establish communication with the students. Only then can you lead them into a lesson.

In covering subject matter, it is helpful to remember that the organization of the subject is always artificial. History, for example, is always chronological because that's how we teach it. History is also here and now, and can even be taught through science fiction. Whatever is taught needs to be broken up into small chunks of no more than eight to ten minutes. Try to remember that the student is constantly asking, "Why should I learn this?"

It is valuable to realize that the traditional classroom organization of tables and chairs prohibits two-way communication. The anthropologist Edward Hall, in his book *The Silent Language,* observed that the distance between two people communicating determines the meaning of the communication.[5] If the distance is greater than 12 feet between speaker and listener, according to Hall, you will get only one-way communication. Middle school teachers often say, "If you aren't close enough to see the color of their eyes, you aren't close enough to teach." Look at the way your furniture is arranged and start adjusting to the needs of the preadolescent.

Middle school teachers face the greatest range in the classroom of any level of schooling. The rule of thumb is that for each year in school, the classroom will have one year of range in achievement, reading, social maturity, and so on. While the fourth grade teacher looks at a four-year reading range, the eighth grade teacher has up to an eight-year range. Beyond the eighth grade, students drop out of school and the range narrows again.

What this means is that in selecting instructional materials, the teacher must plan for diversity in ability, subject mastery, reading comprehension, attention span, background experience, and a host of other variables. Multilevel materials for learning will have to be provided to allow all students to access the lessons. Middle schools often use "interdisciplinary units" as a vehicle to allow multilevel access by a wide range of students at any grade level.

The goals of instruction in a middle school differ from the traditional intermediate model. Historically, traditional intermediate schools (junior highs and middle schools) sought to be like the high school. The curriculum of such institutions was comprised of watered down and junior versions of the high school curriculum. For example, life science in such schools was often baby biology, complete with the dissections and the biological identification plates. True middle schools, in contrast, seek to promote holistic learning and the development of learning skills. The content component of any subject area is wedded to applications in the real world and cross-disciplinary (interdisciplinary) units.

Teachers at this level are focused on general understandings and the development of readiness and motivation for formal learnings. It is important to remember that about 30 percent of those students in the middle school will not complete high school, and for them the middle school is a finishing school. The ability to demonstrate how any subject matter can be used in the real world is a special skill needed by middle school teachers.

Motivating middle schoolers can be difficult if the teacher attempts to standardize instruction. Group book coverage, repetitious drill, lecture and sterile homework are all causes of disinterest for middle school students. By contrast, the teacher who constantly changes the stimuli, who includes humor in learning, who can give both practical and interesting examples of application, and who teaches a few things many ways will be more successful in a middle school.

Middle school teachers who can remember that students did not come to school today to learn a subject, but rather to socialize, will have a clearer understanding of the task at hand. The most important thing for the student is to belong, to be accepted, and to develop an identity. In teaching, lessons need to start where the student is, rather than where the teacher was during the last class meeting. Engage the student, offer challenges in the form of real life problems, and make the learning appealing. For an eighth grade boy, metrics is a dry title until the teacher begins to talk about motorcycles.

Sustaining the attention of a middle school student is often difficult. Their world is changing daily, and there are many things competing for their attention. Yet, an important lesson in the middle school is to learn how to complete work and sustain momentum. Lessons in the middle school should move from point to point, with attainable products resulting from any labor. Many middle schools use mini-courses rather than semester courses so that students don't get lost, or tired, or stop trying due to excessive failure.

Teachers in the middle school need to acknowledge the role of feeling or affect in learning. In order to engage the student in any learning activity, the teacher will have to increase the level of affect in the lesson. Using the learning taxonomies of Bloom and Krathwohl (*Cognitive Domains* and *Affective Domains*), it is easy to see the dependence of higher learning on affective learning. Figure 4.1 outlines the path of this relationship.

Middle school is a time of exploration by the student. Many highly individual traits will emerge during these years, indicating artistic, musical, and creative abilities, and will need to be encouraged by teachers at the classroom level. The authors once saw a band director identify one of his students as a potential track star just by being observant. The band director told a coach, the boy was recruited to the track team, and six years later he was the state champion in sprint races. Think of the middle school years as a time for every teacher to be a talent scout.

Middle school teachers need to be aware of the power of peer groups in the classroom. Being neither a child nor an adolescent, the middle schooler looks to peers to define desirable behaviors. For students, peer groups or cliques and even sometimes gangs are a source of security. All such groups have natural leaders, and teachers should consider these relationships when planning classroom activities. If push comes to shove in a middle school classroom, the student will almost always side with the peer group against the teacher in order to save face with his primary group.

One of the very important skills a middle school teacher must possess is the ability to measure student progress by nonstandardized means. Since the range of progress is so wide and varied in the middle school, it is impossible to judge all students by one standard. Middle schools have utilized a number of techniques to respond to this problem area including multiage groups,

FIGURE 4.1   *Connecting Cognition and Affective Learning*

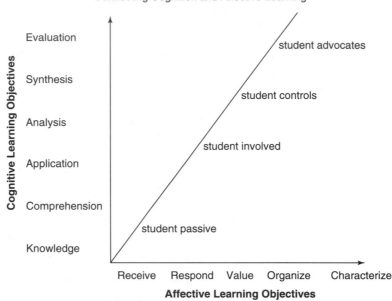

Connecting Cognition and Affective Learning

Note: The use of learning taxonomies like Bloom's cognition and Krathwohl's
affective domain allows teachers to plot expectations for student behavior
in learning. In traditional (low level) teaching, the student is passive, but as
affect is increased, the student becomes the dominant player in learning.

continuous progress curriculums, cooperative learning strategies, and portfolios of student work. Ahead in the near future, personalized Internet assignments will be added. Whatever technique is utilized, the important thing
to remember is that these students are not alike, and there is very little chance
that they will ever be alike in school. We must see each student by his or her
development and assess growth over time rather than achievement to a fixed
and artificial point of expectation.

A final skill of classroom instruction is dealing effectively with classroom
management and discipline. At no other level of schooling can things go wrong
so quickly, and middle school teachers must develop an effective plan to short-
circuit problems. As they say in football, a good defense is a great offense. Teachers who have a successful management plan, including keeping students on
task and managing time, will have fewer discipline problems. Such discipline
problems generally arise when students are uncertain, bored, or frustrated with
the instructional routine.

One key to successful discipline in middle schools is flexibility. Recognizing that any absolute standard will not fit everyone raises the possibility that the

teacher's response to problems may have to be situational. What is disruptive behavior for one student may not constitute disruptive behavior for another. While it is strongly recommended that there be a basic set of rules for any classroom, these rules are simply expectations.

Another critical idea about discipline in the middle school, besides being as flexible as possible, is that such episodes represent a learning experience for the student. When the student leaves school (one-third will leave in the high school years), he or she will have to be responsible for personal behavior. The teacher who makes all the decisions and makes judgments against the student without student participation is not helping the student grow. Middle school is the final time in life when students develop lasting attitudes toward self, work, and life itself.

Any discipline plan should be progressive, rather than absolute, allowing the student to understand the consequences of behavior and reach punishment in incremental steps. Discipline programs should be fair, but the punishments should be of short duration. Students change a great deal in the middle school from month to month.

Finally, there is the new and special situation of inclusion in the middle school classroom. Dating back to the "least restrictive environment" clause of the Education for All Handicaps Act of 1975 (Public Law 94–142), middle school teachers have sometimes accommodated students with categorical special needs. Since 1990, however, there have been new requirements for such students as defined by the Individuals With Disabilities Education Act (IDEA). This new law, superseding 94-142, and its concept of mainstreaming, calls for a much greater presence of special children in regular classrooms. The law states, "[C]hildren with disabilities will be educated with children without disabilities and no separate channels shall be supported except under the direst circumstances." Said simply, all children will be included in the basic classroom, most of the time (Figure 4.2).

The problem for the middle school teacher is that often, if not most of the time, the special teacher will not be present to assist in working with these handicapped children. As the special students are dispersed throughout the school (about 15 percent of any school population), the former special education teacher must divide his or her time among many places. When the special

FIGURE 4.2   INCLUSION DEFINED

To the maximum extent appropriate, children with disabilities, including children in public and private care facilities, are educated with children who do not have a disability, and special classes, separate schooling or other removal of children with disabilities from the regular educational environments occurs only when the nature or the severity of the disability is such that education in regular classes with the use of supplementary aids and services cannot be achieved satisfactorily.

20 United States Code 1412 (5) (B)

teacher is serving a number of classrooms, the model is called "collaborative consultation." If there are many special teachers and a one-to-one relationship can be established between special teacher and regular classroom teacher, the model is called "co-teaching." By far, the majority of schools employ the collaborative consultation model.

So how does the untrained middle school teacher work with multiple handicaps in regular classrooms? In reality, the organization of middle school teaching (discussed in the following chapter) through teams makes inclusion easier than the traditional self-contained classroom model. Middle school teachers who plan together daily can place handicapped students in student groups where they can learn and participate. It is the attitude of the regular teacher that is important to student success. New teachers should just think of these various handicaps as extensions of the general student differences in the middle school. More about these techniques will be discussed in Chapter Seven.

RESEARCH AND THE MIDDLE SCHOOL TEACHER

It should be obvious from the previous section that the middle school teacher will have to possess many exceptional skills to be effective with preadolescents. Some of these skills are general, while others are specific to the middle school years. The growing body of research in education shows that certain teacher behaviors are effective with certain age groups when accomplishing certain tasks. This section looks at some of the areas that seem appropriate to middle school teaching.

Student Home Life

Students today live in homes that differ greatly from 50 years ago. At that time, more than 60 percent of all students lived in homes with two parents, and only one of those parents worked. Today, less than six percent of all students come from such homes. Today, three out of four school age children have mothers in the labor force. In some states, less than one-half of all marriages succeed, and among all children there is better than a 50-percent chance that the child will live with only one parent during the school years. Single parent-headed households, predominantly female, earn less than one-half what a two-parent family earns. About 30 percent of all school children come from homes below the poverty level. Children from single-parent homes have more social problems and more academic problems than do children from two-parent homes.

While the above facts are not a judgment about single parent families in America, they do suggest a different role for a teacher in today's schools. Teachers in middle schools are found in the role of family-teams member, teacher–counselor, and learning partner in exploratory activities. The role of absentee parent has been thrust upon middle school teachers in particular due to the social nature of the preadolescent.

Readings

Epstein, J. "Longitudinal Effects of Family–School Interaction on Student Outcomes," *Research in Sociology of Education, 59,*3 (1986) 171–189.

Guralnick, M. "The Next Decade of Research on the Effectiveness of Early Intervention," *Exceptional Children, 58,*2 (1991) 174–81.

Davidson, N. "Life Without Father: America's Greatest Social Catastrophe," *Policy Review,* 51, (1990) 40–44.

Compensatory Programs

Compensatory programs have been around for nearly 35 years in America and have been shown by research to make a difference. These various services to low-achieving and economically deprived children are necessary since the basis of learning is existing knowledge and prior experience. Children without significant experience or general knowledge, and children without language skills, are poor candidates for higher level learning in the secondary school.

Two major programs found in the middle schools of America are Chapter One (originally Title One) and various ESL (English as a second language) programs. Chapter One has served over five-million students in 45 states at a cost in excess of five-billion dollars. In recent years it has shifted from a student-oriented approach to a school-oriented approach, and has been extended upward through the eighth grade. Teachers in any low-income school will find this program being offered.

ESL and ESOL (English for speakers of other languages) are programs that service language-deficient learners. The Supreme Court Case *Lau* v. *Nichols* found that "it is the responsibility of schools to take action so that non-English speaking students have equal access to educational opportunity." Given the dramatic increase in the number of foreign students in the United States, particularly Spanish-speaking students, it is probable that teacher competence may be measured by the acquisition of a second language in some areas, such as in the Sunbelt states. Cultural awareness also seems a logical staff development topic given these emerging conditions.

Readings

Hubbell, R. 1985. "A Review of Head Start Research Since 1970," Washington DC: Department of Health and Human Services.

Slavin, R. 1989. *Effective Programs for Students At-Risk.* Boston: Allyn and Bacon.

The Learning Environment

Ninety percent of all school expenditures result from the cost of school buildings and salaries. As we enter the twenty-first century, the meaning of "schools" and the meaning of "teachers" will change. Technology will lessen our dependence on only one kind of educational structure and on only one kind of certified teacher. Learning environments are going to change!

We may look back on the end of the twentieth century as a kind of archaic period when students were contained in buildings made up of miniature lecture halls even though the sources of knowledge were plentiful. The average classroom allows only about nine square feet of personal space for each student; a space size more appropriate to a short duration event than a six-hour stay. Most of these rooms totally ignore research on space, color, light, temperature, and a host of other variables that affect learning.

Increasingly, in the next decade, learning spaces will be more defined by access to information than by location. School buildings, as we know them, will begin to give way to learning spaces that may be rehabilitated buildings such as community buildings, old malls and storefronts, and neighborhood learning centers. Teachers, too, may become differentiated with some being learning guides and others being instructional space managers.

The new middle school teacher will need to think hard about what an ideal learning space would look like, and be flexible to these changing conditions. The new learning will be electronic, integrate media, and connect learners throughout the world based on common learning needs. We are entering, indeed, a new ball game.

Readings

Bourke, S. "Relationships Between Class Size, Teaching Practices, and Student Achievement," *American Education Research Journal*, 23 (1986) 558–571.

Weinstein, C. "The Physical Environment of School: A Review of Research," *Review of Educational Research*, 49 (1979) 577–610.

Ability Grouping

Middle schools, unlike the traditional intermediate schools, have moved away from grouping students on the basis of ability alone. Because we recognize that the preadolescent is in transition from a childhood form to an adolescent form, placement on the basis ability alone is impossible. Not only are the capacities of students changing as they pass through this developmental stage, but their development is uneven. The child who wins a national spelling bee competition may be an immature child at the same time. Flexible grouping, cooperative grouping, and regular review of subject ability groups is more appropriate to the middle school design.

It is reinforcing to know that over 1,500 studies have been conducted on ability grouping and the vast majority of them advise against the practice at any level. These studies fail to show the anticipated achievement gains that rationalize the practice, and also document many adverse conditions resulting from ability grouping, such as declines in self-concept, poorer race relations, and lowered academic motivation. This practice which originated in the Boston Public

Schools in 1908, is out of date and very inappropriate for the developmentally appropriate middle school curriculum.

Readings

Hallihan, M. "The Effects of Ability Grouping in Secondary Schools," *Review of Educational Research Journal,* 60 (1990) 501–504.

Kalik, J. and Kalik, C., "Meta-Analysis: Findings on Grouping Programs," *Gifted Child Quarterly, 36,*2 (Spring 1992) 73–76.

Slavin, R. "Achievement Effects of Ability Grouping in Secondary Schools: A Best Evidence Synthesis," *Review of Educational Research Journal,* 60 (1990) 471–499.

Cooperative Learning

More research has been conducted on the practice of grouping students cooperatively (heterogeneous grouping) than any other area. These findings on mixed-ability grouping suggest that teachers can teach a variety of students using a number of grouping patterns, such as games and teams, jigsaws, and group investigations, without a loss in achievement. These findings follow like findings about how various types of tutorial learning, such as peer and cross-age, can be accomplished without a loss of achievement when compared to like-ability grouping.

The majority of studies on cooperative learning have documented positive achievement on standardized tests, improved race relations, higher attendance, and smoother inclusion of special students in middle school classrooms. A rule of thumb for middle school teachers is that you get the same achievement by combining the upper two levels (high and middle) as you do in separating and teaching the high level alone.

Readings

Newman, F. and Thompson, J. 1987. "Effects of Cooperative Learning on Achievement in Secondary Schools: A Summary of Research," Madison, WI: National Center on Effective Secondary Schools.

Slavin, R. "Synthesis of Research on Cooperative Learning," *Educational Leadership* (February 1991) 71–82.

Teacher Expectation

Research shows clearly that how the teacher sees the student determines the expectations that teacher holds for the student's learning performance. Further, teachers act on their expectations in treating students differently in a classroom setting. These findings are important to middle school teachers in areas such as grouping, grading, and discipline, and especially given the changing nature of the middle school pupil throughout the year.

In particular, studies have documented discrimination against poor students, female students, and students of various ethnic origins. Teachers have been found to reward students with learning styles that match their own teaching style, and to penalize those students who don't fit the instructional style of the teacher.

Readings

Good, T. "Two Decades of Research on Teacher Expectations: Findings and Future Directions," *Journal of Teacher Education*, 38 (1987) 32–47.

Sternberg, R. "Thinking Styles: Key to Understanding Student Performance," *Phi Delta Kappan*, 71 (1990) 366–371.

Discipline

Many research studies have addressed classroom discipline, defined as a response to any student behavior that creates a competing vector or direction for the class. Generally, these studies show that discipline techniques used by the teacher affect instruction and are most appropriate when they parallel other instructional activities. Many middle schools use a technique called "assertive discipline" that is a form of group behaviorism. Meta-analyses (studies of studies) have found that this specific program has "no significant difference" in results when compared to other programs or no program at all." Assertive discipline, in the author's opinion, is an inappropriate technique for middle schools.

What does seem true is that middle schoolers respond to peer pressures, not to materialistic rewards, and to individual responsibilities. For middle school teachers, strong classroom management skills and positive classroom climates are the best means of minimizing student disruption in the classroom.

Readings

Cotton, K. "Schoolwide and Classroom Discipline," *School Improvement Research Series*, 5 (1990) 1–12.

Goldstein, W. 1986. "Group Process and School Management," in *Handbook of Research on Teaching*, New York: Macmillan, pp. 430–435.

Using Praise

Most teachers at all levels use praise as a reinforcement tool; they praise assuming that if a pleasant consequence follows a behavior, that behavior is likely to reoccur. Such reinforcement is sometimes true, but not always, and particularly in the middle school classroom. In middle schools, research has shown praise to sometimes embarrass students and to often be perceived by students as a patronizing act by the teacher. Students can even elicit praise from the teacher, says research, by making eye contact and smiling.

What is recommended by almost all research on praise is that it always be contingent upon a specific behavior by the student, and that such praise should be delivered in a confidential or private way if possible.

Readings

Brophy, J. "Teacher Praise: A Functional Analysis," *Review of Educational Research Journal*, 51 (1981) 5–32.

Merrett, F. "Teachers Use of Praise and Reprimands to Boys and Girls," *Educational Review*, 44, 1 (1992) 73–79.

Questioning by Teachers

Questions in the classroom form an intellectual link between the curriculum delivered and student learning. Research since 1970 reveals that classroom teachers ask about 50,000 questions per year and almost all are didactic (question–answer) or procedural in nature. Such drilling often produces listlessness in students.

Middle school teachers should know that questions establish the level of cognitive activity in the classroom. Teachers who learn to wait for an answer (wait time) get better and more complex answers from students. Most teachers wait less than one second for a student response before moving on to the next student. In fact, researchers have concluded that the questions asked by the teacher are most helpful in assessing the teacher's level of thinking about a subject, rather than the students' level of performance or participation.

Readings

Carlsen, W. "Questioning in the Classroom: A Sociolinguistic Perspective," *Review of Educational Research*, 61, 1991, 157–178.

Redfield, D. "A Meta-Analysis of Experimental Research on Teacher Questioning Behavior," *Review of Educational Research*, 51, 2 (1981) 237–245.

Shiang, C. "The Effectiveness of Questioning on the Thinking Process," paper presented at American Educational Research Association, 1989 (ERIC Ed 013 704).

Self-Concept Development

Educators regularly state that self-concept is an important factor in school achievement, attitude toward school, motivation to learn, and social adjustment. While these things are generally supported by studies, in the real world of the classroom things are more complex. There are many kinds of self-concept, such as academic and social, and the age and individual self-concept of the student is a factor in relating this area to school performance. Middle school students, quite naturally, experience a decline in self-esteem while going through puberty.

Academic self-concept results from some combination of performance and reward. Students who have success, who experience feelings of confidence and well-being, and who possess higher expectations for future success, have higher academic self-concepts. Negative academic self-concept results from repeated failure, low teacher expectation, and retention.

Readings

Kurtz-Costes, B. "Self-Concept, Attributional Beliefs, and School Achievement: A Longitudinal Analysis," *Journal of Contemporary Educational Psychology,* 19, (1994) 199–216.

Marsh, H. "Relations Among Dimensions of Self-Attribution, Dimensions of Self-concept, and Academic Achievement, *Journal of Educational Psychology,* 76, 6 (1984) 1291–1308.

Retention

Of all the areas covered by educational research, none is more conclusive and unified in findings as the 800 studies on school retention. Each year, about 10 percent of all public school students are retained, and the odds of being retained in school sometime approaches 50 percent for any given student. In reality, closer inspection reveals that the retainee is usually male, southern, poor, and disproportionately minority. This practice costs public schools 10 billion dollars a year.

Most teachers and parents believe that a second year in the same grade will increase achievement, but this notion is not supported by organized study. Students who are held back may make temporary gains, compared to the like student who is allowed to be promoted, but the gains are short-lived. In the long run, like students who are promoted or retained are indistinguishable except for the negative by-products of the practice. Retainees correlate with low self-esteem, low attendance, behavioral problems in school, and dropping out. A single retention makes the student a 50–50 candidate for dropping out. A second retention makes dropping out a certainty.

Alternatives to retention include practices like transitional promotion, multiage instructional grouping, compensatory learnings, and the like. Middle schools with three-year continuous progress curriculums have no need of such a practice.

Readings

Balow, I. 1990. *Retention: A Failed Procedure,* Riverside, CA: California Education Research Cooperative, pp. 1–35.

Holmes, C. and Matthews, K. "Grade Level Retention Effects: A Meta-Analysis of Research Studies," in Shepard and Smith, eds., 1990. *Flunking Grades: Research and Policies on Retention,* New York: Falmer Press, pp. 16–33.

USE OF RESEARCH ON TEACHING

The available research on teaching is supportive of the middle school use of developmentally appropriate practices in teaching. Teachers who work in middle schools need to know such research and use it to structure their teaching. From the previous section, here is what we know.

Many children today come to schools disadvantaged in language and experience, and these deficiencies often cause them to experience a lack of success in school. For many of these children, the traditional family is not there to support them or reinforce academic orientations. When applied and sustained, compensatory programs work to overcome these disadvantages.

Classrooms structure attitudes and behaviors toward learning. The more affect that the teacher presents through the classroom environment, the more student participation in learning is possible. Highly structured classrooms, evidenced by rows, single text, and lecture, support teacher control and exclude students as participants.

Practices such as ability grouping, behavioristic discipline, low teacher expectation, and retention only serve to emphasize the unfairness and in some cases, the hopelessness, of schooling for some students. Middle school students in particular need success and positive, encouraging adults to guide them through their passage to adolescence.

Sometimes, middle school teachers are unaware of teaching practices that cause students to turn off to learning. False praise and insincere questions make students think that their thoughts and opinions are not valued. Often, teachers fail to understand that simple distance from a student is communication, too.

Finally, there is a body of research that strongly endorses cooperative and success-oriented classrooms. This knowledge reinforces our intuitive understanding that standardized education is inappropriate for the most diverse population in school and that to be successful, middle schools must attempt to individualize learning for each student. Organizational and instructional flexibility is the key to a successful middle school program. Overcoming the fog of words and building creative learning experiences at the classroom level represent the preferred future for middle schools in the twenty-first century.

LEARNING THEORY IN THE MIDDLE SCHOOL CLASSROOM

In addition to research, a strong learning theory can help a middle school teacher be more effective in the classroom. This section describes the positions of well-known learning theorists, explains what they think happens when teaching occurs, and extracts from this wisdom a series of principles for middle school teaching.

Jean Piaget (Swiss)—Learners create new experiences and events and seek to assimilate them into existing cognitive structures, or to adjust their existing cognitive structures to accommodate this new information. Children learn by moving through stages of intellectual development, interacting with and constructing theories about their environment. They struggle with these disequilibriums and create new ways of thinking.[6]

David Ausubel (American)—Learning is an active process. It requires that the learner make a cognitive analysis of potentially meaningful material to determine which aspects of existing cognitive structure are most relevant. Conflicts must be resolved and material reformed to conform to that structure.[7]

Lev Vygotsky (Russian)—Thought is born in words and words are vital to the thought process. The origins of thought are social, coming at first from more capable others. Eventually, the speech becomes internal–silent, rapid, and abbreviated—and the "voice" becomes thought. With time, the processing becomes automatic. Adults provide a context, a "scaffolding" for this learning, in the way they communicate with students.[8]

John Dewey (American)—The aim of education is to develop the power of self-control in each student. The primary source of control does not reside in the teacher, but with the student. School should be child-centered, practical, and unitary. Students cannot develop truth out of their own minds because "nothing can be developed out of nothing." Developing experiences for students, and activities that will guide them, is the task at hand.[9]

Elliot Eisner (American)—Knowing depends on experience. Experiences can be either practical or imaginary. The different forms of representation (subjects) contribute to our ability to extract meaning from our experiences.[10]

Howard Gardner (American)—Inside all learners is an untamed five-year-old mind struggling to express itself and order the world. This intuitive and natural learning tool is not being utilized by schools.[11]

From just a few of the many learning theorists from the twentieth century, it is possible to see that the middle school rests on a firm foundation of beliefs. Some of these foundational beliefs that guide classroom teaching include:

1. Students develop in a natural progression and need activities and materials that are commensurate with their experience and knowledge of the world.
2. Use subjects in school as a tool to teach certain perspectives in life.
3. Allow students to become aware of their own thought processes and teach them strategies for thinking, such as note-taking and brainstorming.
4. Resist the temptation to label students based on our perception of their abilities.
5. Encourage students to work together in forming concepts and developing approaches to problem solving.
6. Vary classroom instruction to allow all students to find a strong medium for personal growth and learning.

7. Connect student developmental tasks with school projects to enhance academic motivation in the classroom.

8. Use teaching episodes to share how students might structure new learnings (scaffolding).

9. Reach out to the community to find natural learning activities that students experience daily.

10. Utilize generic evaluation measures to assess developmental progress by individual students.

PURPOSE AND INSTRUCTIONAL STRATEGY

If any school represents a design for learning, then each classroom must also be purposeful. Middle school teachers must select a way of teaching that contributes to the desired growth in preadolescents. Figure 4.3 illustrates how any kind of learning can be constructed out of instructional strategies.

The idea of possessing knowledge, very important in the middle school because it forms the building blocks for higher level thinking, requires a structured and efficient approach from the teacher. Lecture has a role in introducing information in an ordered fashion. Computer-assisted instruction may represent greater efficiency in laying down foundational skills needed for higher learning. Practice, drill, and homework may be used to structure habits, attitudes, and perceptions.

Since middle school students are emerging into adolescence, they have many things in their cognitive structures that do not fit their childhood perceptions. They are developing a moral code and laying the foundations for interpersonal relations. They have many questions and will make many important decisions during their middle school years. While teachers can answer some of their questions, it may be more important to arm the students to make decisions on their own. The old saying, "Give them a fish and they eat for a day; teach them to fish and they eat forever," seems relevant.

We know that the emerging middle schooler is full of visions, dreams, and creativity. At no other time in life is the ability to make unique associations so unencumbered by experience and expectations. The capability of middle schoolers is impressive and the schools should allow these explorations and growth and see them as natural and healthy.

Finally, the self-centered child of the elementary school is becoming the other-centered young adult. Learning such skills is a long and difficult task. Middle schools can assist in this major developmental task by structuring interactive learning. The peer groups are natural organizations in middle schools and should be used to encourage the development of social skills and cooperative behaviors.

Any middle school, and any middle school classroom, is a blend of these purposes and strategies. Teachers who work in middle schools need to understand the connectedness between their actions and the type of learning that can occur.

FIGURE 4.3   *Purpose and Instructional Strategies*

```
┌─────────────────────────────┬─────────────────────────────┐
│         Mastery             │        Involvement          │
│                             │                             │
│   Practice Strategies       │   Personal Strategies       │
│                             │                             │
│ Teaching Strategies:        │ Teaching Strategies:        │
│ • Command—demonstration     │ • Graduated difficulty      │
│ • Practice                  │ • Peer practice             │
│ Learner's Thinking:         │ • Moral dilemmas            │
│ • Recall                    │ Learner's Thinking:         │
│ • Rehearse                  │ • Introspection             │
│ Curriculum Objectives:      │ • Decision making           │
│ • Skills                    │ Curriculum Objectives:      │
│ • Procedures                │ • Personal and social maturity│
│                             │ • Academic responsibility   │
│          ┌──────────────────────────────┐                │
│          │     Cultural Literacy         │                │
│          │  Presentational Strategies    │                │
│          │ Teaching Strategies:          │                │
│          │ • Lecture                     │                │
│          │ • Program instruction         │                │
│          │ Learner's Thinking:           │                │
│          │ • Labeling                    │                │
│          │ • Storing                     │                │
│          │ Curriculum Objectives:        │                │
│          │ • Recall information          │                │
│          │ • Presentation                │                │
│          └──────────────────────────────┘                │
│   Processing Strategies     │  Problem-solving Strategies │
│                             │                             │
│ Teaching Strategies:        │ Teaching Strategies:        │
│ • Concept attainment        │ • Creative problem solving  │
│ • Concept formation         │ • Synectics                 │
│ • Inquiry                   │ • Creative expression       │
│ Learner's Thinking:         │ Learner's Thinking:         │
│ • Conceptualizing           │ • Generating                │
│ • Verifying                 │ • Applying                  │
│ Curriculum Objectives:      │ Curriculum Objectives:      │
│ • Formulating concepts      │ • Creative products or      │
│ • Critical thinking         │   solutions                 │
│                             │ • Skills                    │
│       Understanding         │         Synthesis           │
└─────────────────────────────┴─────────────────────────────┘
```

Source: Richard Strong, Harvey F. Silver, and Robert Hanson, "Integrating Teaching Strategies and Thinking Styles with the Elements of Effective Instruction," *Educational Leadership* 42 (May 1985): 9–15.

Suggested Goal Statements and Middle School Standards

The authors have previously stated that many middle schools have been a middle school in name only. Over the past 40 years a kind of conceptual fog has kept middle schools from pursuing their philosophies in the classroom. If we use a sort of if–then logic, it is clear what should be occurring and how the teacher can support the middle school concept at the classroom level.

Most middle schools have a goal statement that sketches the parameters of the program concerns. Arcadia Middle School in California, for example, states its purpose in the following manner: "Arcadia Middle School provides a secure learning environment which encourages students in transition to develop their highest academic and personal potential. This environment helps students to become caring, respectful, and responsible citizens in an ever-changing world."

Goal areas that can be deducted from this global statement of philosophy include (a) a secure learning environment, (b) a personal and caring program, (c) high academic performance, (d) a developmentally appropriate program, (e) a program that is concerned with citizenship and community, and (f) a program with interdisciplinary themes.

If we break each of these goal areas down further (if–then), they might be defined in the following manner:

Secure learning environment

> Nonthreatening
>
> Physically safe
>
> Allows for risk taking
>
> Provides an active role for learners
>
> Promotes individual self-esteem

Personal and caring program

> Small classes or groupings of students
>
> Class identity and pride
>
> Individual student and teacher interfacing
>
> Students known on first-name basis
>
> Use of peer learning and tutoring
>
> Physically comfortable surroundings
>
> A sense of community
>
> Individualized learning

High academic standards

Meets and exceeds state requirements

Provides an extended curriculum (grades six through 12 materials)

A variety of assessments

Teaches higher level thinking skills

Uses technological applications

Highly qualified staff

Enriched curriculum

Developmentally appropriate

Uses multiple teaching strategies

Acknowledges learning styles

Incorporates multiple intelligences research

Provides variety of assessment tools (folios)

Citizenship and community

Community learnings

Community academic resource bank

Parental access to curriculum (webpages or other)

Parents as teacher assistants

Community service projects

Parental advisory board

Interdisciplinary themes

Learning skills (reading and writing) across the curriculum

Thematic units

Interdisciplinary teaching teams

Integration of subjects and student behaviors

Applied student assessments

While many other examples could be provided, the reader should be able to take this outline of purpose a step further by asking, "What does the teacher do?" If, for example, the teacher is going to acknowledge the diversity of the middle school student by providing a developmentally appropriate learning experience, then it follows that each individual student will be assessed, that a plan for each individual student will be developed, that appropriate learning materials and teaching strategies will be applied, and that the evaluation of student development will be tailored to the progress of the individual student wherever he or she may be. In a word, the teacher will individualize the curriculum for the student. This commitment by the teacher to promote the middle school philosophy at the classroom level, may also mean that the teacher must become more highly trained and skilled.

MIDDLE SCHOOL LICENSURE

Like the junior high school before it, the middle school could be called the "school without teachers" since so few middle grade teachers are specifically prepared to teach preadolescent learners. Most states offer elementary and high school licenses that overlap with the middle grades, and this common practice results in teachers with either a content focus or a child development focus, but not both.

Over time, the number of states offering some sort of middle school teaching preparation has increased from only two in 1968, to 15 in 1978, and 33 as of a 1992 survey. But this doesn't mean that all of these states have specific preparation programs for middle school teachers. One state, for example, provides certificates for K–3, 1–8, 4–8, 7–9, and 9–12. Naturally, most college students would select the broadest certification (1–8) to increase their employability. A 1992 survey by McEwin found that only five states (Georgia, Kentucky, Missouri, Virginia, and North Carolina) required special licensure to teach in the middle grades.[12]

In reality, this condition means that few new teachers will enter middle school teaching with adequate preparation to implement the middle school philosophy at the classroom level. Most middle schools will be organized to aid teachers in their roles, such as using teams and flexible schedules, but the teachers will not possess the pedagogical skills to carry the program. What can be found in most middle schools is a highly standardized teaching style with rows, textbooks, and tests on Friday in too many rooms. Because the classroom teacher is the final filter on the planned curriculum, the failure of so many middle schools to fully develop can be found in the classrooms.

What this means for the new middle school teacher, and the experienced middle school teacher as well, is that most of what is needed will be learned on the job and in the school. This also means that most middle schools will need to rethink staff development for teachers to include an internal skill-sharing approach. As a foundation for any new teacher, the National Middle School Association recommends the following teacher education components:

Thoroughly knowing the preadolescent learner

Understanding the purpose of middle school organizational components

Developing a broad and interdisciplinary academic background

Learning special methods to teach learning skills, especially reading

Building up a solid set of early field experiences in good middle schools

To this list the authors would add becoming familiar with the issues and the techniques of special educators so that inclusion in the middle school can be more than a slogan. It is encouraging to note that many colleges and universities are now wedding special education certification and elementary/middle certification in their teacher education programs.

SUMMARY

Middle school teachers in the twenty-first century will need to understand the mission of the American middle school and develop the teaching skills to carry out that mission in the classroom. Middle schools possess highly defined preferences for how a child is to be educated and generally endorses the developmentally appropriate instructional orientation. Middle school teachers must share the beliefs that undergird middle school education in order to be effective.

Certain parameters of practice distinguish the middle school from the previous forms of intermediate education. Middle schools see each learner as unique. Middle schools seek to involve the student in her or his own learning. Middle schools endorse a broad and general education at this level. Middle schools encourage interdisciplinary and applied learnings. Instructional strategies in middle schools revolve around the needs and interests of the student. Middle schools will use many instructional tools and strategies to reach learners. Finally, middle schools are dependent upon teachers who can make wise instructional choices based on knowing the nature of preadolescence.

To be successful, middle school teachers must be people–people. They must be able to encourage a "learning set" by providing a caring and supportive environment. Middle school teachers build learning strategies around the growth and development of the student. Middle school teachers are communicators, using both verbal and nonverbal skills to reach students. Middle school teachers will go the extra mile to provide learning materials for students that are appropriate to their developmental level. Middle school teachers understand the motivation patterns of the preadolescent learner. In short, middle school teachers must possess superior teaching skills in order to be effective with this most diverse learning population in school.

Research about teaching is a valuable asset for the middle school teacher. Reading and understanding the patterns associated with home life, compensatory programs, the learning environment, and various techniques of organizing instruction will make the teacher more knowledgeable and productive. Specific knowledge about grouping, teacher expectation, discipline, asking questions, self-concept development, and retention has been provided in this chapter.

Learning theory in the middle school dates from the time of John Dewey and can be found in the words of Piaget, Ausubel, Vygotsky, Eisner, and Gardner. The common thoughts of these luminaries are presented as 10 foundational beliefs that should guide instruction in the middle school.

Finally, this chapter has presented middle school standards as a linking mechanism that ties goal statements to classroom instruction. Middle schools are totally dependent upon the classroom teacher to make middle schools work. Without a firm foundational understanding of what middle schools believe, the teacher in the classroom may easily be dysfunctional.

Like the junior high school before it, the middle school has failed to provide adequate training for its teachers. Only a handful of states require specific middle school training to gain licensure. For the foreseeable future, middle school teachers will have to learn the skills of middle school teaching on the job.

Suggested Learning Activities

1. Develop a list of the behaviors you most admired in your favorite middle school teacher. How does this list compare to the prescriptions presented in this chapter?

2. Develop an outline of training for a successful middle school teacher. What must the teacher be able to do and in what order of importance?

3. Discuss with other members of your class what discipline procedures would be appropriate for a middle school classroom in a true middle school.

Notes

1. David Elkind, *A Sympathetic Understanding of the Child,* (New York: Macmillan, 1978).
2. National Middle School Association, "The Middle Level Curriculum: A Work In Progress," (Fairborn, OH: 1995).
3. Workshop statement, Ishpeming, MI, 1993.
4. Jon Wiles, *Planning Guidelines for Middle Grades Education,* (Dubuque, IA: Kendall Hunt, 1976).
5. Edward Hall, *The Silent Language,* (Garden City, NY: Doubleday Books, 1973).
6. See Richard Gorman, *Piaget: A Guide for Teachers,* (Columbus, OH: Charles Merrill, 1973).
7. David Ausubel, *Educational Psychology: A Cognitive View,* 1968.
8. Vygotsky, *Thought and Language,* 1934.
9. John Dewey, *The Child and the Curriculum,* (New York: Macmillan, 1902).
10. Elliot Eisner, *Cognition and the Curriculum,* (Alexandria, VA: ASCD, 1982).
11. Howard Gardner, *The Unschooled Mind,* (1991).
12. C.K. McEwin and T.S. Dickinson, *The Professional Preparation of Middle Level Teachers,* (Columbus, OH: National Middle School Association, 1995).

Selected References

Gerrick, W. Gregory. 1999. *Affirming Middle Grades Education.* Boston: Allyn and Bacon.

George, Paul and Alexander, William. 1997. *The Exemplary Middle School, 3d ed.* New York: Holt Rinehart Winston.

Kellough, Richard and Kellough, Noreen. 1998. *Middle School Teaching: A Guide to Methods and Resources.* Upper Saddle River, NJ: Prentice-Hall.

Queen, J. Allen. 1999. *Practice in Elementary and Middle Schools.* Columbus, OH: Charles Merrill Publishing.

National Middle School Association. 1977. *The Middle School: A Look Ahead.* Fairborn, OH.

National Middle School Association. 1995. *This We Believe: Developmentally Responsive Middle Level Schools.*

National Middle School Association. 1996. *America's Middle Schools: Practices and Programs—A 25-Year Perspective.* Columbus, OH.

5

Organizing the Middle School Curriculum

A rule of thumb in middle schools:
for each year in school there is one year of range.

A middle school program should reflect the philosophy of the school itself. For this reason it may be difficult to find an identical program in any two schools, even within the same school district. But because of the common goal that drives middle school philosophy—to provide education for 10- to 14-year-olds who are in transition physically, socially, emotionally, and intellectually—certain elements form a unifying thread that runs throughout the successful middle school curriculum.

This chapter will examine each of those elements that give this level of education its identity and vitality. The heart of the chapter is a model on which a balanced program can be designed.

THE BALANCED CURRICULUM

The Association for Supervision and Curriculum Development (ASCD) has described a number of criteria that make for a balanced middle school program. These criteria are summarized below.

Learning experiences should be provided for transescents at their own intellectual levels and relate to immediate rather than remote academic goals. So to account for the full range of students who are at many different levels of concrete and formal operations, a wide variety of cognitive learning experiences should be made available. In addition, learning objectives should be sequenced to allow for the transition from concrete to formal operations. Toward this end, a diversified curriculum of exploratory and fundamental activities should result in daily experiences that will stimulate and nurture intellectual development. For example, opportunities should be provided for development of problem-solving skills, reflective-thinking processes, and awareness for the order of the student's environment. Cognitive experiences should be so structured that students can progress in an individualized manner. That is, as much consideration should be given to *who* the student is and becomes (his self-concept, sense of self-responsibility, and attitudes toward school and personal happiness) as is given to *how much* and *what* he knows. However, within the structure of an individualized learning program, students can interact with one another—social interaction is not an enemy of individualized learning.

Furthermore, notes the ASCD, a curriculum must be flexible enough that all areas taught reveal opportunities for further study, help students learn how to study, and help them appraise their own interests and talents. In addition, the middle school should continue the developmental program of basic skills instruction started in the elementary school, with emphasis on both developmental and remedial reading. A planned sequence of concepts in the general education areas must be promoted, with major emphasis on the interests and skills for continued learning, a balanced program of exploratory experiences and other activities and services for personal development, and appropriate attention to the development of values.

A balanced program must combine and integrate areas of learning to break down artificial and irrelevant divisions of curriculum content. Some previously departmentalized areas of the curriculum should be combined and taught around integrative themes, topics, and experiences. Other areas of the curriculum, particularly those concerned with basic skills that are logical, sequential, and analytical, might best be taught in ungraded or continuous progress programs (discussed in Chapter 3). Inflexible student scheduling, with its emphasis on departmentalization, should be restructured in the direction of greater flexibility.

Methods of instruction should involve open and individually directed learning experiences. For example, students' personal curiosity should be nurtured, with one learning experience inspiring subsequent activities. The role of the teacher should be more that of a personal guide and facilitator of learning than of a purveyor of knowledge. Thus, traditional lecture–recitation methods should be minimized. Also, curriculum and teaching methods must reflect cultural, ethnic, and socioeconomic subgroups within the middle school student population. Grouping of students should involve not only cognitive, but also physical, social, and emotional criteria.

Finally, experiences in the arts must be made accessible so that all transescents can enhance their aesthetic appreciation and creative expression.[1]

Despite much progress over the past 10 years in developing new and exciting programs for emergent adolescent learners, much remains to be done. Whether middle school programs are housed in structures called middle schools or found in upper elementary grades, junior highs, or secondary schools, their focus must be attuned to the developmental characteristics of this unique group of learners.[2]

It becomes clear, then, that the purpose of a middle school is to offer a balanced, comprehensive, success-oriented curriculum that is designed to bridge the gap between the self-contained environment of the elementary school and the departmentalized structure of the high school. It is also intended to provide experiences that will assist students in making the transition from late childhood to adolescence.

Through the introduction of formal academic disciplines and a variety of enrichment and special-interest experiences, the middle school curriculum is more exploratory in nature than is that of the elementary school and is less specialized than the high school program. Thus, because skill development balanced with subject-area content is a primary goal, three major components emerge in the middle school curriculum: subject content, personal development, and essential learning skills.

Students experience learning through a program that emphasizes integration of the four core subject content areas—language arts, mathematics, science, and social studies—and the advisory program. The specifics of what students should learn and how to help them learn are important aspects of *subject content*.

Personal development is designed to foster social, emotional, and moral growth through student-centered curricular and extracurricular activities. This is a schoolwide responsibility that involves the entire staff. To help initiate and implement personal development topics, an advisor program is recommended.

TABLE 5.1 A Balanced Curriculum

Subject Content	Personal Development	Essential Learning Skills
3 years math	Advisory program	School awareness
3 years science	Developmental PE	Community awareness
3 years communication/	Health and nutrition	Reading
language arts	Individual growth	Listening
3 years social studies	Social growth	Speaking
3 years reading	Citizenship	Writing
3 years developmental PE	Creativity	Vocabulary
3 years exploratory courses	Mini-courses	Thinking
	Special interests	Problem solving
	Career education	Decision making
	Exceptional education	Study
		Media
		Map
		Reference
		Test Taking
		Computer literacy
		Computation and calculator

As an outgrowth of its responsibility to refine *essential learning skills* (e.g., reading, speaking, writing, and such) introduced in the elementary school, a middle school program should assist students in becoming more self-directed learners. Specifically this means that proficiency in certain basic skills emphasized in all subject areas is key to each student's ability to function effectively in further schooling and in society.

Table 5.1 illustrates an ideal curriculum: that is, one that synthesizes the three essential components in a balanced middle school curriculum.

JUNIOR HIGH VERSUS THE MIDDLE SCHOOL: SOME DIFFERENCES

The middle school program differs in a number of ways from its predecessor, the traditional junior high. Table 5.2 highlights some of the key differences.

The personal development component of middle school programs focuses on the developmental differences of emerging adolescent learners rather than on their sameness, as is the case with traditional programs.

The subject content element takes into account existing cognitive and psychomotor skills of preadolescent and early adolescent middle graders.

An effective middle school program also emphasizes those essential learning skills that will be needed throughout school life and adult life.

To educate today's emerging adolescent learners, the middle school will be based on a comprehensive curriculum—a program design that in turn is based on an in-depth needs assessment. The next sections of this chapter present se-

TABLE 5.2 *Traditional Junior High Versus Middle School: A Study in Contrast*

Traditional Junior High	Middle School
Based on high school model	Common, academically oriented core curriculum
Mastery of subject matter	Interdisciplinary academic program
Departmentalized academic program	Team concept
Emphasis on the disciplines	Exploratory elective program
Conference periods scattered throughout the day; seven-period day	Teacher planning time; flexible scheduling; extended blocks of uninterrupted time
Full-semester elective	Collaborative and independent self-contained teaching modes
Homogeneous grouping (tracking)	Equal access to all programs by all students
Full athletic program	Student advisory program

lected curriculum sections of the Duval County, Florida (Jacksonville) Middle School Design. The authors served as chief consultants to Duval County in its middle school transition.[3]

A DESIGN PROTOTYPE: DUVAL COUNTY MIDDLE SCHOOL

Philosophy: The Nature and Needs of Early Adolescents

Middle school students are in transition between childhood and adulthood. Therefore, children between ages 10 and 14 have very distinctive needs that set them apart from elementary and high school students. Physically, they exhibit wide daily variations in growth and development and energy levels, especially with the onset of puberty. Intellectually, they have a heightened curiosity about the world around them but are easily distracted and have short attention spans. Socially, they are strongly influenced by peers and challenge authority. Emotionally, middle school students are constantly searching for self-identity. Thus, they need a stable yet flexible environment that will meet their changing needs and promote their academic success.

The Nature of the Responsive School

Middle schools must be flexible, student-centered structures responsive to the growth and educational needs of children in transition. By providing for maximum interaction between teachers and students, middle schools encourage the development of independent thinking skills to ensure that students achieve academic success and develop personal responsibility. Teachers, administrators, and support staff must adopt a nurturing approach that emphasizes and attends to each student as a person. Such a school will have the following characteristics:

- A student-centered focus that enhances academic progress
- An environment that ensures smooth transitions from elementary to middle school and from middle school to high school
- A curriculum focused on students' personal development and on skills for continued learning
- Opportunities to develop constructive, meaningful relationships with peers and adults
- A focus on students' increasing levels of independence, responsibility, self-discipline, and citizenship through effective decision making
- Teachers and administrators who are committed to the education of the emerging adolescent
- A variety of evaluation criteria to assess student progress while maintaining academic excellence
- An emphasis on developing a safe and caring environment that fosters a genuine interest in learning
- Meaningful articulation with parents that encourages their involvement in their children's education

In addition, the effective middle school will provide the following:

- Teachers who are organized into interdisciplinary teams with common planning times and responsibility for the same student population
- Teacher-based advisor programs facilitated by guidance counselors
- Flexible scheduling based on time blocks rather than on fixed-length periods
- Opportunities for individualized learning that lead to the refinement of existing cognitive and psychomotor skills
- A structured exploratory program that includes enrichment, independent study, art, music, career education, foreign language, intramural activities, team activities, and peer-group activities
- Emphasis on basic skills in reading, writing, mathematics, and critical thinking through an integrated curriculum

The Curriculum: An Overview

The middle school will provide a stable yet flexible curriculum to meet each student's academic, affective, and developmental needs while providing an opportunity to participate in an exploratory program. The *goals* of the curriculum are threefold:

1. To foster academic success in all students.

2. To implement an affective program such as the advisor/advisee program.
3. To provide an exploratory program.

Each student will take the following *core curriculum:*

- 3 years of communications including reading, writing, and speaking
- 3 years of mathematics
- 3 years of science
- 3 years of social studies
- 3 years of physical education and health
- 3 years of exploratory electives in art, music, foreign language, and career education courses
- 3 years of the advisory program

Exploratory elective programs will be defined by the following parameters:

- Offerings will vary from school to school based on the school facility, size, and staff.
- Sixth-grade students will be in a different area during each nine-week period. They will be required to choose four different exploratory programs for the year.
- Seventh-grade students will choose from elective courses of one semester or one year in duration.
- Eighth-grade students will choose from elective courses of one semester or one year in duration.
- Possible exploratory elective areas:

  Career education: wood, graphics, metal, power, electricity

  Home economics: food, clothing, child care

  Business: typing, business skills, accounting

  Fine arts: drama, journalism, art

  Foreign language: Spanish, French, Latin

  Music: band, chorus, general music

  Computer: programming, applications, problem solving

Following is a list of *continual (essential) learning skills* that need to be an integral part of all subjects and courses:

- Critical thinking
- Reading
- Social interaction
- Test taking skills

- Writing
- Listening
- Speaking
- Study skills
- Vocabulary
- Problem solving
- Decision making

- Computer literacy
- Reference usage
- Career awareness
- School awareness
- Community awareness
- Citizenship
- Media usage

Curricular Design: A Model for Setting Standards

1.0 Career Education. A hands-on approach allows for personal assessment, technological literacy, and career development. Students will learn the role of technology in the world of work, explore various career fields, and have the chance to set career goals from which they will develop a personal career and educational plan.

 1.01 Experiences that demonstrate the relationship of educational achievement to career opportunities
 1.02 Orientation to standard career clusters
 1.03 Activities that apply basic skills in English, mathematics, science, and social studies to the world of work
 1.04 Participation during each of the three middle school years in exploratory career programs including business, home economics, and technology education
 1.05 Experiences that develop an understanding and appreciation for the dignity and worth of work
 1.06 Assessment of the student's personal aptitudes, interests, and direction toward relating those aptitudes and interests to career fields
 1.07 Individual student development of a four-year educational plan for grades nine through 12 with input from student, parents, and school advisers
 1.08 Participation in manipulative activities with tools, materials, and processes to solve practical problems
 1.09 Access to an occupational specialist for all students
 1.10 The use of computer technology to enhance instruction
 1.11 Mastery of the career education curriculum through frequent use of reading, writing, speaking, and listening skills

2.0 Computers and Technology. As society advances technologically, it is imperative that students in grades six through eight be exposed to technology so as to apply it beneficially in their environment.

 2.01 Computer studies offered to sixth-grade students through the exploratory wheel

2.02 A computer or technology course for seventh-grade students based on the current eighth-grade Computer Literacy Program modified to include in-depth study in the area of computer applications

2.03 Semester courses in computer logic and problem solving, computer applications, and computer programming offered as elective courses in the seventh and eighth grades, should student demand and available facilities warrant such course offerings

2.04 The incorporation of computers and related technology into all areas of the curriculum, in that research indicates that technology is a viable tool for instruction when that technology is used to supplement, not replace, the curriculum

3.0 Exceptional Education. Every student has the opportunity to become an active participant in, and contributing member of society through a program designed to meet his or her specific physical, emotional, intellectual, communicative, social, and vocational needs. No student is separated from the educational mainstream without documented evidence that separation or a more restricted environment is for the student's benefit or is necessary to serve his or her best interest.

3.01 Ongoing process for review and revision of the Individual Education Program (IEP) to ensure that individual needs are met

3.02 Provision of the least restrictive environment that provides successful educational and social opportunities

3.03 Full access to all school programs and activities

3.04 Provision of appropriate therapies, adaptive programs (and devices), and transportation

3.05 Curriculum that focuses on students' functional levels and meets the state and local requirements for promotion

3.06 Provision for various scheduling, mainstreaming, and regular education alternatives to meet individual student needs

3.07 The use of computer technology to enhance instruction

3.08 Vocational evaluation and appropriate opportunities for training and career awareness activities

3.09 Affective curriculum that includes problem-solving and coping skills and encourages appropriate behaviors and self-concept

3.10 Provision for challenging activities that promote reasoned, logical, and critical thought

3.11 Mastery of the appropriate academic curriculum areas through frequent use of reading, writing, speaking, and listening skills

4.0 Fine Arts. Art experiences are valuable as a means of teaching creative problem solving and critical thinking through direct performance as well as indirect study. The middle school student should be exposed to two- and three-dimensional art on the exploratory wheel in order to make choices for further courses of study in the arts. Classroom activities should be integrated with the four primary content areas for arts instruction, which includes creating art forms (production), aesthetics, history, and criticism. Every effort should be made to combine aspects of each major area in every unit of study with appropriate assignments and projects.

4.01 Perceptual skills—identifying potential for subject matter by responding to works of art

4.02 Technical skills—producing works of art that relate to media and technique

4.03 Expressive skills—producing art through meaning, composition, and choice of appropriate tools and techniques

4.04 Critical skills—classroom critique sessions on student work as well as master work providing experiences in making and justifying judgments about the aesthetic quality and merit of works of art

4.05 Art knowledge—offering experiences to learn about historical masterworks through becoming aware of contemporary and local artists and events

4.06 The use of computer technology to enhance instruction

4.07 Mastery of the fine arts curriculum through frequent use of reading, writing, speaking, and listening skills

4.08 Nine-week exploratory art experience for sixth grade

5.0 *Foreign Languages.* The general philosophy of the program is to promote the educational benefits gained through the study of foreign languages and cultures. Foreign language will be offered as a part of the exploratory wheel for sixth graders, emphasizing the comparison and exploration of a variety of languages and corresponding cultures. For seventh graders, foreign language will be offered as an exploratory semester course, emphasizing basic conversation and cultural awareness of a single foreign language. Eighth graders may take either a semester of foreign language or a year-long course, emphasizing preparation for high school foreign language study. As with any elective course, foreign language offerings in any school depend on the facilities available, the student demand for the course, and the presence of appropriate instructional staff.

5.01 Skills in listening and speaking in a foreign language

5.02 Skills in reading and writing in a foreign language

5.03 An appreciation and understanding of the historical and cultural values of people who speak foreign languages

5.04 A better understanding of the student's own language

5.05 An awareness of the value of foreign language as an employable communication skill

5.06 A foundation for continuing the study of foreign languages in high school

5.07 The use of computer technology to enhance instruction

5.08 Mastery of the foreign language curriculum through frequent use of reading, writing, speaking, and listening skills

6.0 Health. In addition to the tremendous emotional, social, biological, and intellectual changes that routinely confront the middle school child, today's students also face a number of potentially fatal threats: substance abuse, AIDS and other sexually transmitted disease, increased incidence of suicide, and an increased rate of teenage pregnancy. Therefore, it is essential that students be provided a strong comprehensive health program throughout the middle school years. That program will be best achieved through the integration of health instruction into the physical education and life science classrooms and into the advisor/advisee program. All teachers responsible for health instruction must receive either adequate health inservices or health certification so as to ensure competent instruction in this essential subject area.

6.01 Substance abuse prevention
6.02 Disease prevention
6.03 Personal health and hygiene
6.04 Human growth and development
6.05 Nutrition education
6.06 Safety and first aid (including CPR)
6.07 Health resources in the community
6.08 Consumer education
6.09 Family living
6.10 Mental and emotional health
6.11 Interpersonal relationships
6.12 Structure and function of the human body
6.13 Mastery of the health curriculum through frequent use of reading, writing, speaking, and listening skills
6.14 A yearly minimum of 45 days instruction in comprehensive health education in physical education

7.0 Language Arts. The study of English language arts develops written and oral communication skills and provides opportunities to practice critical reading skills and writing techniques in order to successfully use these essential skills in other subject areas. Provisions for defined skill development in the area of reading are necessary to enable students to make the transition from "learning to read" through the elementary school basal reading program to middle school "reading to learn" in each of the content areas. Such provisions may best be enhanced through the use of at least one reading resource teacher to service each middle school in terms of providing integrated reading assistance to content area teachers for course-specific reading strategies and to individual students in terms of developmental reading instruction, as necessary. The program should consist of integrated instruction in reading, writing, listening, and speaking skills.

7.01 Instruction in reading comprehension at the literal, inferential, and evaluative levels
7.02 Remediation, enrichment, and developmental reading programs
7.03 A sustained silent reading program involving students and faculty members

7.04 Weekly writing practice and instruction

7.05 A diagnostic approach to writing instruction, including immediate feedback to students and use of students' essays as teaching tools

7.06 Practice in listening and speaking skills, including class discussion, group discussion, teacher–student dialogue, following oral directions, and peer feedback

7.07 Integration of reading, writing, speaking, and listening instruction in the language arts classroom rather than emphasis on isolated skills

7.08 The use of computer technology to enhance instruction, particularly in the area of writing

8.0 Mathematics. Today's adolescents and preadolescents (mostly in grades six through eight) need more academic challenge, particularly a strengthened curriculum in mathematics and science. Higher-order analytical and problem-solving skills should provide the thrust for the mathematics curriculum.

8.01 Applying mathematics to problem-solving situations

8.02 Demonstrating estimation and approximation procedures

8.03 Performing mathematical computations

8.04 Recognizing and applying geometric concepts

8.05 Recognizing and applying measurement concepts

8.06 Recognizing and applying the concepts of probability and statistics

8.07 Demonstrating number sense and operation sense

8.08 Demonstrating knowledge of algebraic concepts, the emphasis on which will be undertaken in advanced seventh-grade classes and in eighth-grade pre-algebra, algebra, and general math courses where a sufficient number of students and adequate facilities justify offering those courses

8.09 Hands-on activities that incorporate the use of manipulatives

8.10 Application of mathematics in other content areas

8.11 Additional challenges and activities for those students who demonstrate the desire and talent to expand their study of mathematics to a technologically related field

8.12 The use of computer technology to enhance instruction

8.13 Mastery of the mathematics curriculum through frequent use of reading, writing, speaking, and listening skills

9.0 Music. Because music is a primary expression of every culture, the middle school music education program is designed to develop student sensitivity, cultural values, and the skills necessary to respond to and enjoy music from an aesthetic standpoint. The sixth-grade music program will consist of general music and music appreciation in the exploratory wheel. Sixth-grade students will be restricted from taking band or chorus during the school day, but there will be opportunities for interested students through afterschool activities. The music course of study will include band, orchestra, and chorus for seventh and eighth graders.

9.01 Providing experiences that will develop a basic understanding of the elements of music and the ability to use the skills and knowledge in music

9.02 Developing basic skills in production, performance techniques, music literacy, and music appreciation

9.03 Identifying similarities and differences in the music of various styles and cultures

9.04 Demonstrating positive participation in music activities through singing, playing instruments, moving, listening, and creating

9.05 Using computer technology to enhance instruction

9.06 Mastering the music curriculum through frequent use of reading, writing, speaking, and listening skills

9.07 Providing nine-week music experience for sixth grade

10.0 Physical Education. The physical education program develops in students an understanding of the importance of living a healthful life, as well as a mastery of individual motor skills, sportsmanship, and physical fitness. In each grade the program consists of a minimum of 45 instructional days of comprehensive health education, which is an integral part of the physical education middle school program. In the sixth grade, these 45 days consist of both an orientation to physical education to discuss the importance of physical education and a comprehensive health education study. Each comprehensive health unit is taught by instructors who have received either health certification or adequate health inservice instruction. The remainder of each year is devoted to participation in a team-sports and life-sports program.

10.01 Health and safety instruction provided initially in the sixth grade, continuing through the middle school years

10.02 Development of motor skills stressed throughout the entire middle school physical education program

10.03 Life sports such as table tennis, badminton, and horseshoes, based on student demand and available facilities

10.04 Opportunities for students to demonstrate skills in individual and team sports

10.05 Emphasis on sportsmanship and healthy, less stressful competition

10.06 Individual student assessment of fitness development strategies for self-improvement

10.07 Intramurals conducted both during and after the school day

10.08 Provisions for students with physical limitations and disabilities, such as adaptive physical education programs

10.09 Use of technology to enhance instruction

10.10 Mastery of the physical education curriculum through frequent use of reading, writing, speaking, and listening skills

11.0 Science. A strong instructional program that emphasizes critical thinking skills and problem-solving skills in science and mathematics is essential. Whereas a general science course structure may not prove as challenging to the middle school student as a focused, content-specific structure, students in the sixth grade will receive year-long instruction in general science with an emphasis on earth science in order to provide instructional continuity from the elementary grades. However, the science curriculum for students in grades seven and eight will consist of year-long courses in life science at the seventh-grade level and physical science at the eighth-grade level. The course content at both of those grade levels will be based on inquiry, problem solving, and process skills.

11.01 Specifically scheduled hands-on laboratory experiences on at least a weekly basis

11.02 Instruction in basic and integrated process skills including observing, comparing, analyzing, classifying, communicating, and experimenting

11.03 Social implications of technological advancements

11.04 Current environmental issues and concerns

11.05 Use of technology to enhance instruction

11.06 Mastery of the science curriculum through frequent use of reading, writing, listening, and speaking skills

12.0 Social Studies. The primary purpose of the middle school social studies program is to enable students to develop those skills needed to function as productive citizens in a democratic society. Because a general social studies course structure may not prove as challenging to the student as a focused, content-specific structure, students in the sixth grade will receive year-long instruction in world history; seventh-grade students will be taught geography; the emphasis in eighth-grade social studies will be U.S. history.

12.01 Provision for reasoned, logical, and critical thought

12.02 Stimulation of career awareness

12.03 Promotion of positive personal development

12.04 Use of technology to enhance instruction

12.05 Mastery of the social studies curriculum through frequent use of reading, writing, listening, and speaking skills

13.0 Special-Needs Programs. Some middle school students face more than the usual number of developmental, economic, and social problems. Special-needs programs heterogeneously group students so that self-worth is realized and opportunities for positive interaction with other students are provided. Programs are also designed to meet individual academic and social needs and to monitor the progress of each student.

Dropout Prevention. Dropout prevention programs target students who are at risk due to apathy, poor motivation, underachievement, and who are overage for their grade level. Special programs that provide a positive environment for social, emotional, and cognitive growth give these students an opportunity to become contributing and participating members of society.

Compensatory Education. Compensatory programs in mathematics and communication will be offered to all students on an as-needed basis.

English Speakers of Other Languages (ESOL). Students with limited English-speaking capabilities require special sensitivity to their unique experiences and needs. These students are provided the opportunity to learn new ways of behaving, learning, and thinking. Opportunities are also provided for discussing, examining, and evaluating conflicting values and norms presented to them by their home and school environments. Proper guidance is available for understanding the differences in expectations and values in order to find a balance between the two cultures so that smooth adjustments can be made to their newly adopted American society.

Program Design: A Model for Setting Standards

1.0 Advisor/Advisee Program. Designed to give each student the opportunity to develop a positive relationship with an adult member of the school staff. An environment is created in which faculty and staff respond to the needs of, and take a personal interest in each student. With the help of parents, teachers, counselors, and advisers, students learn to monitor their academic progress and accept the consequences of their decisions and behavior. Advisers serve as positive role models and provide opportunities for students to develop positive relationships with peers and adults. The program is particularly designed to include topics in health education instruction.

    1.01 All certificated staff included as part of the program

    1.02 Inservice provided to all advisers prior to their participation in the program

    1.03 Program includes, but is not limited to, these topics:

- Study skills
- Substance abuse
- Self-concept
- Decision making
- Goal setting
- Career education
- Interpersonal relationships
- Family relationships

    1.04 Daily uninterrupted advisory sessions at least 25 minutes in length

    1.05 Scheduling and organization flexible enough to meet the needs of each school

1.06 Standard curriculum base developed within each school according to the needs of the student population, from which advisers have the option to select activities that best meet students' needs

1.07 Annual review conducted at each school to monitor program effectiveness in meeting students' needs, input for which is sought from students, advisers, parents, and school administrators

1.08 Specific designee within the school (preferably a guidance counselor) coordinates the advisory program's activities and functions.

2.0 Intramural Athletics Program. Designed to be an outgrowth of the physical education program, the intramural program is meant to assist the student in physical, mental, and social development. The program, which may include interscholastic competition in noncontact sports, provides recreational activities, physical fitness, group loyalty, success, and a permanent interest in leisure-time activities. The program is structured so that *all* students may take part. Some schools and districts may wish to eliminate all interscholastic sports.

Whatever program is developed, it should be limited to seventh-grade and eighth-grade students and should be scheduled only in the afternoons and without postseason play.

2.01 Interscholastic athletic program for boys does not include football. Basketball, soccer, baseball, track, volleyball, and swimming offered depending on student demand and available facilities

2.02 Interscholastic athletic program for girls includes volleyball, basketball, soccer, softball, track, and swimming, depending on student demand and available facilities

2.03 Intramural program exists for all three middle school grades

2.04 Based on student interest, intramural activities include those that parallel interscholastic athletic program and any other sports or activities that the school chooses to offer

2.05 Based on student demand and available facilities, a lifetime sports intramural program includes activities such as badminton, table tennis, chess, and horseshoes

2.06 Intramural activities offered during and after school

3.0 Facilities. Ideally, new schools would be designed and constructed to reflect middle school philosophy. Because this is impractical, however, most new middle schools are housed in older facilities already in operation. Consequently, most make do, keeping in mind that it is the program, not the building, that is the essence of the middle school. Even so, facilities must provide enough flexibility to accommodate interdisciplinary teaming and intramural activities.

3.01 Pleasant and attractive school facilities

3.02 Space is provided for counselor–student conferences

3.03 Appropriate furniture for each learning area

3.04 Accommodations for teaming, including considerations such as close proximity of teamed classes, available space for team planning, and available spaces (large and small) for varied activities

3.05 Sufficient number of rooms both for academic and exploratory and elective classes

3.06 Adequate space and facilities for physical education, intramurals, and athletics

3.07 Adequate space for students' social interaction

3.08 Larger schools are divided into houses to create a small school atmosphere

3.09 Annual reviews determine the most efficient and effective uses of the facilities in matching the structural design with the middle school's program design

4.0 Flexible Block Scheduling. The goal of scheduling is to provide teachers with flexibility in instructional time so as to satisfy students' academic needs. This goal is best achieved by using flexible block scheduling, which involves allocating an amount of time for each area of study. Within each interdisciplinary team, blocks of time are designed for the study of academic subjects (reading/language arts, mathematics, science, and social studies) and separate times for electives/exploratory programs and physical education/health. Teams shift blocks of time to accommodate additional instructional activities as necessary.

The degree of flexibility in blocking areas of time for the study of academic subjects provides progressively higher levels of independence and variety as students progress from sixth to eighth grade. The eighth-grade schedule more closely resembles a traditional junior high school schedule than does the block schedule of the sixth and seventh grades.

4.01 Adequate provision for a flexible daily time schedule

4.02 A block of time (minimum of 225 minutes) assigned to the interdisciplinary team for academic instruction

4.03 Provision for a block of time for exploration and physical education (minimum of 45 minutes for each area)

4.04 Sufficiently variable daily schedule to allow for athletic competition between inhouse student groups or intramural teams during an extended physical education class or for planned activities by an interdisciplinary team of teachers

4.05 Provision for daily interdisciplinary team planning and concerns

5.0 Guidance and Support Services. Providing a strong guidance service is key for middle grade students in coping with their specific (and diverse) problems, which involve self-esteem, peer relations, and the students' own physical changes.

Guidance counseling services are not limited to counselors; they also include support personnel—psychologists, psychiatrists, house administrators, social workers, teacher-advisers, advisory groups, and community programs and resources.

5.01 Guidance staff members participate in team planning sessions and assume a leadership role in all guidance-related aspects of the learning program

5.02 Each school has access to Multi-Agency Community Council (MACC) resources

5.03 Administrators play an active part as support personnel, in addition to accepting discipline responsibilities

5.04 Teachers familiar with the results of testing programs and receive assistance in the use of test results as an instructional tool

5.05 Guidance and support staff assists in orienting the student to the new school, its purposes, facilities, rules, and activities in order to facilitate adjustment to the middle school environment

5.06 Staff provides assistance with small and large group instruction

5.07 Communication occurs with all service personnel within the school for the maximum benefit to students

6.0 Instructional Strategies. The teacher must examine classroom methodology for, and demonstrate a variety of instructional strategies that are designed to meet the specific needs of the middle school student. Such variety encourages student learning and participation.

6.01 Inservice opportunities provided for teachers to examine various teaching and learning styles

6.02 Teachers assess their individual teaching styles

6.03 Teachers assess their own students' learning styles

6.04 Students provided opportunities to learn at different proficiency levels

6.05 Variety of delivery methods accommodate different learning styles

6.06 Balance in strategies allows students some experience in cooperative learning and independent study

6.07 Broad use of the competitive nature of the middle school child to enhance the student's self-concept through formal and informal competitive learning

6.08 Media and concrete demonstrations used regularly in classroom instruction

6.09 Active mechanism exists through which teachers and administrators share ideas and activities

6.10 Program improvement feedback elicited from the instructional staff

7.0 Integrated Curriculum. The purpose of an integrated curriculum is to ensure that middle school students will perceive the relationships among the disciplines, develop a holistic knowledge structure, and transfer learning among disciplines.

7.01 Each team prepares and implements at least one interdisciplinary unit during each nine-week period in which each discipline's application to a common theme is taught

7.02 Core skills in each discipline are reinforced by all other teachers

7.03 Provisions for the display of students' work to show integration of disciplines for a unit of work

7.04 Teams coordinate instructional activities with specialists in an area of study (e.g., speakers, demonstrations, field trips)

7.05 Established team and cross-subject goals

7.06 Coordinated homework and testing

7.07 Common difficulties remedied

8.0 *Interdisciplinary Teams.* Middle school students are organized into interdisciplinary teams. The teaming concept provides for integrated instruction in the core subjects of language arts and communication skills, math, science, and social studies. It also provides a smooth transition from the self-contained classroom of the elementary schools to the departmentalization of the high school setting.

Sharing a common group of students facilitates the extension of educational involvement from the classroom to the home and community. The team becomes thoroughly familiar with each student and therefore is better prepared to address the needs of the whole child and to help guide the student through his or her own life experiences.

Interdisciplinary teaming and block scheduling further provide for the flexible scheduling of students within the team area. The following are standards for team *organization*.

8.01 Teams consist of a balance of two to five teachers selected according to experience, age, race, sex, and special talents and who represent the core academic areas of mathematics, language arts, social studies, and science

8.02 Team assignments made for elective teachers, ESE (Exceptional Student Education—special ed) teachers, and other resource personnel

8.03 Common group of students shared by each team with a ratio of 25 to 35 students per teacher per time block

8.04 Common planning times for all teachers on the same team

8.05 When feasible, additional individual planning time or resource assignment time is provided for each team member

8.06 Classrooms for team teachers are in proximity to each other, depending on available facilities

8.07 Designated team leader coordinates each team and acts as a representative for the team

8.08 Interdisciplinary team controls a block of time

8.09 Interdisciplinary team is responsible for the coordination of curriculum and for the delivery of instruction to the students on its team

The following are standards for the team *functions*.

8.10 Team members plan cooperatively

8.11 Methods developed to enhance the instructional delivery system

8.12 Common pools of information about students are shared among team members

8.13 Teams meet with parents to discuss individual students' academic and developmental progress

8.14 Team members participate in a team meeting at least once each week

8.15 Team members provide support for each other

8.16 Uniform procedures for middle school instruction and classroom management developed and consistently implemented within the team

8.17 Activities planned to foster a sense of team identity and pride among teachers and students

8.18 Implementation of school's advisor/advisee program

8.19 Members of each team interact cooperatively with other members of the school staff (guidance counselors, resource teachers, administrators)

8.20 Interdisciplinary units of instruction developed and implemented

8.21 Action plans developed for individual students who are experiencing difficulties

8.22 Team operates on a consensus basis so that when a decision must be made and agreement has not been reached, the team leader makes the decision based on available input

9.0 *Parent–Community Involvement.* Because of the total-child educational philosophy of the middle schools, parent involvement is essential in defining goals, in educational decision making, and in monitoring their children's studies. In addition, middle schools should have an active public relations program to promote the school within the community and to maintain good community relations. Communities share with parents and middle school staff the responsibility for each student's success by serving as a learning environment and source of instructional resources, by providing opportunities for constructive after school activities, and by ensuring that students have access to health and social services.

9.01 Annual report of staff, parents, and students study and evaluate the progress of the entire school through Parent–Teacher–Student Association (PTSA), Local School Advisory Committee (LSAC), program improvement committees, or other avenues

9.02 Parents have the opportunity to support the learning process at home and at school by involvement in school activities, instructional support roles in the classroom, curriculum planning, disciplinary procedures, and incentive planning

9.03 Open and frequent communication exists between school and parents about the school program and the students' progress, as evidenced by the following:

- Parents' handbook that explains the middle school program
- Individual report cards sent to each student's home
- Parent–student–teacher conferences

- Regular communication updating school activities (e.g., newsletters, calendars)
- Progress reports
- Group activities for parents, including seminars, parents' night, and open house

9.04 Each middle school has a PTA or PTSA program

9.05 Each school has a lay advisory committee representative of various community organizations and businesses (LSAC) to maintain parent and community awareness of educational changes and to provide channels for parental and community input

9.06 Middle school provides service-learning opportunities for students such as visiting a nursing home, helping at a daycare center, or cleaning a park. These activities are designed to enhance and supplement classroom learning, foster meaningful participation in the community, and encourage self-exploration

9.07 Each school establishes a business partnership with at least one business organization in the community

10.0 Shared Decision Making. Decisions that have an impact on the overall school program must involve input from those who are affected. Established by a committee of principals and teachers, the following guidelines are used for school-wide decision making. (The following are district guidelines, not standards.)

10.01 Committee representative of the total school staff will be established at each school and will consist of members selected by a democratic process within areas of responsibility (departments, teams, grade levels, or as otherwise stated)

10.02 Strongly encouraged parent and student participation when deemed appropriate by the committee

10.03 Committee develops the philosophy and establishes and evaluates the goals and policies of the school

10.04 Committee's areas of responsibility may include, but will not be limited to the following:

- Departmental or local school programs
- Development of master schedule
- Recommendation and evaluation of instructional materials
- Development of curriculum
- Facilities and equipment
- Disciplinary plans
- Student activities
- Budget preparation
- Staffing
- Staff development

10.05 Committee will strive to reach consensus on all decisions; otherwise, the principal will make the decision utilizing the committee's input. Daily operational decisions are the responsibility of the principal or designee(s) and will reflect the spirit of this program

10.06 If a school committee requests an instructional delivery system that is at odds with school board policy or collective-bargaining agreements, the school may petition the appropriate agency for a waiver of policy to implement the desired program

11.0 *Staff Development.* A middle school staff is effective only if each employee possesses special understandings, skills, and attitudes in working with middle school students, parents, and community members so as to implement the middle school concept. These personnel see the middle school as neither elementary nor secondary but as an institution designed to meet the special needs of emerging adolescents. In that the schoolwide philosophy is student-centered as well as subject-centered, each staff member's role is to help all students develop emotionally, socially, and academically.

To ensure that educators work effectively with the emerging adolescent, inservice education is essential. The decision to teach the whole child and attend to the developmental needs of the middle school student means that teachers and other staff will be seeking an expansion of their skills.

11.01 All teachers are trained in characteristics of the middle school child, interdisciplinary team organization, advisory strategies and techniques, and curriculum planning and evaluation

11.02 Inservice training in the areas of learning styles, teaching strategies, interdisciplinary units, team leader training, and special training for middle school administrators

12.0 *Transition and Articulation.* The movement of students into, out of, and within the middle school program requires communication and the cooperative effort of all staff. This movement may be between schools, teams, or special education programs. The curriculum requires not only horizontal, interdisciplinary coordination but vertical articulation within the kindergarten through twelfth grade continuum.

Flexible two-way communication is essential, and opportunities for parental involvement are more frequent and more participatory than in the junior high school model.

12.01 Orientation programs for students, teachers, staff, and parents

12.02 Special strengths and talents are utilized through a Teachers Teaching Teachers (TTT) program

12.03 Guidance programs facilitate transition for students and staff

12.04 Teachers and staff schedule interschool meetings on a regular basis with feeder school staffs

12.05 An operative plan facilitates communication between school and parents

12.06 Positive communication occurs in addition to communication that is punitive in nature

12.07 Available school visitations for feeder-school students who are entering as well as exiting the middle school program

13.0 Evaluation. Whereas planning and organization set the stage for the change process, evaluation ensures that change has taken place to the extent desired. The evaluation process therefore will monitor and assess the implementation of the standards in the design.

13.01 Achievement/academic records

13.02 Staff/student attendance

13.03 Parent/student/staff attitudes

ACHIEVEMENT IN THE MIDDLE SCHOOL—A NEW PRIORITY

Middle schools, often caught up in the fallacious argument of the child versus subject matter, are more and more acknowledging that both the needs of the student and academic knowledge and skills are curriculum priorities. For many students, the middle grades are make or break time. Either they acquire the necessary cognitive skills or they will drop out of high school or drift without hope of a successful future. Supporting the need for more cognitive learning, the results of the Third International Mathematics Study (TIMMS) in 1997 revealed that while fourth graders ranked among the top five nations in math and science skills, by the end of the eighth grade, the performance of American middle school students ranked below that of many third-world countries. The achievement gap is most acute among our nation's poorest students who attend rural and inner-city schools.

If a middle school exists where the academic mission is unclear, where there is not a sufficiently rigorous and challenging academic environment for students, and where academic standards vary from classroom to classroom, even those caring educators won't be able to make a difference in the long-range achievement.[4]

Creating a Standards-Based Curriculum in the Modern Middle School

Raising standards of learning that are achieved through schools has become an increasing priority of governments throughout the world. The United States, wanting to maintain its leadership in the global economy, has employed a number of studies and surveys to build a case for national, state and district standards.[5] National Assessment of Educational Progress (NAESP) and the Third International Mathematics and Science Study (TIMSS) initiatives have resulted in improved school planning and management, enhanced school programs, and state and national tests to measure progress in meeting standards.

There are those who make a good argument that teachers should play a far greater role in contributing to the summative assessments for accountability.

Teachers have access to the performance of their pupils in a variety of contexts and over an extended period of time, while sampling pupils' achievement taken under the conditions of formal testing is merely a snapshot of academic progress.

As the standards-driven curriculum emerges, future research needs to include ways in which teachers understand and deal with the relationship between formative and summative roles. There need to be more comparative studies of summative roles as well. Further, there needs to be more comparative studies of the predictive validity of teachers' summative assessment versus external test results.[6]

The next sections will deal with efforts of improving instruction in the various disciplines found in the middle school. At the end of the chapter, numerous sources for further study and updating on subject area standards will be presented.

Improving the Teaching of Science in the Modern Middle School

Efforts of educators to improve the teaching of science are making significant progress as we enter the new century. The goal at all levels of instruction is to focus on content selection and an inquiry approach to teaching that develops deep understanding of content and the ability to think critically.[7]

The National Science Education Standards (NCSES) developed by scientists and science educators under the leadership of the National Research Council addresses both those dimensions.

National Science Standards. In a world filled with the products of scientific inquiry, scientific literacy has become a necessity for everyone. Everyone needs to use scientific information to make choices that arise every day. Everyone needs to be able to engage intelligently in public discourse and debate about important issues that involve science and technology. And everyone deserves to share in the excitement and personal fulfillment that can come from understanding and learning about the natural world.

Scientific literacy also is of increasing importance in the workplace. More and more jobs demand advanced skills, requiring that people be able to learn, reason, think creatively, make decisions, and solve problems. An understanding of science and the processes of science contributes in an essential way to these skills. Other countries are investing heavily to create scientifically and technically literate work forces. To keep pace in global markets, the United States needs to have an equally capable citizenry.

The *National Science Education Standards* present a vision of a scientifically literate populace. They outline what students need to know, understand, and be able to do to be scientifically literate at different grade levels. They describe an educational system in which all students demonstrate high levels of performance, in which teachers are empowered to make the decisions essential for effective learning, in which interlocking communities of teachers and students are focused on learning science, and in which supportive educational programs and systems nurture achievement. The *Standards* point toward a future that is challenging but attainable—which is why they are written in the present tense.

The intent of the *Standards* can be expressed in a single phrase: science standards for all students. The phrase embodies both excellence and equity. The *Standards* apply to all students, regardless of age, gender, cultural or ethnic background, disabilities, aspirations, or interest and motivation in science. Different students will achieve understanding in different ways, and different students will achieve different degrees of depth and breadth of understanding depending on interest, ability, and context. But all students can develop the knowledge and skills described in the *Standards*, even as some students go well beyond these levels.

By emphasizing both excellence and equity, the *Standards* also highlight the need to give students the opportunity to learn science. Students cannot achieve high levels of performance without access to skilled professional teachers, adequate classroom time, a rich array of learning materials, accommodating work spaces, and the resources of the communities surrounding their schools. Responsibility for providing this support falls on all those involved with the science education system.[8]

There are six major areas found in the National Science Education Standards:

I. Science Teaching Standards

The science teaching standards describe what teachers of science at all grade levels should know and be able to do. They are divided into six areas:
   A. Planning of inquiry-based science programs
   B. Actions taken to guide and facilitate student learning
   C. Assessments made of teaching and student learning
   D. Development of environments that enable students to learn science
   E. Creation of communities of science learners
   F. Planning and development of the school science program

II. Professional Development Standards

The professional development standards present a vision for the development of professional knowledge and skill among teachers. They focus on four areas:
   A. Learning of science through content inquiry
   B. Integration of knowledge about science with knowledge about learning, pedagogy, and students
   C. Development of the understanding and ability for lifelong learning
   D. Coherence and integration of professional development programs

III. Assessment Standards

The assessment standards provide criteria against which to judge the quality of assessment practices. They cover five areas:
   A. Consistency of assessments with the decisions they are designed to inform
   B. Assessment of both achievement and opportunity to learn science
   C. Match between the technical quality of the data collected and the consequences of the action taken on the basis of those data

D. Fairness of assessment practices
E. Soundness of inferences made from assessments about student achievement and opportunity to learn

IV. Science Content Standards

The science content standards outline what students should know, understand, and be able to do in the natural sciences over the course of kindergarten through twelfth grade education. They are divided into eight categories:

A. Unifying concepts and processes in science
B. Science as inquiry [K–4] [5–8] [9–12]
C. Physical science [K–4] [5–8] [9–12]
D. Life science [K–4] [5–8] [9–12]
E. Earth and space science [K–4] [5–8] [9–12]
F. Science and technology [K–4] [5–8] [9–12]
G. Science in personal and social perspective [K–4] [5–8] [9–12]
H. History and nature of science [K–4] [5–8] [9–12]

V. Science Education Program Standards

The science education program standards describe the conditions necessary for quality school science programs. They focus on six areas:

A. Consistency of the science program with the other standards and across grade levels
B. Inclusion of all content standards in a variety of curricula that are developmentally appropriate, interesting, relevant to students' lives, organized around inquiry, and connected with other school subjects
C. Coordination of the science program with mathematics education
D. Provision of equitable opportunities for all students to learn the standards
E. Development of communities that encourage, support, and sustain teachers

VI. Science Education System Standards

The science education system standards consist of criteria for judging the performance of the overall science education system. They consider seven areas:

A. Congruency of policies that influence science education with the teaching, professional development, assessment, content, and program standards
B. Coordination of science education policies within and across agencies, institutions, and organizations
C. Continuity of science education policies over time
D. Provision of resources to support science education policies
E. Equity embodied in science education policies
F. Possible unanticipated effects of policies on science education
G. Responsibility of individuals to achieve the new vision of science education portrayed in the standards

Mathematics—Raising the Bar

In an appraisal of the materials standards of 46 states by Ralph Raimi and Lawrence Braden of the Thomas B. Fordham Foundation, 1999, an excellent assessment of mathematics standards is presented.[9] California math standards were rated number one among the states. They even placed ahead of Japan. The standards were judged in terms of clarity, content, and reason as well as negative qualities.[10]

With states taking direction from the national standards of the National Council of Teachers of Mathematics (NCTM), the mathematics curriculum in the middle school comes as close as any content area to a national curriculum. Those standards were presented by NCTM in Curriculum and Evaluation Standards for School Mathematics published in 1989.

One strong argument for more rigorous standards in mathematics came from the Third International Mathematics and Science Study (TIMSS), referenced earlier, that summarized mathematics education at the time as "a mile wide and an inch deep." Thus the reforms in mathematics education called for in the 1989 NCTM standards were still not implemented a decade later. The wake-up call from TIMSS however, and the math standards and frameworks established by the states will no doubt raise the bar in mathematics in the next decade.

Constructionist theory in mathematics points out that in learning, abstraction is the fundamental mental mechanism by which new mathematics knowledge is generated. Abstraction is the process by which the mind selects, coordinates, combines, and registers in memory a collection of mental items or acts that appear in the attentional field.

Understanding mathematics requires more than abstraction however. It requires reflection which is the conscious process of replaying experiences, actions, or mental processes and considering their results or how they are composed. Meaningful mathematics in the middle school must then come from both reflection and abstraction.[11]

The National Science Foundation funded a number of different projects in the 90s for each level of schooling. Those projects are based on rigorous mathematical standards. Table 5.3 lists some of those projects.

Incorporating Language Arts Standards K through Eighth Grade

In 1992, the National Council of Teachers of English (NCTE) and the International Reading Association (IRA), funded by the U.S. Department of Education, began a task to produce standards for Language Arts. In 1996, Standards of the English Language and supporting publications, including standards in practice for sixth through eighth grades were released.[12]

While continuing to foster student reading and writing skills, the NCTE standards also stressed the need for students to read a wide variety of literature representing many time periods, genres and ethnic and cultural groups. The standards also encouraged teachers to recognize student differences and students to see themselves as readers and writers.

TABLE 5.3 NSF-Funded Standards-Based Curriculum Projects

Elementary	Middle Grades	Secondary
Everyday Mathematics, K–6 Everyday Learning Corporation 2 Prudential Plaza, Suite 1200 Chicago, IL 60681 Phone 800–382–7670	Connected Math Project, Grades 6–8 Cuisenaire/Dale Seymour Publications P.O. Box 5026 White Plains, NY 10602 Phone 800–872–1100	Contemporary Mathematics in Context Everyday Learning Corporation P.O. Box 812960 Chicago, IL 60681 Phone 800–382–7670
Investigations in Number, Data, and Space, K–5 Cuisenaire/Dale Seymour Publications P.O. Box 5026 White Plains, NY 10602 Phone 800–872–1100	Mathematics in Context, Grades 1–8 Encyclopedia Britannica 310 S. Michigan Ave. Chicago, IL 60604 Phone. 800–554–9862	Interactive Mathematics Program Key Curriculum Press 1150 65th Street Emeryville, CA 64608 Phone 800–995–MATH (6284)
Math Trailblazers, K–5 Kendall/Hunt Publishing Company 4050 Westmark Drive Dubuque, IA 52004–1840 Phone 800–542–6657	Middle-School Math Through Applications Project (MMAP) Most modules available through self-publishings. Commercial publisher pending. Phone 650–687–7918	MATH Connections It's About Time, Inc. 84 Business Park Drive, Suite 307 Armonk, NY 10504 Phone 888–689–TIME (6463)
	MathScape, Grades 6–8 Creative Publications 1300 Villa Street Mountain View, CA 94041 Phone 800–624–0822	Mathematics: Modeling Our World South-Western Educational Publishing 7625 Empire Drive Florence, KY 41042 Phone 800–865–8540
	Middle Grade MathThematics, Grades 6–8 McDougal Littell 1560 Sherman Ave. Evanston, IL 60201 Phone 800–323–4068 ext. 3206	SIMMS Integrated Mathematics Simon & Schuster Custom Publishing 2055 South Gessner, Suite 200 Houston, TX 77063 Phone 888–339–0529

Much of the literature and research in reading instruction in recent years advocate teachers getting away from the argument of phonics versus whole language. The issue is not whether to teach phonics, but how much and when. There is agreement by most that students need to learn phonics in the context of meaningful written language, not in isolation.

Writing has taken on new importance in many states. Florida tests students in narrative and expository writing in grade four and persuasive writing in eighth and tenth grades. Essays are graded by the state and returned to school districts. In Florida, writing results (as well as reading and math test results) are used to grade schools with rankings from A through F.

In the middle school, personal narrative writing is often used to help students write about personal events that are important in their lives. Students' stories often reflect the real-life dramas of their own lives and teachers and fellow students can help those students deal with those dramas which are shared by those students. Writing and reading aloud essays then can help students construct life narratives, generate questions from those narratives, and conduct investigations to learn about those experiences.[13]

Attacking literacy with technology (e.g., the Accelerated Reader Program) is occurring in modern middle schools. Computer programs that level students in reading and provide comprehension tests after students read a variety of literary genres are commonplace in many middle schools. Students are encouraged to read both for information and fiction. Immediate feedback is provided to students as they continue to test out at higher and higher levels. Students are able to use computers in the classroom after they have finished other assignments. Students are challenged by reading passages for which they have to read for meaning. This high-level thinking approach to reading comprehension is a valuable resource in raising reading levels of students.

Literacy programs in the middle grades that use a variety of technology are not only productive but fun for students. They are individualized and challenging. Coupled with caring and effective teacher instruction and reinforcement, those programs will continue to be valuable tools for middle school educators.[14]

A New Look at Social Studies in the Middle School

Global education, the Internet, and the growing diversity of America's population have led to new ways of instruction in middle school social studies. As we become increasingly interdependent, today's students who will spend a majority of their time in the twenty-first century will need the tools of analyzing information, thinking critically, and problem solving.[15] Those skills are going to be needed as the next generation deals with the complex developments in technology, advances in science, internationally connected environmental issues, and daily interaction with other cultures. Moving from an almost exclusive study of Western Civilization in social studies to a broader history and multicultural approach will be the social studies thrust in the new American middle school.

Tapping the resources of the World Wide Web will be a valued academic enterprise of middle school learners. There are a number of unique reasons to be enthusiastic about the Web and its support of inquiry learning.

1. The Web enables immediate access to a significant volume of content information on a variety of subjects.

2. Multiple perspectives of scientific, social, historical, and literary issues are available for review by students, providing easy resources for practicing critical evaluation of texts and other forms of information.

3. Diverse topics found on the Web can prompt student-generated questions for inquiry.

4. The Web contains a wealth of specialized and unique information that is likely to match students' inquiry interests.

5. Current event information is available, making student inquiry more relevant and exciting.

6. Data sets are available from government agencies and other institutions for inspection or downloading.

7. Information in the form of imagery and sound are available in ever-increasing amounts.[16]

Our next generation of middle school students will need to be educated in all aspects of the global economy and the occupational and professional requirements of that economy. Social studies and history, mired in the past, are being replaced by a far more dynamic program of studies in the new American middle school. There are references of these types of programs at the end of this chapter for further study.

Bilingual Education—A Continuing Debate

As growing numbers of non- or limited-English speaking students enter our schools, bilingual education continues to receive criticism in the national media and the legislatures of our states as well as in Congress. Bilingual education programs include the characteristics of sheltered subject matter teaching and instruction in the first language. Non-English speaking students initially receive core instruction in their primary language along with ESL (English As Second Language) instruction. As those students grow more proficient in English, they begin instruction in math and science and eventually are placed in mainstream classes.

Opponents of bilingual education claim the public is against bilingual education (as in California's continuing struggle) and that there is little evidence that it is superior to all-English programs.

As the authors have experienced in working with many schools having large populations of limited or non-English speaking students (particularly Spanish-speaking students), those students have little access to books at home. Putting books in the hands of those students, encouraging older English-speaking siblings to read to and with them are great assets for limited-English speaking students.

The United States, as it continues to lead in the global economy, must get all its young people into the mainstream and get them there at a faster pace. While many middle school students of limited English have been in the system longer than their young elementary counterparts, and thus have a better command of the English language, waves of new immigrants will continue to enter the middle grades, and the time frame for getting them into the mainstream will be short. The modern middle school must recognize this and build new programs and employ new strategies (particularly using technology) to reach this vital segment of our student population.[17]

The Arts in the Middle School

As middle schools build a balanced curriculum, the arts in the middle school can't be forgotten. Students not only need to acquire cognitive skills, but they need to explore and experience a variety of areas. Music as well as applied and fine arts are important pieces in this process.

Music enhances creativity and promotes social development, personality adjustment, and self-worth.[18] In recent years, brain researchers have claimed that in many cases a study of the arts improves brain development and even enhances skills in other subjects such as reading and mathematics. For instance, brain scans taken during musical performances show that virtually the entire cerebral cortex is active while musicians are playing.

In the other arts, educators believe a comprehensive approach which moves the arts from the fringe to the core of the academic program will enhance students' ability to understand concepts and to express themselves articulately.[19] We know that visual images students see in art act as a springboard to further learning. Sources for such programs are cited in the back of this chapter.

ISSUES IN MIDDLE SCHOOL CURRICULUM

The TIMSS Report and other studies have pointed out the need for a rigorous curriculum for pre and early adolescents in America's middle schools. All of the complexities of adolescent development discussed earlier in the text demand that the middle school make a dramatic change from the past when schools merely coped with developmental changes rather than took advantage of them. The barriers that limit access to curriculum for some students must be removed. There must be high expectations for all children regardless of race, language, gender, or ethnicity. If the curriculum is diluted for those who are poor or have limited-English proficiency, we will never live up to the promise of our democratic society.[20]

How Do Middle School Students Learn Best?

Issues

Three Major Concepts

- Middle school should be a general education school focusing on widely shared concerns rather than increasing specialization and differentiation.
- The curriculum has many demands but its purpose should be to serve early adolescents and their issues.
- The current view that adolescents are victims of their developmental stage should be revised and educators should look at them as human beings with serious concerns about their world and their own development.

Considerations

Within an integrated curriculum, work with students to develop a thematic unit to use in driving the learning activities. To accomplish this:

1. Students should ask questions about themselves.
2. The teacher should identify themes suggested.
3. The teacher should select one theme and identify activities that students might use to answer the questions they asked about it.

This strategy gives students a voice in developing curriculum. The teacher's role changes to that of guide and facilitator. The curriculum is knowledge rich and allows for the integration of affect and cognition. It is the whole curriculum.

How Can Young People Prepare for Today's Changing Economy?

Issues

Students who do not have the resources to attend a college or university are funneled into a general education track in high school. This prevents them from having the skills necessary to be successful at a technical school or to find employment in an upwardly bound employment path. This results in unequal educational and economic opportunity.

Considerations

- Provide more integration of academic and vocational classes.
- Incorporate more academic material into vocational classes.
- Pair academic teachers with vocational teachers to increase academic competencies in vocational courses.
- Make academic curriculum more vocationally revelant (applied curriculum).
- Vertically align vocational and academic courses.
- Follow the Career Academy model.
- Consider a single occupation vocational school.
- Replace departments with occupational clusters.
- Combine departments and occupational clusters.

How Can Students Be More Authentically Assessed?

Issues

How can teachers find out what students really know? How can teachers find out if students are really understanding what is being taught?

Considerations

- Ask for open-ended or extended writing responses.
- Assign extended tasks requiring sustained attention in a single work area carried out over several hours or longer.
- Assign portfolios for students to collect performance-based work.

SUMMARY

The effective middle school program is balanced, comprehensive, and success-oriented. It differs from the traditional junior high program in that the middle school curriculum is developmentally centered; that is, it moves in tandem with the growth and developmental dynamics of the age group it serves.

The balanced curriculum includes three major components: subject content, personal development, and essential learning skills.

The curriculum design of the middle school includes a wide variety of course offerings and experiences, both in core cognitive areas and in the affective and psychomotor domain. This chapter described those program elements found in the middle school and standards used to measure each one.

The program must include a planned sequence of concepts, emphasize skills and interests needed for continuous learning, provide exploratory experiences, stress development of values, and give special attention to personal development of adolescent students.

The key feature of the chapter was a design prototype for a comprehensive and balanced middle school curriculum.

Suggested Learning Activities

1. Develop an outline of a program design for the middle school.
2. What courses and activities would you include in a special-interest program?
3. Prepare a statement for a school board on the need for a skills program in the middle school.
4. Develop a rationale for a balanced program in the middle school.
5. Design an advisory program for your middle school.
6. Present a case for expanding the arts in the middle school.
7. Discuss the pros and cons of a bilingual program.

Notes

1. Association for Supervision and Curriculum Development, Working Group on the Emerging Adolescent Learner, Joseph Bondi, chairman, *The Middle School We Need* (Washington, DC: ASCD, 1975).
2. Charles Cline, Betty White, Michael Walker, et al., *A Middle School Design*, Duval County (Florida) School District, 1990.
3. The authors wish to acknowledge the Duval County School District for its permission to use the material in the first section of this chapter. (The authors served as chief consultants in the middle school conversion development in Duval County.)
4. http://www.middleweb.com/Why Reform.html
5. Paul Black and Dylan William, "Inside the Black Box, Raising Standards Through Classroom Assessment," *Kappan, 80* 2 (October 1998): 139–48.
6. Ibid.
7. Harold Pratt and Jay Hackett, "Teaching Science, The Inquiry Approach," *Principal*, November 1998, pp. 20–22.
8. National Academy of Sciences. View via WWW at http://www.nap.edu/nap/online/NSES/
9. http://www.edexcellence.net/Standards/math.html
10. Wayne Bishop, "The California Mathematics Standards: They Are Not Only Right, They're the Law," *Kappan*, February 1999, pp. 439–440.
11. Michael Battista, "The Mathematical Miseducation of American Youth: Ignoring Research and Scientific Study in Education," *Kappan*, February 1999, pp. 425–433.
12. Rebecca Sipe, "Incorporating Language Arts Standards for Grades 6–8," *Middle Matters, NAESP*, Winter 1998–99.
13. Audrey Appelsies and Collen Fairbanks, "Write for Your Life," *Educational Leadership*, May 1997, pp. 70–72.
14. Michael Blasewitz and Rosemary Taylor, "Attacking Literacy with Technology in an Urban Setting," *Middle School Journal*, January 1999, pp. 33–39.
15. Barbara Cruz, "Global Education in the Middle School Curriculum: An Interdisciplinary Perspective," *Middle School Journal*, November 1998, pp. 26–31.
16. Mark Windschitl and Janey Irby, "Tapping the Resources of the World Wide Web for Inquiry in Middle Schools," *Middle School Journal*, January 1999, pp. 40–45.
17. Stephen Krashen, "Why Bilingual Education?" *Eric Digest*, ERIC Clearinghouse on Rural Education, January 1997, pp. 1–5.
18. Norman Weinberger, "The Music in Our Minds," *Educational Leadership*, November 1998, pp. 36–40.
19. Russ Chapman, "Improving Student Performance Through the Arts," *Principal*, March 1998, pp. 20–26.
20. Nancy Ames, "Rigorous Achievement Standards," *Schools in the Middle*, January/February 1999, pp. 19–21.

Selected References

Dade County School Board. 1991. *Recommended Literature: An Annotated Bibliography of Outstanding Books for Reading Aloud, Class Study, and Independent Reading, Grades PK–12*. Miami: Dade County, Florida Public Schools. (This list contains many multiethnic, multicultural selections.)

Middle School Task Force. 1988. *Caught in the Middle*. Sacramento: California State Department of Education.

National Association of Secondary School Principals. 1990. *Schools in the Middle: A Report on Trends and Practices*. Washington, DC: NASSP.

National Science Teachers Association. 1991. *Science Education for Middle Level Students*. Washington, DC: NSTA.

Wiles, Jon, and Bondi, Joseph. 1990. *The Middle School America Needs*. Tampa: Wiles, Bondi and Associates, Inc.

_____ . 1991. *The Book of Learning Skills and Objectives for Middle Schools*. Tampa: Wiles, Bondi and Associates, Inc.

CHAPTER 6

Developing Instructional Materials

Learning is always a creative process.

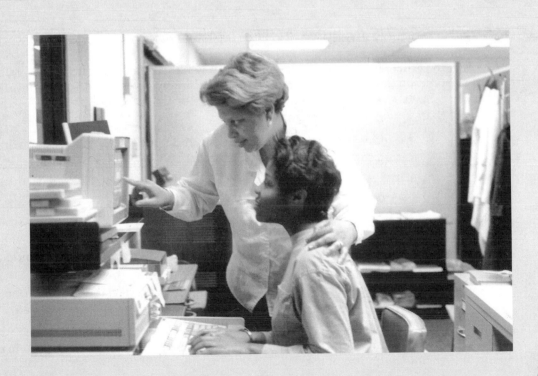

Over the past two decades, American middle schools have been a distinctive form of education because of the dedication to a specific developmental period, the age of preadolescence. In its literature, preadolescence is portrayed as a period of immense change in which each student, as an individual, passes through major physical, social, emotional, intellectual and even moral changes. That literature tells us that students in middle schools are characterized by their differences and, therefore, the curriculum must account for this uniqueness. Implied in these observations is the commitment of middle schools to meeting the needs of each individual student in and out of the classroom.

One of the major differences among middle schools in the twentieth century was in whether they understood and adhered to this instructional logic. Many schools observed by the authors simply adopted the name "middle school" and assumed a number of popular organizational forms such as teams, block schedules, and the interdisciplinary unit, without making the conceptual connection between the words and the forms. Such efforts mocked the efforts of true middle schools to know their students and prescribe for them according to their needs.

In this chapter, the reader will be led through the evolution of instructional design in middle schools including the search for materials that allow these schools to meet the instructional needs of their students in the classroom. Following the theme of this edition, the chapter will also introduce the reader to resources and materials that will guide instruction in the next century using technology as a coordinating medium.

STANDARDIZED VERSUS INDIVIDUALIZED LEARNING

In earlier chapters, the reader has seen how the traditional educational philosophies in the United States have based their programs on a series of assumptions that are, frankly, the antithesis of the middle school philosophy. Among these traditional assumptions are:

- Students are empty or unknowing and teachers are full and knowing.
- The job of the teacher is to develop minimal knowledge in each student.
- All students should possess the same minimal knowledge base to be educated.
- The format of such knowledge (disciplines of study) is known to the teacher.
- Useful knowledge is gleaned from the past and present experiences of man.
- Formal knowledge is to be mastered without deviation or disruption.
- Standardized learning environments, such as those that employ the book or the lecture, maximize learning.
- Examination can be used to enforce standardization and achievement.

For middle schools that converted during the past 40 years without understandings of middle school philosophy, these misconceptions are still applied. Such schools possess no real knowledge of preadolescent development, have no appropriate learning strategy for the preadolescent, continue to use standardized practices despite speaking of the uniqueness of preadolescence, and have high expectations for achievement as measured by standardized achievement tests.

True middle schools, however, have a very different set of assumptions about their purpose that might be stated in this manner:

- Students and teachers are both learners, neither empty nor full.
- The job of the teacher is to guide student development as an individual.
- All students need learning skills and a basis for understanding information.
- The knowledge available to students can be formatted in many ways.
- Useful knowledge is knowledge to be used in future encounters and in problem solving in the everyday world of living.
- Formal learning (disciplines of study) is increasingly difficult to rationalize.
- Flexible learning environments enhance individual student learning.
- Standardized achievement tests are rarely relevant measures of student growth and understanding in the classroom.

For the true middle school, individualization of instruction is a creed, a basic necessity in working with preadolescent learners. Schools that have connected the words of middle school philosophy with the organizational structures and instructional materials used by teachers have promoted the middle school concept and have progressed beyond mere lip service to a set of fundamental premises undergirding intermediate education.

DEVELOPMENTAL APPROPRIATENESS

An important concept in any human-development rationalized curriculum, such as early childhood, gifted education, middle school education, or special education, is the idea of developmentally appropriate learning materials. According to this concept all learners have developing, as opposed to measurable, abilities, and the task of schooling is to match the curriculum to the rate of student development, as opposed to matching the student with other like students. From this perspective, then, middle schools develop educational programs and materials to assist each student in maximizing her or his own development: the individualized educational experiences. In true middle schools there is no goal that all students will be alike or progress at a common pace or achieve at a like level. To possess such goals would mean that the school would attempt to standardize the most diverse group of students in the school ladder. The junior high school, and perhaps the early American middle school failed for trying to do this very thing.

The developmental philosophy, unlike the psychometric philosophy of schools that standardize, acknowledges human diversity, multiple organizational patterns for knowledge, personal learning preferences, and the many instructional methods available to teachers in the classroom. The vision of schooling from the developmental perspective is a teacher who is a guide, providing students with conceptual organizers, learning skills, and intellectual set-ups, and carrying out the act of teaching and learning in a number of environments with a variety of methodologies (see Figure 6.1).

Key to understanding and developing solid middle school instructional programs is the notion of continuous progress curriculum. In the middle school, teachers are confronted with the widest range of growth and achievement found in the school ladder. A rule of thumb is that for each year in school, a one-year range can be found. By this criteria, a sixth grade class should have a six-year reading range, and an eighth grade class might have an eight-year social range. Following the middle school years, many students drop out and the range narrows in the high school. If this is true, and it can be documented in any middle school, then teachers and the curriculum cannot feature a single expected entry and exit point for all students. We must see the students as individuals en route over a long-range continuum of learning.

FIGURE 6.1   *Instructional Method Choices*

Learning centers	Role playing
Collages	Resource people
Models	Field trips
Films	Interviews
Bulletin boards	Debates
Small group discussion	Newspaper articles (want ads)
Exhibits or displays	Brainstorming
Games	Research projects
Scrapbooks	Simulated work activities
Notebooks	Writing letters
Speeches	VTR (Videotaping)
Plays or skits	Unipacs or LAPS
Large group discussion	Committee work
Filmstrips	Overhead and opaque projections
Observations	Demonstrations
Panel discussions	Problem solving
Assigned readings	Decision-making problems
Slides	Radio and TV programs
Puppets	

For years, elementary schools have experimented with continuous progress curriculum (sometimes called nongraded or multiage curriculum). Even at this level, students are not alike and cannot be made alike through standardized instructional practices. By the time students are in the middle years, it is folly to assume that they are coming to the learning experience with common background, experience, knowledge, or skills. The first task of instruction for any middle school is to determine who is attending and what she or he has previously achieved. The school should be prepared for uneven individual development (for example, a student may be a good reader but be poor in math) as well as a horrendous range of achievement and even exposure to learning.

Among the key variables that will differentiate students in the middle school classroom, other than achievement, will be things such as learning anxiety, excitability, preoccupation (daydreaming), insecurity, irritability, emotional instability, attention span, motivation, conceptual clarity, memory development, various small learning disabilities, writing skills, reading skills, and talkativeness. What middle schools desire for each student is "forward progress" during the twelve quarters of the sixth through eighth grade middle school experience.

CURRICULUM MAPPING

A very basic organizational tool in planning instruction for a middle school is to actually map out the middle school experience. Various areas of desired development including personal growth, skills development, and knowledge acquisition, should be detailed, with particular attention to the kinds of information students will be exposed to and whether the purpose of such exposure is to be mastery or conceptual understanding. It has been documented several times in this century such as by the National Education Association in "One Day in the Eighth Grade," and again by the National Middle School Association, that middle school students do not understand what they experience on a given day in school.

It pays huge dividends for school faculties to create simple matrixes and outline what is taught in a subject for each of the twelve quarters of grades six, seven, and eight. When this vertical articulation is completed for each subject, then the various subjects can be coordinated (horizontal articulation) and major ideas or concepts, and key skills can be identified. For example, in the typical middle school metrics is taught in math, science, physical education, home economics, and perhaps other subjects. Also, in the typical middle school, teachers in different subjects don't know that other teachers are teaching the same thing.

If a middle schooler arrives at school and studies verbs and the Battle of Vicksburg, plays volleyball, dissects a frog, and solves basic unknowns in prealgebra, is it so surprising that the student doesn't see the whole of the curriculum? When asked by his or her parents what was learned in school today, a student's most common response is "nothing."

Once the curriculum for the school is mapped, each teacher in every subject must go through a similar planning experience for his or her students. Critical to this planning is the question most often asked by students: "Why do we have to study this stuff?" The answer to this question will reveal the philosophy of the teacher and the learning design of the middle school. For true middle schools, the answer should be that we are preparing ourselves for a life in a rapidly changing world. And since all of the students will be going to different destinations, their need of any single fact or subject will vary.

HOW TEACHERS HAVE RESPONDED IN MIDDLE SCHOOLS

When the first middle schools appeared in the United States in the 1960s, they were really just reformed junior high schools. Listening to early theorists like Alexander, Eichhorn, Vars, and Bondi, these schools recognized the preadolescent period as unique and attempted to respond to the gross human differences present in the middle school classroom. These schools generally rejected the traditional method of accommodating differences, ability grouping, because the students in the middle school are developing and changing. Physical and mental maturation during preadolescence prohibited static grouping practices.

At first, the most creative middle school teachers focused solely on diversifying their methodology. In addition to standardized reading, lecture, and testing, teachers added learning centers, small group discussions, assigned readings, use of resource people, research projects, and decision-making problems, as well as other methods, to enhance the classroom learning.

Early in the middle school movement, it was acknowledged that a single teacher could not deal with the many types of students in the classroom in a satisfactory manner. One early response to the problem of academic diversity was the creation of learning activity packages (LAPs) that allowed each student to progress at her or his own rate through predetermined material. An electronic version of this same idea was the so-called "teaching machine." Later, early computers were used as a kind of electronic textbook. The problem with these responses was that they only dealt with one kind of individualization: rate of coverage. Figure 6.2 by Gibbons indicates other types of concerns when individualizing.

Teachers in early middle schools also responded to the range of academic development in classrooms by finding diversified learning materials. With a six- to eight-year reading range found in most middle school classrooms, this helped students beyond the normal range (high and low) to engage in the curriculum. The addition of supplemental materials presented teachers with some problems in terms of student testing and evaluation.

Finally, in the early 1970s, middle schools began to pull these ideas together in the form of interdisciplinary units (I.U.) of study. These thematic units combined several subject areas, mixed in learning skills, and generally featured

FIGURE 6.2   *Dimensions of Individualized Instruction*

1. *Attendance*	Optional	School not class	Class not subgroup	Mandatory
2. *Materials for study*	Individual choice	Individual prescribed	Subgroup prescribed or discussed	Class/grade prescribed
3. *Method of studying materials*	Individual choice	Individual prescribed	Subgroup prescribed or discussed	Class/grade prescribed
4. *Pace of study*	Individual choice	Individual prescribed	Subgroup prescribed or discussed	Class/grade prescribed
5. *Activity*	Individual choice	Individual prescribed	Subgroup prescribed or discussed	Class/grade prescribed
6. *Decision making*	Student (permissive)	Student and teacher (responsive)	Teacher (active)	Administrative authority
7. *Teaching focus*	Values	Processes	Skill concepts	Content
8. *Teaching function*	Teacher available	Teacher guides	Teacher presents	Teacher directs
9. *Teaching method*	Unspecified discovery (permissive)	Guided discovery (problem solving)	Explanation and discussion	Drill exercise repetition
10. *Environment*	Community	School	Classroom or resource area	Desk
11. *Time structure*	Nonstructured	Fluid	Structured nonstructured	Structured
12. *Evaluation*	Student self-evaluation	Broad assessment	Quantity of work	Exam–class rank
13. *Purposes of program*	Continuous development to maturity	Adjustment	Understanding	Efficient mastery

a student-interest theme for title (see Figure 6.3). What the interdisciplinary unit allowed was for each student to participate in the study of an idea or content in an intellectually honest form, but at their own level of development. A unit on economics, for example, could have some students calculating simple interest on a consumer loan, while other students in the same room could be exploring the debts of the United States.

While elementary teachers have been combining subjects for years in the self-contained classroom, such integration of knowledge bases proved more difficult for the middle school due to the depth of study in simultaneous areas. But,

FIGURE 6.3 Thematic Interdisciplinary Unit Titles

Imagination and Discovery	Sports and Your Identity
Bicentennial	Changing Sex Roles in the Twentieth Century
Sports and You	The Wheel in the Social Development of
Careers in Transportation	Humankind
The Concrete Jungle	Animal and Human Interdependence and the
Humankind Accepts the Challenge of City Living	Necessity for Cooperation
The Law and You	Feeding the Population
International Trade	Evolution: Process of Change
Rural Life	America: The First Two Hundred Years
Communications	How Environmental Factors Affect Shelter
Temporary Living: Camps and Camping	The Civil War and Reconstruction
Greece	Anchors Away to a New World
You Are What You Eat	The World Series
Let's Get Personal	Sports in America
Foreseeing the Unforeseeable	The Pollution Problem
Be It Ever So Humble	Humankind as Consumer
Cities—What You Always Wanted to Know	Then and Now
Shock: A Serious and Dangerous Condition	The Westward Movement
Elections	Westward Expansion
M.A.N.—Minorities Are the Nation	Take Me Out to the Ball Game
Of Mice and Men: An Interdisciplinary Unit	

by combining teachers in common planning and using blocks-of-time schedules to allow the grouping and regrouping of students across subjects, middle schools raised the I.U. to near art form. The downside of the I.U. in some middle schools was that teachers didn't fully understand how they could relinquish their instructional time for these units; they failed to note the change in learning design.

The I.U. was a general learning design, constructed for a conceptual understanding along with some content and skill mastery. Its real intent was to motivate students for future learning, and to accommodate the diversity of the learning population. The idea was sound for middle schools, but required organizational skills often lacking in teacher teams.

In the late 1980s, the practice of cooperative learning was added to the repertoire of middle school teachers, and these small group management skills aided greatly in operating interdisciplinary units and in grouping and regrouping students for various academic purposes.

In those middle schools where teachers and administrators have fully understood the if–then logic of the middle school (if students are diverse, then we must accommodate that diversity), creative learning environments have evolved. Such high-growth environments are contrasted with low-growth environments in Table 6.1.

A final word about those middle schools that have responded with understanding and enthusiasm to the middle school concept must include an observation about school climate. Some intermediate schools fail to recognize the importance of affective orientation on student learning in the classroom. How the student feels about learning contributes or deducts from student motivation

TABLE 6.1 High Versus Low Conditions for Student Growth

High acceptance/respect of pupil ideas	Low acceptance/respect of pupil ideas
1. Pupil ideas are frequently accepted by the teacher. The teacher listens and incorporates pupil ideas in discussion and other learning situations.	1. Pupil ideas are rarely encouraged or accepted. There is little opportunity for discussion, and discussions, when held, are teacher controlled. Pupil contributions are frequently criticized.

High acceptance/respect of pupil's affect	Low acceptance/respect of pupil's affect
2. Pupils' feelings and emotions are accepted by the teacher as long as harm to others is avoided.	2. Pupils' feelings are avoided or discouraged. The teacher is unwilling to recognize expressions and discussions of feelings.

High encouragement/support of pupils	Low encouragement/support of pupils
3. Pupils are encouraged to explore, make suggestions, and so on. An atmosphere of "try it and tell us what happens" pervades the classroom. 4. The teacher is willing to get off the subject when an interesting event or question is raised. At times the question becomes the actual topic.	3. Pupils are discouraged from exploration. The teacher has the one right way of doing things and only that way is accepted. Alternatives are not discussed or tested. 4. The teacher controls the subject at all times. Penetrating philosophical questions are discouraged. The principal aim is to teach the lesson and complete it.

High pupil individualization	Low pupil individualization
5. The teacher attempts to understand and respond to each child's psychological needs. The teacher recognizes that some children may need more direction and control while others may need the opportunity to exercise greater choice. The teacher, therefore, encourages each child to learn and explore in ways that she or he is comfortable with.	5. The teacher denies individual differences and needs and demands conformity. The teacher who demands that every child participate in an open classroom may produce the same low growth conditions as the teacher who provides a lock-step classroom atmosphere. Both strategies are authoritarian and demand conformity at the possible expense of pupil feelings of esteem, control, and connectedness.

High pupil involvement	Low pupil involvement
6. A continuing dialogue with pupils is maintained to involve children in making decisions about their learning (e.g., individual and small group projects, work contracts, and so on), and to help children further clarify what they are learning.	6. The teacher always tells pupils what and how they are to learn. Little room is left for pupil choice and expression.

High teacher genuineness/realness	Low teacher genuineness/realness
7. The teacher is genuine, willing to express ideas, feelings, and experiences and be a real person with students. Where appropriate, teachers share their own ideas and the experiences they have had.	7. The teacher plays a role and maintains a facade that conceals feelings and personal thoughts. A wide emotional gap is maintained between the teacher and the pupil.

Source: J. D. Wiggins and Don English, "Affective Education: A Manual for Growth," (Dover, DE: Department of Public Instruction, 1975), pp. 4–6. Used with permission.

in learning. Student-centered programs as in the middle school create climates or atmospheres that are student friendly and reflect the premise that middle schools are about students, not teachers.

Research on climate conducted over many years identifies some key variables that make up the perception of a person in an organization. Based on this perception, the person will act in a certain way to protect her or his self-interests. Climate is critical to all kinds of motivation, but especially student motivation. In general, such environmental factors contribute to three basic types of motivation: academic, affiliation, and power.

George Litwin and Robert Stringer of Harvard University identified nine such climate variables and conducted research on how they influenced the individual in any organization. By their research, climates can induce feelings of good-will (affiliation), competition (achievement), or conflict (power). Identity, support, and warmth, for example, encourage affiliation in middle schools. Structure, standards, and rewards encourage competition. Conflict, too, can be encouraged by over-structuring, not allowing opinions to be heard, or setting impossibly high performance standards (see Table 6.2).

Having observed these things, we move toward the development of learning materials that are developmentally appropriate for the middle school classroom. These materials are of two kinds, those now available and those emerging through new technologies.

TABLE 6.2 *Key Variables of Organizational Climate*

1. Structure—the feeling that employees have about the constraints in the group, how many rules, regulations, procedures there are; is there an emphasis on red tape and going through channels, or is there a loose and informal atmosphere?
2. Responsibility—the feeling of being your own boss; not having to double-check all your decisions, when you have a job to do, knowing that it is your job.
3. Reward—the feeling of being rewarded for a job well done; emphasizing positive rewards rather than punishments; the perceived fairness of the pay and promotion policies.
4. Risk—the sense of riskiness and challenge in the job and in the organization; is there an emphasis on taking calculated risks, or is playing it safe the best way to operate?
5. Warmth—the feeling of general good fellowship that prevails in the work group atmosphere; the emphasis on being well-liked; the prevalence of friendly and informal social groups.
6. Support—the perceived helpfulness of the managers and employees in the group; emphasis on mutual support from above and below.
7. Standards—the perceived importance of implicit and explicit goals and performance standards; the emphasis on doing a good job; the challenge represented in personal and group goals.
8. Conflict—the feeling that managers and other workers want to hear different opinions; the emphasis placed on getting problems out in the open, rather than smoothing them over or ignoring them.
9. Identity—the feeling that you belong to a company and you are a valuable member of a working team; the importance placed on this kind of spirit.

TABLE 6.2 *Key Variables of Organizational Climate (continued)*

Summary of Findings of Climate Research

The Relationship of Climate Dimensions and Achievement Motivation

Climate Dimension	Hypothesized Effect on Achievement Motivation	Findings	Hypothesis Support	Revised Hypothesis
Structure	reduction	mixed	moderate	—
Responsibility	arousal	consistent positive	weak–moderate	—
Warmth	no effect	some negative	moderate	—
Support	arousal	positive	moderate	—
Reward	arousal	consistent positive	strong	—
Conflict	arousal	mixed	very weak	—
Standards	arousal	mixed	weak	—
Identity	no effect	negative	none	arousal
Risk	arousal	some positive	weak–moderate	—

The Relationship of Climate Dimensions and Affiliation Motivation

Climate Dimension	Hypothesized Effect on Affiliation Motivation	Findings	Hypothesis Support	Revised Hypothesis
Structure	reduction	consistent negative	strong	—
Responsibility	no effect	zero order	strong	—
Warmth	arousal	consistent positive	strong	—
Support	arousal	positive	strong	—
Reward	arousal	consistent positive	strong	—
Conflict	reduction	weak negative	moderate	—
Standards	no effect	some negative	very weak	reduction
Identity	arousal	positive	strong	—
Risk	no effect	some negative	very weak	reduction

The Relationship of Climate Dimensions and Power Motivation

Climate Dimension	Hypothesized Effect on Power Motivation	Findings	Hypothesis Support	Revised Hypothesis
Structure	arousal	strong positive	very strong	—
Responsibility	arousal	positive	strong	—
Warmth	no effect	weak negative	moderate	—
Support	no effect	weak positive	moderate	—
Reward	no effect	zero order	strong	—
Conflict	arousal	consistent positive	strong	—
Standards	no effect	weak positive	moderate	—
Identity	reduction	weak positive	none	no effect
Risk	no effect	negative	very weak	reduction

Source: George H. Litwin and Robert A. Stringer, Jr., *Motivation and Organizational Climate*, exhibits 5.9, 5.10, and 5.11 (Boston: Division of Research, Graduate School of Business Administration, Harvard University, 1968), pp. 90–91. Reprinted by permission of Harvard University Press.

AVAILABLE LEARNING RESOURCES

While it is impossible to list all of those learning materials presently available to middle school teachers, some of the best resources can be identified. These materials are appropriate for preadolescents and will allow the teacher to further individualize instruction for each student she or he encounters.

The National Middle School Association—A beginning point for all resource retrieval for middle schools has to be NMSA. This Ohio-based organization represents state-affiliated and even internationally-affiliated middle schools and has as its mission the dissemination of knowledge about middle school programs. Readers will find print resources on all aspects of middle school organization (schedules, advisory programs, guidance, sports, grouping, and so on), most subject areas, implementation strategies, research summaries, and some staff development materials. NMSA holds an annual conference that features practical applications of middle school ideas.

Association for Supervision and Curriculum Development—Like the NMSA, the Association (ASCD) publishes position papers and produces films and videos on middle schools. Their monthly magazine, *Educational Leadership* has featured articles on middle schools for over 20 years. Also like the NMSA, ASCD has an annual conference during which policy issues and new middle school ideas are featured.

The National Association of Elementary School Principals (NAESP) and the National Association of Secondary School Principals (NASSP)—Both organizations cater to middle school educators as peripheral audiences. Articles in their journals, *The Principal* and the *NASSP Bulletin,* often contain teacher-written articles about middle schools.

In each state, the reader will find a middle school association of developing schools or districts which usually has a communication medium and holds an annual conference. These organizations can be contacted through your state department of education.

Finally, a number of excellent books have been produced over the past 40 years that detail all aspects of middle school development. These classics are featured in the generic bibliography in the appendices of this text.

THE NEW TECHNOLOGICAL RESOURCE BASE

Prior to the emergence of new technologies in the 1990s, it is safe to observe that middle schools in America were stagnating. During the 1960s through 1990s period, the middle school movement had refined instructional delivery to its ability given the limitation of a 30+:1 student–teacher ratio. Team planning, fancy schedules for moving students about, and even colorful and plentiful learning materials in the classroom could not overcome the basic energy demand on a single teacher to try to accommodate all of the pupils in one classroom.

What motivated the authors to rework their 20-year-old classic text, *The Essential Middle School,* into this new edition was the potential impact of these technologies on the middle school learning design. For the first time, middle schools have the tools to meet their promise of individualizing instruction for each student. All of the following tools are Web-based! It is the author's position that any middle school that doesn't move toward such a technological delivery is destined to become increasingly obsolete. The New American Middle School will be born from the 1990s' interactive technologies (see Teacher Resource 11).

Further, and even more important, curriculum development in middle schools, as well as instructional design in classrooms, will be completely dependent on a new kind of teacher who can use these technological resources to make the curriculum relevant and personal for each student. Without such teachers, middle schools will be a historical footnote of the twentieth century.

The Internet

The World-Wide Web (WWW), or Internet, was created in 1969 by the U.S. Department of Defense as ARPAnet to link military sites together. In 1986, the National Science Foundation Network (NSFNET) was created by the U.S. government as a noncommercial network connecting six supercomputer sites. On April 30, 1995, most of the functions of the NSFNET were made available for commercial services and the Internet was born. This network or networks connects all computers in the world into one global communication system.

In the beginning (1995), navigating on the Web required knowledge of UNIX, a special computer language. Soon, browsers or search engines emerged to help users get around on the Internet. These engines such as Yahoo and Magellan use hypertext (http stands for Hypertext Transport Protocol) to provide a multimedia environment combining print, video and sound enhancements. All of these are combined into an Integrated Services Digital Network (ISDN). These browsers, as they are called, search locator addresses and descriptions to provide selected options to the user. Because there are millions of such addresses, some search engines use Boolean search models that look for descriptors in tandem to reduce unrelated information.

Hence, in a very short period of time, teacher access to information on the Internet has become a matter of "point and click" with a mouse using any words that represent what is desired. Of course, as we enter the twenty-first century, voice recognition and internal logic by computers, delivered through your home television set will make searching as easy as asking questions.

The Internet has many search engines for accessing data bases. This instrument will also allow teachers and students to enter into discussion groups and to become members of mailing lists (listserv) for various functions. It will allow teachers and students to communicate by electronic mail (e-mail) with each other, or with students and teachers in distant places.

Teachers and administrators new to the Internet simply have to invest the time to explore this new learning medium. It will first be a novelty, then a habit, soon a tool, and eventually, a new way of learning. Assuming that the reader has access to a computer with Internet access (about $20 per month from home), a good place for educators to start is Web66 <http://Webb.coled.umn.edu> which describes itself as "a catalyst to integrate the Internet into K12 school curricula." In addition to providing a comprehensive list of all kindergarten through twelfth grade schools on the Internet, this site also links out to major educational resources such as:

Library of Congress (http://www.loc.gov/)

Fedworld—100 government agency sites (http://fedworld.gov)

Education Index—links to educational agencies (http://educationindex.com)

CMC Applications-Education—links to 80 educational resources such as ERIC, Educators Usenet, K–12 Armadillo, subject matter resources, and so forth.

For middle school educators, another early site will have to be the Ford Middle School site (http://www.ultranet.com/~fordms/reference.html) discussed earlier. This school is a master site to over 2,500 middle schools in the country with just a click of your mouse.

There are, literally, hundreds of Internet sites that might serve to inform the middle school teacher about what is happening beyond his or her classroom or school. One site dedicated to middle schools is MIDDLE-L@VMD.CSO;MT >UICI.EDU. But others might prove equally interesting:

AFROAM-L@HARVARDA.BITNET—Critical Issues in African-American Life and Culture

ANI-L@UTKVMI.UTK.EDU—Autism Network International

AEELIST@PUCC.PRINCETON.EDU—Association for Experimental Education

CPSI-L@UBVM.CC.BUFFALO.EDU—Creative Problem Solving Institute

EDRES-L@UNBVMI.CSD.UNB.CA—Educational Resources on the Internet

ENGLED-L@PSUVM.PSU.EDU—English Education

GEOGED@UKCC.UKY.EDU—Geography Education List

K12PALS@SUVM.STR.EDU—Teachers Helping Students Find a Penpal

There are, in addition, various listservs for which teachers can subscribe (for free usually) to automatically receive information. In addition to most of those listed above, listservs deal with topics such as academic advising (ACADV @VM1<NODAK>EDU) teaching German (AATG@INDYCMS. IUPUI.EDU) and research on teaching (AERA-K@ASUVM.INRE.ASU.EDU). The reader will note that almost all of these informational sites are university-based.

There are, also, various news groups that can be accessed by your browser with just a short descriptor, such as K12.chat.elementary, K12.chat.intermediate, K12.chat.teacher, K12.chat.health, and K12.chat.science.

Once the reader becomes habitual in surfing the net, the question of utility comes into play. How can I, as a teacher, use this resource to make my middle school classroom a better place for students? The authors would suggest beginning with a vision of what you would like to see in your school and classroom. Start collecting, by printing pages you like, your own portfolio of a model school or classroom. Some recommended best practice sites to begin with are:

A profile of best practices 1998:
http://www.coe.wayne.edu/TSC/es.es.html

Best practices—mission 1997:
http://www.bestpracedu.org/BPE/Statement.shtml

Best practices—global ideas 1998: http://www.bestpraceduc.org.

Best practices—math and science 1997:
http://www.bestpracedu.org/BPE/mathscilit.shtml

Best practices—school to work: http://www.state.nj.us/education/bp-ss/ stw1.htm

The authors would also suggest that the teacher begin collecting useful tools or sites that he or she may want to reference later. These can be saved on your home or school computer by clicking on "favorites" on your screen menu when viewing. Some sample resources are:

Learning Web—A collection of teacher-help sites and sound curriculum ideas
www.learningweb.org

Virtual School Archives—Through shareware.com, some 250,000 software programs are available free. The browser Yahoo also has archives (OS/2 and Unix) for your use
http://metalab.unc.edu/cisco/schoolhouse/computer/archives.html.

Essential Reference Sites—Websters Dictionary, Barletts Familiar Quotations, Britannica Encyclopedia Online, Old Farmer's Almanac, Roget's Thesaurus, and many others all free and at your fingertips (http://www.ultranet.com/~fordms/reference.html).

Assistive Technology Resource Page—The Missouri Department of Education provides information, training, and technical assistance to teachers over this site. Included are how to write IEPs, a center of technological publications, software archives, and a list of vendors for educational resources.

Resources for Emotional and Behavior Disorders—Offered by George Washington University, this interactive site allows teachers to ask questions and receive free consultations, as well as to leave tips for other teachers. Parent education resources are also offered.

Special Subject Curricula—Math projects for middle schoolers at four centers (http://tiger.coe.Missouri.edu/~mathed/M3/curricula) and a sample science curriculum for sixth, seventh, and eighth grades (http://bvsd.K12.co.us/cent/course/sciencec.html).

Instructional Tutorials—Learning hands-on how to do e-mail, utilizing the Microsoft Internet explorers, and to browse using the Netscape Navigator tutorials (http://www.hom.net/~wrmstech/wrmshome/tutorials/tutorials.htm).

Creating and Publishing Your Own Web Page—Includes how to create a web page, add images, add hyperlinks, and actually publish your web on the Internet (http://www.mpls.K12.mn.us/northeast/creatingwebpages.htm).

USING THE COMPUTER IN THE CLASSROOM

Before the Internet, schools used computers like an electronic textbook. Students would pass through programmed materials using a disk or loaded software. Skills were taught in computer labs where all students learned the same things together. After 1995, with the advent of the Internet, all of this changed. Because of individual access, and hypertext, e-mail, and other miracles, students could now learn as individuals on the web. The dream of John Dewey, progressive educators, and middle school educators was suddenly attainable.

One of the earliest attempts to demonstrate the new power of computer learning was the Global Schoolhouse Project, funded by the National Science Foundation from 1993 to 1995. This project linked school students around the world in a number of collaborative projects including "Alternative Energy Sources," "Solid Waste Management," "Space Exploration," and the study of "Weather and Natural Disasters" (http://K12.cnidr.org/gsh/projects.html and w.w.w.gsn.org). These interactive curricula showed that children in places such as Florida and Sweden could communicate daily, live, even visually, about anything they wished to study. The Web was truly world wide.

An example of such multidistrict learning in the United States is presented by a number of Montana school districts that had their students follow the progress of Lewis and Clark in the fall of 1998. Along the trail, various districts learned about the historic Glades Creek Campsite, Indian long house construction, the importance of salt works, and other topics tied into their local history. Each district shared via the Internet with other districts and then stayed tuned for reports from down the trail. The lieutenant governor of Montana and the governor of Idaho were active partners in this investigative venture (http:// www.hellgate.K12.mt.us/middle/clark/index.htm).

Another example of taking the curriculum onto the web can be found in the Main Street Middle School (Montpelier, Vermont) Lake Champaign Study called Eco-Peers Project. This project had a path (lesson sequence and timeline) that sought to answer certain basic questions about the aquatic life in the Lake Champaign basin. It included two 90-minute simulations, an interactive problem-solving activity, a student-created newspaper, and opportunities for students to choose from a variety of acceptable sites for enrichment (http:// ps.k12.vt.us/msms/grade//overview/index.htm).

Another interesting application of instruction on the computer is the Mead Mills Middle School (Northville, Michigan) after-school program. This school posts its Tuesday and Thursday program schedule on its home page giving the title, the sponsor teaching the program, the dates, and the requirements. Such a page could be updated daily (the daily demand schedule) and registration for available spots could be handled online (http://mmwww.northville.k12.mi.us/ Mini.htm).

In one Florida Middle School (Manatee Middle, Naples, Florida), teachers use the Internet and a webpage to explain instructional practices to parents. For example, the middle school practice of "looping" was featured in April of 1999 (http://manateemiddle.org/manateemiddle/looping.htm). This connecting also suggests a more intensive role for parents in the instructional programs of twenty-first-century middle schools.

One of the more exciting examples of middle school instruction going online comes from Centennial Middle School in Colorado <http://bvsd.k12.co.us/cent/ Newspaper>. In this school *Vocal Point,* a student-driven, collaborative electronic newspaper, is designed, managed, and maintained entirely by student volunteers. The newspaper creates a forum for the analysis of ideas of middle schoolers. Presently, students from Colorado, Minnesota, Oklahoma, Texas, and Canada interact on this webpage. Teachers and other students can critique student work, and links in the articles take readers to supplemental information sites. Sample topics in 1999 included "people who impact our world," "great inventions of the 20th century," "rights," "outer space," and "major events affecting youth."

From these few examples of the new middle school instructional resources, it can be seen how teachers will be teaching in the first part of the twenty-first century.

1. They will communicate with students and parents by e-mail, and they will seek to educate students by passive measures on webpages. (For examples, see teaching civility to middle schoolers at Andalusia Middle School [http://199.88.17.100/kyle/new%Folder0/020(2)/amsafe.html]

or communicating a desire for tolerance among students at Smithtown Middle School in St. James, New York [http://www.smithtown.k12. ny.us/midlschl/TolerancePledge.htm]).

2. They will send students to specific educational sites to supplement other classroom work. Included in these instructional supplements are sites such as the NASA telelectures, CNN newsroom, online newspapers, AT&T Learning Network, the World Classroom. (Structured curriculum activities in subject areas can be found at global@glcdallas.tx.us) or the National Geographic Society Kids Page, http://www.archkckcs.org/ sstudies.htm.

3. Once involved, teachers will develop specific "triptiks" for individuals or small groups, much as the authors are doing in this chapter by saying "go look at this." These destinations, like any instructional materials, must be previewed and programmed, but can be saved for future students once created.

4. While many middle school teachers like to pretend that preadolescents are really adolescent, they aren't. For this reason, many of the sites thought more appropriate for late elementary school can serve as motivators and rewards in middle schools. The Ford Middle School in Acushnet, Massachusetts (http://www.ultranet.com/~fordms/ kidspage.html), uses their kidspage to entice learners. Some of the favorite sites are: Goosebumps: Enter If You Dare, Experience the Magic of Disney, Visit to the Crayola Factory, The Yahoo Link to the Comics, The Barbie Doll Page, Kidscom: A Playground for Ages 8–14, A Virtual Tour of Dinosaurs, Volcano World, Sports Illustrated for Kids On-line, Animation, Sound, and Pictures from Warner Brothers, and Homework Page: Searching For a School Project.

5. Teachers and teams can also create both interdisciplinary unit frameworks and exploratory learnings on their webpages. One such school presently listing the access routes to selections is Welches Middle School in Mount Hood, Oregon (http://www.teleport.com/~alexan/ explore.htm).

6. Electronic Field Trips—Many middle schools are fearful of liability in taking students on field trips, but since the late 1990s, it has been possible to take an array of exciting field trips throughout the world from your school. The Virtual Schoolhouse (http://metalab.unc.edu/cisco/ trips.html) offers access to some wonderful adventures including Treasures of the Library of Congress, Nanoworld—The World Magnified 1000 Times, Journey to Yosemite, and a visit to the Paleolithic Painted Caves in Pont-d'Arc, France. Also, students can visit world class museums, such as Le Louve in Paris, the Ontario Science Museum, and the Vatican Exhibit in the Library of Congress. Finally, students can take virtual field trips to art galleries such as The Heard Museum of Native American Art, the Pacific Film Archives at the University of California at Berkeley, and the Oriental Institute Art Museum at the University of Chicago.

7. For more advanced students, teachers may allow free exploration of Internet sites by topic using search engines, much as most students will do at home. In school districts where there is anxiety about the trouble sites on the Internet, filtering services can be purchased. The Harbor Lights Middle School in Bandon, Oregon, for example, uses the N2H2's BESS Internet Proxy Service to safeguard students from unwanted information (http://www.coos.k12.or.us/~hlms4415/filter. html).

Finally, as we enter the twenty-first century, there are numerous ISDN products connecting computers, television, audio, and information resources that can be accessed by middle school teachers developing instructional materials. Satellite television opportunities include IDEANET, Satellite Educational Resources Consortium (SERC), Satellite Telecommunications Educational Programming (STEP), TI-IN Network, Livenet, and a host of related delivery media that offer full courses into the classrooms of America.

While continuing such listing would require a full book, the reader can see that a new and very rich field of instructional resources lies within the small electronic boxes found in 98 percent of all American schools and in many classrooms. There is no question, none, that this is the learning medium of the future in middle school education, and teachers will have to master the Internet in order to remain as teachers.

What strikes the authors, following a 35-year career in middle school education, is that from this point on, teachers will be America's curriculum developers. No university, no publishing company, can provide such a service to teachers in a timely manner. Also, after 35 years of trying to organize to meet the needs of each student in our middle schools, we finally have the tool to accomplish our mission and fulfill our philosophy.

Prerequisite to becoming the instructional programmer, teachers in American middle schools will have to become knowledgeable about their subjects, the students they teach, and the medium they must master. Teachers will be asked to decide, to make hard choices, about the purpose, form, order, and application of learning experiences they create. It promises to be a very exciting time to be a teacher in the middle school.

On the horizon, of course, are further technological inventions and miracles. New video applications with computers, in particular, promise to make visual face-to-face learning between any two persons on earth a reality within the decade. Language translators (like Babelfish) will eliminate language barriers. Our students and their teachers will soon be part of a global learning community.

SUMMARY

Middle schools are committed to meeting the needs of each student experiencing preadolescence. Implied in such a commitment is the need to individualize learning at the classroom level. Overcoming the traditional standardization of instruction has been a major challenge to middle school educators in the twentieth century.

The traditional curriculum in American education viewed the students as unknowing and in need of structured learning. In such schools, knowledge was formatted for essential learning and minimal skill acquisition, and the learning environment was characterized as highly standardized and structured. In order to meet individual needs of middle schoolers, the new middle school will need to be characterized by instructional flexibility and greater student choice and participation in learning. Middle schools must connect the words of their philosophy to instructional practices if they are to survive in the twenty-first century.

Middle schools have attempted to use organizational tools and delivery media to achieve individualization. Flexible schedules, team planning and teaching, exploratory wheels, interdisciplinary units and other such means acted to break down structure and uniformity, but the high student–teacher ratios precluded true individualization.

In the late 1990s, middle school teachers have been given wonderful new teaching tools that will allow middle schools to deliver on the promise of a personal and relevant curriculum for preadolescents. Already, some 2,500 leading middle schools have discovered the uses of the Internet for enriching the curriculum. Highly interactive, integrated curriculums are beginning to emerge under the leadership of classroom teachers. The new technological resource base for teachers is both exciting and challenging.

In the near future, teachers will use the Internet and other telecommunication devices to alter instruction in at least seven ways: (1) to communicate directly with students and parents, (2) to supplement conventional educational teaching, (3) to build specific destination roadmaps for student learning, (4) to reward and motivate students by using "softer" learning sites, (5) to create whole and supplemental learning sites such as exploratory short-courses and interdisciplinary units, (6) to allow students to explore by taking electronic field trips, and (7) to provide students opportunities for independent study using the Internet, with or without filtering services.

Middle school teachers in the twenty-first century will be the developers of curriculum materials. In order to be adequate in this role, teachers will need to know their subject matter, their students, and technology in superior ways.

Suggested Learning Activities

1. Based on the observations in this chapter, develop a description of a school you know in terms of how it is transitioning to a technological future.

2. In order for an experienced middle school teacher to practice in the new middle school of the twenty-first century, what must be learned?

3. Visiting some of the Internet sites listed in this chapter, create your own portfolio of ideas you like and would want to see in your school.

4. Make a list of issues that might result from these new technologies, such as the problem of grading student learning.

Selected References

Books

Commission on Behavioral and Social Sciences and Education. 1999. *How People Learn: Brain, Mind, Experience and School.* Chicago, IL: National Academy Press.

Jostens Learning Corporation. 1995. *Educating Jessica's Generation: Learning, Technology, and the Future of K–12 Education.* Highland Park, IL: Jostens.

Kearsley, G. 1985. *Training For Tomorrow: Distributed Learning Through Computers and Communication Technology.* Barnstable, MA: Addison-Wesley.

Tapscott, D. 1997. *Growing Up Digital: The Rise of the Net Generation.* New York: McGraw-Hill.

Articles

Cobb, T. 1997. "Cognitive Efficiency: Toward a Revised Theory of Media," *Educational Research and Development,* vol 45, no. 4.

Websites

For new "wearable technologies": http://www.news.com/News/Item/0,4.26783.00.html

For technology statistics: http://www.astd.org/vitual_community/research

For knowledge management: http://www.ntgi.net/ntg/y2k/info/kmartcls.htm

For lesson plans on the web: www.workcentral.com

For criticism of technology: http://www.zd.net.com/anchordesk/story/story_2082.html

CHAPTER 7

The New Full-Service Middle School

Knowing depends on experience.

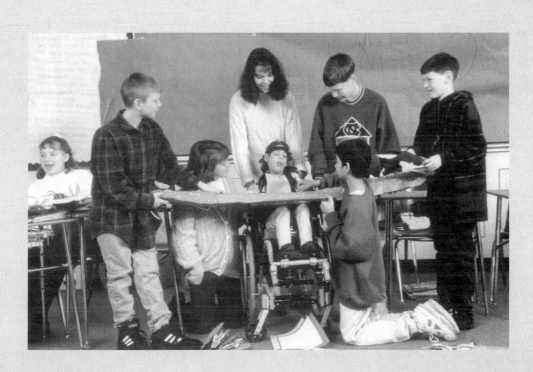

Full service schools are based on the notion that no single magic bullet can substantially improve the lives of at-risk children and their families. Full service schools unite families with community agencies, coordinate referrals for services of those agencies, and assist families in overcoming any barriers to student achievement and success.

This chapter examines a number of components that can result in a quality education for pre- and early adolescents. Of particular importance is how the school works with parents, community and community agencies to promote the welfare of special-needs youngsters as well as those in the mainstream.

THE ROLE OF FAMILIES IN THE FULL-SERVICE SCHOOL

All too often, there is an adversarial relationship between families having children with disabilities and schools. There are barriers that prevent parent involvement in schools. Some school environments actually discourage parent involvement. Some teachers are intimidated by the prospect of working with parents. Reasons for this include lack of time and inadequate training for teachers in how to build appropriate parent involvement. Threats of lawsuits of parents with special needs children also make teachers and administrators shy away from parent involvement.

However, schools are increasingly being held accountable for providing meaningful opportunities for families to become involved in decision making and assessing school accountability. Numerous educational reform mandates have expanded the role of home-to-school relationships to insure that schools are working together with parents.

The GOALS 2000: Educate America Act (U.S. Department of Education, 1994); the Individuals with Disabilities Education Act (IDEA) (National Association of State Directors of Special Education, 1997); and the Improving America's Schools Act of 1993 (U.S. Department of Education, 1993) are just a few of the mandates that place the responsibility squarely on schools for providing parents with the information and assistance necessary to become effective partners in education.

Each legislative enactment is reinforced by a wealth of empirical evidence supporting the benefits of parent–teacher collaboration. There is a strong belief that empowered parents function more effectively as proactive (versus reactive) advocates for their children.

IDEA AND INCLUSION

On May 15, 1997, The Individuals With Disabilities Education Act (IDEA) (P.L. 101–476) was reauthorized by Congress. Although the law maintained provisions public schools had been practicing for years, several mandates have had a direct impact on delivery of services to students with disabilities. There is increasingly more site-based responsibility for increased accountability for general and special education students in a unified model for delivery of educational services.

The child find assurance of IDEA requires that local education agencies (LEAs) develop procedures for locating and evaluating eligible students with disabilities. While many educators associate this requirement with identification of preschool children for early intervention, it also applies to school-age students including those who have not graduated through age 21.[1]

Students with disabilities placed in private schools are entitled to a proportional amount of IDEA funds and services. The services may be provided on site at private schools including parochial schools.

Under IDEA, all students with disabilities must be included in state and district assessment programs, and alternative assessments must be provided to students who can't participate in standard assessments. The requirement of an individualized education plan (IEP) must also be maintained. The IEP must now include an explanation of the extent, if any, to which the child will not participate with nondisabled children in the regular class and in activities that are extracurricular or non-academic.[2]

Disabilities That Qualify Children and Youth for Special Education Services Under the Individuals with Disabilities Education Act (IDEA)

The Education of the Handicapped Act, Public Law (P.L.) 94–142, was passed by Congress in 1975 and amended by P.L. 99–457 in 1986 to ensure that all children with disabilities would have a free, appropriate public education available to them which would meet their unique needs. It was again amended in 1990 and the name was changed to IDEA.

IDEA defines "children with disabilities" as having any of the following types of disabilities: autism, deafness, deaf–blindness, hearing impairments (including deafness), mental retardation, multiple disabilities, orthopedic impairments, other health impairments, serious emotional disturbance, specific learning disabilities, speech or language impairments, traumatic brain injury, and visual impairments (including blindness). These terms are defined in the regulations of IDEA, as follows.

1. Autism: A developmental disability significantly affecting verbal and nonverbal communication and social interaction, generally evident before age three, that adversely affects educational performance.

2. Deafness: A hearing impairment which is so severe that a child is impaired in processing linguistic information through hearing, with or without amplification, which adversely affects educational performance.

3. Deaf–Blindness: Simultaneous hearing and visual impairments, the combination of which causes such severe communication and other developmental and educational problems that a child cannot be accommodated in special education programs solely for children with deafness or children with blindness.

4. Hearing Impairment: A hearing impairment, whether permanent or fluctuating, which adversely affects a child's educational performance but which is not included under the definition of "deafness."

5. Mental Retardation: Significantly subaverage general intellectual functioning existing concurrently with deficiencies in adaptive behavior

and manifested during developmental period, which adversely affects a child's educational performance.

6. Multiple Disabilities: Simultaneous impairments (such as mental retardation/blindness or mental retardation/orthopedic impairment), the combination of which causes such severe educational problems that the child cannot be accommodated in a special education program solely for one of the impairments. The term does not include children with deaf–blindness.

7. Orthopedic Impairment: A severe orthopedic impairment which adversely affects a child's educational performance. The term includes impairments caused by a congenital anomaly (such as clubfoot or absence of some member), impairments caused by disease (such as poliomyelitis or bone tuberculosis), and impairments from other causes (such as cerebral palsy, amputations, or fractures or burns which cause contractures).

8. Other Health Impairment: Having limited strength, vitality or alertness due to chronic or acute health problems such as a heart condition, tuberculosis, rheumatic fever, nephritis, asthma, sickle cell anemia, hemophilia, epilepsy, lead poisoning, leukemia, or diabetes, which adversely affects a child's educational performance. According to the Office of Special Education and Rehabilitative Services' clarification statement of September 16, 1991, eligible children with ADD may also be classified under "other health impairment."

9. Serious Emotional Disturbance: (I) A condition exhibiting one or more of the following characteristics over a long period of time and to a marked degree, which adversely affects educational performance: (A) an inability to learn which cannot be explained by intellectual, sensory, or health factors; (B) an inability to build or maintain satisfactory interpersonal relationships with peers and teachers; (C) inappropriate types of behavior or feelings under normal circumstances; (D) a general pervasive mood of unhappiness or depression; or (E) a tendency to develop physical symptoms or fears associated with personal or school problems. (II) The term includes children who have schizophrenia. The term does not include children who are socially maladjusted, unless it is determined that they have a serious emotional disturbance.

10. Specific Learning Disability: A disorder in one or more of the basic psychological processes involved in understanding or in using language, spoken or written, which may manifest itself in an imperfect ability to listen, think, speak, read, write, spell, or do mathematical calculations. The term includes such conditions as perceptual disabilities, brain injury, minimal brain dysfunction, dyslexia, and developmental aphasia. The term does not include children who have learning problems that are primarily the result of visual, hearing, or motor disabilities, or mental retardation, of emotional disturbance, or of environmental, cultural, or economic disadvantage.

11. Speech or Language Impairment: A communication disorder such as stuttering, impaired articulation, a language impairment, or a voice impairment, which adversely affects a child's educational performance.

12. Traumatic Brain Injury: An injury to the brain caused by an external physical force, resulting in total or partial functional disability or psychosocial maladjustment, or both, which adversely affects educational performance. The term does not include brain injuries that are congenital or degenerative, or brain injuries induced by birth trauma.

13. Visual Impairment, Including Blindness: A visual impairment which, even with correction, adversely affects a child's educational performance. The term includes both children with partial sight and those with blindness.

Table 7.1 illustrates common student characteristics of emotionally handicapped, learning disabled and educationally mentally handicapped children.

TABLE 7.1 Common Characteristics of Children with Learning Disabilities/Handicaps

Common Student Characteristics	Emotionally Handicapped	Learning Disabled	Educable Mentally Handicapped
Developmental	Normal development of early childhood skills	Delayed language and/or motor development	Delayed early skills (physical, intellectual, emotional, social)
Intellectual	Slow/normal to gifted intelligence	Slow/normal to gifted range on IQ tests	Poor performance on verbal and nonverbal IQ tests
Academic	Learning difficulties due to emotional overlays Need for structured directions and consistent expectations	Major discrepancy between two academic areas Needs variety of materials and techniques	Academic skill mastery slower than normal (1/2 to 3/4 rate of average student) Needs constant repetition
Learning	Difficulty in applying what they have learned Poor task completion	Highly distractable Poor organizational skills Poor processing of information High level of frustration Poor time concepts	Kinesthetic/concrete learner Poor time and space concepts
Personal/Emotional	Low self-esteem General pervasive mood of unhappiness/depression	Fear of failure Emotional highs and lows Low self-esteem	Difficulty in coping with or adjusting to environment Loving disposition
Social	Unsatisfactory interpersonal relationships Fears associated with personal or school problems sometimes causing withdrawal or acting out behaviors	Negative social behaviors Social isolate	Immature social behaviors Poor social judgment

Six Principles of IDEA

Free Appropriate Public Education (FAPE)

"The term 'free appropriate public education' means special education and re-lated services that (A) have been provided at public expense, under public super-vision and direction, and without charge; (B) meet the standards of the State edu-cational agency; (C) include an appropriate preschool, elementary, or secondary school education in the State involved; and (D) are provided in conformity with the individualized education program required under section 613(d)." [Section 602(8)]

Appropriate Evaluation

One of the most significant changes in IDEA 97 relates to how the evaluation process should be viewed. "The committee believes that a child should not be sub-jected to unnecessary tests and assessments . . . and the LEA should not be saddled with associated expenses unnecessarily." (U.S. Government Committee on Labor and Human Resources, p. 19)

Evaluation activities should include gathering information related to enabling the child to be involved in and progress in the general curriculum or, for preschool children, to participate in appropriate activities.

Individualized Education Program

"The term 'individualized education program' or 'IEP' means a written statement for each child with a disability that is developed, reviewed, and revised in accor-dance with section 614(d)." [Section 602(11)]

Least Restrictive Environment (LRE)

The presumption that children with disabilities are most appropriately educated with their nondisabled peers and that special classes, separate schooling, or other removal of children with disabilities from the regular educational environment oc-curs only when the nature of severity of the disability is such that education in reg-ular classes with the use of the supplementary aids and services cannot be achieved satisfactorily.

Parent and Student Participation in Decision Making

"The Congress finds the following: . . . Over 20 years of research and experience has demonstrated that the education of children with disabilities can be made more effective by . . . strengthening the role of parents and ensuring that families of such children have meaningful opportunities to participate in the education of their children at school and at home." [IDEA 97, Findings, 601(c)(5)(B)]

Procedural Safeguards

Safeguards to ensure that the rights of children with disabilities and their parents are protected, that students with disabilities and their parents are provided with the information they need to make decisions about the provision of FAPE, and that procedures and mechanisms are in place to resolve disagreements between parties.

Section 612(a)(5)

"(5) Least Restrictive Environment.—

"(A) In General.—To the maximum extent appropriate, children with disabilities, including children in public or private institutions or other care facilities, are educated with children who are not disabled, and special classes, separate schooling, or the removal of children with disabilities from the regular educational environment occurs only when the nature or severity of the disability of a child is such that education in regular classes with the use of supplementary aids and services cannot be achieved satisfactorily.

"(B) Additional Requirement.—

"(I) In General.—If the State uses a funding mechanism by which the State distributes State funds on the basis of the type of setting in which a child is served, the funding mechanism does not result in placements that violate the requirement of subparagraph (A).

"(II) Assurance.—If the State does not have policies and procedures to ensure compliance with clause (I), the State shall provide the Secretary an assurance that it will revise the funding mechanism as soon as feasible to ensure that such mechanism does not result in such placements.[3]

INCLUSION

Clarification of Terms

The terms *mainstreaming* and *inclusion* are often used interchangeably in education today. This inconsistency in usage has led to some confusion about what educators mean when they talk about inclusion or full inclusion. Mainstreaming is the practice of educating the disabled student in the general education classroom. Inclusion is a newer term used to describe the placement of students in regular classes for all or nearly all of the school day; mainstreaming is often associated with sending a student from a special education class to a regular class for specified periods. Although in some inclusion models students are mainstreamed only part of the day, students in full inclusion programs remain in the general classroom for the entire day.

Mainstreaming, Inclusion, and Law

The Regular Education Initiative (REI) is the movement through which the increased practice of mainstreaming has been highlighted. Followers of the REI contend that the removal of the disabled student from the general education classroom systematically creates two ineffective educational programs. Proponents of the REI feel that regular education can accommodate all students.

Through the Individuals with Disabilities Education Act (IDEA) and Section 504 of the Vocational Rehabilitation Act, a free and appropriate public education (FAPE) is mandated for students with disabilities. The placement of disabled students must be in the least restrictive environment (LRE), which is the environment closest to the general classroom in which the student's individual needs can be met. Availability of different placement options is required to ensure the appropriateness of an individual's program. This placement can be a special class, resource room, or the general classroom with or without consultative services. Decisions about placement take place during the development of the individualized educational program (IEP).

Although law requires that students with disabilities be placed in the least restrictive environment, it is not mandated that students be mainstreamed. For example, a full inclusion model may be restrictive for a student who requires intense remediation in reading. It is for this reason that a variety of service options must be made available to disabled students.

Research

To date, approximately 80 percent of students with learning disabilities receive the majority of their instruction in the general classroom. Although critics have claimed that there is no support for providing service in special education programs, there is evidence that some students benefit from such placements more than they would were they in regular classrooms. There is not yet any definitive evidence that supports or rejects the effectiveness of inclusion practices. There has been, however, a massive amount of federal money poured into inclusion research and the results of those studies should be made available in the near future.[4]

Although no consensus exists about the definition of inclusion, it is generally considered a movement to merge regular and special education so that all students are educated in general education classrooms.[5]

There are several terms associated with inclusion:

1. **Full Inclusion**—Students with disabilities who receive their entire education within the general education setting. This is sometimes called mainstreaming.

2. **Partial Inclusion**—The practice of educating students with disabilities in general education classrooms for some portion of the school day, while they spend the other portion of the day receiving instruction in a special education classroom or resource room outside of the mainstream.

3. **Mainstreaming**—The practice of providing a student with disabilities with some of his or her education in a general education classroom. Often used synonymously with "partial inclusion."

4. **Integration**—Used in a variety of ways within the literature, may mean either inclusion or mainstreaming. The context of the discussion determines its meaning.

5. **Neighborhood School**—The public school a child would normally attend if he or she did not have a disability.

6. **IEP—Individual Education Plan**—All students with a disability must have an IEP with a list of all services available to that child. It must:

   a. be reviewed and revised annually

   b. have parental involvement

   c. state the level of the child's performance, goals, and progress

   d. contain an "impact statement," explaining how the child's disability affects the child's ability to learn

   e. state "major life goals" for future employment and independent living

   f. suggest a remedy for behavioral problems

   g. provide accountability for learning, including goals and objectives with measurable indicators.

What Do the Laws Say about the Education of Children and Youth with Special Needs?

The first federal laws designed to assist individuals with disabilities date back to the early days of the nation. In 1798, the Fifth Congress passed the first federal law concerned with the care of persons with disabilities. This law authorized a Marine Hospital Service to provide medical services to sick and disabled seamen. By 1912, this service became known as the Public Health Service. However, prior to World War II, there were relatively few federal laws authorizing special benefits for persons with disabilities. Those that did exist were intended to address the needs of war veterans with service-connected disabilities. This meant that, for most of our nation's history, schools were allowed to exclude—and often did exclude—certain children, especially those with disabilities. Since the 1960s, however, there has been a virtual avalanche of federal legislation that relates directly or indirectly to individuals with disabilities, particularly children and youth. The numerous court decisions rendered, and state and federal laws passed since the 1960s, now protect the rights of those with disabilities and guarantee that they receive a free and appropriate, publicly supported education.

There have been many heroes and heroines in this effort, most certainly the families of children with disabilities. The positive changes in the laws and the attitudes of the public toward those with disabilities would not have occurred without the active and persistent involvement of many dedicated people over the years. Today, people with disabilities have accomplished more than ever dreamed possible, due to increases in the number and quality of programs, better trained professionals, continuous research in education, information dissemination and technical assistance, and the collaboration between parents and professionals to obtain the best education possible for the nation's children and youth with disabilities.

As evidence of these changes, in 1997 over 5.5 million children and youth with disabilities received special education and related services under the Individuals with Disabilities Education Act (IDEA) (U.S. Department of Education, 2000).

Court Decisions Clarify Least Restrictive Environment (LRE)

The U.S. Court of Appeals for the 4th Circuit recently adopted a slightly different standard in *Hartmann* v. *Loudoun County* (1997). The court stated that the LRE requirement of the IDEA established a preference for inclusion, not an inflexible federal mandate. The court listed three situations in which a school district does not have to educate a student with disabilities in a general education classroom. Mainstreaming is not required if:

1. a student with disabilities will not receive educational benefits from a regular classroom;
2. any marginal benefit would be significantly outweighed by benefits obtained only in a separate instructional setting; or
3. the child is a disruptive force in the general education classroom.

In order to make a decision on placement in the general education classroom, the individual student's unique needs must be considered. The planning team that develops the student's Individual Educational Plan (IEP) must first determine what educational services are required, and then where they can be most appropriately delivered. The IEP must address both academic and non-academic needs like social development or communication. At the same time, consideration must be given to whether the student's presence in a particular setting would significantly interrupt the education of the other students, whether by disruptive behavior or by requiring an inordinate amount of the teacher's time.[6]

Reading Comprehension and Learning Disabilities

Reading is a problem for very many students with learning disabilities. Ability to read influences the child's success across the curriculum and success in later years. Comprehension in reading, which is the ultimate goal of reading instruction, presents a problem for students with learning disabilities. They may lack skills in any or several of the following areas:

- Students need to be able to *decode* fluently.
- Students need to recall specific stated information from a reading passage. This refers to *literal comprehension* of the text.
- A second area involves *sequencing,* which requires students to identify the order in which events occur in a passage. This recall skill is important to gaining comprehension.
- Differentiating main ideas and details is used in the process of *summarization.* This aids in retention of information.
- *Inference* requires students to examine stated relationships in the passage to draw conclusions. This involves higher order thinking skills.
- As students progress in reading they encounter more complex *sentence structure* that includes higher level vocabulary and grammar knowledge.

- Students should be encouraged to develop *critical thinking* skills through reading instruction. Readers will be able to analyze and verify information they encounter.[7]

IMPLEMENTING INCLUSION IN THE MIDDLE SCHOOL CLASSROOM

Inclusion into a regular education classroom is the right of all special education students, regardless of their grade level. However, it is not of equal benefit to all students. At the middle school level, some special education students benefit most from being included in a regular education classroom while others benefit most from a self-contained or resource classroom.

A clear message needs to be given that people with disabilities are capable and should be integrated into the world. It should not be advocated that "one size fits all" when making decisions about where disabled students should be educated. Educational placement decisions for students with disabilities are made at the local level and must be based on the needs of the individual student.

Successful inclusive middle schools have been described by The Council of Exceptional Children as addressing leadership, establishing a sense of community, establishing standards, accountability, and changing professional roles. They also call for a variety of services and flexible learning environments to meet student needs.

Inclusive middle schools and classrooms utilize flexible groupings, authentic and meaningful learning experiences, and developmentally appropriate curricula accessible to all students. Even though full inclusion is a goal, a continuum of educational options is present within inclusive schools and classrooms to provide choice and to meet the individual needs of each child. Inclusion and cooperation are emphasized within each option, and there is less reliance on pull-out education programs.

Teaching Models and Methods in Inclusion

Peer-mediated approaches are designed to provide direct instruction to special education middle school students in the regular classroom. A peer-mediated approach can be defined as one in which peers present prompts or task trials, monitor tutee responses, use error correction procedures, and provide help. This approach is highly structured and based on teacher goals and the classroom curriculum. Examples of peer-mediated practices would include peer tutoring, cooperative learning, and social skills training.

Peer tutoring programs have been successfully implemented across a variety of student populations (at-risk, economically disadvantaged, LD, and ED), students in the same grade (same-age students), and older students with younger students (cross-age).

One of the most promising ways of encouraging appropriate interactions among special education middle school students in the regular classroom is to provide tasks that require cooperative effort. The basic principles fundamental to cooperative learning include simultaneous interaction, positive interdependence, and individual accountability.[8]

In middle school, social skills training focuses on the problem of delayed or lack of social skills that are functional and appropriate for successful social interaction with peers. When selecting student goals for social skills training, the teacher must consider the existence of ethnic differences both within and between children of different cultures as well as differences in developmental and cognitive abilities. By incorporating these considerations, social skills training will be sensitive to cultural and developmental issues; it will also address both skill and performance deficits.

Middle school students need teachers who will incorporate instructional strategies in their teaching styles to aid the special education student in the regular classroom. Helpful strategies include modifications in the manner and rate of presenting new materials; bring the student closer to the teaching, allowing more time for students to complete their assignments; provide frequent and direct encouragement; teach highlighting to help with recall; build awareness of self and others; teach positive behavior and asking for help.[9]

INTERVENTIONS THAT WORK WITH STUDENTS WITH SPECIAL NEEDS

Lesson Presentation

- Pair students to check work.
- Write key points on the board or on an individual pad for the child.
- Provide peer tutoring.
- Provide visual aides.
- Provide peer notetaker and photocopy needs.
- Make sure directions are understood; ask student one-on-one to repeat directions.
- Break up lesson into short segments.
- Provide written outline.
- Allow student to copy lesson plans.
- Have child review key points orally.
- Teach through multisensory modes.
- Use computer-assisted instruction.
- Include a variety of activities during each lesson.

Physical Arrangement of Room

- Seat student near teacher.
- Seat student near a positive role model.
- Stand near the student when giving directions.

- Avoid distracting stimuli, such as an air conditioner or a high traffic area.
- Increase distance between the desks.
- Place masking tape on the floor to mark student's "personal space."

Assignments

- Give extra time to complete tasks.
- Simplify instructions; be brief and clear.
- Distribute worksheets one at a time.
- Reduce the reading level of the assignment.
- Allow student to tape record assignments.
- Provide a structured routine in written or picture form.
- Provide study skills training and learning strategies.
- Give frequent short quizzes; avoid long tests.
- Allow typewritten or computer assignments.
- Use self-monitoring devices, such as a clock or timer.
- Reduce homework assignments.
- Don't grade handwriting for students with motor problems.

Organization

- Provide peer assistance.
- Assign a volunteer homework buddy.
- Allow student to have an extra set of books at home.
- Send a daily or weekly progress report home.
- Develop a reward system.
- Provide student with a homework assignment notebook.
- Periodically spot check student's desk for unwanted articles.
- Keep limited materials in student's desk.

Behaviors

- Praise specific behaviors.
- Use self-monitoring strategies.
- Give extra privileges or awards.
- Keep class rules simple and clear.
- Make prudent use of negative consequences.
- Cue student to stay on task, such as by using signs or nonverbal motions.

- Mark student's correct answers, not mistakes.
- Implement a classroom behavior management system. (Use a behavior contract for specific areas targeted.)
- Allow student time out of seat to move around. (The student can run an errand or exercise.)
- Ignore inappropriate behaviors not drastically outside classroom limits.
- Allow legitimate movement.
- Increase immediacy of reward; gradually wean as student improves.
- Implement time-out system in the room, via a neighbor's class, or in the office.
- Be consistent yet fair.

Test Taking

- Allow open book exams.
- Give exams orally.
- Give take home tests.
- Use more objective items; assign fewer essays, if needed.
- Allow answers to be given on a tape recorder.
- Give short segments within time frames.
- Read items to student.

Special Considerations

- Schedule counseling with guidance.
- Provide special escort on field trips.
- Arrange for inservice for teacher on specifics of student handicap.
- Provide social skill instruction.
- Develop intervention strategies for transitional periods, such as lunch, P.E., hall, music, and library.
- Alert bus driver.
- Suggest intervention through guidance for child study team referral.

PROMISING PRACTICES FOR ALL MIDDLE SCHOOL CHILDREN IN THE FULL-SERVICE SCHOOL

Character Education

Character education is based on the premise that good character is not formed automatically. It is developed through a sustained process of teaching, example, learning, and practice.

Character education is helping young people know, care about and act on core values such as fairness, honesty, compassion, responsibility and self-respect. Although character education in children is primarily the responsibility of families, it is also the shared responsibility of communities, schools, and religious institutions.[10]

Even though there is often dispute on what values should be taught and by whom, there are a core set of ethical values that all can agree on as vital to pre- and early adolescent students. These may take the form of lists of basic character traits and life skills.[11] Examples are positive attitude, self-control, patience, cooperation, and caring.

Learning about character can be tied to academic standards published by states by connecting character traits with figures in literature and social studies.

Helping students assume responsibility for school culture takes place primarily through character education. As Americans looked on in horror at school shootings in 1998 and 99, much of the aftermath dealt with how those involved in the violence perceived their school culture as being excluding and indifferent.

School staffs can give students opportunities to practice moral behavior and foster caring relationships, but they must be proactive in the process. Programs must also involve parents and the community. Programs must not simply be add-on programs. They should integrate core values with the existing curriculum and integrate community services into the school day.

One example of integrating core values into the curriculum is to use reading and social studies to bring students into moral discourse by asking questions that demonstrate connections between their reading and their own experiences.

Character education does not need crises or violence to justify itself. Effective character education programs can create a closer connection between classrooms and life experiences and produce a true sense of community among students.[12]

Social and Emotional Learning Programs

Social and emotional learning faces attitudinal roadblocks of educators who dismiss such learning as the latest fad, claiming that teachers already address those needs every day. Although this may be true, there are those who argue that organized programs to develop social and emotional skills will result in long-term behavior changes and positive life outcomes.[13]

Emotional well-being is a predictor of success in academic achievement, employment, marriage, and physical health.

Daniel Goldman, author of the bestseller, *Emotional Health*, cites five dimensions of emotional intelligence that need to be incorporated in everything we do in school for both students and adults:[14]

1. **Self-awareness**—We need to know our strengths and limits and how to be decisive.

2. **Handling emotions generally**—Impulsive behavior has social consequences: boys are three to six times more likely to be violent by the end

of adolescence; children who are chronically sad or anxious in elementary school are most likely to end up as substance abusers in adolescence during periods of experimentation.

3. **Motivation**—An important element of motivation is hope, having a goal, knowing the small manageable steps it takes to get to that goal and having the zeal or persistence to follow through. We can teach students how to set goals, how to persevere, and how to work toward high achievement.

4. **Empathy**—Knowing how someone else feels is a fundamental human ability seen even in infants and small children. Playground bullies are examples of people who seem to lack empathy. Even those students can be taught social skills such as how to take turns and ask about feelings of others.

5. **Social skills**—Social skills can be contagious once taught. As noted previously, even bullies benefit from instruction in social skills. Schools that have environments that foster emotional intelligence are schools in which caring adults exist, including teachers, parents, community mentors and others who daily intervene with students.

Special Programs to Benefit Gifted Students

Gifted programs are carried out in a number of ways. In one type of program students receive core courses with regular students and then spend time with other gifted students in a pull-out program. In another gifted students stay in regular classrooms but teachers tailor the curriculum to their needs. In still another students leave their regular schools for several hours to attend a separate gifted school housed sometimes in museums, outdoor classrooms, or even at community colleges. Finally there are gifted schools (often magnet schools) that house students for the total day. Another version of gifted education is gifted magnet programs housed in regular schools that offer highly specialized and challenging courses to gifted students.

Gifted is most often combined with talented in a program description that reads "gifted and talented." Many magnet programs cater to talented youngsters in music, fine arts, science, or physical education.

In a particularly interesting twist, many schools today are adopting practices of gifted programs into general education as part of the reform movement which encourages the teaching of higher order thinking skills.[15] As higher standards are adopted and the tests that go with them, all students are expected to pursue more rigorous content. Opportunities for students to develop gifted behaviors rather than merely to find them or certify them are becoming the focus in the modern middle school.

As emerging adolescents grow, they develop identities that they will carry with them for a lifetime. If we can stop labeling gifted and nongifted students and view all students as having certain giftedness, then all students can achieve success in school. Looking at individual strengths rather than weaknesses and building on those strengths, as occurs in gifted programs, should be the standard in the entire middle school program.

Conflict Resolution

Modern middle schools are laboratories for conflict resolution. A promising trend in modern middle schools is the implementation of conflict resolution programs, most often in the form of a peer mediation program. A peer mediation program is a method for negotiating disputes and finding resolution that combines the needs of the parties in conflict instead of compromising those needs. It's a way for students to deal with differences without coercion. If students become empowered to resolve their differences peaceably, they will behave more responsibly.

Students who serve as peer mediators receive special training. Shifting responsibility for appropriately solving school conflicts from adults to young adults frees both teachers and administrators to concentrate more on teaching than discipline.

Mediation is voluntary. Students may request mediation when they are involved in a dispute, or they may be referred by teachers, administrators, or parents. When both parties agree to mediation, assigned mediators are sent to the Mediation Room "peace table" to act as a facilitator between the two disputants. Mediators are trained to assist those in conflict to solve their own problem.

Figure 7.1 presents a student information sheet outlining how the peer mediation program works.

FIGURE 7.1   Peer Mediation

Having a conflict?

—Has someone "chewed" on you or does not know when enough is enough?
—Did someone say "Just wait and I'll get you after school?"
—Did "he say"' that "she said" that "you said" and a rumor is going around the school?

What is mediation?

—Mediation is a chance for you to sit face to face and talk, uninterrupted, so each side of the dispute is heard. After the problem is defined, solutions are created and evaluated. When an agreement is reached, it is written and signed.

What is a student mediator?

—A student mediator is one of your peers who has been trained to conduct the mediation meeting. The student mediator makes sure the mediation session is helpful and fair. Your fellow students were selected to help you resolve differences because they might better understand your point of view.

Are there any rules in mediation?

To make the process work, there are a few simple rules:

 1. Mediation is a process that both students choose.

Continued on next page

FIGURE 7.1 *Peer Mediation, continued*

2. Everything said during a mediation is kept confidential. What is said in the room stays in the room.
3. In mediation, students take turns talking and no one can interrupt.
4. The student mediator does not takes sides.

If I have a conflict, how do I go about getting it mediated?

It is very easy to request a mediation. Mediation request forms may be picked up from the **Student Affairs Office, Guidance Office,** or a **teacher.** You will be notified of the time and place of mediation.

Why should I try mediation?

There are many reasons why mediation will be helpful to you. Here are a few:
1. Conflicts that do not get resolved often end in fights, which result in suspension.
2. Conflicts that do not get resolved often result in hurt feelings, which could cause you to lose friends.
3. You will learn to choose a peaceful, responsible way to solve your own problems without an adult doing it for you.
4. Mediation will help you develop mutual respect and clear communications.
5. Mediation makes school a more positive place to learn and grow.

CREATING SAFE AND DRUG-FREE SCHOOLS

The issue of school safety is a shared concern. Schools, communities, businesses, parents and students have to work together to develop a disciplined environment where learning can take place. Providing safe and drug free schools is a cornerstone for achieving world-class education.[16]

From 1980 to 2000, homicides by juveniles involving a firearm increased nearly threefold. In addition, during the same period, the number of juveniles arrested for weapons violations increased 125 percent. Where guns are the weapons of choice, youth violence becomes deadly.[17]

Surveys by the Centers for Disease Control and Prevention in the late 1990s found that one in twenty students indicated that he or she had carried a firearm, usually a handgun. Other surveys by the Office of Juvenile Justice and Delinquency Prevention, U.S. Department of Justice confirm that there is an increased propensity among young people to carry guns.[18]

The epidemic of gun violence in schools in the late 1990s only reinforced young people's notion that they must be prepared to fire back. As schools have tightened security dramatically in recent years, guns may not be carried into schools as often, but they are readily accessible nearby.

Promising Practices

To effectively address the rising levels of juvenile crime, especially youth gun violence, participants from all community sectors, public and private, are beginning to work collaboratively and comprehensively to reduce the incidence of violence in schools. A number of approaches have been taken, can be supported, or should be initiated to address the increased access to and use of guns by young people. These practices are listed below as (1) prevention programs, (2) intervention programs, and (3) comprehensive initiatives.

Prevention Programs. The majority of youth gun violence prevention programs involve instruction carried out in schools, community-based organizations, and physicians' offices. They emphasize the prevention of weapon misuse, the risks involved with the possession of a firearm, and the need for conflict resolution and anger management skills. Educational programs often use videotapes to support their presentation of the tragic results of gun violence and may also include firearm safety instructions, public information campaigns, counseling programs, or crisis intervention hotlines. Key elements of a gun violence prevention program may include:

- Creating an interagency gun-free school committee.
- Standardizing antiweapon policies and procedures for an immediate response for gun-related incidents.

Classroom Strategies. The Center to Prevent Handgun Violence has developed a school-based curriculum that has been used extensively across the country and has been evaluated by the Education Development Center with positive results. The Straight Talk About Risks (STAR) program at the Center to Prevent Handgun Violence is a comprehensive school-based program designed to reduce gun injuries and deaths with prevention activities for children and their families. Through STAR, students also learn how to make better, safer decisions and resolve conflicts without violence through role playing, goal setting, and the development of leadership skills.

Gun Buy-back Programs. Weapons Watch was organized by the mental health center of the Memphis School District, the Memphis Police Department, and Crime Stoppers. Weapons Watch was implemented to get children involved in ridding their schools of weapons. A hotline was established for students to call anonymously with information about a classmate who brings a weapon to school. Students are rewarded if the information leads to the confiscation of weapons and the arrest of the classmate who brings a weapon on campus.

Public Education Campaigns. Fresno's Youth Violence Prevention Network campaign in California is unique because it directly involves young people in delivering an anti-gun violence message. Previously known as Radio Bilingue, the Network is the result of a collaboration among Chicano Youth Center, House of Hope, Save Our Sons and Daughters, and End Barrio Warfare. Violence prevention activities include developing gun-free zone programs in city parks and neighborhoods, school emergency response and mediation teams, youth conferences, and youth leadership programs.

Intervention Programs. Police and sheriff's departments have been instrumental in supporting gun violence prevention and intervention programs. As part of drug education, public safety, and violence prevention efforts, police officers and sheriffs across the nation have worked collaboratively with schools to present critical information on gun violence to young people and, simultaneously, to develop more effective and interpersonal relations with young people.

Community Law Enforcement Programs. The Illinois State Police School Security Facilitator Program identifies jurisdictions with concerns about school violence. Representatives from all community programs that play a role in addressing problems of youth crime and violence are invited to attend a five-day team building and education program. Part of the curriculum deals directly with the interdiction of guns in schools. Teams return to their communities to educate others on youth violence issues and to implement specific strategies for violence reduction. While no short- or long-term evaluation of this program has been implemented, anecdotal information from prior participants indicated some degree of usefulness and success.

Gun Market Disruption and Interception. The Kansas City Weed and Seed program is a joint effort of the U.S. Department of Justice, the U.S. Attorney, and the Kansas City, Kansas, police department. The program focuses police efforts in high-crime neighborhoods on traffic violations, curfew violations, and other infractions of the law. Despite the fact that previous police campaigns have drawn protests of discrimination, the gun intercept program in Kansas City has not. Police have involved community and religious leaders in initial planning, and neighborhoods have made requests for greater police activity.

Diversion and Treatment Programs. In Pima County, Arizona, the Juvenile Diversion Program has set up a firearms prevention course for youngsters who are not hard-core delinquents but who have been referred to juvenile court for firing or carrying a gun, and for young people at risk for being involved with guns. At least one parent is required to attend the monthly sessions. During the course, the assistant prosecutor informs the juveniles and their parents about gun laws. Parents are given instruction on safe gun storage. By agreeing to take the course, the youth do not have their cases adjudicated and are not placed on probation; however, they do acquire a juvenile record.

Gun Courts. A special type of court called a gun court has recently been established by Providence, Rhode Island, to focus on gun crimes. All gun crimes are referred to a single judge who processes cases on a fast track. Gun courts have cut the processing time of gun crime cases in half.

Alternative Schools. The Second Chance School in Topeka, Kansas, is a voluntary half-day instructional course for students who have been expelled for possession of weapons or assaulting a staff member. Students engage in studies of math, social science, and language skills, participate in some recreational activities, and are required to participate in community service. Depending on the seriousness of the offense, students attend the program for one semester of one year. To date, 90 percent of the students enrolled have successfully completed the program. The program has been operating for three years and has developed partnerships with juvenile courts, the public schools, the police department, and the recreational department.

Comprehensive Initiatives. In Atlanta, the Center for Injury Control at Emory University is working together with the community, State and local governments, and with Project Pulling America's Cities Together (PACT) to analyze the magnitude, extent, and characteristics of youth firearms violence and to develop a broad-based strategy for addressing the problem. The planned intervention includes a three-part strategy: (1) to reduce the demand for firearms through a comprehensive community education program; (2) to reduce supply by promoting safe storage of firearms and by increasing law enforcement efforts to interdict the illegal gun market; and (3) to provide aggressive rehabilitation to decrease recidivism among juvenile gun offenders.

In Dade County, Florida, the Youth Crime Watch program, mandated for all schools by the Miami school board, was created in 1984 to extend the neighborhood watch concept to schools. The Gun Safety Awareness Program targets kindergarten through twelfth-grade students and their parents, examining causes of handgun violence and teaching the consequences of being arrested. The curriculum is supplemented by area Youth Crime Watches, school resource officers, and police officers. Parents attend training workshops on handgun safety awareness. Metal detectors are used unannounced at selected schools, and students caught with guns are referred to juvenile or adult court and recommended for expulsion and assignment to an alternative school. Awareness levels among youth and parents about the need to prevent handgun violence have increased in Dade County as a result of this comprehensive program.

State Legislation

In May 1995, the State of Texas enacted legislation that would both remove students who brings guns to school and who commit other serious offenses from their regular school and provide a safety net for those youths so they are not on the streets. Each school, in cooperation with the juvenile board of each county, must adopt a student code of conduct and provide an alternative education program. When a student is expelled, the school must notify juvenile court. Juvenile boards and schools establish what support services are to be given to these expelled youths. In counties where the population exceeds 125,000, the juvenile board must offer a juvenile justice alternative education program. School districts and local juvenile boards meet regularly to coordinate efforts. For more information, contact the Texas Juvenile Probation Commission at 512–912–2402.

Federal Legislation

In August 1994, the Youth Handgun Safety Act (Title XI, Subtitle B) (P.L. 103 322) was passed as part of the Omnibus Violent Crime Control and Law Enforcement Act. It prohibits the possession, sale, or transfer of a handgun or ammunition to a juvenile. The law includes a number of exceptions, such as farming, hunting, and other specified uses. The Gun-Free Schools Act (P.L. 103 382) (GFSA), enacted in October 1994, requires that local educational agencies implement a policy "requiring referral to the criminal justice or juvenile delinquency system of any student who brings a firearm or weapon to a school served by such an agency." Under the Gun-Free Schools Act, each state receiving assistance under the Elementary and Secondary Education Act (ESEA) must have a law requiring that any student who brings a firearm to school be expelled from school for a period of not less than one year. The local chief administering officer may modify the expulsion requirement on a case-by-case basis.

Even though reducing youth gun violence is a federal priority, the primary responsibility is on the state and local level. The federal role must be to encourage and assist communities by providing support based on sound information gathered nationally on effective approaches to intervention and prevention.[19]

Action Steps for Schools

Some of the ways in which schools can ensure safety and discipline are:

- Establish a team of educators, students, parents, law enforcement and juvenile justice officials, and community and business leaders to develop a plan for creating a safe, disciplined, gun- and drug-free school.
- Develop a Safe School Plan based upon an examination of problems and resources and a review of strategies that work.
- Ensure that students are engaged in school work that is challenging, informative, and rewarding. When students are fully engaged and absorbed, they are less prone to violence and less likely to be disruptive.
- Work with law enforcement's and juvenile justice agencies' support in reporting violations of weapons policies as well as other delinquent or criminal behavior.
- Take immediate action on all reports of drug use or sales, threats, bullying, gang activity, or victimization. Anyone caught bringing a gun to school should be reported immediately to the appropriate law enforcement agency.
- Create an environment that encourages parents and other adults to visit the school and participate in the schools' activities. Develop a sense of community within the school.
- Encourage staff to treat each other with respect and to act as good role models.
- Encourage community members to support schools in their community and to participate in school programs and services that promote the safety of students and all school staff.
- Work with community groups and law enforcement officials to keep schools open after normal operating hours so that students and their families have places where they can engage in productive, well-supervised, and safe activities. Help create safe corridors to and from school.
- Involve youth in program and policy development.

- Offer programs that teach peaceful, nonviolent methods for managing conflict to students and their families, as well as to staff.
- Work with the media to make the public aware of the crime and safety issues that confront the schools. Provide accurate assessment of school crime and violence to the public.
- Learn about effective practices based on research and proven programs used in other districts. Share the knowledge.
- Monitor implementation and progress of the Safe School Plan, making improvements based on what is learned as well as on new developments in the field.[20]

INSTRUCTION AND DISCIPLINE FOR THE EXCEPTIONAL EDUCATION STUDENT

With inclusion in school, regular teachers for the first time are being exposed to behaviors formerly dealt with exclusively by special education teachers. Early in this chapter the authors discussed a number of topics relating to the inclusion process.

Teaching students with disabilities, one still has the chief responsibility of promoting student achievement and dealing with classroom discipline whether those children are in isolated classrooms, mainstreamed, or part of an inclusion model.

There are some teaching practices for special education students that are critical to student learning.

1. In introducing a lesson alert students to key questions that need to be answered.
2. In presenting a lesson proceed in small steps at a fairly rapid pace, signal transition between main points in the lesson, and ask higher order, challenging questions.
3. Set high standards for student participation, redirect student questions back to the group, and encourage peer interaction and cooperation.
4. Provide accurate and rapid corrective feedback on homework assignments, reteach when necessary, and test frequently using a variety of evaluation strategies, particularly alternative assessments.[21]

Curbing School Violence

Discipline problems often are blamed on special education students, but current records show that the majority of students involved in violent acts are not special education students. However, there is some question as to whether or not these students may be eligible for seriously emotionally disturbed (SED) services.

To curb school violence, schools need to offer a full continuum of services. Violent students are more likely to erupt in inclusive or crowded classes where they may not receive a structured setting or individualized curriculum. Behavior management training is vital for all adults in a school, and parents, schools, and the community must work together to enact programs to meet the multiple needs of violent students.[22]

Though records show that most students who are violent are not special education students, experts disagree as to whether or not violent students (who may be classified as socially maladjusted) should be identified as emotionally disturbed. In some districts, students identified as socially maladjusted do not qualify for special education services. Where some schools shy away from identifying students who are emotionally disturbed because they feel it carries a stigma, other schools are quick to identify students in SED, saddling them with a label that follows them for their entire educational career.

Violent behavior in children touches all economic statuses. Because of the breakdown of the family, lack of community support systems, and economic necessity (both parents working), by middle school, some children are raising themselves. This can often lead to problems of disrespect, noncompliance and truancy.

A variety of classroom management skills are needed by teachers to help students change behaviors. They include:

1. Making sure students are physically comfortable.
2. Having the curriculum at an appropriate age level.
3. Teaching problem-solving skills so that students can apply a conflict resolution process to problems that occur in academic and social education.
4. Developing proper consequences for the behavior a teacher wants to change.
5. Giving students more positive than negative feedback.
6. Making sure that students can achieve the goals set by the teacher and themselves.[23]

A Guide to Safe Schools

Most schools are safe. Fewer than one percent of all violent deaths of children occur on school grounds. A child is far more likely to be killed in the community or at home, but no school is immune as we saw with the school shootings across America in the late 1990s.

There are early warning signals related to violence and discipline problems. Some of those signs may or may not indicate a serious problem. They don't necessarily mean that a child is prone to violence toward self or others.

Educators and families can increase their ability to recognize early warning signs by establishing close, caring and supportive relationships with children and youth.

We know from research that most children who become violent toward self or others feel rejected and psychologically victimized. The Columbine shootings in 1999 illustrate this point.

The following warning signs are presented with two qualifications. They are not equally significant, and they are not presented in order of seriousness. The signs might include:

1. Social withdrawal
2. Excessive feelings of rejection
3. Excessive feelings of isolation and being alone
4. Being a victim of violence
5. Feelings of being picked on and persecuted
6. Low school interest and poor academic performance
7. Expression of violence in writings and drawings
8. Uncontrolled anger
9. Patterns of impulsive and chronic hitting, intimidating, and bullying behavior
10. History of discipline problems
11. Past history of violent and aggressive behavior
12. Intolerance for differences and prejudicial attitudes
13. Drug use and alcohol use
14. Affiliation with gangs
15. Inappropriate access to, possession of, and use of firearms
16. Serious threats of violence[24]

School Uniforms

School uniforms have been touted by many, including President Clinton, as an effective way to reduce discipline problems in schools. Although initial claims of districts, such as Long Beach in 1998 and 99, that uniforms dramatically reduced discipline problems were impressive, later studies indicated that uniforms alone without other effective discipline measures would not do the job. School districts wanting to target particular clothing of students, such as that which is gang-related or offensive, have often gone to a single uniform requirement. Legal challenges still are being made to across-the-board district mandates on uniforms.

Dealing with Racial and Ethnic Tension

There are a number of steps to take toward restoring order when racial or ethnic tension erupts among students in school. First, respond immediately when harassment occurs among two or three students to avoid further escalation and before it triggers dangerous events such as stabbings or shootings. Second, anticipate escalation, especially if the community has a history of racial or ethnic hostilities, or if the school hasn't dealt with incidents in the past adequately. Third, acknowledge when the problem is racial or ethnic and begin working toward a resolution. Fourth, follow school policies already formulated for dealing with perpetrators and supporting victims. Last, investigate and question participants and observers and get support from community agencies. It is important to know and execute state laws and local school board policies. Know how to call immediately, secure the school, calm the public, and counsel the children and handle the crisis with integrity.

Conclusion

Violence in schools has increased in recent years for a variety of reasons, from abusive parents to poverty to exposure to violence in the media. Many prevention techniques have been tried through various programs in schools, such as peer mediation and social skill training, with varying degrees of effectiveness. It seems that a combination of good prevention lessons combined with strict and consistent consequences involving everyone in the school setting and involved parents are the most effective ways to decrease incidents of school violence. Violence in schools is definitely an issue in the news and on the lips of parents and educators. Children need to feel safe in schools and in traveling to and from school. This is a continuing obligation of the modern middle school. [25]

MULTICULTURALISM

The population of American schools is becoming increasingly multicultural. Since the early 1980s, the majority of students in public, inner city schools have been African-American and Hispanic.[26] Entering the new century, about 45 percent of students in American schools are non-Caucasian. In large school districts and large states, such as California, New York, Texas, and Florida, there is or soon will be no majority group of students in public schools. Unfortunately, only 13 percent of all teachers are nonwhite. Implications are many. For instance, studies have indicated that teachers tend to interact with, call on, praise, and intellectually challenge white (particularly male) students more than African-American or Hispanic students. Also, minority students' contributions to class discussions receive less attention when compared with those of majority students. A concern of many minority parents is that Euro-American teachers will not reflectively and critically question the social, political, historical, or cultural tradition of their own educational experience and thereby replay the hidden curriculum taught to them—one which includes messages about individual students (for instance, portraying Mexican-Americans as farm workers). Hispanics or Latinos represent the largest proportion of undereducated individuals of any group in America—one half of Hispanic-origin adults have less than a high school education.[27]

Building Multicultural Perspective Into the Curriculum

Even though educators may believe in the need to create partnerships with parents, if the educational process is to be successful, efforts to involve minority parents, especially Latino parents, pose challenges for many schools. Many mainstream teachers working in linguistically and culturally diverse classrooms do not know the languages of students, nor do they know much about the culture of the parents. Tapping into the funds of knowledge of parents in the community will not only provide a legitimate way to involve parents, but also will broaden the multicultural content of the curriculum.

One strategy that works is for teachers to have their students carry out oral history projects for which parents and other members of the community integrate their knowledge into the social studies curriculum of the school. Oral history is defined simply as the recollections and reminiscences of living people about the past. It is a historical inquiry that is undertaken by interviewing the individuals about events they had experienced. It is a "living history" of different cultures. It also does much to build the self-concept of students sharing family history.[28]

Interdisciplinary units of instruction are also useful tools for building a multicultural perspective. Different countries can become topics for such units. For example, "Greek History" not only looks at early Greek civilization, but the art, music, food, and history of modern Greeks.

Effective teaching and continuous reflection mediated by culture serve as the foundation for construction of a culturally responsive curriculum. Culturally responsive teachers give attention to the needs and cultural experiences of the students they teach. They value students' personal cultural knowledge and use their students' prior knowledge and culture in teaching. Teachers use a variety of instructional techniques such as the use of student ideas, frequent feedback, demonstrations, summarizing, and reinforcing. Finally, they link with parents as they plan, deliver and evaluate instruction.

THE EMERGING ROLE OF PARENTS

As discussed in the previous section, parents of minority children are vital links in the success of their children in school. The same can be said for parents of all students. As students leave childhood and enter adolescence, the needs of and functions of parents change. Adolescence is often marked by bickering, disagreements, emotional tensions, and minor conflicts with parents over the everyday details of family life, such as doing chores, getting along with siblings, or doing homework.

The roles of the family established during childhood help to maintain a sense of equilibrium. During adolescence, teens often upset the equilibrium with demands for more freedom or material needs such as clothing. During this time teens are looking for a different kind of support from their family, and this is often a stressful time until a new system of equilibrium is established. The following are changes that can be expected in the family system: There will be a shift from the parents providing nurturing, protection, and socialization to the child, to providing support and direction for the teen. Teens look to parents for approval and guidance in forming standards, values, and educational or occupational goals. Acceptance, active understanding, and parental expressions of individuality and connectedness can help the teen to mature without feeling left out or alienated from his or her family.[29]

David Elkind, the great child development scholar reminds us that the "nuclear family (two parents, one working and one at home with children) has changed with new demographics. There are many more nontraditional families today. The post-modern family or permeable family has two parents working, single-parent families, adoptive families, remarried families, and so on. The permeable family is more fluid, more flexible, and obviously vulnerable to pressures from outside itself. It mirrors the openness, complexity, and diversity of our contemporary lifestyles."[30]

As we enter the new century, a shift from the permeable family to the vital family is occurring. Recent statistics show that young people are marrying later and having fewer children. They are trying in their own lives not to make the mistakes their parents made. They want relationships to work. They don't want to go through divorce. Growing numbers of women, particularly professional women, are opting to stay home while their children are young. These events bode well for the family.

In reviewing the literature on the influence of parent involvement in education, the authors have concluded that many researchers over-interpreted their findings. For instance, when variables other than parent involvement are included in a study, student ability and school climate have substantially stronger relationships with achievement than parent involvement. However, parent involvement appears to account for 10 percent to 20 percent of the variance of achievement, which is important. Based on a review of all the aspects of parents' involvement that have been studied, parents' expectations of their child's success in school consistently has the strongest relationship with achievement.[31]

REACHING OUT TO THE COMMUNITY

In 1998, Congress approved 40-million dollars in grants to support after school programs in legislation under Title X of Improving America's Schools Act, known as the 21st Century Learning Centers. In addition, districts, states, foundations and business partners have also funded after school programs.

Connecting with the community remains one of the primary goals of the modern middle school.

The evidence of need for after school programs can be found in statistics that show the most violent hour for juvenile crime is between 3 P.M. and 4 P.M. That is the time when children are home from school, but their parents are still at work. With changes in society, perhaps the schools' mandate to provide a safe environment does indeed extend beyond the last bell.

In the early part of the twentieth century, very few adolescents went on to high school. Most went directly into the workplace—in the factory, farm or mine. Young people were needed in the workforce of the day. Today the need for those young people in the workforce does not exist. Jobs are temporary, minimum-wage jobs and jobs with little future for monetary gain. From less than 10 percent of students finishing high school in 1900 to a national goal of 90 percent finishing in 2000, we have come full circle from the industrial age to a high-tech era demanding highly educated young people. The connection between school and work is no longer immediate. However a connection between school and community can be made on a different basis—that of a partnership in learning, both academic and social.

The extension of the school day beyond the last bell can occur when the school reaches out to the community in full partnership, where school buildings, city buildings (such as libraries and recreation centers), government, and private agencies are joined together with one purpose—to nurture and support young people as they grow into adulthood.

Schools can create programs that respond to the unique needs of middle-grade students and their families. Families can engage middle-grade students in active decision making. In Fort Worth, Texas for example, the Vital Link Program places sixth graders in more than 140 businesses for several hours each morning during a one-week internship. The goal is for the students to understand career opportunities in a variety of fields through hands-on experience.

Schools can also provide professional development on promising practices and family involvement programs and empower front line workers to make key decisions that connect middle graders' families with needed services. For example, the Kentucky Education Reform Act mandates youth service centers in middle schools serving economically disadvantaged students. A wide range of services are available through local agencies there.

The *Boston Globe,* in a story written in September 1998, announced that the number of after school programs in Massachusetts had surged to 726 programs, a growth of 44 percent in four years.

There are many other examples of positive connections between school and community. Community District 3 in New York City provides families with home learning kits that reinforce instruction, and the Parent Center staff in Natchez, Mississippi, demonstrates materials and activities that families can use to work with their children at home. Finally, Project REACH at Beck Middle School in Georgetown, South Carolina, uses community members as instructional resources. Listings of such programs are available in ERIC microfiche collections in more than 900 locations worldwide and can be ordered through EDRS: 800–443–ERIC.

SUMMARY

Successfully implementing the full service middle school requires that its goals and purposes be clearly understood by students, teachers, parents, and the supporting community. A strong message in this chapter is that today's society requires much more of our schools than an 8:30-to-3:30 day. The full service school is now the rule rather than the exception with various ranges of services provided by those schools.

A common ingredient of the full service school is providing the most appropriate and least restricted learning opportunities for all students, particularly those with handicaps. A substantial portion of the chapter deals with the Individuals With Disabilities Act (IDEA). Rules, terms, and examples of student characteristics of students with handicaps are presented in the chapter. Inclusion is also dealt with in detail in the chapter.

Included also in Chapter Seven are examples of promising programs in the full service middle school including character education, social and emotional learning programs, programs for the gifted, and conflict resolution including peer mediation.

A major goal of the modern middle school is to create a safe and drug free school. Examples of successful programs to accomplish that goal are dealt with extensively in the chapter.

As the population of America's schools becomes increasingly muticultural, a prime responsibility of the modern middle school is to include strategies that build a multicultural perspective in the curriculum. Strategies are included in the chapter.

Finally, the important roles of parents, family, and community are stressed throughout the chapter. Parents are vital links in the success of their children in school.

The roles of the family established during childhood change dramatically for youngsters as they emerge from childhood to adolescence. The new American family is also much different than before, and that requires a new kind of outreach for American middle schools. Examples of such outreach programs are presented throughout the chapter and in detail in the last section.

Suggested Learning Activities

1. Write a handbook for students and parents outlining the goals and purposes of the full service middle school.

2. Survey the community to identify all the programs available to middle school students.

3. Conduct a needs assessment for your faculty on the types of discipline programs they feel would be successful for middle school students.

4. Organize a panel discussion of parents, students, and teachers to discuss the pros and cons of school uniforms.

5. Develop an outreach program for your school to get better involvement of parents, community, and private agencies involved in the learning program.

Notes

1. Brenda Williams and Antonis Katsiyanris, "The 1997 IDEA Amendments: Implications for School Principals," *NASSP Bulletin,* January 1998, pp. 12–18.
2. Mitchell Yell, "The Legal Basis of Inclusion," *Educational Leadership,* October 1998, pp. 70–73.
3. National Information Center for Children with Disabilities (Washington, DC: (NICHCY) 2000) http://www.nichy.org
4. Curry School of Education, "Learning Disabilities," http://curry.edschool.virginia.Edu/Curry/dept/cise/category/id.html
5. *NICHCY News Digest,* Interim Update, January 2000.
6. Yell, "Legal Basis for Inclusion."
7. Curry School of Education, "Reading Comprehension," http://curry.edschool.virginia
8. Michael Coutinho. *Inclusion: The Integration of Students with Disabilities.* California: Wadsworth, 1995.
9. J. Smith. *Inclusion: Schools for All Students.* California: Wadsworth, 1998.
10. Character Education Partnership, Washington, DC, 2000.
11. Tools for Building Character, http://www.infowest.com/sites/w.washcoed/bloomingtonh/tbc.html
12. Ibid.
13. Maurice Ellias, et al. "How to Launch a Social and Emotional Learning Program," *Educational Leadership,* May 1997, pp. 15–19.
14. Daniel Goldman, *Emotional Intelligence* (New York: Bantam Books, 1995).
15. Joseph Renzulli, "A Rising Tide Lifts All Ships—Developing the Gifts and Talents of All Students," *Kappan,* October 1998, pp. 105–111.
16. "Creating Safe and Drug-Free Schools—An Action Guide," http://www.ed.gov./offices/OESE/SDFS/actguide/intrhtml
17. Ibid.
18. U.S. Department of Justice, "Juveniles and Violence," *Fact Sheets* (1995–2000). Washington, DC.
19. Ibid.
20. Ibid.
21. Melanie Sikorski, Richard Niemiec, and Herbert Walberg, "A Classroom Checkup—Best Teaching Practices in Special Education," *Teaching Exceptional Children,* 10 September 1996, pp. 27–29.
22. Council of Exceptional Children (CEC)—Special Focus—"The Discipline Problem—And Ways to Deal With It," http://www.cec.sped.org/bk/focus/1906.htm.2000
23. Ibid.
24. "Early Warning Signals, Timely Response—A Guide to Safe Schools," http://www.mir.org/cecp/guide/files/4.htm.2000
25. Joan Curcio and Patricia First, *Violence in Schools, How to Proactively Prevent and Defuse It* (Menlo Park, CA: Corwein Press, 1993).
26. U.S. Department of Education National Center for Educational Statistics, 2000.
27. U.S. Department of Education National Center for Educational Statistics, 2000.
28. Irma Olmedo, "Family Oral Histories for Multicultural Curriculum Perspectives," *Urban Education,* 32 1 (March 1997): pp. 45–62.
29. http://www.parentsplace.com/readroom/authors/Dell/except.html, 2000
30. Marge Scherer, "On Our Changing Family Values: A Conversation with David Elkind," *Educational Leadership,* 53 7 (April 1996).
31. Ron Thorkildsen and Melanie Stein, "Is Parent Involvement Related to Student Achievement? Exploring the Evidence," *Kappan Research Bulletin,* 22 (December 1998): 17–20.

C H A P T E R

8

Designing the New American Middle School

The future of tomorrow's society can be found in today's middle school youth.

Americans have always searched for the perfect school: an environment that is nurturing, yet fosters independence; allows for the natural mistakes of learning, yet encourages academic excellence; provides guidance on appropriate behaviors and personal choice, yet does not assume a parental role; and in the process, produces a potential workforce of highly skilled, motivated workers with the ability to solve problems creatively, work independently or as a part of a team, and maintain America's leadership in the global economy. A tall order? Absolutely! Yet we must keep trying!

The 1997 National Commission on Teaching and America's Future report, "What matters most: Teaching for America's Future," asked that the nation get serious about standards for reinventing teacher professional development as a means to that end.[1]

In addition, the Goals 2000 developed in 1994 (listed below) are very explicit about the need for a better educated youth in America.

GOALS 2000

1. **School Readiness:** By the year 200, all children will start school ready to learn.

2. **School Completion:** By the year 2000, the high school graduate rate will increase to at least 90 percent.

3. **Student Achievement and Citizenship:** By the year 2000, all students will leave fourth, eighth, and twelfth grade having demonstrated competency over challenging subject matter including English, mathematics, science, foreign languages, civics and government, economics, arts, history, and geography, and every school in America will ensure that all students learn to use their minds well, so they may be prepared for responsible citizenship, further learning, and productive employment in our nation's modern economy.

4. **Teacher Education and Professional Development:** By the year 2000, the nation's teaching force will have access to programs for the continued improvement of their professional skills and the opportunity to acquire the knowledge and skills needed to instruct and prepare all American students for the next century.

5. **Mathematics and Science:** By the year 2000, United States students will be first in the world in mathematics and science achievement.

6. **Adult Literacy and Lifelong Learning:** By the year 2000, every adult American will be literate and will possess the knowledge and skills necessary to compete in a global economy and exercise the rights and responsibilities of citizenship.

7. **Safe, Disciplined, and Alcohol- and Drug-Free Schools:** By the year 2000, every school in the United States will be free of drugs, violence, and the unauthorized presence of firearms and alcohol and will offer a disciplined environment conducive to learning.

8. **Parental Participation:** By the year 2000, every school will promote partnerships that will increase parental involvement and participation in promoting the social, emotional, and academic growth of children. The full text of these goals may be found at <http://www.edgov/legislation/Goals>.

REALIZING THE PROMISES OF STANDARDS-BASED EDUCATION

The Standards movement became a major force in the last decade of the twentieth century. As well as national standards, mainly developed in content areas, states and districts across the United States have developed standards for student learning that describe what students should know and be able to do as a result of their schooling. The standards are intended to provide educators with the guidelines for curriculum and teaching that will ensure that all students will be successful in the highly technical and global society. But questions remain as to how standards are shaped, whether they will support more ambitious teaching and greater success levels for students or create higher rates of failure.[2]

Florida is a state which jumped on the accountability bandwagon early. In 1991, the Florida Legislature committed itself and the state to long-term systematic change with the *Blueprint 2000 Act.* The act created the Florida Commission on Educational Reform and Accountability. In 1995, the State Board of Education developed criteria for critically low performing schools based on student scores in reading and writing on nationally normed tests and in writing on a new Florida writing test, "Florida Writes!"

School Improvement plans were mandated for low achieving schools and Department of Education assistance provided those schools.

In 1996, the state had developed its own tests in reading and mathematics, "The Florida Comprehensive Assessment Test (FCAT) to go with the Florida Writes! examination. Students were tested in fourth, eighth, and tenth grades.

By 1999, the state not only began grading schools A–F, but expanded FCAT testing to other grades and allowed parents of "F" schools with vouchers to remove their children from those schools.* Under the legislation, students did not have to return even if the school later became an "A" school. Standards for schools passing were also raised.

During the period of 1995 to 2000, Florida also developed the *Florida Sunshine Standards* with benchmarks spelled out at grade levels in reading, writing, and mathematics. Grade level tests followed with tests expanded to other content areas.

The reader can update himself or herself on Florida's accountability efforts by accessing the DOE home page http://www.firn.edu/doe. Additional information can be found at the School Improvement Knowledge Network http://www.state.fl.us/sac.

---

*A district court has found the voucher program to be unconstitutional. An appeal is planned by the state of Florida.

FIGURE 8.1   Pick a Number

If there were a test on education statistics, Florida's graduate rate would be a multiple choice question and the correct answer would be "all of the above." The rate ranges from 95 percent to 52 percent depending on how it is calculated. Below is a sampling of graduation rates as calculated by the federal government and the state.

95.7%	Based on high school seniors only, it means better than nine of ten high school seniors actually graduate. This rate is found in the Florida Department of Education's School Indicators Report.
80.1%	The U.S. Department of Education's "completion rate" is taken from census data, and shows the percentage of 18- through 24-year olds who said they completed high school.
73.2%	Divides the number of graduates by the number of ninth graders four years earlier. Does not account for students who transfer, so it could result in rates in excess of 100 percent. Does not account for students who withdrew for home schooling or students who die after ninth grade. This is Florida's current method for calculating graduates.
65.3%	Based on a system tracking individual students over four years. This "cohort graduate rate" accounts for students who transfer out or withdraw to attend private school or for home education. Does not include graduates who get certificates of completion rather than standard diplomas.
57.8%	The official federal graduation rate, this differs from Florida's current method in that it does not include students who get a GED.
52.2%	Tracks individual students over four years. This "adjusted cohort rate" adjusts for new students transferring into a school after ninth grade.

Source: Tampa Tribune and Jacksonville Times-Union.

It is interesting, though, that Florida is a state that has a tough time determining its graduation rate. In 1999, the *Tampa Tribune* and the *Jacksonville Times-Union* printed the data in Figure 8.1.

More Is Not Better in Standards Documents

In reviewing official documents generated by the 50 states and professional subject-area organizations, one is struck by the sheer volume of the documents. Some of them are not only written in language that no one understands, but contain such quality that it would take a 10-hour teaching day to cover the material in them.[3]

"Less is more" according to many educators. Students learn more when we teach less—but teach it well.[4]

If standards are bloated or poorly written, no one will realistically teach or even hope to adequately assess them. As with curriculum documents in the middle part of the twentieth century that attempted to be all things to all people, we made the same mistake with standards documents at the end of that century.

In the case of standards, more is not better. Quantity does not necessarily mean quality. One might learn from the statements of the Third International Mathematics and Science Study (TIMSS) that pointed out U.S. mathematics textbooks attempted to address 175 percent more topics than German textbooks and 350 percent more topics than Japanese textbooks. Yet both German and Japanese students significantly outperformed the United States in mathematics. The same was true in science in which U.S. science books attempted to cover 930 percent more than German texts and 433 percent more than Japanese texts. Again, both German and Japanese students significantly outperformed American students in science. Critics of U.S. standards have described them as "a mile wide and an inch deep."

Clearly, U.S. schools can benefit from decreasing the amount of content covered and teach that content in greater depth. Teacher morale and self-efficiency would certainly improve.

Finally, simply stating that all students should perform task *m* at level *t* won't accomplish anything without proper instruction and assessment.

Aligning Assessment with Standards

Schools that must meet standards can benefit if they start with standards that can be assessed. If schools focus teaching on standards actually contained in current state norm-referenced or criterion-referenced assessment, they can be more efficient. Many existing state standards will never be assessed.

State and standardized tests don't always measure what teachers believe is important, yet they remain yardsticks for how teachers and schools are measured in this era of accountability.

Assessment is simply the process of gathering, describing, or quantifying information about performance.

There are six steps for designing assessments:

1. Clearly state the purpose for the assessment, and do not expect the assessment to meet purposes for which it was not designed.
2. Clearly define what it is you want to assess.
3. Match the assessment method to the achievement purpose and target.
4. Specify illustrative tasks that require students to demonstrate certain skills and accomplishments.
5. Specify the criteria and standards for judging students' performance on the task selected.
6. Develop a reliable rating process that allows different raters at different points in time to obtain the same results, or allows a single teacher in a classroom to assess each student using the same criteria.[5]

Samples of Assessment Activities Around the United States

In addition to the Florida samples stated earlier, other states also have state assessment programs. Samples are listed below:

Oklahoma
ITBS (Iowa Test of Basic Skills)
Administered to third and seventh grade students

PASS (Priority Academic Student Skills)
(Oklahoma Core Curriculum Tests)
Administered to fifth and eighth graders in mathematics,
science, reading, history, and writing.

Idaho
Idaho Direct Writing Assessment
Administered to fourth and eighth grade students
Idaho Direct Mathematics Assessment
Administered to fourth and eighth graders

Maryland
MSPAP (Maryland School Performance Assessment Program)
Administered to third, fifth, and eighth graders in reading,
writing, language usage, mathematics, social studies,
and science
CDTBS5 (California Test of Basic Skills)
Administered to second, fourth, sixth, and eighth graders in
reading, language, and mathematics

New York
CTBS (California Test of Basic Skills)
Administered to first through eighth graders
Test of Cognitive Skills
Administered to second through eighth graders
PEP (New York State Pupil Evaluation Program)
Administered to third and sixth graders in reading
and math
Administered to fifth graders in writing
PET (Program Evaluation Test)
Administered to fourth graders in science
Administered to fifth graders in writing

Colorado
CSAP (Colorado Student Assessment Program)
Administered to third graders in reading
Administered to fourth graders in reading and writing
Administered to fifth graders in mathematics

North Carolina
EOG (End of Grade Tests)
Administered to third graders in reading and math
Administered to fourth graders in reading, math, narrative
writing, and open-ended questions in reading and math
ITBS (Iowa Test of Basic Skills)
Administered to fifth graders

Texas
TAAS (Texas Assessment of Academic Skills)
Administered to fourth and eighth graders in writing

Administered to third, fourth, fifth, sixth, seventh, and eighth
　　graders in reading and mathematics
Administered to seventh graders in social studies and science
Vermont
Student Portfolios in Writing and Mathematics
Maintained by fourth, fifth, and eighth graders
Standards-Based Standardized Tests in Reading, English, and Mathematics
Administered to second, fourth, and eighth graders

ASSESSMENT COMES IN MANY FORMS

Assessment is a widely diverse word. Assessment comes in many shapes, forms,
sizes, and languages. Within today's schools, the key issue with assessment is to
find the right method by which we can effectively evaluate children. Students
learn through many different modalities, so should they be evaluated in a manner that supports their strengths and indicates weaknesses? Assessment is an issue in today's schools that allows for many responses.
　　The following is a collage of the many variations in assessment form:

**Teacher-made assessments designed by one teacher or a group of
teachers.** Teacher-made assessments are likely to reflect what was actually
taught to a greater degree than tests aimed at a wider audience or broader
range of control. Teachers are the primary source of custom-made
assessments because they know the learning outcomes or objectives, the
instructional plan, and their students' needs better than anyone.
Observations. Observation is used as a methods of assessment when
actions speak louder than words. In observation assessment, teachers
gather data not by asking for information, but by watching closely. The
students simply perform by action. Observation is commonly a
diagnostic decision made about individual students, their strengths,
weaknesses, and needs.
Assessments by commercial test publishers. These go hand-in-hand
with math, reading, science, social studies, and English programs.
Standardized tests through publishers are often provided as a quick
convenience to teachers after certain material is taught. These are
based on measurement-driven information. Commonly these
assessments take the form of true/false, multiple choice, or matching
questions.
State-produced assessments like Florida's. The writing test is an
example of this assessment form. The student's ability to write, assessed
at three different points result as an indicator of the effectiveness of the
teacher, the student's ability, and the Florida Writing Objectives program
itself.

Alternative assessments. These require students to actively construct meaning rather than passively regurgitate isolated facts.

Authentic assessments. These permit pupils to show what they can do in a real situation. Another name for authentic assessments are "performance-based assessments."

Performance-based assessments. These are assessments in which pupils carry out an activity or produce a product to demonstrate their knowledge and skill.

Demonstrations. These might take the form of a math tournament, individual science experiment, or collaborative group project.

Portfolios. Portfolios are purposeful, systematic, well-organized collections of student materials. Students add to and subtract from their material within the portfolio based on a continual evaluation of self-improvement. Progress is based on evaluation of documents within the portfolio.

Exhibitions. These can be musical performances, dramatic presentations, or spelling contests. These are examples of authentic or performance-based assessments.

Essays, classroom oral presentations, and journal writing. These are more examples of alternative assessments.

There is a growing consensus that new assessments are needed to measure a broader range of abilities and to give teachers and schools better information about student progress and achievement. Many educators are developing assessments that engage students in real-world tasks rather than in multiple-choice exercises and that evaluate them according to standards and criteria that are important for actual performance in a given field. These assessments use a broad range of performance, including essay examinations, oral presentations, collections of written products, solutions to problems, records of experiments, debates, and research projects by individuals and groups. They also include teacher observations and inventories of students' work and learning.

Many teachers who have pioneered the use of performance assessments confirm that such assessments provide information critical to responsive teaching: information about how students think, what they understand, and the strategies they use in learning.

Performance assessments create a comprehensive picture of what students know and can do, demonstrate their progress, and indicate areas of learning that need attention. When schools provide this kind of information to teachers, students, and their families, they are being accountable for their work in ways that support the attainment of high standards.

Hammond (1997) suggests that academic success for a greater range of students will be facilitated by initiatives that:

- Encourage the use of teaching strategies and practices that create bridges between students' diverse abilities, language, backgrounds, and experiences and common curriculum goals;

- Use standards and authentic assessments as indicators of progress for improved teaching, not as a gateway to grade transition;
- Encourage the design of grouping structures that create extended, intensive teacher–student relationships;
- Provide teachers with professional learning opportunities that build their capacity to teach in ways that reflect contemporary understanding of learning, to use sophisticated assessments to inform teaching, and to meet differing needs; and
- Develop strategies for accountability that examine the appropriateness and adequacy of students' learning opportunities and create levers and supports for school change.[6]

Culturally Sensitive Assessment Programs

Imagine an assessment system in which teachers have a wide repertoire of classroom-based, culturally sensitive assessment practices and tools to use in helping each and every child learn to high standards, in which educators collaboratively use assessment information to continuously improve schools; in which important decisions about a student, such as readiness to graduate from high school, are based on the work done over the years by the student; in which schools in networks hold one another accountable for student learning; and in which public evidence of student achievement consists primarily of samples from students' actual schoolwork rather than just reports of results from one-shot examinations.

However, these ideas are at the core of *Principles and Indicators for Student Assessment Systems, 1997,* developed by the National Forum on Assessment and signed by more than eighty national and local education and civil rights organizations.

The seven principles endorsed by the Forum are:

1. The primary purpose of assessment is to improve student learning.
2. Assessment for other purposes supports student learning.
3. Assessment systems are fair to all students.
4. Professional collaboration and development support assessment.
5. The broad community participates in assessment development.
6. Communication about assessment is regular and clear.
7. Assessment systems are regularly reviewed and improved.

Assessment to enhance student learning must be integrated with, not separate from, curriculum and instruction.[7]

STANDARDS GUIDE IMPROVEMENT OF TEACHING

As stated earlier, the 1997 National Commission on Teaching and America's Future stressed standards for improving teaching. With national, state, and local standards making their way into classrooms, school officials are belatedly recognizing that the rise or fall of standards-based reform depends on the quality of professional development that surrounds its implementation.[8] Policymakers understand that it is unrealistic to expect that teachers on their own will somehow be able to make sense of the numerous national and state standards without unprecedented amounts of support.

Linda Darling-Hammond, executive director of the National Commission on Teaching and America's Future points out that educators are facing greater challenges than ever before. Not only are schools being asked to help students meet higher academic standards, but they are expected to meet the wide-ranging needs of the most diverse group of learners ever educated in public schools of any nation. The new basics demanded by the knowledge that society requires all students to have, rather than that previously reserved for only the talented top tenth include:

- To understand and use complex materials
- To communicate clearly and persuasively
- To plan and organize work
- To access and use resources
- To solve sophisticated mathematical and scientific problems
- To create new ideas and products
- To use new technologies in all of these pursuits.[9]

Researchers have expressed serious concerns about the academic ability of teachers since the 1920s, pointing out that those college students who major in education have consistently earned lower scores on standardized tests than their college peers.

Another concern more recently has been the growing demand for teachers and the gender and ethnic homogeneity of the teacher workforce. In 1999, nine out of 10 public school teachers were white and three in four were female.

With increased student standards have come increased teacher standards and standardized teacher tests. Minority candidates have traditionally scored lower than their white peers on such tests. This leads to fears that testing teachers will deny a disproportionate number of minority candidates access to the profession. Some view this as a choice between higher standards for teachers or increased supply and diversity of teachers.[10]

From 1995 to 1997, Educational Testing Service (ETS) and ACT undertook a research study that examined the profile of those seeking a teaching license. That study confirmed that the teaching profession will be largely white and that white women will constitute a majority of the teaching profession at the beginning of the twenty-first century. It also suggested that the pool of candidates applying to colleges of education does not reflect the diversity of the kindergarten through twelfth grade student population.

When SAT scores were compared of students entering the college of education, those students' scores averaged 485 verbal and 479 mathematics. This compared with 505 verbal and 511 mathematics for all students.

On teacher tests, 82 percent of white students had passing scores while 46 percent of African-American candidates passed with Asian and Hispanic passing marks falling in between. In recent years, the gap between white and Hispanic candidates has widened while the gap between white and African-American passing has narrowed.

Professional Development for Principals

Programs in school leadership abound. However, many of those programs consist of workshops which assume that principals' effectiveness will improve more or less automatically as a result of their attendance at the programs/workshops.

If principals are indeed to make a genuine difference in schools, principals will need the leadership skills that will help students and teachers achieve the high standards expected in today's modern society.

The Annenberg Institute for School Reform has focused on improving professional development for principals. Its work centers on seven core beliefs:

1. Principals' learning is personal and yet takes place most effectively while working in groups.
2. Principals foster more powerful faculty and student learning by focusing on their own learning.
3. While we honor principals' thinking and voices, we want to push principals to move beyond their assumptions.
4. Focused reflection takes time away from administrative work, and yet it is essential.
5. It takes strong leadership to have truly democratic learning.
6. Rigorous planning is necessary for flexible and responsive implementation.
7. New learning depends on protective dissonance.[11]

At the core of school reform is the teacher whose knowledge and skill can tip the balance in favor of improved student achievement. The same holds true for the school principal.

Standards are about providing a way for all students to access quality education; they are also about principals working with teachers to develop a standards-aligned curriculum to ensure that students learn more and teachers teach more effectively.

Standards affect every level of the school system. Table 8.1 illustrates responsibilities of each component of a standards-driven school district, Broward County, Florida, the nation's fifth largest school district.

TABLE 8.1 Broward County Public Schools—What it Means to be a Standards-Driven System

A standards-driven system has identified content standards, performance, and an accountability system to insure that students and adults master these standards. When a standards-driven system is functioning effectively, all system components, accountability, standards of service for student achievement, standards of student services, and standards of professional development, are interrelated and focus on the mastery of standards. All stakeholder groups support the components at varying levels based on their identified roles and responsibilities.

Roles and Responsibilities

Students	Classroom Teachers	Principals
Understand standards	Know contents standards and core curriculum competencies at appropriate levels	Know content standards and core curriculum competencies at appropriate levels
Understand their gap in relation to mastery of standards	Diagnose student needs using data	Know appropriate strategies
Take responsibility for their own learning	Prescribe appropriate strategies to teach content standards, core curriculum competencies, and self assessment	Diagnose student and teacher needs based on data
Use technology to improve their own learning	Develop an instructional management plan that moves a diverse student population toward mastery, and integrate appropriate technologies	Analyze student data to determine mastery of student outcomes
Master content standards and core curriculum competencies at appropriate proficiency levels, as evidenced by scores on norms-referenced and criteria-referenced tests and other appropriate assessments	Assess for mastery	Allocate resources to support standards implementation
Work and learn collaboratively with others, including students and other people of varying age levels, and business and community partners	Integrate technology into the delivery of instruction and instructional management	Create an effective school culture focused on implementation of standards
Participate in and create a classroom environment in which they can learn and teachers can teach	Record and report student progress toward mastery	Develop an adult learning plan that organizes time, opportunity, and resources to provide job-embedded professional development
Make appropriate choices based on diploma requirements and Student Code of Conduct	Implement SOSS standards	Provide ongoing teacher feedback linked to assessment based on quality implementation
Self-assess progress toward mastery	Create learning climate that is safe, orderly and responsive to student needs	Form partnerships to enhance student mastery of standards
	Implement a personal professional development plan as an integral part of teacher work and determined through an individual needs assessment	Provide daily leadership, support, and oversight monitoring
	Demonstrate proficiency in knowledge and skills linked to increased student achievement and job performance	Ensure that instructional management plan and SIP move students toward mastery

Area-Based Administrators	Innovation Zones (Leadership Team)	Support Personnel School/Area/District
Know content standards and core curriculum competencies at appropriate levels	Develop a system to define a common commitment to rigorous performance outcomes, analyze and desegregate data, diagnose gaps, and formulate plans to address standards of service and increase achievement for all students pre-K through adult	Coordinate the development of rigorous standards and periodic revision
Analyze schools' progress toward standards	Create a learning community with a commitment to clearly defined standards and high expectations	Define mastery
Allocate resources to support standards implementation	Maintain a safe and orderly learning environment in which teachers can teach and students can learn	Communicate standards to all stakeholders
Create an effective area culture focused on implementation of standards	Develop school, parent, and community partnerships which support readiness to learn and provide enhanced learning opportunities	Align assessment with standards
Organize personnel to facilitate a coordinated, Zone-based support system	Establish the community initiatives for families concept of Level I, II, and III support of students and families through the Innovation Zones	Align results-driven staff development with standards
Participate in training on results-driven professional development	Establish effective leadership that develops ownership in Zone initiatives for all stakeholders and improves student achievement and school effectiveness	Align resources to support mastery of standards
Assist the schools in organizing time and resources to provide job-embedded professional development	Initiate and refine Innovation Zone strategic planning in order to establish a constancy of purpose and provide a quality education for all students, pre-K through adult	Use technology to provide data on achievement of standards and support instructional management
Provide daily leadership, support oversight and monitoring	Integrate technology to provide a seamless pre-K through adult learning process	Monitor the implementation of the standards-based curriculum
Monitor implementation of results-driven professional development		
Provide ongoing feedback linked to assessment based on quality implementation of standards		
Ensure that principals implement a standards-driven system through a direct link to professional development and evaluation		

Institutions of Higher Learning	Business/Community	Parents/Community	Superintendent
Know and understand the standards-driven system and the interrelated impact on all institution demands	Know and understand the standards-driven system and how it is applicable to education and real world problems	Know and understand the standards-driven system and how it is applicable to the education of their child(ren)	Set clear and rigorous expectations for a standards-driven system for all students and staff supported by a well-defined accountability system
Integrate the use of technology in all levels of training	Endorse students as meaningful outcomes	Provide home environment which supports student learning	Establish a focus on teaching and learning and a climate of accountability based on standards
Work in cooperation with the school district in the development of programs based on standards to educate, train, and retrain teachers, student support personnel, and school administrators	Provide work-based educational experiences for students as part of school to career	Engage in dialogue about teaching and learning	Recommend policies and performance standards: Standards of Practice, Standards of Service for Student Achievement, Standards of Student Services, Accountability, and Public Engagement
Commit resources to the educational partnership	Participate and communicate through appropriate structures, such as School Advisory Council, vocational and adult advisory boards, and systemic partnerships to assist the schools in implementing a standards-driven system	Collaborate with school personnel in mastery of standards for their child(ren)	Recommend budget allocation and manage resources to support standards-driven system
Provide interdisciplinary preservice consistent with standards of student services	Provide health and human services in or in close proximity to schools	Participate and communicate through appropriate structures, such as School Advisory Council, PTA, and parent conferences	Define critical shortage areas
Provide coursework that promotes integrated delivery of support services	Jointly plan and deliver health and human services through the Community Initiative for Families (CIF)		Effect change to support standards-driven system
Assign field-experience students to schools based on an agreement between partners to maximize teaching and learning	Provide release time for employees to volunteer or to participate in their child's education		Develop legislative program to recommend to the board and advocate on behalf of that program
Recruit underrepresented groups, and develop programs in critical shortage areas	Assist with the development of appropriate training		Engage the public and communicate standards-driven system to community at large
Collaborate in grant development and implementation	Provide work experiences for teachers		
Assess professional development needs of university students and develop a professional development plan			
Ensure teacher mastery of strong content knowledge and pedagogy			

School Board	Media	State/Federal
Adopt policies which support a standards-driven system	Know and understand school and district challenges and issues and their impact on the community	Define national and state goals and standards
Adopt performance standards and assessment policy for triad of standards	Communicate important information to the community concerning school and district challenges and accomplishments	Encourage and provide support for local educational agencies to implement standards
Organize system to provide Zone support	Work with school and district staff to obtain and communicate accurate information	Align federal and state programs to support student mastery of standards
Allocate resources to support a standards-driven system	Respect and abide by school and district policies and procedures which protect student and staff safety, welfare, and privacy	Provide resources and support for all mandates
Approve partnerships which enhance student mastery of standards	Report on local, state, and national educational issues on a regular and consistent basis	Require research-based pedagogy for instructional material adoption
Encourage institutions of higher learning to adopt policies to support standards	Teach and correlate educational information, trends, and challenges, and their relevancy to Broward County Public Schools and Broward County	Generate public support for challenging educational standards
Initiate legislation to support standards-driven system	Base reporting on accurate data, information, and impartial observation	Provide leadership on assessment issues by establishing performance standards
	Evaluate responding regularly based on the highest professional standards and community expectations	

IMPLICATIONS OF A STANDARDS-DRIVEN CURRICULUM

While advocates for mandated curriculum standards typically claim only potentially positive consequences, there are potential negative consequences as well. Some of those cited by critics of standards-driven curricula include:

1. The potential for restricted, even poor curricula based on standards even as most of the state standards advise that mandated curriculum standards should not constitute all of the emphasis for the specific curriculum.

2. The eroding of local control as states develop and mandate standards, often mirroring national standards.

3. Differences in grading styles of teachers as they implement standards.

4. Demands by some states to allow nonteachers and noneducators to be principals with the premise that any good executive can monitor implementation of standards.

5. The call to eliminate tenure of teachers and to base performance and incentives simply on tests results of students that teachers teach during the year.

6. The call to eliminate social promotion and mandate retention of students, which will increase the challenges to teachers having large numbers of over-age, disaffected students in their classes. Since many of the retainees will be in poverty areas, this will only increase the problems of those teachers.

7. With all students held to the same standards, those teachers in inner city schools will flee those schools leaving only inexperienced, and in many cases, uncertified teachers in those schools.

8. With Valued Added Assessment, in which teachers are given a grade on the increases of student scores, the potential for cheating by teachers increases. This potential will increase further as monetary incentives are provided for teachers who raise test scores (such as in 1999, California implemented a fifty-million-dollar bonus program for teachers with high test score increases).

9. Where states provide vouchers for students in poor achieving schools (such as in 1999, Florida provided funds for vouchers for students in "F" schools—a grade based on scores of students on state tests), public schooling may be in jeopardy.

CREATING A CARING COMMUNITY IN SCHOOLS

Results of national surveys have indicated that every generation coming of age since the 1950s has been less trusting than the previous one. Furthermore, the most distrustful members of our society are the youngest, those 10- to 23-years old.

We can look at the many reasons for such distrust—breakup of the family, mobility of our society, the influence of television, or the waning feeling of national solidarity after the conclusion of World War II. However, with school children, particularly pre- and early adolescents, schools must be caring communities where trust can be built. The caring community in a school has to include a partnership with parents and the larger community that houses the school.

Creating a school in which students want to be is a challenge in all schools. The modern American middle school must be such a school. What kind of school contributes to a positive climate and caring community?

1. A school that offers a sense of security and belonging
2. A school where students are seen as persons worthy of respect
3. A school that seeks to provide a safe environment for building student–teacher relationships
4. A school that has places for students to sit, relax, and enjoy the school
5. A school where students have a variety of options and choices for courses and activities
6. A school where the underlying norms for students and teachers are collegiality, improvement, and hard work
7. A school where success, joy, and humor abound
8. A school that reaches out and touches parents and other citizens in powerful, meaningful ways. "No cow ever gave milk because a farmer sent her a letter" is a comical but powerful message that means we can't promote parent and community involvement through bland mass mailings and lifeless meeting announcements.

Self-Esteem—A New Look

For decades, promoters of the self-esteem movement have asserted that low self-esteem is responsible for many of our students' social and academic problems. Their prescription was to give students heavy doses of praise and to assure them that they were special even if their performance was mediocre or poor.

It is true that people are more likely to succeed if they believe they will, and students are no exceptions. They also will wilt under heavy criticism. However, it is important that teachers point out students' mistakes so they can correct them and learn from them. Those are natural and important components of teaching and learning.

Clearly self-esteem can't be separated from achievement. If students are told they are doing well regardless of their performance, either they won't believe it or they will see no reason for doing the hard work necessary to learn. Students need to be helped to achieve in real ways, and that will give them a solid basis for self-esteem.

Although self-esteem enthusiasts would argue that violent people suffer from low esteem which is masked by their arrogance, there is no evidence linking low self-esteem and violent behavior, though many researchers have sought to make that connection.[12]

Furthermore, it doesn't make sense to assume that high but unfounded self-esteem is a mask for low self-esteem. When comparing scores of American versus Japanese and Chinese students in math, studies show American students achieved less. However, the Americans felt just fine about their performance and their self-esteem was very high.

With self-esteem as with many other movements in American education, supporters often insist that their claims are based on research. Parents and educators must address those claims by asking "what research?"

THE ROLE OF TECHNOLOGY IN THE NEW AMERICAN MIDDLE SCHOOL

It isn't the presence of computers in a school or classroom that makes a difference, it's what students and teachers do with them that counts.

Technology holds great potential for moving school reform forward, but to date, the research evidence of its impact on student achievement in general is sparse. One reason may be that conventional research methods, such as comparisons on studies of standardized test scores and report cards, may not be sensitive enough to detect the kinds of learning gains technology can afford, such as improved higher-order thinking skills, visual literacy, creativity, resourcefulness, sense of efficiency, or motivation for learning.[13]

Student Information

Student information systems now available allow schools to automate all the repetitive tasks performed by administrators on a day-by-day basis: entering attendance, recording discipline, enrolling new students, generating report cards and transcripts, and creating master and student timetables. Sensitive data are protected by multilevel password systems.

Comprehensive student and demographic information is stored on well-organized screens for quick entry and retrieval of information. Student files can include address information, contacts, health, transportation information, and photographs. Almost all data can be printed on custom reports and kept updated, and discipline trends can be recorded in each school.

Teachers are working out of electronic grade books for use on teacher desktops. Teachers can electronically record grades on individual assignments throughout the year. At the end of the term when grade cards are due, consolidated grades can be transferred to the school report.[14]

Internet Use

Schools are major stockholders in the effort to make Internet use safe and rewarding for students. Schools already teach children personal safety, fire safety, and bicycle safety. Students in the modern middle school also need to be taught Internet safety—and responsibility.

In attempting to block objectionable content, many schools have installed filtering software, but what has been learned is that no technology is fail-safe. Further, blocking may severely restrict desirable communications and information and face challenges on constitutional issues.

The abundance of commercial websites also poses a challenge for students on the Internet that creates a reaction where distinctions among information, advertising, entertainment, and promotion are blurred. In addition, there are Internet sites that collect personal information from students.

The near-total saturation of schools by Internet means that children are going online faster in classrooms than families are at home. Schools, then, must be responsible to ensure that children bring home a set of Internet-appropriate behaviors. Children lead other family members into computer use.

The Internet and Its Impact on School Libraries and Media Centers

The Internet is a wonderful source of information for research and projects, and it provides its user with access to libraries other than his or her own school's and many information databases.

Progress in incorporating the Internet into classes and libraries has been slow to this point. This is mainly due to a lack of awareness of the Internet's potential and importance as a current information tool.

When it is used for its potential, together librarians and teachers can develop online projects that will allow students to do research, develop their own projects on the Internet, use e-mail, and become more aware of the technology that is used today and will be the basis for technology in their future.

Technology and Other Training for Teachers Using the Internet

Schools typically begin the process of integrating new computer technology into their curricula by soliciting community input, securing the necessary funding, and then organizing a technology team to select hardware and a curriculum committee to select software. But all too often, principals soon discover new computers not in use in many classrooms. That's because so much technology planning concentrates on hardware and software instead of on staff development needed to make teachers knowledgeable and comfortable with computers.

For any technology implementation plan to be successful, it must allocate sufficient time and resources for a focused staff development program. Many schools are discovering that traditional models of staff development—particularly one-time inservice training for the entire family—are ineffective for teaching computer use and for helping teachers develop methods to use computers as instructional tools. Innovative staff development programs are needed to meet teachers' diverse and ever-changing technology needs.[15]

The Web itself offers a host of unique opportunities not only for teachers to become proficient in technology, but many other ways to engage in professional development. At the simplest level, teachers can participate in professional discussion through e-mail, or they can immerse themselves in the activities of a "virtual professional center." Examples of each possibility are discussed next.[16]

- Andy Carvins' EdWeb site bills itself as a "hyperbook" that focuses on educational reform and technology. Among its many components is a list of over 100 education-related "listservs." These topical, automated mailing lists facilitate the exchange of ideas and information to a large number of individuals with similar interests. Topics range from media and technology to early childhood education. The page includes basic information on how the lists operate and how to subscribe.

  http://edweb.gsn.org/lists.html

- EdWeb also offers an online tutorial for teachers who want to learn to create their own webpages. The tutorial covers design bases and includes HTML quizzes at the end of each lesson.

  http://edweb.gsn.org/thmlintro.html

- The American Association of School Librarians' ICON-nect site holds all sorts of resources to help teachers and their students learn the skills necessary "to navigate the Information Superhighway." Online courses include basic Internet skills, using search engines, and information literacy. The "Curriculum Connections" section includes "carefully selected and annotated" references to research and reference sites in many subject areas. The site also includes information on available mini-grants and a "Kids Connect" area where kindergarten through twelfth grade students can request reference assistance from volunteer school librarians.

  http://www.ala.org/ICONN/index.html

- Teachers who would like to try participating in an online discussion might like to check out the "Forum" section of the Association for Supervision and Curriculum Development. These discussions are asynchronous, so teachers can read and post contributions at any convenient time. Recent topics included integrated curriculum, block scheduling, democratic schools, violence prevention, technology in schools, arts education, and service learning.

  http://www.ascd.org/

- At the most complex end of our continuum is "Tapped In" a "virtual professional development center" under development at SIR, International. The site describes itself as follows:

TAPPED IN is a shared teacher professional development (TPD) workplace patterned after a real-world conference center. Teachers with diverse interests, backgrounds and skills can share experiences, engage in mentoring and collaborative work, or simply meet their colleagues. TPD organizations can maintain their own agendas (institutes and workshops), while enabling their teachers to benefit from a range of expertise, ideas and resources that not one organization could provide by itself. Membership is free for teachers, educators and researchers.

http://www.tappedin.sri.com/

Distance Learning

Distance learning has brought a myriad of learning opportunities into our schools. At the University of Colorado, teachers can receive an M.B.A. through a special online program called Course Connection. Students can tune into Stanford University's Center for Professional Development to see real-time lectures on science and engineering. Others can take a course at MIT thanks to a new partnership between PBS, the Business Channel, and MIT. Elementary students in rural Indiana review books they have read with students from a classroom across the country using a newly created distance learning network.

With distance learning technology, we can virtually take our students to exotic lands, our staff to important training sessions, and our administrators to vital and valuable meetings. Examples of means to find the information you need to introduce your school to the vast, exciting world of distance learning and video conferencing follow.

Network/Conferencing System
3M Visual Systems Division
6801 River Place Blvd.
Austin, TX 78726–9000
800–328–1371
www.3M.com

A videoconferencing solution for remote gatherings.

IMAGINA, Inc.
921 SW Washington Street, Suite 410
Portland, OR 97205
800–909–6537
www.imagina.comIntraNewstand2.0

Allows schools to build secure cyberforums for teacher training or cooperative student projects.

NEC AMERICA, INC.
1555 W. Walnut Hill Lane
Irving, TX 75038
800–832–6632
www.eng.nec.com

Virtual On-Line Advanced Remote Education (VOLARE)
A distance learning training program with full voice-over capabilities.

AT&T51
Peach Street Center, NE
Atlanta, GA 30303
800–232–1234
www.attt.com

Offers teleconferencing and video conferencing systems.

MITEL Corporation
350 Legget Drive
Kanata, ON, Canada K2K 1X3
800–648–3579
www.mitel.com

A local area networking system allowing computers within a school and at remote sites to be networked.

NORTEL
200 Athens Way
Nashville, TN 37228
800–466–7835
www.nortelnetworks.com

Symposium Multimedia Conferencing.

Increasing Communication Between Parents and Schools Through Technology

There are many ways that technology can be used in the realm of education as far as parent–teacher communication is concerned. Technology will make it easier for teachers and parents to understand each other when conference situations are hampered by everyday events. It will also allow the teacher to have the parent experience activities in the classroom in a real world setting that may not take place at school. Homework may be affected as well. There is no end to the ways that technology can be used in education to improve communications.

Sometimes parents cannot attend conferences when necessary. A technology that could bring teachers and parents together via the computer is online chatting using the same communication online software. Online chatting means a two-way interactive exchange takes place through telecommunications via the computer. This is not an exchange of spoken words. Instead, as many people as needed may participate from remote computers and are able to send messages back and forth. In the chat mode, part of the screen will display outgoing messages. At the same time, there is another part of the screen that shows the incoming messages.

Teleconferencing is similar to online chatting yet it involves pictures and voices. Video cameras capture pictures that are then transmitted and displayed on the other computer screens in the conference. Voices are transmitted over the computer hook-up as well. This allows the conference to take place in real world time and contributes to better understanding and ease of communicating.

Videotapes are another way for parents and teachers to communicate. Videos are being used at some schools to allow the parents to see what events are taking place in the classroom instead of just hearing about them. Videos can include valuable information: how parents can help their child succeed in school, what materials to purchase for projects, and descriptions of special programs and curricular units. After-school sessions, parent information sheets, and calendars can be emphasized through the use of video to improve awareness of events taking place in the class.

Webpages are being used as well to enhance parental communications. Parents who have computers can access sites on the World Wide Web that show information about the class that their child may be in. Classroom schedules, notes home, homework assignments , and field trip pictures are just a few things that may be featured on the pages. Curriculum links may also be put on the pages so parents can access them to enhance the children's understanding of subjects and units at school.

Spoken Language Translation

Since classrooms are made up of multiple ethnic backgrounds, teachers sometimes encounter a language barrier in communicating with parents. A technological development that may help overcome this problem is the Spoken Language Translation program. This program automatically translates words spoken by human beings in one language to computer-spoken words in another language and could fill in for human translators. Continuous speech or computer-generated spoken words are produced by text-to-speech or digital audio playback depending on the particular application requirements. Current demonstration systems translate spoken English to computer-spoken Spanish, Korean, or Mandarin Chinese, and spoken Spanish or Mandarin Chinese to computer-spoken English. The applicability of spoken language translation to various law enforcement situations is being evaluated. It is very realistic to think of the applications to other situations than law enforcement, and the school environment is one of those possibilities. This program would allow teachers to communicate with parents who may not speak the same language. This would allow for schools with no one knowing certain languages to communicate with students and parents and to bring down the communication barrier that may hinder community relations.

Examples of Innovative Technology in Schools

In the modern middle school, technology is a vital component in the educational process. Administrators, teachers, parents, and students are all directly affected by the integration of technology in our world. To facilitate the process of integration in the school, the application of technology serves three purposes:

1. Providing students with innovative and effective instructional experiences and the resources for demonstrating student learning,
2. Providing teachers with proper training and continuous technical support, and
3. Providing parents with useful and prompt communication.

One of the many exciting experiences for students and teachers, exercised primarily in math and science classes, is the application of graphing calculators and the Calculator-Based Laboratory (CBL) from Texas Instruments, as found at Easton Middle School Maryland. The CBL is a hand-held battery-operated unit used to collect real world data. Students are able to measure position, velocity, acceleration, force, temperature, light, and sound, using probes. After retrieving this data, graphs can be created to represent the results of an experiment. Along with these tools, the use of monitors, VCRs and video cameras are also available to collect and present data for classroom illustrations of math and science concepts. These meaningful learning experiences heighten student interest, promote active learning, and contribute to students' understanding of the scientific process. The National Council of Teachers of Mathematics (1989) discusses the value of such modeling problems: "students who are able to apply and translate among different representations of the same problem situation or of the same mathematical concept will have at once a powerful, flexible set of tools for solving problems and a deeper appreciation of the consistency and beauty of mathematics."

Computers are available for student use in all classrooms at the Garden Gate School in California. A few of the many activities that are provided by computer access include: composing writing projects such as designing a monthly newsletter for the school, using spreadsheets to create charts that manipulate data, and creating multimedia presentations. According to some studies, multimedia stations with a scanner, color printer, and Internet access furnish students with design experiences that develop important cognitive and social skills. Moreover, multimedia presentations promote a constructiveness approach through peer collaboration, a highly valued instructional strategy. Other technological learning opportunities involve creating digital portfolios useful for student-led conferencing and learning the importance of copyright laws. When the entire class needs simultaneous access to computers, a computer lab is available for teachers to sign up and use.

Another innovative program offered to teachers and students has been modeled at J. W. Fair Middle School in San Jose, California. This program allows students to utilize and check out lap-top computers. Before students can use the lap-tops, students and parents must attend a training session. Because of the lap-tops' portability, they are taken on field trips, shared among classrooms, and carried home. The Beaufort County School District in South Carolina has also reported increased student and teacher motivation with their lap-top program making them indispensable.

Because Internet and intranet services are available in all classrooms and in the computer lab, many functions for students, teachers, and parents are within reach. Teachers and students can participate in distance-learning projects using the Internet and video-conferencing equipment available in the computer lab. Teachers and parents have the ability to communicate quickly and conveniently using e-mail services accessible through the school website. This website is designed and maintained by students and teachers using Microsoft's Front-Page 98 web-authoring tool. The website contains information for students and parents including information about the school, guidance services that include links to other websites as well as teacher webpages, and interactive teaching elements to encourage frequent browsing. Student project descriptions and deadlines, homework updates, and individual grade and progress reports are also accessible using passwords.

Another remarkable application of technology at many middle schools is the morning announcement program using the closed-circuit AV network. Students are responsible for writing, directing, and broadcasting the daily morning announcements. Additional uses of this equipment includes taping special events, and video productions. This is just one more opportunity for students to feature their creative products and develop meaningful life skills.

Programs alone will not guarantee the success of available technology. In fact, research indicates that the difference between effective and ineffective use of technology in schools largely depends on the training of teachers. Teachers in the middle school continuously must be offered classes to learn new ways computers can change their instruction. Teachers should be provided opportunities for self-exploration and sharing expertise with colleagues. Mentoring and coaching programs are effective tools for new teachers. To support the modern middle school's commitment to technology and training, substitute teachers can be provided for staff development, and release-time can be rewarded to teachers as an incentive.

Successful integration of technology in any school is an enormous endeavor. The modern middle school is committed, as illustrated in the technological applications described above, to supporting research-based innovations.

EDUCATION AND POWER IN THE GLOBAL ECONOMY

The new American middle school must face up to the challenges of the new century. In its 40-year history from 1960 to 2000, the middle school evolved into a school that recognized developmental changes and needs of emerging adolescents and built a myriad of programs for those changes and needs. The focus on student needs came early through such publications as ASCD's *The Middle School We Need* and *Making Middle Schools Work,* organizations such as state and national leagues of middle schools, and state and national conferences devoted to the middle school.

The last decade of the twentieth century saw another evolution of the middle school, that of the academic foundation school for high school and beyond.

In particular, the challenges of technology and the global economy forced the realization that the age-old argument of the child-centered school versus the content-centered school was now a moot argument. National and state standards, state testing, and achievement comparison of American middle-grade youth with those of other countries hastened the push toward a stronger content emphasis in the middle school. During the same 40 years of the evolution of the middle school, America saw social changes, including the breakdown of the family, slipping moral values, increased diversity, and mobility, unlike any experienced in the history of the United States. A caring school, yet a highly focused academic school is emerging for the middle school in the new century—a century of interdependence and a global economy.

Continuing Changes in America's Public School Education System

After two decades of status quo in American education, states and school districts have seen traditional roles redrawn to permit the creation of alternative forms of public education. School boards increasingly are beginning to work with schools in their districts that they neither run nor own.[17]

Districts are being urged to break the mold of conventional designs with models like the "New America Schools."

There are private alternatives in which private schools are commercial, selling their services directly to families. Home schooling is another alternative. Home schooling, brought on by parents' concerns about safety, is being enabled by electronic technologies that can bring a full curriculum right into the living room. Vouchers allow for the public to pay for educating students in private schools.

Unlike private schools, public schools can't charge tuition, teach religion, or select their students. Public alternatives include magnet schools and charter schools.

Contracting has followed a trend of governmental agencies in turning over all or parts of programs to private contractors. Entire schools have been contracted out to commercial firms such as the Edison Project. Other firms sell programs such as, Sylvian Learning sells a reading program to public schools.

Contracting should not be confused with privatization. Contract schools are still part of public education paid by public funds and are accountable to the school districts.

Charter Schools may be sponsored by other public bodies such as community colleges, universities, and cities. Charter schools are chartered for a limited term and freed from most rules and regulations. The charter school is autonomous and a discrete legal entity. A charter may be revoked earlier than the charter period if a school board finds that a school is not run properly.

Lease back of school buildings is yet another example of private involvement in public schools. Private companies can build and own school buildings and then lease them back to school boards. The building can then be used for a variety of commercial purposes by the private contractor.

Globalizating the Curriculum

As we meet the challenges of the global economy where work, workforces, products and ideas are globally intertwined, students should be taught the values of human rights, dignity, self-reliance and social justice and how they are and should be applied on a global scale.[18]

Human and universal values cover all attitudes and beliefs of the individual and humanity as a whole. We can help students stretch their identity beyond their own ethnic, national, and religious groups and understand the value of people who are different from themselves.

Global systems identify our interdependence. As we work in a global economy, the world becomes a more closely knit community. Technology has shortened the distances around the world, and global issues and problems are transitional and not isolated. They require cooperative and well-thought-out direction.

SUMMARY

In 2000, none of the goals listed in the Goals 2000 document (drafted in 1994) were realized. Although Americans still view those goals as very important, and we have made progress in reaching them, the resources, strategies, and will to meet them are still lacking. We must continue to work to reach those goals and not accept anything less than excellence in our schools.

Because of technology, for the first time in American history, education is seen as a direct gateway to the acquisition of power. Power used to belong to persons who produced goods or owned property. Power, traditionally based on goods and property, now to an astonishing degree stems from intellectual power.

In the twentieth century, it took an enormous labor force and kingdoms of land to build powerful enterprises such as a railroad. In the new decade of the twenty-first century, power comes from the minds of people through the World Wide Web.

Public schools are open-system organizations and by their nature are open to public policy demands and mandates. Those policies and demands are imposed by diverse coalition groups, court systems, and legislative bodies at the local, state, and national levels.

Schools today are standards-driven and they are being measured by state assessment tests. State standards are based on national standards (see groups producing these standards under Selected References at the end of the chapter). With standards and tests have come alternative delivery systems for schools, both public and private.

The explosion of technology has brought new and exciting ways for students to learn, facilitated record keeping for schools, and forced the re-tooling of our teaching staffs. Challenges of how to use the technology and information generated through technology remain with us.

Finally, the globalization of our economy and shrinking world have brought on the need for globalizating the curriculum. Helping students increase their understanding of ethnic and religious groups beyond our own borders and helping them see our economic and social interdependence will be an important mission of the new American middle school.

The mission of the modern middle school has changed dramatically and we must ensure that it succeeds.

Suggested Learning Activities

1. Prepare an outline of the standards and assessment tests your middle school will face in the school year.

2. Write a paper listing various types of assessments found in the modern middle school.

3. Develop an inservice plan to prepare teachers for using technology in the modern middle school.

4. Develop an outline of a global curriculum for your middle school.

5. Organize a panel discussion on the topic "Challenges of Privatization."

Notes

1. Stephanie Hirsh, "Standards Guide Staff Development," *Journal of Staff Development, 20* 2 (Spring, 1999), 45.

2. Linda Darling-Hammond and Beverly Falk, "Using Standards and Assessment to Support Student Learning," *Kappan,* November 1997, pp. 190–99.

3. Mike Schmoker and Robert Marzano, "Realizing the Promise of Standards-based Education," *Educational Leadership, 56* 6 (March 1999) pp. 55–61.

4. F. N. Dempster, "Exposing our Students to Less Should Help Them Learn," *Kappan,* vol. 74, no. 6, 1993, pp. 432–37.

5. North Central Region Educational Laboratory: http://www.ncrel.org/sdrs/areas/issues/methods/assessment/as7sele.2.html

6. Linda Darling and Beverly Falk, "Using Standards and Assessment to Student Learning," *Kappan,* November 1997, pp. 190–99.

7. D. Monty Neill, "Transforming Student Assessment," *Kappan,* September 1997, pp. 34–58.

8. Stephanie Hirsh, "Standards Guide Staff Development," *Journal of Staff Development, 20* 2 (Spring 1999), 45.

9. Linda Darling-Hammond, "Quality Teaching: The Critical Key to Learning," *Principal,* September 1998, pp. 14–21.

10. Andrew Latham, Drew Gitomer, and Robert Ziomack, "What The Tests Tell Us About New Teachers," *Educational Leadership, 56* 8 (May 1999), 23–28.

11. Paula Evans and Nancy Mohr, "Professional Development of Principals: Seven Core Beliefs," *Kappan,* March 1999, pp. 530–32.

12. Albert Shanker, "Where We Stand—Love Ya!" *New York Times,* 23 February 1997, p. 7.

13. US Office of Educational Technology: http://www/edgov/Technology/Focus/edfocus3.html

14. US Office of Educational Technology: http://chancery.com/products/winschool.nuiu

15. Donna Benson, "Technology Training: Meeting Teachers' Changing Needs," *Principal, 76,* January 1997, pp. 17–19.

16. Michael Simkins, "Teachers Go Online for Staff Development," *Thrust for Educational Leadership,* 27 7 (May/June, 1998): 19.

17. Ted Kolerire, "What are the Alternatives?" *Principal,* May 1998, pp. 61–65.

18. James Hendrix, "Globalizing the Curriculum," *The Clearing House,* May/June 1998, pp. 305–308.

Selected References

GOALS 2000

National Education Goals
http://www.ed.gov/legislation/GOALS2000/TheACT/ sec102.html

Content Standards Contracts

New Teacher's Guide: Raising Academic Standards
http://www.ed.gov/pubs/TeachersGuide/raising/html

Steps for Designing Assessments

Select and/or Design Assessment that Elicit Established Outcomes
http://www.ncrrel.org/sdrs/areas/issues/methods/assessment/as7sele2.htm

State Assessment Information

Colorado: A Teacher's Guide to the Colorado Assessment Program
http://connect.colorado.edu/connect/publications/teachers/index.html

Idaho: Idaho Department of Education
http://www.sed.state.id.us/instruct/SchoolAccount/StateTesting.htm

Maryland: Queen Anne's County Public Schools
http://boe.qacps.k12.md.us/boe/TESTS.HTM

New York: Montauk Public School
http://www.516web.com/school/montauk/test.htm

North Carolina: The NC Testing Program Under the ABC's Plan
http://www.dpi.state.nc.us/account...y/testing/abcs testing program.html

Vermont: Vermont Department of Education
http://www.state.vt.us/educ/assmt2.htm

Improving America's Schools Act

Financing Education in a Climate of Change (pp. 9–10)
Burrup, Brimley, and Garfield, 1999

CHAPTER 9

Instruction in the New Middle School

Preparing students now for the next generation.

In Chapter 1, the authors spoke of a new age in schooling in which the teacher and the student would have very different roles from that found in the twentieth century. According to the authors, the coming years will allow educators in the middle grades to achieve what has only been dreamed of since the time of John Dewey; a natural school, focused on the learner, where the curriculum would allow for creative expression. In such a school, competence would be based on the skills of application as well as on the act of knowing. Dewey dreamed of a school where the student could have the freedom to investigate, where there would be choices in what to study, and where students would develop a growing consciousness, an ability to meet and solve problems that he or she might confront in later life.

The ideas for such a school have been fermenting for nearly a century in America, and the new technologies that continue to implode into our schools will allow the development of a very exciting curriculum. The new middle school teacher will need a thorough understanding of these possibilities in order to adjust to the yet-to-be-determined changes ahead. In this chapter, the authors will attempt to project those new conditions and how teachers and schools will change to meet them.

ESTABLISHING NEW LEARNING ENVIRONMENTS

The time has come for middle school teachers to climb into the new boat. The use of the new interactive technologies and various forms of distance learning are promoting a breakdown in the traditional curriculum and the old instructional delivery systems. Among teachers, already, there is a veritable chasm between early adopters of these technologies and their less enthusiastic peers.

New educational learning environments can be contrasted with the older more traditional environments in a number of ways. One such list, provided by the National Educational Technology Standards group (http://cnets.iste.org/condition.htm) uses ten dimensions to assess the change:

Traditional Learning Environment	New Learning Environment
Teacher-centered instruction	Student-centered instruction
Single-sense stimulation	Multisensory stimulation
Single-path progression	Multipath progression
Single media	Multimedia
Isolated work	Collaborative work
Information delivery	Information exchange
Passive learning	Interactive participative learning
Factual, literal thinking	Exploratory, inquiry-based learning
Reactive student response	Proactive student initiation
Isolated and artificial context	Authentic, real-world context

These are not just words on a page, but rather a promise that is unfolding because of new technologies. The new curriculum in the middle school will be constructed by teachers and students, and will provide them with frameworks and standards to guide them in establishing enriched learning environments supported by technology.

Traditionally, the dissemination medium for learning in America has been the classroom. Under such a centralized model, adapting curriculum to student needs is difficult. With the new technologies, it is possible to construct a generative model (constructivist) for instruction. In this environment, learning will be characterized by students who create real-life learning tasks, who elaborate on those tasks by exploring informational sources, and who represent new ideas or insights by reaching conclusions or producing products.

Four premises will undergird the new instructional patterns that are already emerging:

1. **Learning will be active.**—Students will manipulate, observe, explore, discuss, compare, experiment, and likewise be full participants in the teaching–learning process.

2. **Learners will make choices.**—In the new way of learning, students will make instructional choices from a rich and varied menu of learning experiences and possibilities.

3. **Learners will take a greater responsibility for planning and learning.**— The student in the middle school can already learn without the teacher using computer technologies. It is inconceivable that the teacher's 3,500-year-old role of controlling student learning can be maintained.

4. **Learning will be tailored to the individual student.**—Students learn best when they can relate their personal experiences and perceptions to the learning task. The new middle school learning environment will allow the student to learn through a variety of media.

It is instructive for teachers and educational administrators to be aware of how this same set of technologies is impacting other walks of life. For example, the 1998 Techlearn Annual Report on the Learning and Technology Industry (techlearn-trends@lister.masie.com) lists the following key trends in business:

- 92 percent of large organizations are implementing networking.
- 41 percent have placed education online for employees.
- Workers are beginning to have higher computing and learning capacity at home than they do at work.
- Companies are choosing from best-option vendors outside of companies.
- Learners are experiencing training alternatives outside the workplace.
- Alternative approaches to training are being explored.
- Annotated books are being provided for faster learning.
- Of particular interest to teachers is the explosive growth in K–12 homework sites.

GAINING PERSPECTIVE

The changes in technology, with the influence on learning, can be overwhelming to any classroom teacher. In many respects, teachers are physically captive inside the old classroom on a daily basis and unable to even find time to learn about the changes happening around them. It is essential that new teachers enter the field of teaching computer literate and prepared for a professional lifetime of study.

The computer industry is the fastest developing industry in the history of the world with technology doubling every 18 months at present. This observation by Gordon Moore of Intel (Moore's Law) suggests that any computer technology could grow 100 times in power within a decade. Because of cost alone, it is unlikely that schools will ever be on the cutting edge of technology, but rather will make informed choices as "second wave" buyers. Teachers will need to be able to choose wisely from the many options available to them. These options are dynamic and will continue to change every year the teacher is in service.

In reality, teachers in future middle schools will be the final filter on the development of curriculum and any choices concerning instructional delivery. The teacher will interface with technologies in one of three ways:

1. **Enhancing** and enriching the existing curriculum—for example, the enlargement of subject matter and content learning can be designed by the teacher by providing tools, learning sites, and applications and simulations.

2. **Extending** the existing curriculum—here the teacher is helping the student to go beyond the limitations of the existing school structures without seriously interrupting those structures. Networking, distance learning, and content retrieval are all examples of such extension.

3. **Transforming** the curriculum through technology—changing the basic structures, such as organization and schedules, of the school to make learning more personal and relevant. Obvious as a target is the grade level steps of existing schooling, the idea of subject mastery as opposed to a skills-based curriculum, and the acceptance of a totally individualized curriculum for each child based on IEPs and evaluated on portfolios.

Teachers in the new middle school will begin to understand that learning can now occur across space and time. The new learning will use integrated systems and interactive learning systems such as the Internet. The old idea that learning is linear (point-to-point) can be replaced by a nonlinear orientation. Said another way, rather than moving from A to B to C, we can start at any of these points and make tangential links to other learnings. While such a view of knowledge may open an intellectual Pandora's box at the high school level, the middle school familiarity with interdisciplinary instruction will make this transition easier.

At the present there are some very obvious ways in which the new technologies can enrich and improve learning in middle schools:

- To upgrade curriculum, knowledge and structures using resource retrievals such as political maps, encyclopedias, and census data.
- Allow teachers to access banks of lesson plans (http://www.ASCD.org/index).
- To attack basic skill mastery through personalized computer coaching.
- To provide electronic communication from school to home (parents and students) as well as world-wide student-to-student communication.
- Use of LANs (learning activity networks) within a school for special functions such as "brain bowls" or chess championships.
- To monitor student progress and record teacher grades.
- To analyze data for instructional decision making (standardized test analysis).
- For live and face-to-face video conferencing with persons in other places.
- To poll parents and involve them in curriculum development and delivery.
- For teacher-to-teacher inservice across schools, districts, states, and nations.
- For the instant updating of teacher-developed text materials.

Our list could be expanded well beyond these obvious applications, but the point for the reader to comprehend is that all of these and other adaptations are already taking place in middle schools in America—*now!* Further, all of these new and exciting applications are retrievable, *now,* from your own school and, in many cases, from your own classroom.

BEGINNING THE NEW MIDDLE SCHOOL—INSTRUCTIONAL THEORY

The origin of all changes toward a new middle school will be the basic instructional or learning theory that undergirds practice. Such theory is philosophically based, reflecting beliefs about how people learn and how they should be taught. One such statement recently released by the Commission on Behavioral and Social Sciences and Education (1999) addresses the special nature of children as learners in their "key findings":

- Humans have a disposition to learn in certain domains, and children actively engage in making sense of their worlds.
- Children lack knowledge and experience, but not reasoning ability.
- Misinformation can impede school learning, so teachers need to be aware of the ways in which children's background knowledge

influences what they understand. Such awareness will help anticipate learning difficulties.

- Teachers notice features and meaningful patterns of information not noticed by novice learners.
- The organization of knowledge by the teacher reflects a deep understanding of the subject matter.
- Expert knowledge by the teacher cannot be reduced to sets of isolated facts but, instead, are best demonstrated by the context of applicability of knowing.
- Technologies can help students visualize difficult-to-understand concepts.
- Technologies allow access to a vast array of information for the student.
- Technologies are interactive allowing continuous refinement of understanding.

This set of assumptions about the student and the teacher may or may not be correct, but they illustrate the beginning of a formal theory of instruction. This is something that middle school teachers possess intuitively, but if not formalized this set of beliefs may become distorted by environmental influences. For example, most middle school teachers pay lip service to the uniqueness of the preadolescent learner, but use standardized techniques in instruction (lecture) and evaluation (standardized tests).

As the assumptions about learning are formalized into if-then statements, a pattern or instructional model begins to emerge. One model that uses technological support, by McKenzie, likens the instructional process to a AAA Triptik (http:// w.w.w. fromnowon.org/eschool/adult.html):

Assumptions (fundamental beliefs)

1. The learner may make choices.
2. The learner must take responsibility for planning, acting, and growing.
3. Learning is a personal journey of growth and discovery.

Strategies

Begin all learning with an assessment of where the student is at this point.

Network with other teachers to gain a greater understanding of the student and lesson.

Perceive yourself as a technology mentor.

Build short duration tutorials for your students from websites.

Be available to provide human assistance and adult guidance to the student.

Be prepared to intervene when the teaching moment presents itself, indicated when the student asks the prerequisite question of "how" or "why."

Provide for "home alone" follow-up by suggesting further activities for students on their own computers.

Develop a list of books (in-depth thinking) that support your subject area and the lessons being learned.

Encourage the student to use distance learning to contact others and go beyond the school curriculum.

Emphasize application and problem solving. Teach students the skills of information retrieval and of data analysis.

From this model, the reader will quickly see that the new middle school teacher will be the primary curriculum developer and instructional designer. As stated earlier in this book, schools are nothing but an instructional design; they organize to teach in a certain pattern. Because middle schools in the United States have such a strong child-centered philosophy, new ways of teaching are called for. If the reader doesn't feel comfortable with the McKenzie design, then he or she should attempt to outline the teacher–student relationship. How does it go? If the middle school believes X, then how should the teacher behave to promote learning?

STUDENT INVOLVEMENT

Because middle school theory sees the student, rather than the teacher, as central in the learning process, it is necessary to engage the student in both planning and activating the curriculum. Students can be involved in determining curriculum goals, selecting course content, choosing methodology, carrying out activities, retrieving materials, and conducting assessments. In short, students can have an active role in teaching as well as learning, and in middle schools the ideal teacher would also be a learning partner.

In 1989, the widely read statement by the Carnegie Foundation, *Turning Points*, projected the kind of teacher to be needed in the twenty-first century, and that profile matches the prescription being drawn in this chapter. The report called for the active involvement of the young adolescent in the teaching–learning situation. It called for a curriculum built around themes, rather than the mastery of content knowledge. It proposed instruction in which students "inquire, associate, and synthesize" information and have opportunities to "discuss, analyze, express opinions, and receive feedback from peers. Teachers, in such a school "view themselves as facilitators through which young people construct knowledge themselves" (p. 43).

In 1995, the National Middle School Association wrote a position paper called *In This We Believe,* and this paper noted that because of the young adolescents' drive toward independence, "curriculum that challenges must enable them increasingly to guide the course of their education. Consonant with their varying capacities to handle responsibility, students must be nurtured in making choices and decisions about curricular goals, content, methodology, activities, materials, and means of assessment. In addition, they should have opportunities for involvement in team governance that emphasizes student initiative and responsibility" (p. 22).

"How is this done?" the reader may ask. According to an untitled article by the National Middle School Association (http://nmsa.org/cmplanning.htm) such involvement results when the teachers take the students seriously as partners in learning, and when they ask the student to participate! The old "boat" believed that the teacher was the "knower" and the student the "learner." The new "boat" sees the teacher and learner as mutually involved in the process of learning.

Over 50 years ago (1948), Alice Miel suggested a technique for student and teacher planning that is today referred to as "negotiating the curriculum." In this model, four questions structure communication between the teacher and the learner (or in the case of cooperative learning, among students):

1. What do we already know? (What don't we need to learn?)

2. What do we want to or need to find out? (What are our questions?)

3. How will we go about finding out? (What information or resources will we access?)

4. How will we know when we've found out? (How much do we need to know?)

Such a set of questions fits hand-in-glove with the general interdisciplinary theme format sometimes used by middle schools. It allows each student to identify a personal learning agenda, complete with individualized goals, materials, activities, and assessments (see Figure 9.1). At the same time, teachers in the middle school can overlay the basic tracks, choice categories, and requirements. Teacher planning teams are broken into student–teacher and even student–student planning teams as the process unfolds. The curriculum can be organized around skills to be mastered, chunks of basic foundational knowledge, concepts or major ideas, or even the developmental tasks experienced by the preadolescent on a daily basis. Figure 4.3 in Chapter 4 illustrates five conceptions of instructional purpose and sketches the teaching strategies that might promote such learning. The reader will note that all five of these strategies could be used with the same content or subject matter.

NEW TECHNOLOGIES AND LEARNING STYLES

At the beginning of the twenty-first century, a new way of communicating and learning poses a challenge to any educator who continues to operate a highly

FIGURE 9.1   *Choices in Unit Development*

Length of Unit—day, week, month, semester
Unit Objective—exposure, familiarity, mastery, analysis, application
Unit Location—classroom, resource center, school grounds, community, field trip
Grouping Patterns—individual study, paired study, cooperative teams, small group
Media of Delivery—lecture, readings, films or videos, computer, speakers, debates
Preferred Interaction—problem solving, discussions, individual research, creativity
Student Evaluation—tests, work samples, portfolio, conferences, products, diaries,
                            demonstrations

controlled instructional delivery system in schools. The Web, Internet relay chat, CUSeeMe, ICQ, desktop video conferencing, and FTP (file transfer protocol) all point to a revolution in instruction and the design of learning. These new media, and others to follow, suggest that the 3,500-year-old-control of learning by teachers may be nearing the end. What appears to be emerging in only the last decade, is an era of distributed learning in which teachers, students, and instructional materials will be separated by time and space. As such, the study of the teaching–learning act will change from looking at the behaviors of teachers to the study of how students learn, and how student learning styles can be accommodated.

A real distributed learning environment, first envisioned by Kearsley in 1985, would allow educators to meet the century-old goal of individualizing the learning experience for each child. Such a learning design would counter those many intervening variables that have plagued teachers for years in the classroom: the differences in intelligence, personality traits, prior knowledge, learning preferences, and others. If middle school teachers knew how to use the Internet technologies, such a transformation to the new age of learning could begin. An understanding of the role of technology and the meaning of "learning styles" are prerequisite to the journey.

The Role of Technology

There has been an avalanche of technology in the final years of the twentieth century, and teachers and administrators in middle schools have had to react to these wonders without a principle to guide selection. Each year something new and exciting supersedes the previous year's new and exciting item and, in the meantime, this continuous effort to be high tech in schools is distorting the school budgets and skewing the schools' curricula. In this sense, technology has not been good for schools because it has distorted the existing system. Computers, for example, can cover information in a fast and attractive visual format, presenting the classroom teacher with something of a savant in terms of traditional lecture format teaching.

But while these machines have threatened many teachers, they have also piqued the curiosity of the better teachers who have recognized that the new Internet technologies might provide a truly space age learning tool if the power of the instrument could be captured. So far, all of these technologies have made learning more exciting, but they have not done much to promote organized learning in formal school settings; they have not demonstrated their capacity to simultaneously teach each student as an individual in a manner appropriate to that student's individual capacities.

The reader may ask, "Is this really possible?" The authors believe that, in fact, not only is this possible but the use of technologies to promote individualized learning is probable within the coming decade. However, the cost of these new learning wonders cannot be justified to simply speed up the transmission of knowledge in the old and traditional ways of educating. Only if schools transition to a new learning design, a new relationship between the teacher and the learner, can technology further improve learning in schools.

It is likely that the future computer will have the ability to assess learner preferences and program itself to teach the student in a medium and pattern that is best for the student. While, in fact, no instrument to do this has yet been built, it has been conceptualized and is being researched at IBM and other leading companies. The key to this development is refocusing teaching and learning on the student, not the teacher. Research on how we learn, ATI (aptitude by treatment interaction) research, can assist in defining the optimal learning conditions for each student.

While in the infant stages of development, ATI research notes differences in learner behaviors that every classroom teacher will recognize. Seven heavily researched variables and the inferred or suggested teaching strategy for each preference follows:

1. **Field dependent versus field independent learning**—The field dependent learner attends to the stimulus (teacher, textbook) but finds it hard to locate the exact information they are seeking because they give equal importance to all stimuli in the environment. Field independent learners find it easier to attend to information they are seeking and quickly locate what is to be captured. Children are generally more field dependent and field independence increases with age and education received.

   Suggested Strategy—for field dependent learners provide orienting strategies, graphic organizers of content, embedded questions throughout learning, and cues such as advanced organizers. For field independent learners provide an abundance of learning resources, allow inquiry and discovery in study, and give minimal guidance.

2. **Cognitive Flexibility**—Measures of the ability of the student to ignore distractions and focus on incoming stimuli (teacher talk, computer programs). Flexible students are not easily distracted and are better at preventing irrelevant responses. By contrast, the constricted student is susceptible to cue distractions and is also resistant to cognitive style modifications.

Suggested Strategy—The constricted learner tends to maintain a perceptual set long after the appropriateness or effectiveness ends. Such learners resist change in style or methodology. By contrast, changing the cognitive style requirements for those evidencing flexibility poses no problems. A direct form of instruction is favored by the constricted learner, while autonomy and inductive learning are best for the flexible learner.

3. **Impulsivity versus Reflectivity**—Learners either respond quickly to stimuli or they reflect upon it. Those students with impulsivity tend to respond faster and commit more performance errors. Reflective students, by contrast, take longer to process incoming stimuli but make fewer errors. The reflective student is generally more anxious and lacking in self-confidence than those who are impulsive.

Suggested Strategy—Highly structured learning such as computer-assisted learning will increase the achievement of impulsive learners. Highly structured lessons with small chunks are recommended. By contrast, for those students who are reflective, low structured learning is recommended.

4. **Focusers versus Scanners**—Focusers are learners who are passive and concentrate on a narrow band of information at any time. Scanners, by contrast, are active participants with the information they encounter and often explore the elements of the information received. Focusers often jump to conclusions based on what they perceive, whereas scanners are less susceptible to making a quick first impression.

Suggested Strategy—For the focuser, keep the field of information simple, presenting one topic at a time in a linear fashion. Use simple graphics. For scanners, use many types of information and stress broad information fields.

5. **Narrow or Wide Band Width**—Students can be differentiated by whether they have a narrow or broad band width in learning. A narrow band width is characterized by excluding items and forming narrow classes of information. The wide band width learner will, by contrast, often over-generalize and include too many items. The band width of individuals tend to narrow with age, and the narrower band width often possesses greater attention to detail.

Suggested Strategy—To promote greater learning in the student with a narrow band width, give the student specific details and request that he or she generalize. For those possessing a broad band width, require the student to extrapolate information and give a deductive sequence in their explanations.

6. **Verbalizers versus Visualizers**—Verbalizers like to use words, either through reading or listening to receive incoming stimuli. Visualizers

prefer pictures, graphics, and diagrams. These preferences represent their style of learning.

Suggested Strategy—For verbalizers, non-illustrated texts, outlines, and concrete sequencing of information is suggested. For the visualizer, video games, interactive TV, computers, and other graphics are recommended.

7. **Serialists versus Holists**—Serial learners approach information by concentrating on narrow details. Holists, by contrast, use global or thematic strategies. Often the serialist fails to make connections between data (can't generalize) while the holist is severely short on details.

Suggested Strategy—With the serialist learner, tutorials may be helpful, while for the holist, simulations and games are recommended. Serialists like regular feedback while they learn, while the holist likes to draw inferences from information.

For the computer industry, the future will be a software program that interacts with the learner (even measuring where the student is looking during the assessment) and eventually "types" that student. Then, based on a universe of other such assessments, prescribes to itself which program or which branches of the program to provide for the learner. In a perfect world, the computer will adjust the program in up to 30 ways to accommodate the learner and will do so for each and every learner who interacts with it. In short, the computers of the near future will individualize the instruction offered to the student.

LEARNING STYLES AND PLANNING

From the previous account, we can see that the individual learning preference of the student in the twenty-first century middle school will be an important variable in planning learning episodes. The prescription for someone who is field dependent, cognitively flexible, reflective, possessing a broad band width, a visualizer, and holistic is quite different from that for a student who is field independent but constricted, impulsive, a narrow categorizer, verbal, and a serialist learner. In fact, any mix of these preferences would call for a unique learning prescription. In order for teachers to understand why they must leave the standardized model for all students and move toward a personal and individualized model of teaching, an understanding of these learning styles is needed.

Educators often use the terms learning style and learning preference interchangeably although they are not the same thing. A learning style is a construct, usually self-reported, that summarizes a series of preferences held by the student. A learning preference, by contrast, is a behavior that can be observed. For the immediate future, the authors believe that teachers should concentrate on the learning preferences of students, rather than styles of learning, in their role as instructional designer.

Learning style models such as Kolb, Dunn and Dunn, Hill, Gregorc, and Hanson and Silver, are useful in thinking about these many differences in student preferences. All such models are derived from the work of Carl Jung (pronounced Young) who completed the first characterization in 1921. Dunn and Dunn, for example, is a widely referenced model that addresses environmental, sociological, emotional, and physical variables. Like most of these inventories, Dunn and Dunn assumes that, once informed, the teacher will make adjustments based on knowledge gained. Like most such systems, the Dunn instrument gives the teacher too much data regarding a multitude of things like light, motivation, structure, learning groups, learning media, and teacher motivation. The complexity of these systems makes research of their reliability and validity difficult.

For the teacher in the standard twentieth-century middle school classroom with 30–35 preadolescent learners, such instruments make for interesting workshops but are poor resources for what to do on Monday. But the authors believe that these widely cited instruments and style indicators can sensitize middle school teachers to the fact that different patterns of instruction can be provided and that technology will be an ally in this effort. The days in which an individual teacher with a room full of children had to calculate such variables is ending.

PUTTING THE PIECES TOGETHER

This chapter has introduced the reader to a logic that might be summarized as follows:

1. Individual students are unique, having different backgrounds, intelligences, cognitive patterns, and learning receptors.
2. Middle schools promote a constructivist learning theory that calls for an individualized and adaptive approach.
3. Technology has evolved in the past decade to allow distributed learning.
4. Distributed learning is supportive of individualized instruction.

Stated simply, new technologies will allow middle schools to reach their goal of adapting learning for each student.

By the year 2005, one billion persons will be on the Internet, and it can be assumed that most middle schoolers will have access to learning outside of school. While high tech businesses dream of computers that can teach an unlimited number of persons in an individualized manner simultaneously, middle school educators will edge toward the future by adapting what they now do. The most important thing to recognize is that we must move to the next level because our students are going to learn by technological media in the future. This transition at the middle school level will occur during the career of the reader!

As we move into a media-driven mode of learning, we can see that the learner's reception will be based on his or her learning preferences. Each person (including teachers) has a preferred medium or way of learning. A multimedia approach in the middle school classroom will enable us to meet the learning needs of more students. Media will influence instruction in numerous ways. For example:

1. Students will have choices and will not all do the same things.
2. Media will have an effect on the feelings of students about what they learn.
3. Teachers will be able to color information by the choice of media.
4. By combining learning experiences, teachers can suggest cause and effect relationships (call them lessons).

In days gone by, the teacher could call upon numerous media such as the chalkboard, textbooks, bulletin boards, flipcharts, newspapers, movies, television, filmstrips, overhead projections, radios, phonographs, cassette tapes, multimedia kits, and learning systems. There is nothing new about teachers using media. However, teachers in the past were severely restricted in their use of media by the fact that they were the sole activating agent for such media. Because of this dependence relationship between the possible media and the single teacher, media was usually singular in use and intended for all learners. Another limitation on the use of these media was the unspoken goal of keeping all of the class of learners together in their progress.

The new technologies change both of these conditions. First, they are interactive and the classroom teacher is not essential to their use. This fact calls into question what role the teacher is to play. This will be dealt with in a moment. A second and more momentus change is the fact that these technologies are so constructed that keeping all of the learners together would be virtually impossible. This is a new era of buttons and mice and voice recognition instruments, and once students begin to interact with the media (particularly the Internet), there is no common denominator to their experience.

For these two reasons, some teachers fear the computer and interactive technologies as a job threatening force, and this will be true to the extent that the teacher seeks to control all learning and standardize all experiences had by the students in her or his classes. For these teachers, technology can only mean a serious decline in their authority and their esteem. Because their students hold different views of technology (it's been there all their lives), the resistant teacher will be increasingly obsolete. Such a teacher will find the first ten years of the twenty-first century a terrible experience.

But middle school teachers, who for 40 years have observed how unique each child is, and who preach flexibility in instruction and broad-based curriculum, will embrace these new media once they understand their potential. The new interactive technologies will allow the middle school teacher to have a number of new roles that will be both rewarding and exciting.

One new role for the middle school teacher will be that of tutor. Rather than lecturer (the sage on the stage) the new middle school teacher will be a one-on-one or one-on-two tutor (the guide on the side). The exact nature of this role will be determined by whether the teacher electronically monitors all students working (like Hollywood Squares) and tutors electronically, or whether students will be working in individual project format and the teacher will drift around as a co-learner.

A second new and exciting role for the middle school teacher in the twenty-first century will be that of curriculum designer. By the end of the twentieth century, many teachers had been restricted to being program managers using fixed and externally developed materials. Standardized testing had accelerated this declining role for the classroom teacher by the end of the 1990s, to the point at which many teachers wanted to quit the profession. In the new era, however, the same teacher will be a decision maker who chooses technological experiences for students (developing the Triptik) and serving as a guide through the endless galaxy of the Internet websites. Of course, in order to play this role the teacher will need to possess solid knowledge about computers and have a thorough understanding of why her or his subject is being taught.

A third and fascinating role will be leading students in the study of their community. Much as John Dewey dreamed of in 1900, students can learn to think and act by learning about real things in their own communities and throughout the world. Virtual field trips, chat rooms, and interactive video have made reaching out an attainable goal. Relevance of the curriculum, always a problem, disappears when the student and the community are interactive.

Finally, like no time before in the past 3,500 years, each middle school teacher will be a philosopher. The power of the new media that the teacher selects to influence students and determine their perceptions of life are magnified. Each teacher will have to understand that the time-tested honor of influencing the lives of children will be played out in new dimensions. For the teacher, a moral code and a vision of what is best learned will be prerequisite to the teaching experience.

NEW MIDDLE SCHOOLS IN TRANSITION

At the time of this writing, 2,664 American middle schools have webpages and are entering the interactive learning era. This represents about one-fifth of all middle schools in our nation. These schools are redefining what knowledge is:

> Knowledge is an active process of construction, not a simple replication of information from external sources.

Schools entering this new learning era should seek to construct (design) learning environments in which learners can thrive, adapt, respond, and change themselves. This generative school would meet Dewey's dream of a place where children could have the freedom to investigate, where they would have choices in what to study, and where they would develop an ability to meet and solve problems that they might encounter in the future.

Back in the early 1990s, the National Science Foundation sponsored a project called Global Schoolhouse to demonstrate the potential of high speed Internet connectivity in the public school classroom. The project consisted of connecting schools and students nationally and internationally using the Internet, and modeling classroom applications of Internet tools and resources. Collaborative research was conducted between the schools and the students using a variety of Internet tools including live video conferences. One such school was the Guy B. Phillips Middle School in Chapel Hill, North Carolina (http://k12.cnidr.org.gshwelcome.html). The Global Schoolhouse Project, completed in December of 1994, demonstrated the new power of technological learning.

Schools or teachers wishing to become informed about the new middle schools can begin with some generic sites that are links to an overwhelming amount of information. The authors suggest that you begin with the Virtual Schoolhouse (http://metalab.unc.edu/cisco/schoolhouse/principal). This site tells you and your principal how to get connected.

Another early site for those getting into the new middle school would be the Ford Middle School in Acushnet, Massachusetts (http://www.ultranet.com/~our-school. html). This small school of 375 sixth, seventh, and eighth graders is also the master website for all other middle schools. The schools are organized by region, state, and city so that the reader can select some near enough to be credible or to visit. The site Web 66 at the University of Minnesota is another such master site for middle schools.

For descriptions of active and technological middle schools, the authors recommend Maryville Middle School in Tennessee (mms@ci.maryville,tn.us) and Ferndale Middle School in Michigan (www.ferndale.K12.Mi. US/jrb/best/magic.html.#1). Three other beginning sites of interest are CyberSchool (cyberschool@4j,lane.edu) in Eugene, Oregon, a discussion of futuristic technology for learning (http://www.Nttopenlab-unet.ocn.ne.jp/13e.html), and the website (http://www.ncsa.uiuc.edu/IDT/html/start.html) that provides a strategic flowchart for the construction of a twenty-first century middle school. To get your middle school in touch with these and other reforming middle schools, send an e-mail to MiddleWeb@middleweb.com. To join an electronic discussion group about middle schools, e-mail to midyears-l@scu.edu.au.

One school that serves as a model for a technological program is the Shandin Hills Middle School in California (http://www.territories.com/SHMS/tech.htm), whose mission statement reads: "To provide students with the optimal facilities and technology to develop skills in problem-solving, accessing information, and communicating as responsible citizens in the global community." The school has over 180 computers throughout the school, a technology lab, technology workstation, and uses video, laser disc, and liquid crystal technologies in instruction.

Another school widely known for its technological thrust is the Horace Mann Middle School in Miami, Florida (http://www.facenet.org/May99/virtual.htm). Horace Mann is moving rapidly toward the paperless classroom (http://hmms.dade.K12.fl.us/cossi), where student assignments, readings, and tests are all online. At the school, teachers are beginning to replace standard textbooks with lessons from other teachers pulled from the web (http://www.webteacher.org).

There are, of course, emerging virtual schools where there is no building and there are no live teachers. The Florida High School being developed by the Department of Education (http://fhe.net/fhsweb.nsf/body?open) is one such effort. The high school diploma over the Internet project in Alaska (http://www.jsd.K12.Ak.US) or (www/schools/dzh/dzh.html) is another. While the authors have not found a virtual middle school, to date, it is virtually certain one will soon emerge.

Having oriented yourself to the emergence of new middle schools, you may wish to sample specialty schools that demonstrate the range of possibilities for middle schools in the twenty-first century. The following are recommended sites:

Educational Resources for Middle Schools, the Marie Hastings School in Lexington, Massachusetts (webkeeper@poorhouse.lexington.ma.us)

The middle school as a community school with apprenticeships, community service, and intergenerational projects, The Puget Sound Community School in Bellevue, Washington (http://www.pscs.org)

A world-wide partnership school between Buffalo, New York, and Kanazwa, Japan, (http://www.webnexus.com/users/worldwise endeavors/)

A multi-age, developmentally appropriate school at the middle level (http://www. moreland.K12.ca.us/Discovery/index.html). Another middle grades program where the middle schools tutor the elementary students on computers at the P.K. Yonge School in Gainesville, Florida (www.pky.ufl.edu/about/default.html)

A school where parent volunteers sign up over the Internet, Salk Middle School, Spokane, Washington (http://wwwsd81.K12.Wa.US/salk/unique/parvolu/htm)

A residential school where kids are practicing organic education, in Corvallis, Oregon (fhschool@corvallis.K12.or.us)

A network of school sites where the students communicate visually using cameras on their computers' CU-See Me School Sites (http://www.peddie.K12.nj.us)

A school where there is a computer for every child, Choice 2000 charter School, Perris, California (http://choice2000.org)

Schools that are using long-distance learning as an alternative to standard electives, (http://www indianapolis.in.us/pike/training/pages/media.htm)

Schools that are assigning homework electronically, Westerville, Ohio (http://www westerville.K12.oh.us/emerson/index.htm)

Schools that are doing collaborative projects with other virtual schools, Williamsport, Maryland (http:// isaac.williamsport.K12.md.us)

A school that is conducting faculty discussions about schedules, buildings, and other topics online, Wayland, Massachusetts (http://www wayland.K-12.ma.us/middle_school/teachers/fac_discussion.htm)

While these sites indicate the diversity and richness of the new middle school applications of technology, the ultimate interest should be in how these media can help middle schools individualize and personalize learning for preadolescents. The following entries are some favorites uncovered by the authors:

Visit the "sidewalk chalk festival" at Bernardo Heights Middle School in San Diego, California (http://powausd.sdcoe.K12.ca.us/pusdhhms.)

Kids can take the eighth grade state basic skills test in reading or math over the Internet at Northeast Middle School in Minneapolis (http:// www.mpls.K12.mn.us/northeast/index.html)

Students, parents and teachers can access the lunch menu, daily announcements, school map, test dates, and a host of data online at St. Cloud Middle School in Florida (http://www.scms.osceola.K12.fl.us/ navigation/index.html)

Desert Mountain Middle School in Phoenix, Arizona runs a microsociety where students study subjects and apply them during the "marketplace" portion of the day. Technology is used to integrate the subjects into the marketplace (http://www.dvusd.K12.az.us/DVUSED/SCHOOLS/ dmms.html)

At Middlesex Middle School in Darien, Connecticut, students of the month have their pictures on the school webpage as a reward for good work (http://www.darien.ct.us/middlesex/stu_month_apr.htm.)

At Freeport Middle School in Maine, the school webpage is sponsored by the Merchant's Association and, of course, L.L. Bean (http:// fms.freeport.K12.me.us/)

And finally, a favorite, at Centennial Middle School in Boulder, Colorado you can watch the science classes "live" through the webcam, and you can also browse through student essays on the award-winning *Vocal Point* virtual magazine. http://bvsd.K12.co.us/schools/cent/ centennial.home.html.

The reader can easily observe that the move to leave the old middle school and enter the new middle school has already begun. The journey promises to be exciting as teachers and administrators redefine education for the twenty-first century.

SUMMARY

For over a century, some educators have dreamed of creating a school to serve students. Like the junior high school before it, the middle school has struggled to develop such a school without proper tools. High pupil–teacher loads, standardized testing, resource shortages, and an absence of know-how have prevented the full development of the middle school concept. Now, with the arrival of interactive technologies, teachers finally have the tools to build such a school.

The new school will be student-centered, multisensory, multimedia, collaborative, exploratory, authentic, and directed by students. Teachers and students will construct learning opportunities by enhancing, extending, and finally transforming the school of today. In the new school, learning can occur across space and time, and the traditional parameters of a book, a teacher, and a classroom will melt away. The transition in middle schools will be completed when the assumptions about learners are translated into a theory of learning.

The middle school teacher in the new middle school will be a guide and a community relations person and a curriculum designer. The universe of knowledge on the Internet must still be directed, and it will fall to the teacher to create the paths or Triptiks for students. Teachers will soon learn that the choices among media will enhance or color the meaning of such information. Teaching will be choosing, directing, and encouraging.

Recognizing that learning preferences among students are real will lead the teacher to technologies. These media are the intervening variable in instruction, and the better the choice of technology, the better the learning opportunity for the student. While middle school teachers have always had medium choices, it is the new technology to manage learning that is so important.

It is now obvious that this new learning era will evolve and many middle schools are experimenting with how technology can enhance their curriculum. The interaction among these schools, and the teachers in them, will quickly disseminate the best of practice in the United States.

Selected Learning Activities

1. Using the leads in this chapter, visit five web sites where active middle schools are moving toward a technological future. What do these schools seem to have in common?

2. Spending only one hour, use the generic web sites (Web 66, Ford Middle School) to browse the web. Begin collecting ideas for your school of the future.

3. Discover who Marshal McLuhan is. Why are his thoughts of value to middle school teachers?

4. Reach out and contact another middle school teacher outside of your district on some subject of interest to you. Summarize how it feels to have such new powers.

Selected References

Bennett, Frederick. 1996. *Computers as Tutors: Solving the Crisis in Education.* 12 March 1997 (www.cris.com/~faben 1).

Berman, S. and Tinker, R. 1997. "The World's the Limit in the Virtual High School." *Educational Leadership,* vol. 55, no. 3 (November 1997): 52–54.

Cohen, R. and Holzman-Benshalom, Y. 1997. "Multimedia in Junior High." *Educational Leadership,* vol. 55, no. 3 (November 1997): 64–66.

Davis, S. 1997. "How Mastering Technology Can Transform Math Class." *Educational Leadership,* vol. 55, no. 3 (November 1997): 49–51.

Debenham, J., and Smith, G. 1994. "Computers, Schools, and Families: A Radical Vision for Public Education." *T.H.E. Journal,* vol. 22, no. 1 (February 1994): 58–61.

Dede, C. 1997. "Rethinking How to Invest in Technology." *Educational Leadership,* vol. 55, no. 3 (November 1997): 12–16.

Dillon, R. and Sternberg, R., eds. 1986. *Cognition and Instruction:* FL: Academic Press.

Ehrankranz, Ezra. 1995. "Design for Flexibility: Today's New Schools Can Be State of the Art in 2055," *Electronic School,* February 1995 (http://www.access.digex.net/~nsbamags).

Elias, M., Zins, J., Weissberg, R., Frey, K., Greenberg, M., Haynes, N., Kessler, R., Scwab-Stone, M., and Shriver, T. 1997. *Promoting Social and Emotional Learning: Guidelines for Educators.* VA: ASCD Publications.

Fund, J. 1998. "Politics, Economics, and Education in the 21st Century." *Imprimis,* vol. 27, no. 5 (May 1998).

Hasselbring, T., Goin, L., Taylor, R., Bottage, B. and Daily, P. 1997. "The Computer Doesn't Embarrass Me." *Educational Leadership,* vol. 55, no. 3 (November 1997): 30–33.

Herndon, J. 1994. "School as Waystation on the Information Superhighway." *T.H.E. Journal,* vol. 22, no. 2 (August 1994): 78–82.

Hiem, S. 1995. "Stafford County Schools Use Partnerships to Blaze Hi-Tech Trail." *T.H.E. Journal,* vol. 22, no. 8 (March 1995): 53–55.

Jensen, E. 1997. *Brain Compatible Strategies.* CA: Turning Point Publishing.

Jensen, E. 1998. *Teaching with the Brain in Mind.* VA: ASCD Publications.

Lonergan, D. 1997. "Network Science: Bats, Birds, and Trees." *Educational Leadership,* vol. 55, no. 3 (November 1997): 34–36.

Luskin, B. 1996. "Toward an Understanding of Media Psychology." *T.H.E. Journal,* vol. 23, no. 7 (February 1996): 82–84.

Mann, L. 1997. "Designing the Learning Environment." *ASCD Education Update,* vol. 39, no. 6 (September 1997): 1–5.

Mohnsen, B. 1997. "Stretching Bodies and Minds Through Technology." *Educational Leadership,* vol. 55, no. 3 (November 1997): 46–48.

Niguidula, D. 1997. "Picturing Performance with Digital Portfolios." *Educational Leadership,* vol. 55, no. 3 (November 1997): 26–29.

Pool, C. 1997. "A New Digital Literacy: A Conversation with Paul Gilster." *Educational Leadership,* vol. 55, no. 3 (November 1997): 6–11.

Razik, T. and Swanson, A. 1995. *Fundamental Concepts of Educational Leadership and Management.* Upper Saddle River, NJ: Prentice-Hall.

Rothstein, R. and McKnight, L. 1995. "Architecture and Costs of Connecting Schools to the NII." *T.H.E. Journal,* vol. 23, no. 3 (October 1995): 91–96.

Sager, M. 1998. "Polk May Log On to Internet School." *The Tampa Tribune,* Saturday, 20 June 1998, p. 12.

Scanlon, Mary. 1995, 1997. "Making Connections: How Technology Acquaints Students With Their Communities," *Electronic School,* September 1995, Also see 21 March 1997 (http://www access.digex.net/~nsbamags).

CHAPTER 10

Evaluation of New Middle School Programs

Diversity and flexibility go hand in hand.

If there has been one weakness associated with the American middle school during the past 35 years, it must be that evaluation was never a serious component of development. Failure to evaluate middle school programs has blurred their special mission in the eyes of school boards and the public at large. Is a middle school a grade level arrangement, or is it a special instructional program for the preadolescent?

There are four areas that are generally reviewed in evaluation at any level: programs, processes, products, and personnel. Middle school programs are fairly easy to validate in terms of organizational components (see Table 10.1). Does the school have a flexible schedule, teaching teams, interdisciplinary curriculum, guidance component, and other such standard items? (See Figure 10.1.)

The study of processes, especially instructional processes, presents the evaluator with a greater problem. The choice of instructional methods and media can only be rationalized in terms of what the educators are trying to do with students. Why, for example, are middle schools so concerned with providing guidance to resident preadolescents? The answer, of course, is that the preadolescent is completely preoccupied with self, and the needs of selfhood are primary and prerequisite to satisfying school needs. As any middle school teacher knows, physical and social concerns dominate the middle school classroom.

Products of middle school classrooms are equally troublesome due to the fixation of our society with standardized test scores. At the least, middle schools must achieve as well as standardized intermediate schools, but this target is a minimum for the middle school. If middle schools are designed and delivered to help the preadolescent learner grow and develop as an individual, the product of such an education must be individually measured. Portfolios and other evidences of learning must supplement or even replace the more standardized measures.

Finally, assessments of personnel in a middle school must be expanded beyond the judging of teacher competence to also include the student and his parent(s). It has been estimated by researchers that the parent is as important as the teacher to student achievement. Additionally, the attitudes and motivation of the student are critical to school success. Personnel evaluation is broader in the middle school.

TABLE 10.1 Design Outline for School Evaluation

Approach	Focus	Procedure	Questions
Program Design	Conceptual/ Structure	Validation of Goals/ Purposes	Do we have the kind of program intended?
Program Process	Operational/ Technique	Problem Analysis/ Checklists	Is the program we have efficient in delivering services?
Program Product	Structured Feedback	Testing and Survey	Does the program work? Are there desired outcomes?
Program Personnel	Observation/Analysis	Review/Redesign	Are personnel making a direct contribution to the planned program?

Jon Wiles & Joseph Bondi, *Supervision: A Guide to Practice*, 5th ed., Charles Merrill, Columbus, Ohio, 2000, p. 175.

FIGURE 10.1 *Middle School Program Analysis*

Directions:

Please check those items that are descriptive of the middle school program at your school.

Philosophy and Goals

_____ 1. A formal middle school-oriented philosophy exists and is accepted by principal and teachers.

_____ 2. The goals of the middle school program reflect a three-part thrust: personal development, skills for continued learning, and education for social competence.

_____ 3. Philosophy and goals are developed based on an assessment of the needs of students attending the school.

Organization

_____ 4. The middle school day is flexibly scheduled using large blocks of time and modular time arrangements.

_____ 5. Teachers are organized into interdisciplinary planning/teaching teams that share a common group of students and planning period.

_____ 6. Teaching teams are located in physical proximity to one another.

_____ 7. Parent involvement/community involvement is built into the school curriculum.

Curriculum/Organized Learning

8. The formal program of organized learning includes the following components:

_____ Core academic learning consisting of language arts, mathematics, social studies, and science.

_____ Remedial and enrichment opportunities such as gifted programs.

_____ Exploring electives to expose new fields of knowledge and expand aesthetic and creative horizons.

_____ Career education components for all students.

_____ Physical development and health education for all students.

_____ Student-initiated elective choices in art, music, and other related areas.

_____ A required course in the area of computer literacy.

9. General skill development is planned and included in major subject areas including:

_____ Reading

_____ Spelling

_____ Writing

_____ Library use skills

_____ Problem solving

_____ Finding and organizing information

_____ Critical and creative thinking

10. A continuous progress approach to learning is present and does the following:

_____ Assesses each student at entry level on a continuum of course objectives.

_____ Has ongoing monitoring to determine each student's readiness to progress in curriculum.

_____ Allows student to attain proficiency in skills and performance objectives at rate/level that matches the student's instructional needs.

_____ Assesses student performance based on progress through a skill-and-objective continuum.

11. Schoolwide advisement programs are present and do the following:

_____ Include a separate, planned nonacademic program

_____ Include direction by guidance counselors

_____ Have a regularly scheduled group activity

FIGURE 10.1   *Middle School Program Analysis (continued)*

_____ Involve all certified personnel, staff, and support personnel
_____ Provide ongoing personal interaction between staff (adviser) and students (advisee)
_____ Maintain a teacher/pupil ratio of less than 1:20
_____ Provide individual guidance opportunities when needed

12. A physical development/health program is present and is characterized by the following:

_____ Experienced by all students
_____ Students grouped on basis of development rather than grade level
_____ Intramural program available to all students and organized around skill development
_____ Formal health program to assist students in understanding and accepting physical and intellectual changes in themselves and others
_____ Health screening and monitoring for all students
_____ Graduated physical education program according to student development

Instructional Patterns

_____ 13. Students are grouped by intellectual, social, and/or physical characteristics in classes.

_____ 14. A variety of instructional methods are used in classes at any given time.

_____ 15. Instructional strategies other than lecture are used in most classrooms.

_____ 16. Varied instructional materials are regularly used in most classrooms.

17. There are interdisciplinary team planning/teaching approaches that provide for the following:

_____ Teachers of different subjects meet during scheduled time to coordinate instruction for common groups of students.
_____ Teachers of different subjects meet during scheduled time to monitor progress of common groups of students.
_____ Teachers of different subjects teach common group of students within a block of time and group/re-group students to meet varied instructional objectives.
_____ Teachers of different subjects participate in delivery of interdisciplinary units on periodic basis.
_____ Teachers of different subjects meet together with parents of individual students to discuss the student's program.

Jon Wiles and Joseph Bondi, *The Essential Middle School*, 2nd ed. Macmillan/Merrill, Columbus OH, pp. 329–30.

To begin to assess a middle school as a program with organization, involving people, and resulting in products, we must begin with the following objectives that the middle school purports to serve:

1. To facilitate a smoother articulation between the various levels of the school ladder.

2. To create a plan of staff utilization that will maximize the personal and professional development of teachers.

3. To facilitate new teacher education programs based on career opportunities in this special area.

4. To facilitate the introduction of needed specialization in the upper elementary years by using team teaching and special instructional centers.

5. To provide for more realistic and effective guidance through the use of teacher counselors and planned guidance sessions.

6. To create a social and physical environment free from the pressures of competitive athletic programs and highly organized social activities typical of junior high programs, and one that requires less dependence upon adults than typical elementary programs.

7. To promote a greater degree of individualization through encouraging pupils to progress at different rates through different programs by using independent study plans and self-pacing materials as well as newer media of instruction.

The following hypotheses might be tested in the evaluation of a middle school:

1. The middle school will provide a rich program of exploratory experiences.

2. There will be fewer and/or less intense social and psychological problems found in middle school students than age-mates in other types of schools.

3. Middle school students will develop more adequate self-concepts than age-mates in other types of schools.

4. Pupils in middle schools will become more self-directed learners.

5. Middle school graduates will succeed better in high school.

6. There will be less teacher turnover in the middle school.

7. Teacher morale will be higher in the middle school.

8. The organization of the middle school will facilitate more effective use of special competencies and interests of the teaching staff.

9. The average daily attendance record of middle school students will exceed that of pupils in conventional schools.

10. Teachers in the middle school will use a greater variety of learning media than teachers in conventional schools.

11. Patrons of the middle school will hold more positive attitudes toward objectives and procedures of the middle school than patrons of conventional schools.

12. Achievement of middle school students on standardized tests will equal or exceed that of pupils in conventional schools.

EVALUATION AS A SYSTEM

Like the instructional program for students, the evaluation program in a middle school must be comprehensive if it is to achieve its objective—*promote better learning*. Like the curriculum, the instructional pattern, and the operation of the school, evaluation should be a product of the objectives of middle school education. Middle school evaluation must be systematic if it truly is to assess the effectiveness of the program[1] (see Fig. 10.2).

FIGURE 10.2   *How Evaluation Contributes to Effectiveness*

1.	Makes explicit the rationale of the program.
2.	Provides basis to collecting and analyzing data.
3.	Allows conclusions about effectiveness.
4.	Prepares evidence to rationalize decision making.
5.	Suggests ways in which to implement decisions about improvement.

The primary question in designing systematic evaluation in the middle school is "education for what?" The middle school has been identified as a school "designed to promote personal growth and development in preadolescent learners." That single purpose defines the parameters of middle school evaluation. Evaluation serves to answer this question: Is preadolescent development being promoted?

As we seek to answer this question, our evaluative focus shifts to the learning design created to achieve this end, and to the arrangements for learning that have been made. In doing so, middle school evaluation goes beyond the areas of student growth, identified in Chapter Three, to include a much broader range of concerns. Personnel, facilities, learning materials, rules and regulations, and all other program planning considerations become concerns of evaluation. Evaluation in the middle school is defined by the purposes and activities of the middle school program.

One way of viewing evaluation is as a feedback or corrective mechanism. Here the goals of the school are translated into objectives which in turn create a program design. Student learning, for instance, is structured into activity which have distinct foci. As evidence is gathered and analyzed, discrepancies between desired outcomes and real outcomes are discovered and adjustments in program are made. Goals are refocused and the feedback cycle is renewed (see Figure 10.3).

Another way to approach middle school evaluation would be to use evaluation as a means of "validating" program goals and objectives. In this approach, evidences are gathered to justify specific facets of the program and these facets or subsystems collectively comprise the evaluation program. Examples of such subsystems are student performance, teacher effectiveness, program design, resource utilization, facilities usage, policies and regulations, parent and community feedback, and staff development programs (see Figure 10.4).

An example of how this approach might work can be drawn from the middle school's concern with teaching academic processes. If, for instance, students were not demonstrating growth in study skills, each area or subsystem could be analyzed for probable cause. For example, materials for teaching skills are inadequate, or teachers need additional training in teaching reading.

By combining these two approaches to evaluation, a school can develop a means of regularly assessing its programs and taking corrective actions where findings are not satisfactory. Some guiding questions in each of the above mentioned areas are provided for study.

FIGURE 10.3   The Evaluation Cycle

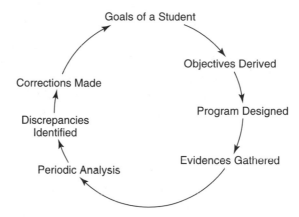

Source: Jon Wiles, *Planning Guidelines for Middle School Education.* Kendall Hunt, Dubuque, IA, 1976, p. 71.

FIGURE 10.4   Areas of Evaluation

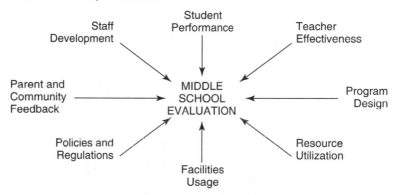

Source: Jon Wiles, *Planning Guidelines for Middle School Education.* Kendall Hunt, Dubuque, IA, 1976, p. 79.

Program Design

The overall design of the middle school program can be assessed from both an external and an internal vantage point. Viewed from the perspective of the school district in which the middle school is located, the following questions seem pertinent:

1. Is the middle school concept as described consistent with the overall philosophy of the district and its leaders?
2. Does the middle school articulate (fit) with the preceding elementary programs and the high school programs which follow?
3. Are the resources allocated to the middle school, such as building, staff, monies, and materials, commensurate with those given to other levels of schooling?

From an internal perspective, concern for the program design would focus on the structure of the curriculum and the learning opportunities for students. The following questions might guide such an analysis:

4. In what ways does the curriculum actually provide for the intellectual, physical, social, and emotional differences of students?

5. What materials and equipment contribute to the development of skills, interests, abilities, and special talents of students?

6. By what means are all of the learning experiences in the school integrated with one another?

7. What provisions are made for student growth and development in health, personality, and character?

8. How are learning activities individualized to meet student needs and interests?

9. What special provisions have been made to insure the mastery of basic learning skills?

10. What adjustments in the organization of the school have been made to promote a climate for exploration?

Facilities Usage

Regardless of the age or condition of the facility in which a middle school program is operated, much can be done with a facility to support the advancement of activities. Schools should be built or converted in anticipation of program needs.

Although some facility concerns in the middle school are more obvious than others, such as using a building that promotes flexibility and physical movement, that allows for variable grouping of students, and that encourages cooperative planning and teaching, others are subtle. The following questions may assist in illuminating facility-usage evaluation in the middle school:

1. Does the allocation of space in the facility, both in location and in volume, reflect program priorities?

2. Is space utilization in the facility flexible enough to allow for individualized instructional activities?

3. Is the instructional resource center (IRC) centrally located and readily accessible to teaching spaces?

4. Are the noisy spaces relatively isolated from needed quiet areas?

5. Is the entire building stimulating in its spatial and color orientation?

6. Are all available spaces, like stairwell corners and foyers, being used to educate and communicate with students?

7. Is there a sufficient number of special focus areas in the facility like darkened projection areas, storage areas for projects, common areas, and areas for private conversations to promote program objectives?

8. Is the administrative area accessible to students, teachers, parents, and visitors?

9. Are provisions made for the display of students' work, such as tackboards and cork strips in the hallways?

Resource Utilization

The allocation and utilization of resources, both human and material, is a problem area for many middle schools. An all too familiar pattern is seen in territorial rights established in buildings, or available resources allocated to favored segments of a program. Middle schools must use all available resources judiciously to promote their programs. The following questions suggest some areas worth analyzing:

1. Is there a clear relationship between the allocation of funds and materials in the school and the curricular objectives of the program?

2. Are staff members assigned to positions in the program according to function and talent rather than by credential?

3. Are high-priority areas like skill building given sufficient support in the form of staff and consumable materials?

4. Are immediate resources available to support innovative instructional techniques?

5. Is there an established means of assessing future resource needs and planning for their acquisition?

Policies and Regulations

Few middle schools regularly view administrative policy and regulation from a program objectives standpoint. Yet, no other single area in a middle school is so important in setting the tone or climate for learning. It is important in evaluation that the following questions be asked:

1. What policies and regulations are absolutely essential to the operation of a middle school?

2. What existing rules or policies might contradict the spirit of the middle school concept?

3. How might policy-setting and regulation enforcement best be handled to promote the objectives of the school?

Student Performance

Since the terminal objectives of the educative process, in any school at any level, are concerned with student performance or behavior, this area of evaluation is generally given more attention by parents, teachers, and administrators than any other phase of schooling. In the middle school, as students are evaluated, the folly of redefining the purpose of education must be avoided while still retaining the old yardsticks of measurement.

Middle schools must evaluate student performance in areas that are truly important—areas suggested by the conceptual image of the middle school design. A comprehensive evaluative approach is needed to match the comprehensive educational program. The following questions may assist in the development of such an approach:

1. Is student evaluation perceived and conducted as a measure of personal development for each student?
2. Is student evaluation both systematic and continuous in nature?
3. Is the student fully involved in the evaluation and measurement of her or his own growth and development?
4. Is the reported student evaluation social–personal as well as academic?
5. Is the evaluation of student progress related to her or his own ability and previous performance?
6. Are parents actively involved in the evaluation of their children?
7. Is the gathering of evaluative data comprehensive in nature, such as a combination of periodic testing, student self-report files, teacher–pupil conferences, and observations?
8. Is student progress reporting directional in nature, indicating where improvement is needed?
9. Is student progress reported to parents in a positive manner with emphasis on growth as shown in the following scheme?
   C   = Commendable Achievement
   S   = Satisfactory Achievement
   I   = Improving
   N   = Needing more work
   NA = Not Applying

Teacher Effectiveness

Teachers in the middle school are more than simply a resource, they are in fact the medium or delivery system through which the middle school sends its message. Without the full support of the teaching staff, the middle school will falter under the weight of ambition. Full effectiveness from each member of the instructional staff is needed. Evaluation of teacher effectiveness might center around the following questions:

1. Have the talents and abilities of all staff members been fully explored and catalogued?
2. Are members of the instructional and support staffs working where they believe they can be most effective?
3. Are there organizational and administrative constraints on teaching styles in the school?
4. Is there an active mechanism by which teachers can share ideas and activities with other teachers?
5. Is there an established means for program-improvement input by the instructional staff?
6. Does the administration use a mechanism for reviewing teacher growth?

Team Effectiveness

Teachers in middle schools are often organized into teams. Procedures must be developed to analyze the strengths and weaknesses of the team approach. Evaluation must include the role of the team leader. Evaluation of team effectiveness might center around the following concerns:

1. Team climate—Does the team display cooperation and teamwork?
2. Team goals—Does the team use integrative, constructive methods in problem solving rather than a competitive approach? Are team goals understood by all teachers in the team?
3. Team contract—Has the team put into writing the expectations of its members regarding meeting times, reviewing performance, and building agendas?
4. Team leadership—Does the team leader provide leadership in facilitating communication within the team and with other teams? Does the team leader coordinate curriculum planning by the team and provide resources, both human and material, for the team?

Staff Development

In the middle school evaluation schemata shown earlier, staff development was seen as a corrective device for program improvement. Rather than a regularly scheduled or unfocused treatment which characterizes many inservice programs, staff development efforts in the middle school attack real problems faced by educators. The following questions suggest a possible evaluative focus:

1. Are there monies budgeted for staff development efforts during the school year?

2. Do staff development needs arise from analysis of other areas of evaluation such as student performance and teacher effectiveness?

3. Can staff development efforts be conducted on short notice during the school year?

4. Do teachers regularly have a chance to critique staff development activities and suggest areas of future need?

Parent–Community Feedback

Perhaps the most important dimension in the middle school evaluation system is that which monitors the reactions and interest of parents and the community in which the middle school is located. Without support from both of these groups—at a minimum, tacit support—the programs of the middle school cannot fully succeed.

Involvement of the community, like involvement of parents, is a matter of degree as well as frequency. The following questions may assist in evaluation of this part of the middle school program:

1. Were members of the community involved in the original study of the middle school concept and the drafting of formative documents?

2. Is there presently in existence a citizens committee at the school whose major function is to communicate to parents and to the community about programs at the school?

3. Are members of the community regularly kept informed, through school dissemination efforts, of changing programs or changes in operation?

4. Can citizens actively participate in school functions at a meaningful level of involvement?

Each of these components of the evaluation system is important in terms of program improvement and increased performance by those actively engaged in the operation of the school. All components are interrelated and crucial to other areas. A simple evaluation baseline is shown in Figure 10.5.

Student Evaluation

Perhaps the greatest challenge to the new middle school is developing a program of evaluation that reflects the personal nature of the middle school curriculum. Like the curriculum, the goals of student evaluation must be broad. Like the curriculum, student evaluation must be individualized. And, like the curriculum, the goals of student evaluation should focus on relevance of any achievement to the life of the student.

Surveys by the authors indicate that middle schools are attempting to go beyond report cards and standardized achievement tests in assessing student growth. For example, in Mesa, Colorado, the Assessment Home Page reveals the following outline:

FIGURE 10.5   *Evaluation Baseline*

---

1. *Discipline:* Number of referrals by school and grade—corporal punishment
2. *Achievement:* Stanford and SSAT Reading/Math Listening Range by school—
       Percentage of skill passage by school
3. *Grading:* Percentage of grade awarded by subject, grade, and school
4. *Attendance:* Quarterly ADA averages—baseline
5. *Student Mobility:* By school—internal and external
                            Transportation report
6. *Low/High SES:* Lunch programs
                      Migrant programs
                      Chapter 1 eligibles
7. *Vandalism:* By school
8. *Age of Students:* By school, sex, race
9. *Teacher Experience:* Form
10. *Student–Teacher Attitudes:* Form
11. *10th Grade Follow-Up:* Form
12. *Instructional Practices:* School visits
13. *Facilities:* School visits
14. *Instructional Resources:* Supervisors

Mission—To lead all students to reach their individual potential by rigorously pursuing and evaluating achievement of high academic and ethical standards in a disciplined and nurturing environment.

Principles for Assessing Student Learning. The assessment of student learning begins with educational values.

Assessment is most effective when it views learning as multidimensional, integrated, and revealed performance over time.

Assessment requires attention to outcomes but also and equally to the experiences that lead to those outcomes.

Assessment fosters improvement when representatives from across the educational community are involved.

Assessment leads to improvement when it begins with issues of use and illuminates questions that people really care about. (For a complete statement see <http://www.mesa.k12.co.us/assessment>.)

In an adequate evaluation system, student learning might be assessed by looking at work habits and academic skills, social attitudes and evidences of adjustment, measures of physical and mental health of students, knowledge acquisition and achievement, creativity and interest expansion, aesthetic appreciation developed, self-esteem and the development of a personal code of values, and various evidence of critical thinking attainment. In other words, a comprehensive review of progress directed toward the question, "How is this student developing?"

EVALUATION IN THE NEW MIDDLE SCHOOL

While traditional criteria for existing middle schools suggest a comprehensive and flexible approach, the new technological middle schools of the twenty-first century will need highly individualized assessment designs. In these new middle schools, teachers will create instructional materials, and the degree of individualization for each student will be much greater. Districts will need to anticipate these changes to help teachers to prepare for this coming era.

As stated earlier, curriculum "frameworks" and "learning objectives" will guide teachers in their selection of learning experiences for students. All learning objectives should be specific to the following points:

1. Learning is defined in terms of global outcomes using measures such as the cognitive and affective taxonomies of Bloom and Krathwohl to target the desired results of instruction.

2. All learning should include thinking and problem-solving skills to emphasize that middle school learning is about life in the future and after school.

3. Affect (emotion) should be employed as a criterion for selecting learning opportunities for middle schoolers. The higher the affect present, the more lasting or impressionable the learning episode.

4. Learning objectives should be sequential and within the scope of the curriculum. This is especially important when using the Internet due to the many enticing and interesting topics available.

5. Objectives should imply a level of attainment or a range of attainment, but not standardize such growth. Underestimating student capacity, as well as overestimating student capacity is a regular problem in many middle school classrooms.

6. All objectives should suggest evidences of participation or attainment, with the majority not being of the pencil-and-paper test variety.

As teachers begin to develop curricula (units, triptiks, exploratories) there are certain evaluative criteria to be followed:

1. Concepts should guide any content selection. Middle schools feature "big" learnings and detail is often forgotten.

2. Content is usually "sampling" rather than mastery oriented. We select a piece of literature as representative of a kind of literature rather than good in itself.

3. Information should be developmentally appropriate for middle schoolers.

4. Information should be current and accurate. When using the Internet, the teacher must remember that there is no quality control agent.

5. The scope of the learning is defined. With Internet learning, the information horizon is limitless. The student must have guidance in selection of experience.

6. Content, on the Internet, is always connected to more content, especially using search engines. Teachers should draw "information webs" or maps for the student with search guide words provided.

In terms of instructional design, teachers must understand that learning changes behavior. When we program a learning episode, we expect something to happen. The accidental curriculum is dangerous because it trivializes formal learning and suggests that all information is equally important. The following guidelines might aid in evaluation of instructional plans:

1. All teaching strategies recognize and acknowledge that students have individual learning styles and preferences.

2. Lessons that are for self-directed learning should be defined by time and anticipated attention span.

3. There should be order or logic to all groups of lessons, and this order should reflect an overall curriculum plan for the subject or year.

4. Until individual student work habits are known, an instructional pace should be suggested for each student (expectations for learning materials).

5. Teachers should be able to build in optional learning activities and suggest peripheral learning paths for better students.

6. Middle school learning designs can be for groups of students (LANS) and should always show applications of the principles, concepts, or skills learned.

Selection of instructional materials is a very important part of any evaluation component. As we enter the age of Internet learning, we must be cognizant of the fact that materials on the Internet are extensive, dynamic, and easily accessible. The ultimate use of such "information superhighway" materials will be found in the meaning attached to the materials, not in the access to the materials. Use of computers allows the processing of information: deleting, adding, connecting, and constructing knowledge. Without guidance, students can easily become overwhelmed and lost as learners. The teacher role in the new middle school will be greatly enhanced.

Many teachers the authors speak with are anxious about students in their classrooms taking unguided learning trips on the Net. Providing the students with the appropriate addresses, "bookmarking" menu items on the browser, and even using existing "projection devices" to see what students are viewing will make early use of Internet materials less stressful for the teacher. The following guidelines are also suggested for evaluating criteria:

1. Select materials thought to be motivators for individual students.

2. Do not get trapped in using only the computer. Use books, films, and other media to engage students. Like television, computer viewing is hard on the eyes and has been shown by research to irritate some students.

3. Make sure the student understands the connection between suggested materials.

4. Use the Internet to supplement teacher lessons, not vice versa.

5. Try to ascertain the appropriate print size and reading difficulty for any assigned materials.

6. Do take advantage of materials and plans recommended by state and national agencies. Most of these subject area plans are on the Web.

7. Be on the lookout for inaccurate, false, or enticing information on the Internet. Remember, there is no filter beyond the classroom teacher for the new technological curriculum materials.

In addition to these suggestions, the authors would observe that the new middle school teacher needs to see himself or herself as in charge of learning. Over the past 20 years, publishing companies have taken away much of the control of learning in America's classrooms by producing "teacher-proof" learning systems. The advent of Internet technology changes all that—the teacher is once again in charge!

Teachers in the new middle school must become expert on understanding the philosophy and the instructional criteria if they are to design learning once again. Middle school students are unique, and instruction in the middle school is not like that at the elementary or secondary school.

Finally, teachers need to see evaluation of instruction as an assisting venture that makes learning more and more purposeful. The questions suggested in the preceding section are helpful, guiding questions, designed to sharpen the instructional focus of the classroom teacher.

NEW STANDARDS FOR THE MIDDLE SCHOOL

As we enter the twenty-first century, the authors predict that a new and more responsive middle school will evolve. Frankly, this must happen if the middle school is to survive! In a nutshell, everything has changed in terms of teaching and learning since the Internet became available to us in 1995. The curriculum, including what is offered, how it was developed, who developed it, how it's accessed or delivered, and the role of the teacher of students is uniquely new.

A century-old promise of intermediate educators to build an instructional program for a unique learner, the preadolescent, can now be fulfilled. The middle school can declare itself once and for all and be consistently progressive in its philosophy and its programs. The network of emerging technological middle schools is awesome and can only become more powerful through synergy.

Given these changes, new middle schools must clarify their mission and update their standards for evaluation. The authors would offer the following list for the consideration of readers and middle school leaders.

The Middle School Will

A. Use communicative technologies to redefine school learning.
1. Will provide each student with developmentally appropriate materials.
2. Will individualize learning for each student.
3. Will deliver learning experiences at the level of student readiness.
4. Will allow each student to experience continuous progress in learning.
5. Will group students instructionally by purpose, not progress.

B. Develop a new and exciting exploratory curriculum.
1. Will expand on the natural growth of each student.
2. Will teach skills of access, assessment, and application.
3. Will stress an action learning format.
4. Will be future oriented, focusing on learning to solve problems.
5. Will be "high growth" in design, allowing for student expression.

C. Feature teachers who have transitioned to twenty-first century learning.
1. Teachers will be guides to and designers of learning.
2. Teachers will be the chief developers of curriculum.
3. Teachers will be at the center of a world learning community.
4. Teachers will train and be trained by other teachers.
5. Teachers will be lifelong learners.

D. Possess evaluation measures that are relevant.
1. Evaluation will be a joint venture with teachers, parents, and students.
2. Evaluation will reflect the comprehensive nature of middle school education.
3. Evaluation will assess individual students as individuals.

SUMMARY

Evaluation has always been a problem for the American middle school. The failure to address assessment and develop an evaluation system to measure what the middle school advocates has blurred the lines between middle schools and other forms of intermediate education. Evaluation in middle schools should be comprehensive and balanced, addressing programs, products, processes, and personnel.

Evaluation in a middle school is best perceived as a system with all parts interacting with other parts. The effort to evaluate results in school leaders and teachers being able to make decisions based on information, not hunches. A list of questions that could structure evaluation in eight key areas is provided for the reader's study.

Student evaluation is an especially difficult area for middle school teachers due to the diversity of the students. Since middle schools recognize the uniqueness of students and the diversity of their background and achievements, a standardized evaluation design is both unfair and inappropriate. The philosophy of the middle school calls for flexibility in the design of student evaluation.

The new middle school, with communication technology, will have to be very flexible in assessing students. In developing an individualized assessment plan for all students, certain guidelines will prove helpful. The authors suggest general guidelines for learning objectives, selection of curricula, instructional planning, and evaluation of classroom instruction.

Finally, the authors propose new standards for the twenty-first century middle school. These standards reflect and reaffirm a century-old effort to serve the needs of the preadolescent learner.

Suggested Learning Activities

1. Identify evaluation practices found in today's middle schools that are either philosophically inconsistent or developmentally inappropriate.

2. Develop a list of questions that would guide the evaluation of a middle school in your district. What purpose does such evaluation serve?

3. Construct an instrument for evaluating parent participation in a middle school program. What criteria guides this instrument?

4. Collect evaluation report cards or forms from a local middle school. How would you change these forms to more adequately represent instruction in a new twenty-first century middle school?

Notes

1. Jon Wiles, *Planning Guidelines for Middle School Education* (Dubuque, Iowa: Kendall/Hunt Publishing Company, 1976), pp. 71–79.

Selected Resources

Resource A
Obtaining Background Information About Students

SCHOOL DATA SHEET

Enrollment (Research Department Enrollment Survey):

ADA (Research Department) 7th/8th grade:

Teacher Absence Ratio, May—June pay period (ratio = absences per teacher per month):

Number of Low Socioeconomic Recipients (Junior high school students eligible to receive free or reduced lunch):

Number of Gifted/Other Special Students (State Report Matrix):

Student Mobility (In/Out—School records indicating check-in and check-out patterns as percentage of total enrollment):

Corporal Punishment (Research Department) from: _____ :

Suspensions, out-of-school (Program Evaluation Department):

Expulsions, school records (Research Department):

Dropouts, 9th graders only in junior highs:

Grade Distribution (Negative if more than one-half classes show 25% failure on 40% gaining or grade of D or F in classes):

Achievement, SSAT grade 8 (CTBS—Reading/Writing/Math = total battery as compared with district average):

LEARNING BEHAVIOR CHECKLIST

Directions: For each sentence beginning, check as many responses as seem to apply to you most of the time. If none apply, fill in the blank that reads "other."

1. When a teacher lectures in class,
   _____ a. I listen carefully and take notes which I study later.
   _____ b. I listen carefully and try to take notes, but they never help much.
   _____ c. I try to listen, but I get bored and my mind wanders.
   _____ d. I listen, and I learn a lot, but don't bother taking notes.
   _____ e. I use the time to read or do homework for another class.
   _____ f. I frequently talk, write notes, or just goof off.
   _____ g. I hope to get the notes from someone else later.
   _____ h. I daydream or sleep and hope I can get the same information from the book or from discussions.
   _____ i. Other _____

2. When I read an assignment in class,
   _____ a. I always read it carefully and study it hard.
   _____ b. I change the way I read (fast or slow, skim or study), depending on what the teacher says is the purpose for reading it.
   _____ c. I read it as fast as I can just to get it over with.
   _____ d. I read it slowly but don't learn much.
   _____ e. I wait until a friend is finished and ask what it was about.
   _____ f. I just read the first few paragraphs.
   _____ g. I never finish in time.
   _____ h. I always finish early.
   _____ i. I never read, period, because I'm a poor reader.
   _____ j. I read it, but don't remember it later.
   _____ k. I take notes as I read to study later.
   _____ l. Other _____

3. When we work in small groups in class,
   _____ a. I work harder because I can talk to other people.
   _____ b. I don't work much, but enjoy talking to my friends.
   _____ c. I try to work hard, but the others in the group don't usually listen to me.
   _____ d. I usually end up doing most of the work.
   _____ e. I don't participate much, but I pay attention and learn a lot by listening.
   _____ f. I *sit* in the group, but do the work by myself.
   _____ g. I enjoy it, but don't seem to learn as much.
   _____ h. I enjoy it and learn more than working alone or hearing lectures.
   _____ i. Other _____

LEARNING BEHAVIOR CHECKLIST *(continued)*

4. When I work by myself in class,
   _____ a. I work harder because it is easier for me to concentrate.
   _____ b. I talk to friends instead of working.
   _____ c. I don't enjoy it much, but I probably learn best.
   _____ d. I borrow answers whenever possible since I don't learn much this way, anyhow.
   _____ e. I wait and figure out the answers during discussions.
   _____ f. I just zip through to get done in a hurry and don't worry about it much.
   _____ g. I do my best, but it takes me such a long time!
   _____ h. Other _____

5. When I have assignments that aren't due for several days,
   _____ a. I usually forget to do them.
   _____ b. I do them right away just to get them done.
   _____ c. I put them off until the last possible minute and then rush through them.
   _____ d. I really worry about them even if I do put them off.
   _____ e. I like them because I have plenty of time to do them at my own rate.
   _____ f. I just copy them anyway, so it doesn't matter when they're done.
   _____ g. I wish they were due sooner because I need pressure to make me work.
   _____ h. Other _____

STUDENT INFORMATION SHEET

Name_____ Nickname _____
         Last   First   Middle

Student Number _____

Address _____

_____ Zip _____

Phone Number _____

I live with my   mother _____   father _____   stepmother _____

                stepfather _____   grandparents _____   other _____

Father's name _____ Occupation _____

Father's place of business _____ Phone _____

Mother's name _____ Occupation _____

Mother's place of business _____ Phone _____

List the names and ages of your brothers and sisters.

_____ _____   _____ _____

_____ _____   _____ _____

_____ _____   _____ _____

My birthdate is _____
                Month   Day   Year

I was born in _____
               City   State

Do you wear glasses to read books? _____

Do you wear glasses to read the chalkboard? _____

Do you have difficulty hearing from the back of the room? _____

How much time do you spend on homework each night? _____

My favorite subject is _____.

The subject I like least is _____.

My hobbies are _____.

After school I like to _____

_____.

When I finish high school, I would like to _____

_____.

Resource B
Middle School Parent Survey (Excerpt)

MIDDLE SCHOOL PARENT SURVEY

How would you rate this school on these qualities?

	Excellent	Good	Fair	Poor
1. Friendly and interested teachers	1	2	3	4
2. Emphasis on basic skills	1	2	3	4
3. Strong principal leadership	1	2	3	4
4. Supportive and involved parents	1	2	3	4
5. Good student discipline	1	2	3	4
6. Quality of teaching	1	2	3	4
7. Students excited by learning	1	2	3	4
8. Opportunities for enrichment	1	2	3	4
9. Library services	1	2	3	4
10. School/community relations	1	2	3	4
11. Reporting of pupil progress	1	2	3	4
12. Communication with parents	1	2	3	4
13. Meeting needs of individual students	1	2	3	4
14. Addressing the developmental needs of students (physical, social-emotional)	1	2	3	4

• • •

Please indicate how much you agree or disagree with the following statements:

	Strongly Agree	Agree	Disagree	Strongly Disagree	Don't Know
15. The principal of this school sets high academic standards for students.	1	2	3	4	5
16. The principal of this school sets high standards for student behavior.	1	2	3	4	5

	Strongly Agree	Agree	Disagree	Strongly Disagree	Don't Know
17. My child's teachers expect him/her to do well academically.	1	2	3	4	5
18. The principal communicates well with parents.	1	2	3	4	5
19. A positive feeling exists in this school.	1	2	3	4	5
20. My child's academic needs are being met.	1	2	3	4	5
21. The principal takes responsibility for the effectiveness of the instructional program.	1	2	3	4	5
22. Decisions about what happens to students in this school are made by the principal, teachers, and parents working together.	1	2	3	4	5
23. Parents and teachers work together to monitor homework.	1	2	3	4	5
24. Parent–teacher conferences result in specific plans to improve student classroom achievement.	1	2	3	4	5
25. My child receives adequate individual attention from his/her teachers.	1	2	3	4	5
26. My child is treated fairly in class.	1	2	3	4	5
27. My child enjoys what he/she does in his/her classes.	1	2	3	4	5
28. The lunchroom at this school is orderly.	1	2	3	4	5
29. I am aware of the consequences of my child's not obeying the rules at this school.	1	2	3	4	5
30. Students at this school are generally well-behaved.	1	2	3	4	5
31. I feel my child is safe from physical harm in this school.	1	2	3	4	5
32. Students at this school generally appear respectful of their teachers.	1	2	3	4	5
33. Students at this school generally appear respectful of their principal.	1	2	3	4	5

MIDDLE SCHOOL PARENT SURVEY (continued)

	Strongly Agree	Agree	Disagree	Strongly Disagree	Don't Know
34. In my child's classes there is a positive feeling that helps students learn.	1	2	3	4	5
35. My child's classes are generally orderly and quiet.	1	2	3	4	5
36. Goals and priorities for this school are clear.	1	2	3	4	5
37. My child's teachers let me know how my child is doing in school.	1	2	3	4	5
38. My child enjoys going to this school.	1	2	3	4	5
39. I expect my child to do well academically.	1	2	3	4	5
40. My child has friends at school with whom he/she feels comfortable.	1	2	3	4	5
41. There is at least one staff member who has a close, supportive relationship with my child.	1	2	3	4	5
42. I have specific reasons to be concerned about my child's exposure to drugs and alcohol at this school.	1	2	3	4	5
43. The school building is neat, bright, clean, and comfortable. It is a source of school pride.	1	2	3	4	5
44. My child is respected by students from different races and backgrounds.	1	2	3	4	5
45. My child has opportunities to socialize with students from other races and cultures.	1	2	3	4	5
46. I know whom I would call to correct a situation in which I felt that my child was discriminated against.	1	2	3	4	5
47. My child's courses have included students from differing races and cultures.	1	2	3	4	5
48. My child feels welcome to participate in any school activities that he/she is interested in.	1	2	3	4	5

	Strongly Agree	*Agree*	*Disagree*	*Strongly Disagree*	*Don't Know*
49. My child socializes with students from other races and cultures.	1	2	3	4	5
50. My child's courses include opportunities to learn about many races and cultures.	1	2	3	4	5

51. How would you rate the academic ability of your child compared with other students at this school?

My child's ability is much higher.   1

My child's ability is somewhat higher.   2

My child's ability is about the same.   3

My child's ability is somewhat lower.   4

My child's ability is much lower.   5

52. Do you expect your child to attend college?

Yes _____   No _____

53. Please list steps that this school could take to become more sensitive to differing races and cultures.

a. _____

b. _____

c. _____

54. Please list three things you like about this school.

a. _____

_____

b. _____

_____

c. _____

_____

55. Please list three things you would like to see improved at this school.

a. _____

_____

b. _____

_____

c. _____

_____

Resource C
Inservice Design and Workshop Models

C

INSERVICE/STAFF DEVELOPMENT ACTIVITIES
(DADE COUNTY)

Middle School Inservice/Staff Development Committee

Chair:	Ms. Elvira Dopico
Members:	Dr. Kenneth Walker, Dr. Joseph DeChurch, Dr. Ed Trauschke, Ms. Karen Dreyfuss, Ms. Margaret Petersen
Consultants:	Dr. Jon Wiles, Dr. Joseph Bondi
Purpose:	To develop an inservice/staff development plan to train, orient and inform all persons responsible for the successful implementation of the middle school program in Dade County.
Impact Groups:	School board
	Senior staff
	District subject area supervisors
	Area administrators
	Middle school principals, assistant principals, counselors
	School support staffs, including clerical, security, custodial, and bus drivers
	Parents
	Community groups/persons

INSERVICE/STAFF DEVELOPMENT ACTIVITIES FOR MIDDLE SCHOOL TRANSITION

Group	Activity	Time Frames	Person(s) Responsible
School Board	a. Reporting to (progress report) b. Information and updating	June 1989, 1990, 1991, 1992	J. Fernandez P. Bell Management team Coordinating committee Wiles–Bondi

Group	Activity	Time Frames	Person(s) Responsible
Senior staff	a. Information and updating	As needed	J. Fernandez P. Bell Wiles–Bondi
District staff/area administrators	a. Orientation– training	Spring, Fall 1988	Wiles–Bondi
Other school administrators (elem.–high school)	b. Information and updating	As needed	Wiles–Bondi
Middle school principals, assistant principals, counselors	a. Leadership training in scheduling, leadership, working with teams, building parent and community involvement	Spring preceding implementation of middle school program	Wiles–Bondi
	b. Information and updating	Ongoing	J. DeChurch Wiles–Bondi
Middle school teachers	a. General training in 50-hour middle school training components	1988–1992	K. Walker K. Dreyfuss M. Petersen Subject area supervisors Training teams Wiles–Bondi University—other consultants
School support staff, clerical, custodial, security, bus drivers	Orientation and information	1988–ongoing	J. DeChurch K. Dreyfuss J. Gilyard
Parents	Orientation and information	1988–ongoing	J. DeChurch
Community groups/individuals	Information	1988–ongoing	P. Bell J. DeChurch

Training Components for Teachers

A. Three 10-hour training components developed by Wiles–Bondi for teachers:
1. The Middle School and Middle School Student
2. Teaming and Interdisciplinary Instruction
3. Strategies for Adviser/Advisee Program

INSERVICE/STAFF DEVELOPMENT ACTIVITIES
(DADE COUNTY) (continued)

B. Two additional 10-hour components developed by Teacher Education Center (TEC) staff and Wiles–Bondi. This will provide a total package of 50 hours of training leading to middle school endorsement (for those eligible) and internal Dade County middle school certification. These two components will be taught by local university consultants and others. They are as follows:

4. Teaching Strategies in Middle School (English, science, math, social studies, art, etc.)
5. General Strategies for Teaching in Middle School. This component will include topics for teaching critical thinking, teaching decision-making skills, designing positive classroom management and assertive discipline programs.

Training Program for School Administrators

A separate 10-hour training component for school administrators developed by Wiles–Bondi will include topics such as scheduling, school leadership, working with teams, and community involvement. This component will allow principals, assistant principals, and district and area staff to update skills in middle school leadership.

Orientation and Information Components

Orientation and information components for the board, district, senior staff, supervisory staff, area staff, school site administrators, coordinating committee, and parent and community groups will be developed by the management team, middle school coordinator, and consultants. These components will begin in 1988 and be ongoing.

Delivery of Training and Orientation/Information Program

Delivery of teacher training components 1–3 will occur through the TTT (Teachers Training Teachers) Model with the consultants training the training teams to deliver each of the three components. Training in these components began in 1988 and will be ongoing. Components 4 and 5 will be regularly scheduled by the TEC beginning in 1989 and will be ongoing. The 10-hour leadership component will be regularly scheduled and taught by the consultants beginning in 1989 and will be ongoing.

Recordkeeping, Monitoring, Support, and Certification

Recordkeeping, monitoring, support, and certification will be the responsibility of the Bureau of Human Resource Development.

Overall Goal

Our goal is for Dade County to have *the* nationwide model for a middle school training program. Dade County will train 100% of our middle school teachers and administrators and set in motion a sustaining program for all new personnel. In addition, orientation and information components will be developed and delivered to orient and update all school personnel, parents, and community individuals on the middle school concept.

Committee Members: Linda Cugini, Barbara DeSue, Jana French, Peggy Kring, Genevieve Oliver, Marlene Rasmussen, Franklin Smith, Dorothy Williams

Consultants: Dr. Jon Wiles, Dr. Joseph Bondi

Purpose: To develop an inservice/staff development plan to train, orient, and inform all persons responsible for the successful implementation of the middle school program in Dade County.

Inservice/Staff Development Activities

Group	*Activity*	*Time*	*Person(s) Responsible*
School board	Progress report	November 1989, 1990, 1991	Larry Zenke Management team Coordinating committee
District/staff area superintendents	Orientation–training	Fall 1989/ongoing	Wiles–Bondi
Other administrators (Elem.–high school)	Information and updating	Spring 1990/ongoing	Wiles–Bondi
Middle school principals, assistant principals, counselors	a. Leadership training in scheduling, leadership, working with teams	January–February 1990/ongoing	Wiles–Bondi
Middle school principals (24)/vice principals/counselors/assistant principals	a. Leadership Training II	April–June 1990	Wiles–Bondi
	b. Information	Ongoing	Management team Wiles–Bondi
Middle school training team	a. Trainer inservice	Fall 1989/ongoing	Wiles–Bondi Staff development coordinator Teacher Education Center
Middle school teachers/staff	a. General training in June; 40-hour middle school training component	November–1989–1990/ongoing	Training team Teacher Education Center Staff development coordinator

INSERVICE/STAFF DEVELOPMENT ACTIVITIES
(DADE COUNTY) (continued)

Group	Activity	Time	Person(s) Responsible
School support, staff, clerical, custodial, bus drivers	Orientation and information	1989/ongoing	Barbara DeSue Staff development coordinator
Parents	Orientation and information	1989/ongoing	Barbara DeSue Staff development coordinator
Community groups/individuals	Information	1989/ongoing	Barbara DeSue Staff development coordinator Committee members

The Staff Development Coordinator will release two newsletters, one in the winter of 1990 and one in the spring of 1991.

TEACHER/ADMINISTRATOR TRAINING MODEL
(DUVAL COUNTY)

TRAINING COMPONENTS FOR TEACHERS–ADMINISTRATORS

A. Four 10-hour training components for teachers/administrators:
1. Characteristics of the Middle Grade Student and Middle School Program
2. Organization of Instruction (Teaming) in the Middle Grades
3. Counseling the Middle Grade Student
4. Middle Grade Curriculum: Planning and Evaluation

Delivery of Teacher Training components 1–4 will occur through the TTT (Teachers Training Teachers) Model with the consultants training the training teams to deliver each of the four components. These components will be scheduled through the TEC and will begin in 1989 and will be ongoing. Components 5 and 6 will be regularly scheduled by the TEC office and middle grades staff development coordinator beginning in 1990 and will be ongoing. Training in components 7, 8, and 9 will be regularly scheduled through the TEC and the middle grades staff development coordinator.

B. Five additional 10-hour components are:
5. Teaching Strategies in Middle School (math, English, art, social studies, science, etc.)
6. General Strategies for Teaching in Middle School (will include topics for teaching critical thinking skills and designing positive classroom management techniques)
7. Team Leader Training
8. Utilizing Interdisciplinary Units
9. Trainer Component (Teachers will be trained to deliver the 40-hour inservice.)

C. Training program for school administrators will include:
10. Leadership in Middle Schools I: A 10-hour general training component for school administrators, developed by Wiles–Bondi, will include general topics such as scheduling, school leadership, working with teams, and community involvement. This component will allow principals, assistants, and district and area staff to update skills in middle school leadership.
11. Leadership in Middle Schools II: A 10-hour training component for middle school administrators (principal, vice-principal, assistant principal) developed by Wiles–Bondi will focus on identified needs of administrators. This component will permit work on a real schedule, building organization, curriculum, team organization, and leadership strategies.

Recordkeeping, monitoring, support, and certification will be the responsibility of the staff development coordinator.

PRESERVICE AND INSERVICE: RECOMMENDATIONS

TEACHER EDUCATION EXPERIENCES

A. Underlying Principles: In addition to guidelines for the three phases of teacher education—general education, individual specialization, and professional preparation, the following underlying principles are suggested:

  1. Middle school teacher education should promote continuity of educational experience. All aspects of the teacher education program should be closely interrelated to provide a meaningful professional experience for the prospective middle school teacher.
  2. Middle school teacher education should ensure the development of personal qualities as well as professional abilities.
  3. Middle school teacher education should be highly personalized. It is important that the individualization of instruction sought for the middle school also be a goal of middle school teacher education.
  4. Middle school teacher education should be a simultaneous blending of didactic instruction and practical experience. Practical experiences should be coordinated with didactic course work to provide meaningful professional education experiences for prospective middle school teachers.
  5. Middle school teacher education should use those principles, techniques, and materials appropriate to middle school teaching insofar as they are consistent with the level of understanding and maturity of prospective middle school teachers.

B. General Education: Middle school teacher preparation should include sufficient experiences of a general or liberal education nature to qualify the teacher as a literate, self-directed learner, able to understand and interpret current developments in a changing society.

C. Individual Specialization:

  1. As early as possible in the teacher education program, teacher candidates should have opportunity to study the operation of schools at different levels, so that the individual's choice of middle school specialization is based on special interest in work at this level.
  2. Each middle school staff member should have both breadth and depth in preparation. The depth of preparation should be in a curriculum or service in which the person could function as a specialist in team teaching or other instructional organization appropriate to middle school-age children.
  3. Specialization should be planned for each middle school teacher in terms of his interests, competencies, and pattern of college courses to ensure an adequate preparation in the field of specialization.
  4. Some experiences in the field of specialization should parallel the school laboratory experiences described below, so as to provide adequate opportunity for relating general professional preparation and individual specialization. Periodic reviews of each teacher competencies should be used in determining further training needs.

D. Professional Preparation:

  1. Basic to the entire program of teacher education for the middle school is study of the characteristics of middle school-age children. In that continuous and prolonged experience in working with these children is desirable in the program, a

combination of laboratory observation, case study, and systematic instruction seems indicated.

2. The middle school teacher should participate in a middle school laboratory experience program for at least one year. These experiences would include observation of teaching and learning situations; involvement in parent conferences and school–community activities; participation in team planning, team teaching, and evaluation, and other differentiated staff arrangements: direct instruction of individuals, small groups, and variable-size classes, and participation in schoolwide and special-interest activities. The program should include both extensive and intensive phases to provide experience with a wide variety of instructional situations.

3. The school laboratory experience should be paralleled by, or include, experiences of a curricular and instructional laboratory type. These experiences would include preparation of curriculum objectives, plans and units, and instructional materials; practice in use of a variety of instructional media and resources; development of tests and test analyses; and the use of systematic observation, simulation, and other techniques for developing teacher skills.

4. Paralleling the laboratory experiences should be a professional seminar devoted to developing professional understandings, skills, and attitudes for working in the middle schools. Seminar participants (in addition to teacher candidates and college professors) might include supervising teachers in the laboratory situations and resource personnel as needed and as available. Experiences in the laboratory settings would be analyzed with attention to alternative procedures, relationships between schools and units within particular schools, and in general the application of theory and research to practice. The seminar would include opportunities for grouping participants both by curriculum area and across roles.

PROGRAM ADMISSION

A. Preservice:
   1. The institution has a procedure for identifying and selecting candidates for admission to the program for middle school teachers. Sections II and III of these guidelines are used in developing the procedure for admission.
   2. Procedures for admission include criteria relating to selection, placement, and retention.
   3. Procedures provide for individual assessment utilizing Section II of these guidelines as criteria. They also provide for a design of an individual program for the applicant that is based on his needs as revealed by this assessment.
   4. The assessment should include the capacity of the candidate to complete the program; familiarity with the objectives of the program; an understanding of the competencies, attitudes, and skills needed in the middle school teacher; and an initial commitment to teaching the middle school child.
   5. Procedures provide for candidates to enter the program after completion of an undergraduate program in another area of concentration.

PRESERVICE AND INSERVICE: RECOMMENDATIONS (continued)

B. Inservice: The inservice teacher, for all practical purposes, is admitted to the inservice program of a school district when that school district employs the teacher to teach in a middle school. However, admission to certain parts of the inservice program for middle school teachers should follow an organized procedure:

1. The local education agency or school has a cooperatively developed procedure for assessing the inservice needs of middle school teachers.
2. Procedures provide for individual assessment based on Section II of these guidelines and the system's ability to improve the needs revealed. Assessment only includes the competencies in Section II of which the local system is capable of improving through inservice education.
3. Procedures provide for the cooperative development and use of the assessment procedures by teachers, supervisors, and administrators.
4. Procedures provide for candidates to use both the local education agency's inservice education program, and institution-based programs.

FOLLOW-UP OF PROGRAM PARTICIPANTS

A. Preservice:

1. There is a planned program for assessing changes in attitudes and behavior of students as they move through the program.
2. The program utilizes the results of the assessment procedures to revise individual student programs.
3. Personnel in cooperating schools participate in the education process.
4. Evaluation of the effectiveness of the program is accomplished through evidence obtained from former students, the schools in which they work, and the Department of Education. This evidence is based on the stated objective of the program.
5. The follow-up program includes early leavers as well as those who complete the program.
6. A record of revisions in the program includes the follow-up data on which the revisions were based.
7. Data appropriate for preservice/inservice program articulation are shared with the cooperating school system.

B. Inservice:

1. There is a planned program of evaluation of the effectiveness of each inservice education component.
2. The assessment of competencies developed in the program includes not only changes in teacher behavior, but an assessment of the resultant changes in student behavior.
3. A record of revisions of inservice education components includes the evaluation data on which revisions were based.
4. Personnel from teacher education institutions participate in the evaluation of the program.
5. Supervisors, principals, and teachers participate in the evaluation of the program's effectiveness.

TRAINING CATEGORIES

In an effort to provide top-quality administrative training, we will divide our training into three specific categories (Beginning, Intermediate, and Advanced). This will allow us to focus our efforts to meet the specific needs of individual schools. The following is a description of the three categories with an explanation of the type of district support attached to each.

Advanced

This category of schools will open their doors in September with a master schedule that reflects *true* interdisciplinary teaming in *all* grade levels within the school.

District Support

1. Salary supplements for team leaders and advisory leader (contingent on state funding)
2. Salary supplement for an advisory leader—if schoolwide advisory program exists (contingent on state funding)
3. Summer training for administrative staff (generic and technical assistance)
4. Training of teacher training cadre
5. District support services
6. $6,000 for interdisciplinary team development

Intermediate

This category of schools will open their doors in September with a master schedule that reflects *true* interdisciplinary teaming in *one* or *more* grade levels. *Or,* this group comprises those schools that will revise their master schedules during the first semester so that *true* interdisciplinary teaming will be in place in *one* or *more* grade levels during the second semester.

District Support

1. Salary supplements for team leaders (contingent on state funding)
2. Salary supplement for an advisory leader—if a schoolwide advisory program exists (contingent on state funding)
3. Summer training for administrative staff (generic and technical assistance)
4. Training of the teacher training cadre
5. District support services
6. Some portion of the $6,000 for interdisciplinary team development (exact amount determined by the school principal and the middle school office)

Beginning

Those schools will use the 1989–1990 school year as a planning and training year. They will train staff and use the 1989–1990 school year to develop a master schedule, which will allow for full-scale interdisciplinary teaming during the 1990–1991 school year.

TRAINING CATEGORIES (continued)

District Support

1. Summer training of administrative staff (generic and technical assistance)
2. Training of the teacher training cadre
3. District support services

CATEGORIES

Advanced	*Intermediate*	*Beginning*
Arvida	Allapattah	Brownsville
Campbell Drive	B. T. Washington	Carver, G. W.
Carol City	Centennial	Hammocks
Citrus Grove	Hialeah	Highland Oaks
Cutler Ridge	Miami Lakes	Kennedy, J. F.
Drew	Richmond Heights	Lee, J. R. E.
Edison	Thomas Jefferson	Mann, Jan
Filer	Westview	Marti, Jose
Glades	W. R. Thomas	McMillian, H. D.
Homestead		North Dade
Horace Mann		Palmetto
Kinloch Park		Riviera
Lake Stevens		Rockway
Madison		Southwood
Mays		South Miami
Miami Springs		West Miami
Nautilus		
Norland		
North Miami		
Palm Springs		
Parkway		
Ponce de Leon		
Redland		
Ruben Dario		
Shenandoah		

ADMINISTRATOR TRAINING MODEL

Premise: Principals should receive *useful,* hands-on training. Training configuration must be taken in order:

1. Middle School Development (Component "A")
   A. Role of intermediate education
      How is it different and why should it be different?
   B. Middle school curriculum: establishing a philosophy; establishing a climate; focusing the learning design; establishing major curriculum developmental tasks

2. Effective Administration of a Middle School (Component "B")
   A. Development of an action plan based on a needs assessment
   B. Determination of progress points and observable criteria
   C. Elements of the basic middle school components
   D. Building the administrative team
   E. Special problems of the new middle school administration

3. Leadership and Change in a Middle School (Component "B")
   A. How to create change
   B. Meeting with resistance and overcoming challenges
   C. Leadership theory in practice
   D. Inservice training needs and the development of a yearlong implementation plan

4. Retooling the School and Staff (Component "C")
   A. Prepare ways to orient teachers to middle school
   B. Develop orientation presentation
   C. A new look at the middle school classroom
   D. How to humanize instruction (total development versus subject priority)
   E. Learning styles/instructional strategies
   F. Organizing the classroom for instruction
   G. Teams and team leaders—what are they and what do they do?
   H. Obstacles/challenges/helpful hints

5. Developing a Middle School Curriculum (Component "D")
   A. Scheduling process
   B. Issues and concerns
   C. Hands-on training
   D. Adviser/advisee

ADMINISTRATOR TRAINING MODEL (continued)

Training with a different edge (for assistant principals) includes:

1. Middle School Model/Philosophy (Component "A")
   A. Role of intermediate education
   B. Focusing on the learning design
   C. Major curriculum developmental tasks

2. Supervision of the Middle School (Component "B")
   A. Teams/team leaders/department heads
   B. Team leader council
   C. Interdisciplinary planning/implementation/setting
   D. Setting expectations, adviser/advisee, etc.

3. Retooling [Same as principals, plus supervision of team leaders] (Component "C")

4. Scheduling (Component "D")

ADMINISTRATOR TECHNICAL ASSISTANCE TRAINING

Teams of two to three training principals will be assigned to work with schools on an individual basis. Each school will set its own schedule for technical assistance with its assigned principal training team. Technical assistance will be offered throughout the summer and will include these areas:

A. Scheduling	G. Intramurals
B. Teaming	H. Needs assessment
C. Adviser/advisee	I. Action plan
D. Interdisciplinary instruction	J. Follow up
E. Curriculum	K. Inservice
F. Exploration	

TEACHER COMPETENCIES SELF-APPRAISAL

Name _____ School _____

Date _____ Grade _____

Directions: Below are a list of competencies deemed important for effective teaching in the middle school. Please examine each competency and appraise your own abilities in this area. Indicate whether the competency is an area of strength, adequacy, or weakness for you. Do so by using the following code to mark the boxes to the right of the competency: S = Strength, A = Adequacy, W = Weakness.

At the end of the list, you are asked to select several competencies for further professional development. The competencies that you select may be strengths that you wish to capitalize on, or weaknesses you wish to erase.

PART ONE: MIDDLE SCHOOL TEACHER COMPETENCIES   APPRAISAL

A. Competency Area: Interpersonal Relationships
   1. The teacher manages the classroom with a minimum of negative or aversive controls. _____
   2. The teacher creates a climate in the classroom which rests somewhere comfortably apart from an authoritarian tenseness or a laissez-faire chaos. _____
   3. The teacher uses himself (herself) as a tool in promoting the personal growth of students and colleagues. _____
   4. The teacher's relationships with colleagues, administrators, and supervisors are harmonious and productive. _____
   5. The teacher is aware of the needs, forces, and perceptions which determine his (her) personal behavior. _____
   6. The teacher accepts behavior, and values individuals and groups which depart from his own. _____

B. Competency Area: Basic Instructional Skills
   1. The teacher exhibits variety as a basic facet of instruction both during the hour and from class to class. _____
   2. The teacher uses a multimedia approach. _____
   3. The teacher maintains a balance between teacher-directed learning and student-directed learning. _____
   4. The teacher individualizes instruction in the classroom. _____
   5. The teacher promotes student self-direction, initiative, and responsibility. _____
   6. The teacher selects learning activities and executes them in a way that promotes student interest and involvement. _____

TEACHER COMPETENCIES SELF-APPRAISAL *(continued)*

PART ONE: MIDDLE SCHOOL TEACHER COMPETENCIES	APPRAISAL

7. The teacher's efforts in curriculum and instruction proceed from a problem-solving framework, involving the students in relevant inquiry.   _____

8. The teacher plans lessons thoroughly and in advance, using specific objectives and smooth transitions from one lesson to another.   _____

9. The teacher utilizes a variety of group sizes and devices in instruction.   _____

10. The teacher possesses skill in asking questions which encourage student thinking beyond the level of "recall."   _____

11. The teacher avoids common pitfalls of expository teaching, such as in faulty speech patterns, pacing the room, use of chalkboard, physical appearance of the classroom, etc.   _____

12. The teacher knows about and applies modern learning theories in the classroom.   _____

C. Competency Area: Curriculum

1. The teacher knows what is relevant to the lives of students and finds ways to include it in the curriculum.   _____

2. The teacher chooses curriculum materials that are appropriate for the learning abilities and styles of the students.   _____

3. The teacher, individually or with a team of teachers, involves students in interdisciplinary studies.   _____

D. Competency Area: Relationships with the Community

1. The teacher establishes positive relationships with the parents and families of students.   _____

2. The teacher works at understanding, accepting, and being accepted by members of the subcultures in the school and in the community.   _____

3. The teacher is interested in and participates in affairs of the community and school.   _____

E. Competency Area: Understanding the Student

1. The teacher understands the intellectual nature of middle school youth.   _____

2. The teacher understands the physical nature of middle school youth.   _____

3. The teacher understands the socio-emotional nature of middle school youth.   _____

F. Competency Area: Commitment to Middle School Teaching

1. The teacher is enthusiastic and vigorous in the daily activities of teaching middle school youth.   _____

2. The teacher understands the middle school concept and attempts to apply it in the classroom, and in the school as a whole. _____

PART TWO: AREAS FOR DEVELOPMENT

Please list below the numbers of the competencies which you have selected for further development. They may be either strengths or weaknesses, and you may select more than five or fewer than five.

1.

2.

3.

4.

5.

TEACHER SURVEY OF EXPERIENCE AND STAFF DEVELOPMENT NEEDS

Instrument: Teacher Survey Form (administered to 6–8 teachers, counselors, and administrators)

Findings: This questionnaire was designed to gather data from the above-mentioned sources regarding experience and training. The findings include:

Degrees:	22% hold a B.A. degree
	28% hold a B.S. degree
	39% hold a Master's degree
	8% hold a higher degree
Years of service:	22% over five years
	42% over ten years
	22% over twenty years
Years in middle school:	33% over five years
	44% over ten years

Skills identified as most useful in implementing the middle school concept include:

1. Dealing with motivation and discipline problems in the classroom
2. Effective teaching strategies
3. Understanding characteristics of middle school students
4. Strategies for dealing with low achievers
5. Techniques for guiding and advising students

TEACHER SURVEY OF EXPERIENCE AND STAFF DEVELOPMENT NEEDS (continued)

Implications:

1. Middle school teachers represent a veteran, highly trained staff. Almost half of the teachers surveyed have ten or more years in middle school; however, one-fourth of these teachers do not have middle school certification.
2. Teachers are anxious to improve skills relating to discipline, motivation, and advising students. In order to do this, they need a clearer understanding of middle school students and strategies for working with them at all levels.
3. Inservice and staff development should continue to provide teachers with retooling skills needed to carry out an effective middle school program and provide means to gain proper certification.

TRAINING: OBJECTIVES, ACTIVITIES, AND EVALUATION

Number: 5–01–49–2–13

Inservice Points: 60

General Objective: To identify the characteristics of the middle school; to identify the needs of and develop a curriculum for the middle school students

Specific Objectives: At the conclusion of training, each participant will be able to:

1. State the rationale for the middle school
2. Examine the history of the development of the middle school
3. Develop a program description for the middle school
4. Describe the physical, social, emotional, and intellectual development of students between the ages of ten and fourteen
5. Suggest specific program needs suggested by growth and development characteristics of emerging adolescent learners
6. Develop a block schedule, given the number of teachers and students in their middle school
7. List the advantages and disadvantages of a nongraded structure
8. Plan a lesson for a block of time in their classrooms
9. Learn to use the thirteen-category Flanders System of Interaction Analysis and Gallagher–Aschner System for Analyzing Classroom Questions
10. Develop a system for dealing with classroom discipline
11. Identify the ten most important teacher competencies for the middle school

12. List the advantages and disadvantages of team teaching
13. Develop a team agenda
14. Practice teaming skills
15. Learn the steps necessary in developing an interdisciplinary unit of instruction
16. Outline the steps of a needs assessment
17. Learn to state Level I, II, and III goals and learning objectives
18. Identify the major skills, concepts, and content in their subject for grades 6 through 8
19. Learn to diagnose needs of creative and talented students
20. Master the sequential skills in the Wiles–Bondi skill clusters for creative thinking
21. Develop and teach one or more skill-learning activities in the Wiles–Bondi Creative Thinking Skills System
22. Develop and implement a series of guidance exercises for their students that will enhance their self-understanding and respect for others
23. Practice learning skills and other skills necessary for serving in an advisory role to middle school students
24. Learn what persons and agencies are available to assist the classroom teacher in working with students having special school and home problems
25. Develop and teach a creative learning lesson
26. Plan and implement several new classroom activities for that unit
27. Present a plan to restructure the seating arrangement of the classroom and utilize other school spaces for their students in teaching the learning unit
28. Develop a plan for a learning center in their classrooms
29. Develop strategies for working with students with special needs
30. Develop a plan to enhance the learning environment for middle-level students
31. Identify and sequence the steps necessary in planning a middle school
32. Develop an instrument to judge the effectiveness of a middle school. The instrument will examine both curricular and instructional practices

Description/Activities:

Objectives 1 through 3: Participants will view the film "Profile of a Middle School," write a philosophical statement defending the middle school design, and develop a parent information brochure outlining the essential elements of a middle school.

Objectives 4 and 5: Participants will develop procedures for studying students in their middle school and develop one instrument to carry information about student needs and interests in their school.

Objectives 6 through 8: Given enrollment and the staffing pattern of a middle school, participants will develop an actual middle school schedule. In groups of four or five, participants will organize a week's activities for a block of instructional time.

TRAINING: OBJECTIVES, ACTIVITIES,
AND EVALUATION (continued)

Objectives 9 through 11: Participants will practice using certain instruments utilized in assessing classroom instruction and develop an actual set of discipline procedures they will use in the classroom. Case studies will be provided to examine in detail teaching–learning situations found in middle schools.

Objectives 12 through 15: Participants will role-play in team meetings and work together in interdisciplinary teams to develop an outline for an interdisciplinary unit.

Objectives 16 through 18: Participants will work individually and in teams to analyze the curriculum of the middle school, focusing on the subject areas they are teaching. A skill continuum or checklist will be developed for each subject area represented by the participants.

Objectives 19 through 21: Participants will develop a series of learning activities utilizing the Wiles–Bondi Creative Thinking Skills System and organize several learning activities that will enhance the creative thinking skills of their students.

Objectives 22 through 24: Participants will structure a series of guidance activities. Role-playing techniques will be used to acquaint teachers with actual student–teacher roles and expectations.

Objectives 25 through 30: Participants will utilize existing classroom materials and teacher-made materials to develop a learning unit. The unit will require the development of innovative classroom activities and a restructuring of the physical arrangement of the classroom in which the unit is being taught.

Objectives 31 and 32: Participants will work in small and large groups to develop a planning checklist for those organizing a middle school and also develop an evaluation instrument for judging the effectiveness of a middle school.

Evaluation:

Objectives 1 through 3:   Participants will

—list the essential elements of a successful middle school.
—explain the rationale for the middle school.
—design a program description for their own middle school.

Objectives 4 and 5:   Participants will

—discuss characteristics of adolescent learners and implications for effective school level programs.
—describe the physical, social, emotional, and intellectual development of students between the ages of 10 and 14.
—list and develop appropriate instructional strategies for middle-level learners.

Objectives 6 through 8:   Participants will

—list advantages of interdisciplinary teams with regard to the instruction of middle-level learners.
—develop an appropriate block schedule and flexible time schedule for middle school students.
—list the advantages and disadvantages of a nongraded structure.
—plan a lesson for a block of time in their classrooms.

Objectives 9 through 11:   Participants will

—list kinds of teaching strategies appropriate for preadolescents.
—discuss appropriate classroom questioning techniques.
—discuss necessary competencies for the middle school teacher.

Objectives 12 through 15: Participants will

—list advantages and disadvantages of team teaching.
—develop an agenda for a team meeting.
—list, discuss, and practice effective teaming skills.
—list the steps used in developing an interdisciplinary unit of instruction.

Objectives 16 through 18: Participants will

—analyze curriculum and discuss its impact on middle-level learners.
—develop appropriate goals/objectives for middle-level instruction.
—identify skills, concepts, and activities to achieve specific learning levels.

Objectives 19 through 21: Participants will

—list activities/strategies that develop thinking and creativity in middle-level students.
—discuss the sequential skills used in developing higher thinking.
—develop and teach an activity which addresses higher/creative thinking in middle-level students.

Objectives 22 through 24: Participants will

—list support personnel with expertise in counseling middle-level students.
—list and practice skills necessary for serving in an advisory capacity.
—develop, assemble, and practice a series of activities designed to enhance the self-concept of middle school students.

Objectives 25 through 30: Participants will

—implement a plan designed to enhance the learning environment for middle-level students.
—design and implement a creative learning unit.
—plan classroom activities for the unit mentioned above.

TRAINING: OBJECTIVES, ACTIVITIES,
AND EVALUATION (continued)

—design a plan to fully utilize classroom space in a variety of ways.
—develop a learning center for use in their subject area classrooms.
—plan activities for students with special needs.

Objectives 31 and 32: Participants will

—develop a list of criteria with which to evaluate their team/school effectiveness.
—identify a sequence of steps for use in planning a middle school and critique their own school.

Participants and consultants will assess the degree to which specific objectives have been addressed by the component activities.

Pretests and posttests designed by the instructor(s) will be administered to each participant. Mastery of the component will be demonstrated by a minimum score of 80 on the posttest.

A workshop evaluation form will be administered to all participants to assess their perceptions of the training received.

Coordinator: District staff development director/middle school supervisor

TEACHERS TRAINING TEACHERS (TTT) WORKSHOP IN TEAMING AND INTERDISCIPLINARY INSTRUCTION

AGENDA

I. What Is Teaming? Advantages and Disadvantages of Teaming

II. How Teams Make Decisions
1. Autocracy
2. Voting
3. Consensus

III. Team Building
1. Expectations of team members
2. Expectations of team leader
3. Expectations of principal, assistant, counselors
4. Working with special-area teachers
5. Goals for your team

IV. Goals for Your Team Students
1. Achievement
2. Team spirit
3. Attendance

V. Developing a Discipline Plan for Your Team

VI. Evaluating Team Effectiveness

VII. Working Tasks
1. Profile folders
2. Recordkeeping
3. Scheduling students
4. Who's who in our school
5. Team agenda—minutes
6. Day one, week one, month one tasks

VIII. Developing an Interdisciplinary Unit

IX. Materials Needed
1. *Teaming in the Middle School* (Wiles–Bondi)
2. *Designing Interdisciplinary Units* (Wiles–Bondi)
3. Tear-off sheets, marking pens, masking tape

WORKING TASKS

1. Profile folders
2. Schedules for students; grouping, regrouping
3. Traffic patterns: lunch, changing classes

TEACHERS TRAINING TEACHERS (TTT) WORKSHOP IN TEAMING AND INTERDISCIPLINARY INSTRUCTION *(continued)*

4. Place and schedule of team meeting: physical resources
5. Scheduling of administrators, counselors, media, and other support persons in school and outside school
6. Rules for use of staff support persons—secretary, custodians
7. Communication with special-area teachers—exceptionalities teachers
8. Plans for adviser/advisee
9. Recordkeeping—files
10. Team rules for students
11. Roles of team members
12. Roles of team leader
13. Team agenda
14. Plans for reaching goals
15. Rules for communicating with parents
16. Orientation of students—communications to parents
17. Day one
    Week one
    Month one
18. Curriculum maps
19. Determination of ID topics
20. Plans for first ID unit
21. Evaluation
22. Inservice follow-up

SAMPLE TRAINING CERTIFICATE

NASSAU COUNTY PUBLIC SCHOOLS

MIDDLE SCHOOL
TRAINING CERTIFICATE

awarded to

_____

FOR SUCCESSFULLY COMPLETING
THE PRESCRIBED COURSE OF STUDY FOR

MIDDLE LEVEL EDUCATION

Given this _____ day of _____ ,20 ___

Craig Marsh	Eugene W. Grant	Dr. Joseph Bondi
Superintendent	Director of Middle Education	Middle School Consultant

Resource D
Middle School Design Parameters (Excerpts), Dade County

DESIGN PARAMETERS FOR THE MIDDLE SCHOOL IN DADE COUNTY PUBLIC SCHOOLS

PREPARED BY THE MIDDLE SCHOOL DESIGN COMMITTEE

John Moore, Co-chairperson
Principal, Cutler Ridge Middle School

Murray Sissleman, Co-chairperson
President, United Teachers of Dade (UTD)

Thelma Davis, Principal
Madison Middle School

John Gilbert, Principal
Norland Middle School

Michael Jones, UTD

Al Maniaci, UTD

Dorothy Mazine, Teacher
Miami Springs Middle School

Kim Rubin, Teacher
Nautilus Middle School

Pat Tellis, Asst. Principal
Drew Middle School

Dan Tosado, Principal
Centennial Middle School

Developed under the direction of the Middle School Office—J. L. DeChurch, Executive Director. Consultant services provided by Jon Wiles and Joseph Bondi.

FOREWORD

The Middle School Design Report was developed through a collaborative effort between staff of the Dade County Public Schools and members of the United Teachers of Dade (UTD). This collaboration represents the continued effort of the district and union to work together for the betterment of education in Dade County's public schools.

The *Design Report* is to be considered a working blueprint that allows individual school communities maximum flexibility in developing programs and implementing the philosophies of the middle school.

The document is the result of the work of an ad hoc committee formed to provide a model for education to all middle schools in the district. The model recommends a shared philosophy and identifies programs and components, objectives, standards, and evaluative criteria for all middle schools.

The Dade County School Board has adopted a four-year plan to convert all its intermediate-level schools to fully functioning middle schools by 1991–92. This four-year conversion process utilizes a Curriculum Management Plan (CMP) as a guide. The CMP focuses on using needs assessment, developing a clear set of goals, tying school needs to program needs, involving teachers, administrators, union, parents, and community, and providing an analysis of progress to the general public.

It is the hope of Dade County Public Schools that this type of long-range planning and collaborative working arrangement will allow us to accomplish our goal of "National Excellence in Middle Grades Education."

Joseph A. Fernandez
Superintendent of Schools

EXECUTIVE SUMMARY

Design of the DCPS Middle School

The design parameters for middle school education in the Dade County Public School (DCPS) System are described in the accompanying document.

The document sets forth the essential parameters of an appropriate middle-grades education program in Dade County. Information is presented in three ways:

1. Critical Elements: narrative text explaining critical aspects of our middle school program
2. Design Checks: specific questions or criteria, which school-site practitioners may use to monitor progress during the transition
3. Perspectives: charts and diagrams showing the relationships between significant elements of the middle school program

The Critical Elements Summarized

The middle-grades education program has important functions different from the elementary and high school programs.

Middle school students (transescents) have special needs that identify them as a unique group in the K–12 learning continuum. Specific philosophical approaches, educational strategies, and school organizations are effective during this period. Twelve critical elements are needed in the DCPS middle school:

1. The philosophical core of the middle school education program is based on the following beliefs:
   □ Every child can learn.
   □ Middle school is a key experience whereby students learn that the various disciplines and subjects are all related to people's search for understanding (i.e., "big picture" or holistic knowledge structure).

DESIGN PARAMETERS FOR THE MIDDLE SCHOOL IN DADE COUNTY PUBLIC SCHOOLS *(continued)*

- □ Learners must feel physically and psychologically safe for our educational goals to be achievable.
- □ Thinking skills instruction is a middle school responsibility.
- □ Respect for every child's individual differences must be maintained.

2. To accomplish its mission, the middle school curriculum has three interwoven and connected threads:
   - □ The pursuit of academic excellence as a way to achieve social competence in a complex, technological society
   - □ The pursuit of self-understanding and personal development
   - □ The pursuit of continuous learning skills

3. The traditional academic core must be taught in a way that ensures the following:
   - □ Students recognize the relationships between such disciplines as math, language arts, science, and social studies and can transfer learning from one discipline to another.
   - □ Students recognize that their exploratory and developmental experiences are related to the academic core and are a way to broaden each individual's insights and potential for personal growth.

4. The middle school curriculum contains a variety of exploratory experiences (into disciplines beyond the academic core), which will enable students to:
   - □ Recognize, through exploratory experiences, that there are a multitude of routes to take to understanding and successful independence
   - □ Sample fields they may wish to pursue in greater depth in high school or beyond
   - □ Develop a realistic overview of talents, aptitudes, and interests
   - □ Begin to develop talents and special interests in a manner that provides balance and perspective

5. Thinking skills expand in scope and nature during the middle grade years. Although problem-solving strategies need to be part of the K-12 learning continuum, formal instruction in critical and creative thinking skills is essential in the middle grades program.

6. Middle school students need someone to whom they can relate as an adviser and guide during transescence. Middle schools provide such advisers and ensure that advisers and advisees have time to work on the developmental issues of early adolescence.

7. Middle schools integrate academic knowledge and skills through use of interdisciplinary teaching teams. The structure of such teams may vary widely from school to school, but the essential elements are common planning time and teaching the same group of students.

8. Teachers of the academic core and of the exploratory/developmental programs work together to foster transfer of learning from one discipline to another, enhance application of basic skills, and help students develop a "big picture" on the scope and nature of people's efforts to understand themselves and the environment.

9. The exploratory program is provided in a variety of ways in addition to formal classes. These may include minicourses, clubs, special activities, and interest-group meetings built into the school day at regular intervals.

10. Inservice education and methods for teachers to share insights and information are an important part of the middle school conversion.

11. Instructional delivery strategies used at the middle grades allow for the developmental traits of the students. Cooperative learning strategies, accommodating different learning styles, recognition of attention span limitations, and understanding the transescent's preoccupation with personal development issues are all needed in the middle-grades program.

12. The middle school must develop a closer relationship with the parents and community and serve as a guide to each student's departure from childhood and embarkation on the route to adulthood and citizenship.

The middle school transition and the professionalization of teaching are complementary efforts to improve the educational programs we provide our young people. Within the parameters, which set the goals of middle-grades education, school sites should have as much flexibility as possible in structuring programs and experiences to meet the needs of students in their feeder pattern.

Sample Proposal for Organizing a Middle School

PROPOSED ORGANIZATION: GUIDELINES

All middle schools consist of students, teachers, time, space, and media/curriculum. This outline proposes general organizational standards for a middle school that address teacher grouping, student grouping, time, staffing, and facilities (space).

GENERAL ORGANIZATIONAL STANDARDS

Organization within the middle school is such that a smooth transition may be made from the self-contained classroom of the elementary school to the departmentalized high school. Provision is made to meet the unique social, academic, and personal needs of children as they emerge from childhood into adolescence. Flexibility in time utilization, and in the grouping of students and teachers, is provided to allow for balanced instruction.

1. Teacher Grouping
   - Teachers are organized into interdisciplinary teams to provide instruction in the core subjects of reading, language arts, science, mathematics, and social studies.
   - The interdisciplinary team serves a common group of students.
   - The interdisciplinary team controls a block of time.
   - Interdisciplinary team members are assigned classrooms that are in close proximity to one another.
   - Interdisciplinary team members have a common planning period.
   - A member of the interdisciplinary team shall be designated as team leader.

2. Student Grouping
   - Students are organized by grade levels.
   - Each grade level is divided into teams of approximately 90 to 135 students as is compatible with the interdisciplinary instructional team.
   - Provision is made for instruction at differing ability levels, at differing skill levels, and in different interest areas.

3. Time
   - Provision is made for a flexible daily time schedule.
   - A block of time equivalent to five 45-minute time segments (225 minutes) is assigned to the interdisciplinary team for academic instruction.
   - A 90-minute block of time is provided for exploration and physical education activities.

SAMPLE MIDDLE SCHOOL STUDENT SCHEDULE

The day schedule contains seven 45-minute periods, one 25-minute A/A period, one 25-minute lunch period, and accumulative passing times (total of 25 minutes). The total student day is 6 hours 30 minutes (as blocked below):

25 min A/A	225 min Academic Block	25 min Lunch	45 min Enrichment	45 min P.E.	25 min Passing

STAFFING STANDARDS

An effective middle school is dependent on professional and nonprofessional staff who possess special understanding, skills, and a positive attitude in working with middle school students, parents, and community members. An effective middle school staff supports, understands the need for, and implements the middle school concept. These personnel see the middle school as neither elementary nor secondary, but as an institution designed to meet the special needs of emerging adolescents. The schoolwide philosophy should be student-centered, not subject-centered. Each staff member's role is to help all students develop emotionally, socially, and academically. Recommended administrative staffing pattern (school of 1,200 students):

1. Administrative Staff
   - One principal
   - Two assistant principals

2. Support Staff
   - Three grade coordinators (10-month contract with provisions for contract extension)
   - Guidance counselors; recommended counselor/student ratio is 1 to 350
     (*Note:* Special consideration given for additional staffing for exceptional education centers housed at some schools.)
   - Media
   - Alternative education
   - Nurses
   - Aides
   - Psychologist
   - Social worker
   - Police liaison
   - Additions (school volunteers)

3. Teachers
   - Team teachers
   - Exploratory education teachers
   - Exceptional education teachers

PROPOSED ORGANIZATION: GUIDELINES (continued)

FACILITIES STANDARDS

The instructional program and the organizational pattern of the middle school dictate the facility requirements. Facilities should allow for varied instructional experiences, support the middle school concept, and meet the needs of personnel and support staff.

1. Essential Considerations
    - Increased attractiveness by use of color schemes and graphics
    - Adequate instructional space and equipment for each curricular program
    - Clustered interdisciplinary team instruction rooms
    - Team planning/work/conference area
    - Flexible classroom space
    - Computer instruction area
    - Alternative education area
    - Clinic area
    - Closable stalls in boys restroom and girls restroom
    - Adequate area for physical education and recreational activities
    - Private shower and changing facilities for boys and for girls
    - Exceptional education/student services

2. Desirable Considerations
    - Inhouse television capability
    - Adequate acoustical treatment (ceiling tile, floor covering, etc.)

DEVELOPING A TEAM PHILOSOPHY

Dear Principal:

During our team leader workshop, we developed a list of fifteen questions that will help define teaming in our pilot middle schools. We have asked that our participants meet with you to discuss these items. Thank you for your input into this planning process.

1. What is teaming at our school?

2. What is the composition of teams?

3. What is the role of team members?

4. What is the role of the team leader?

5. How will we make decisions?

6. How will we solve "big" problems?

7. What things should teams *not* do?

8. What are the most important tasks of our teams?

9. How will we form teams?

10. How often should teams be formed? Reformed?

11. What steps lead to team success?

12. What is our time frame for team development?

13. How can we evaluate team progress?

14. What do we expect from this effort?

15. How will we motivate team members?

CURRICULUM MAPPING GUIDELINES

1. Introduce concept to coordinators.
2. Pull together vertical mapping—coordinators.
3. Introduce and validate the mapped curriculum—coordinators and lead teachers.
4. Look for logical connectors (horizontal). Identify by six weeks. (Lead discipline each six weeks.)
5. Select a six-week link and develop interdisciplinary unit.
6. Introduce concept of mapping to interdisciplinary teams in all schools—coordinators and lead teachers.
7. Each team selects a six-week link and develops an interdisciplinary unit.
8. Build bank of interdisciplinary units.
9. Network units/instructional strategies (printed media, electronic media).
10. Establish review group to monitor, update, and revise existing mapped curriculum.
11. Train administrators at school level in monitoring mapped curriculum.
12. Include all other disciplines in interdisciplinary approach.
13. Evaluate total process.

SAMPLE INTERDISCIPLINARY (THEMATIC) UNIT

Grade: Six

Grading Period: First nine weeks

Title of Interdisciplinary Unit: Contributions of ancient civilizations

Content: To acquaint students with the contributions of ancient civilizations on modern culture.

Math	Language Arts	Science	Social Studies	Health
Numeration	Reading	Plants	Rise of Civilization	Interpersonal Relationships
Integers	Writing	Animals	Ancient Civilizations	
Measurement	Thinking			Personal Health Practices
Decimals/ metric	Speaking			
	Listening			Substance Abuse Prevention
Geometry				
Graphing				Human Growth and Development
				Disease/AIDS Education
				Safety/First Aid/CPR

GENERALIZATION/CONCEPTS

Renumeration is the foundation of any mathematical system.

Positive and negative numbers can be used to describe the world.

Measurement involves primary and intermediate students in measuring metric units of time, money, capacity, weight, and temperature. In addition, intermediate students are involved in working with perimeters, areas, volumes, and measuring angles.

Sharing common human experiences assists in defining one's own humanity and in developing a positive self-concept.

Literature is a reflection of its historical era.

Personal values are enhanced through exploring the values of others.

Functional literature provides the skills necessary and/or relevant to business and personal management.

The environment depends on plants to maintain the balance of life.

The study of plants includes the structures, the reproductive systems, and the process of photo-synthesis.

All animals are classified as vertebrate or invertebrate.

Knowledge of the structure and function of human systems increases the awareness of health problems associated with these body systems.

People alter their environment to meet their needs.

People whose basic needs are met begin to develop a more complex culture.

Development of shared language, religion, and government unifies a culture.

Relationships within the family and among peers affect potential well-being.

Knowledge of personal health practices is basic for potential development.

SUGGESTED INTERDISCIPLINARY UNIT FORMAT

A. Theme/Cover Sheet
   □ Title
   □ Names of unit developers
   □ School

B. Introduction Sheet
   □ Information for the teacher
   □ Background information for the student
   □ Acknowledgments

C. Goal Statement/Broad Objectives

D. Specific Objectives for Each Subject Area

E. Activities and Materials
   □ Glossary
   □ Classroom activities
   □ Student record sheet
   □ Homework and enrichment materials
   □ Resources
   □ Evaluation procedures
   □ TAP (advisory program) activities
   □ Culminating events/activities
   □ Bibliography

F. Calendar/Schedule

G. Modifications/suggestions sheet/student evaluation/teacher evaluation
   □ Involvement of other subject areas:

INTERDISCIPLINARY TOPICS: SUGGESTIONS

Imagination and Discovery	Of Mice and Men: An Interdisciplinary Unit
Bicentennial	Sports and Your Identity
Sports and You	Changing Sex Roles in the Twentieth Century
Careers in Transportation	The Wheel in Human Social Development
The Concrete Jungle	Animal and Human Interdependence and the
People Accept the Challenge of City Living	Necessity for Cooperation
The Law and You	Feeding the Population
International Trade	Evolution: Process of Change
Rural Life	America: The First Two Hundred Years
Communications	How Environmental Factors Affect Shelter
Temporary Living: Camps and Camping	The Civil War and Reconstruction
Greece	Anchors Aweigh to a New World
You Are What You Eat	The World Series
Let's Get Personal	Sports in America
Foreseeing the Unforeseeable	The Pollution Problem
Be It Ever So Humble	People as Consumers
Cities: What You Always Wanted to Know	Then and Now
Shock: A Serious and Dangerous Condition	The Westward Movement
Elections	Westward Expansion
MAN: Minorities Are the Nation	Take Me Out to the Ballgame

FLEXIBLE BLOCK SCHEDULE: A SAMPLE

Adviser/Advisee, Study Skills, and Silent, Sustained Reading Block
Academic Block □ Language arts □ Social studies □ Math □ Science
————Lunch————
Activity and Special-interest Block
Physical Education Block
Exploratory Block

SAMPLE LETTER TO PARENTS

Dear Parents:

We welcome you and your child to Team II. Teaming is an instructional program in which four teachers share their resources and expertise. It provides better instruction and classroom experiences. Teaming also gives students and teachers the feeling of belonging to a small group that has common goals and whose members are supportive of each other. It provides the opportunity for you as parents to join with students and teachers in sharing ideas, plans, information, and activities.

Successful team teaching is based on common and consistent rules for behavior. Our team rules for this school year are as follows:

1. Respectfully enter and leave the classroom.
2. Be on time to class—be seated.
3. Be prepared for work.
4. Listen carefully, answer respectfully.
5. Allow others a turn to speak—be patient.
6. Be considerate of others—no interruptions.

7. Stay seated in your own space.
8. Complete your work.

Your team teachers will be Ms. Brown, Mr. Green, Ms. Smith, Mr. Jones.

We all look forward to having you work with us in making this a productive year.

_____

Please indicate you have read, and discussed with your child, our common team goals by signing below and returning this section tomorrow.

Date _____   Parent's Signature _____

                                         Student's Signature _____

TEAMING PROCESSES: A CRITIQUE

	Always	Sometimes	Never
Agenda used			
Remained on task			
Good listeners			
Ideas and decisions clarified			
Decisions summarized			
Meeting critiqued			
Opportunity for everyone to speak			
Evidence of domination			
Ideas accepted			
Mutual respect			
Trust			
Decisions reached by consensus			
Freedom to express ideas			

TOPICS DISCUSSED

_____ Content planning   _____ Student concerns
_____ Content evaluation   _____ TLC Minutes
_____ Teaching strategies   _____ Organizational concerns
_____ Grouping or placement of students   _____ Parent involvement
Other: _____

_____

_____

TECHNIQUES FOR EFFECTIVE TEAM MEETINGS

1. Plan meetings cooperatively.
2. Acknowledge the schedules of others.
3. Provide ample lead time.
4. Keep a portion of the agenda open.
5. Stay on task.
6. Keep presentations/discussions short and to the point.
7. Make space ready and presentable for the meeting.
8. Eliminate distractions.
9. Schedule time to socialize if possible.
10. Feed the troops.
11. Value humor.
12. Learn to read silence.
13. Manage hostility.
14. Respect differences.
15. Protect confidentiality.
16. Stretch for closure.
17. Invite participant feedback.
18. Retire useless practices.

Middle School Instructional Checklist

MIDDLE SCHOOL INSTRUCTIONAL CHECKLIST

Directions. This instrument is to be used during a ten- to fifteen-minute classroom observation. The observer is to place a check in the space beside those items that *are observed or present.* Items not observed or present are to be left blank.

School _____ Subject Area _____

Teaching Is Personal

_____ 1. Student work is displayed prominently in the classroom.

_____ 2. Teacher/student-made bulletin boards rather than purchased displays are in use; ideally, bulletin boards are activity-oriented.

_____ 3. There is a seating pattern other than straight rows.

_____ 4. Living objects (plants, animals) are found in classroom.

_____ 5. Teacher moves about room freely while instructing.

_____ 6. Teacher calls students by first name without difficulty.

_____ 7. Constructive student-to-student communication is allowed during class.

_____ 8. Teacher uses specific praise and encourages comments frequently.

Teaching Is Individualized

_____ 9. Multilevel texts or materials are in use for instruction.

_____ 10. Some students are doing independent research or study in classroom.

_____ 11. Learning centers are present in the room.

_____ 12. Students are working on assignments together in small groups.

_____ 13. Supplemental learning materials are available in the classroom for student use.

_____ 14. Student work folders are used by teacher for work management.

_____ 15. Skill continuum cards are kept on individual students.

_____ 16. Instructional activity allows for creative or multiple outcomes over which the student has some choice.

Teaching Skills Are Utilized

_____ 17. One-to-one conferences with students in the classroom.

_____ 18. Diversifies instructional approach or method during observation.

_____ 19. Utilizes small groups to increase learning.

F

MIDDLE SCHOOL INSTRUCTIONAL CHECKLIST (continued)

_____ 20. Groups and regroups students for instructional purposes.
_____ 21. Teaches at varying level of difficulty around an idea or concept.
_____ 22. Stylized learning materials for the group.
_____ 23. Uses real-life illustrations or examples during instruction.
_____ 24. References student interests or needs during instruction.
_____ 25. Maintains student discipline through nonpunitive behavior.
_____ 26. Uses student–teacher contracts for learning.
_____ 27. Works with other teachers across subject-matter lines.
_____ 28. Teaches general study skills while instructing.
_____ 29. Uses teacher-made interdisciplinary units during instruction.
_____ 30. Uses questioning techniques that encourage participation.

Instructional Activities and Materials

BROAD-UNIT TOPIC: A MATHEMATICS CONTINUUM

   I. Origin of Various Numeration Systems (Words, Symbols, and Their Meanings)

  II. Whole Numbers
- A. Recognition of Whole Numbers (Each student should be able to read or write any number to one-billion)
- B. Prime, Composite, and Relatively Prime Numbers
- C. Computation and Related Problems of Application in Equalities and Inequalities
  1. Addition
  2. Subtraction
  3. Multiplication
  4. Division

III. Fractions
- A. Basic Understanding of the Fraction Concept
- B. Computation and Related Problems of Application in Equalities and Inequalities
  1. Addition
  2. Subtraction
  3. Multiplication
  4. Division
  5. Ratio and proportion

IV. Decimal Fractions
- A. Basic Understanding of the Decimal Fraction Concept
- B. Computation and Related Problems of Application in Equalities and Inequalities
  1. Addition
  2. Subtraction
  3. Multiplication
  4. Division

  V. Percent, Interest, etc.
- A. Meaning of Percent (%)
- B. Computation
- C. Application

G

BROAD-UNIT TOPIC: A MATHEMATICS CONTINUUM (continued)

VI. Statistical Graphs—Bar, Circle, Picture, Broken Line, and Smooth Line
    A. Reading and Interpreting Graphs
    B. Construction of Graphs from Given Data

VII. Metric System
    A. Length—Meter
    B. Capacity—Liter
    C. Weight—Gram

VIII. Geometry
    A. Nonmetric Geometry
        1. Basic terminology (ray, curve, polygon, parallel lines, etc.)
        2. Elementary constructions
    B. Metric Geometry
        1. Perimeter
        2. Area
        3. Volume

IX. Directed Numbers
    A. Basic Understanding of Directed Number System
    B. Computation and Related Problems of Application in Equalities and Inequalities
        1. Addition
        2. Subtraction
        3. Multiplication
        4. Division

X. Eighth-Grade Algebra
    A. Four Basic Operations of Whole Numbers and Rational Numbers
    B. Solution Sets for Equations and Inequalities (All Types)
    C. Word Problems—Reading, Interpretation, and Translation of Data to Variable Expressions
    D. Polynomials—Basic Operations of Monomials and Polynomials, Powers
    E. Factoring
    F. Quadratic Equations
    G. Algebraic Fractions—Simple and Complex
    H. Graphs and Analytic Geometry
    I. Systems of Linear Equations
    J. The Real Number System
        1. Meaning of square roots
        2. Computation and simplification of square roots
        3. Equations with irrational solutions

RESEARCH, ENRICHMENT, AND DEVELOPMENT
(RED) PROGRAM

Management of time and class schedules in a middle school provides the time which can be used in a program of interest activities, developmental or remedial activities, and research activities. Such a program is often called ER & R, or Special Interest, or Enrichment Class. Since our school colors are red and white, and since Research-Enrichment-Development produced the acronym RED, our program became known as the RED classes.

By shortening each of seven periods by a few minutes, we developed an "R Day" schedule for use on the days that these classes meet.

Surveys of students and faculty members produced the list of activities attached. The A-B-C lists apportion participation among the activities and ensures a variety of experiences for the students.

Registration for RED classes was effected through the three academic centers by reserving one-third of the membership of each class for each center. Every care was taken that all students took part in RED classes, and their satisfactory participation was recognized with a certificate.

RED PERIOD COURSES

Below are described the various special-interest courses being offered in the RED period. Read them over carefully, discuss them with your council teacher and with your parents, and make a list of the numbers of the ten courses you are most interested in. Bring your list of numbers and this description sheet back to Council Group.

Activity Number

1. *Applied Mathematics:* A study of the applications of mathematics to social studies, science, athletics, art, home economics, and mechanics. Activities in mapping, use of the slide rule, and independent study and research.
2. *Babysitting:* Those who successfully complete this course will receive a Red Cross certificate identifying them as a certified babysitter.
3. *Basketball—Basic Fundamentals:* Learn and improve your basic skills in basketball through skill drills and game playing.
4. *Beginning Backgammon:* Learn an exciting new game. Develop strategy and compete with other students.
5. *Beginning Typing:* This course is designed to present an introduction to the keyboard and development of correct typing techniques. These skills might be a good way to improve your papers and grades. Students in 8th grade Business Careers *should not* sign up.
6. *Cheerleading:* This course is designed for all cheerleaders. They work on improving their cheers and help others learn cheers. (Cheerleaders will work with 40 additional students every six weeks.)

RESEARCH, ENRICHMENT, AND DEVELOPMENT
(RED) PROGRAM (continued)

7. *Cheerleading Clinic:* Open to all students who would like to learn cheers and to improve their cheerleading ability.

8. *Chess—Advanced:* This course is for students who already know the moves and rules of the game. Emphasis will be on strategy and improving skills.

9. *Chess—Beginning:* Learn the basic moves and explore the fascinating game of chess.

10. *Creative Stitchery:* An exploration of various kinds of sewing with emphasis on handwork. Crewel, embroidery, needlepoint, and patchwork will also be included.

11. *Creative Communication—Art and Speech:* Participants will do speech and/or art activities such as children's storytelling, puppet theatre, and choral reading. Culmination of activities should be visits to other schools and local organizations to present programs.

12. *Creative Writing:* Do you want to write creatively and with purpose? In this course you will create short stories, personal journals, poetry, and biographies. Some may even compose a novel. Depending on this group's work, we may publish a literary magazine containing your best work.

13. *Current American Issues:* To research current American issues for presentation to the rest of the group. Students will be divided into approximately four committees for work on various current problems. Examples of topics are overpopulation, pollution, and the state of the economy. Each group will give a presentation to the class.

14. *Debate:* Students learn to organize their ideas and arguments in a formal manner with the correct debate procedure. Important issues of the day such as politics, environment, and sports will be used in this activity.

15. *Developmental Math:* Acquire a better understanding of the world of math, increase basic skills, and improve your grades. Teacher recommendations required.

16. *Developmental Spanish:* Improve your skills in this subject and improve your understanding of Spain and the Spanish language. Teacher recommendation required.

17. *Dissection—Internal Affairs:* Learn techniques of dissecting by starting with the lower forms such as mollusks and insects. Then progress to more advanced life such as fish and frogs.

18. *Emergency Treatments:* Students learn how to care for someone who has had a heart attack or other emergency. This course could save your life.

19. *Environment—Get Involved:* This course deals with environmental concerns. The activities will be set up to prepare the student to become involved in the functions of his city.

20. *Everything You've Always Wanted to Know About and Not Had Time to Investigate:* This course will offer the opportunity to work on a subject of interest to you from comic strips to archeology. Goals will be determined by contract between students and teacher.

21. *Experiments Can Be Fun:* Interested in science? Want to do some fun experiments? Here's something that offers a little instruction and a lot of doing. Make things like an electric quiz board, a fire extinguisher, a 002 boat, and more.

22. *Foreign Language Newspaper:* Improve that language! Help design and publish a foreign language newspaper. Make cartoons, puzzles, and illustrations.

SAMPLE RECOGNITION CERTIFICATES

NORCO TEAM PRIDE

HAPPY BIRTHDAY

BONANZA

TO BE USED FOR EXEMPTION FROM ONE DAY'S
CLASSWORK OR HOMEWORK ON THE DAY OF
BEARER'S BIRTHDAY OR A SUBSTITUTE DAY.
MANY HAPPY RETURNS.

BIRTHDAY _____   SIGNATURE _____

NORCO TEAM PRIDE

HOORAY

NO HOMEWORK

THE BEARER OF THIS CERTIFICATE IS HEREBY ENTITLED TO USE IT IN
EXCHANGE FOR ONE DAY'S HOMEWORK WITHOUT FEAR OF
CHASTISEMENT, DEFAMATION OF CHARACTER, OR BODILY HARM.

TEACHER SIGNATURE _____

DATE USED _____   SIGNATURE _____

DISCIPLINARY NOTICE TO PARENTS

_____ has engaged in the following unacceptable behavior:

I have taken the following steps to correct this behavior:

_____ A thorough discussion of the team discipline plan with the entire class

_____ A verbal warning

_____ A conference with the individual student

_____ Time out

_____ Parent contact (phone conference or letter to the parent)

_____ Detention

_____ Parent conference with the team, perhaps including a dean or administrator

In spite of all my efforts, the student continues to exhibit unacceptable behavior. Therefore, I have requested administrative intervention in the matter.

Sincerely,

Date _____   _____

(Signature)

STUDENT RECOGNITION REFERRAL

Date _____   Time _____

Student's Name: _____   Grade _____   Period _____

Referred by: _____

1. Reason for Referral (check as appropriate):

_____ Respect for others   _____ Always on time to school/class
_____ Classroom participation   _____ Exhibits good manners
      and completion of assignments   _____ Shows concern for other students/others
_____ Possession of classroom materials   _____ Other
_____ Any act which promotes the orderly
      conduct of a class, a bus, the school,
      or school function

2. Each reason checked is to be supported by factual comments. (Use reverse side if needed.)

3. Action by Teacher/Faculty Member
_____ Acknowledged with student
_____ Phone call to parents
_____ Written communication to parents
_____ Acknowledgment submitted for school bulletin
_____ Other

4. Action by Administrator
_____ Acknowledged in conference with student
_____ Phone call to parents
_____ Written communication to student
_____ Formal letter of recognition to parents
_____ Other

_____
                                    Signature

COMMUNITY INVOLVEMENT TECHNIQUES

1. *School Board Meetings:* School board meetings should be a central place for the members of the community, educators, and board members to exchange ideas about their schools. Meetings must be scheduled for the convenience of all members.

2. *Citizen Advisory Councils:* Advisory councils provide excellent opportunities for members of the community to meet with school officials and educators and discuss new issues and situations. Advisory councils can also be developed for special-interest areas such as sports, music programs, current issues, transportation, and many more.

3. *Volunteers and Aides:* The community has many people who would like to assist the schools. Often they are retired and have a wealth of knowledge and available time. Volunteers have an opportunity to see what is taking place in the schools while students have an opportunity to work with the not so young.

4. *Adult and Continuing Education Programs:* Less than one-third of the U.S. adult population have children in school today. These people are also taxpayers and want to see a return on their money. Evening and adult classes can be offered for academics as well as for recreational reasons.

5. *Community Coordinator:* Many school districts are now employing a professional advertising/promotion coordinator. Frequently, this responsibility is placed with the superintendent or another high-level administrator, who often is too busy or inadequately skilled at promoting programs.

6. *Schools as Community Centers:* This is not a new concept, and many more schools now work hand-in-hand with the local government to utilize the schools to the fullest. Both parties share expenses and facilities, and both realize greater financial savings while improving the community's contact with the school and its activities.

7. *Adopt-a-School Programs:* Although there is some disagreement concerning the name, the idea remains the same. Specific schools will be supported by partner businesses.

8. *Administrators and Principals:* Administrators may be in the best position to obtain community support for a district or a school. Administrators should become involved in community activities, organizations, and clubs. If an administrator strongly believes in good community–school relations, these bonds usually exist. The opposite holds true as well.

9. *Teachers:* Although the most important individual in the educational system, the teacher is usually overlooked as a resource speaker to represent the school to the community. Teachers and their discussions concerning their schools do have great impact on how a community perceives the school.

10. *Open House and Parent Visitations:* Most educators will agree that a school enjoying a great deal of parental involvement usually provides a better climate for learning. These schools are also perceived to be doing better.

11. *Newsletters and Releases:* Schools and individual teachers should prepare newsletters for parents and the community. They should be distributed in grocery stores, doctors' offices, and other high-visibility locations.

Planning Considerations

CURRICULUM MANAGEMENT PLAN (CMP)
MODEL: HIGHLIGHTS

1. Needs Assessment
   - Of the school and the community

2. Philosophy and Goals
   - Determined by students, administrators, teachers, parents, community, board
   - Based on needs of students and community

3. Curriculum
   - Based on needs and philosophy
   - Includes defined sequence of content, concepts, skills
   - Provides for all levels of learners
   - Includes skills continuums, checklists for progress
   - Provides balance between personal development and skill and content acquisition
   - Provides for uniform, articulated curriculum for K–12

4. Instructional Program
   - Management system to assure implementation
   - Grading and reporting system follows curriculum
   - Articulated guidance program smooths transition
   - Materials are current and appropriate

5. Organization
   - Self-contained classes, teaming, departmentalization used when appropriate
   - Flexible rather than static grouping of students
   - Maximum time-on-task for teachers and students

6. Staff
   - Only qualified teachers employed
   - Responsibilities for all are clearly identified
   - Systematic inservicing for teachers and administrators
   - Systematic evaluation of teachers and administrators

7. Facilities
   - Flexible spaces to meet a variety of instructional programs and organizational structures
   - Lab and computer areas provided for high-tech training

H

CURRICULUM MANAGEMENT PLAN (CMP)
MODEL: HIGHLIGHTS (continued)

8. Evaluation and Reporting
   - □ Checkpoints for monitoring student progress (K–12)
   - □ Norm-based and criterion-based testing for progress
   - □ Reporting system that shows clearly extent of student progress in each grading period
   - □ Grading system that matches curriculum

9. Budget
   - □ Resources allocated based on alignment with plan

COMPREHENSIVE PLAN FOR MIDDLE SCHOOL
DEVELOPMENT (EXCERPTS)

DUVAL COUNTY PUBLIC SCHOOLS, 1990–1995

CMP Committees

The organization of the middle school conversion will feature four primary committees under the direction of a general oversight committee known as the Coordinating Committee. Other ad hoc committees will be employed as needed to design programs and coordinate changes.

The *Coordinating Committee,* a select committee of about 30 members (key citizens and school personnel), will oversee the entire four-year conversion process. The role of the Coordinating Committee will be to ensure that smooth progress is maintained in moving from a junior high structure to the middle school structure. Tools used by the Coordinating Committee include a Management Plan (based on needs assessment data), four primary committees, and a series of ad hoc committees. The primary committees will include: The Design Committee, the Program Development Committee, the Staff Development Committee, and an Evaluation Committee.

The Design Committee, consisting of about 10 members, will establish general standards or specifications for all 50 middle schools in the district. These standards will be arrived through a study of needs assessment data and input from both the professional literature and the public.

The *Program Development Committee,* a committee of about 20 members, will translate the standards of the Design Committee into quality indicators for all aspects of middle school programming. Specific ad hoc committees will be formed to define subject areas and special programs such as mathematics, computer literacy, or physical education.

The *Staff Development Committee,* consisting of about 10 members, will recommend and plan inservice for teachers, administrators, and parents connected with the 50 middle schools. Inservice planning will be based on needs assessment data, the program design, and local school plans for conversion.

The *Evaluation Committee,* consisting of five members and assigned staff members from the Program Evaluation Section, will monitor the progress of the conversion process throughout the four-year period. Periodic reports from the Evaluation Committee to the Coordinating Committee will assess the accomplishment of tasks.

The governance structure calls for the four primary committees to report findings and recommendations to the Coordinating Committee. The Coordinating Committee in turn will make recommendations for conversion through periodic reports to the Board. The Board will then set policy to be implemented by the Superintendent and the staff.

The role of the Management Team in the conversion process will be unique. The Management Team will serve as a liaison between the Coordinating Committee and the Board for purposes of planning, policy formation, research allocation, and policy implementation. The Deputy Superintendent will coordinate this mediating role between the professional staff and the various committees of the conversion process. The Consultants will provide general advice and input through the Management Team and will serve as a resource to the committees and the Board.

CMP Tasks Timetable (*Sample*)

Program	*Activity*	*Person(s) Time Frame*	*Responsible*	*Costs*
Middle School Program Design 8.0	Training of team leaders for 1990–1991	July 30– July 31, 1990	Wiles–Bondi	Stipends for team leaders (2 days × 6 hrs. × number of participants) Materials—$2,000 (provided by Wiles–Bondi as part of contract)
Middle School Program Design 12.0	Study/ development of K–5 pilot technology program— selected sites	1990–1991	Charles Cline Michael Walker Betty White Wiles–Bondi Selected participants from district/ community	None
Middle School Program Design 3.0	Five-year plan (1990–1995) for renovation, construction of schools to house grades K–5, 6–8, 9–12 by 1995– to board	Summer, 1990–1991	Board Dr. Zenke Charles Cline Management team	To be determined by board, superintendent, management team

SCHOOL-BASED STANDARDS (SAMPLE)

Standards	*Date Achieved*	*Person(s) Responsible*

XIII. Flexible block scheduling—
The goal of scheduling is to
provide teachers with a
flexible instructional block
of time to satisfy students'
academic needs.

   A. Provision is made for a flexible
daily time schedule.

   B. A block of time is assigned to
the interdisciplinary team for
academic instruction.

   C. A block of time is provided for
exploration and physical education.

   D. An established time is set aside
each day for adviser/advisee
(between 25 and 30 minutes per day).

   E. Provision is made for varying the
daily schedule to allow for club
and intramural activities to occur
during the regular school day for
all students.

   F. Provision is made for interdisciplinary
team planning each day.

* * *

   G. The interdisciplinary team is
responsible for the coordination
of curriculum and for the delivery
of instruction to the students on
its team.

	Standards	Date Achieved	Person(s) Responsible
H.	Members of the team plan cooperatively.		
I.	Common pools of information about students are shared among team members.		
J.	Teams meet with parents to discuss individual student's academic and developmental progress.		
K.	Team members participate in a team meeting at least once a week.		
L.	Team members provide support for each other.		
M.	Activities are planned to foster a sense of team identity and pride among teachers and students.		
N.	The school's adviser/advisee program is implemented.		
O.	Interdisciplinary units of instruction are developed and implemented.		
P.	Action plans are developed for individual students who are experiencing difficulties academically or socially.		
Q.	The team operates on a consensus basis, so that when a decision must be made and agreement has not been reached, the team leader will make the decision based on available input.		

BOOKLET FOR PARENTS (SAMPLE "LAYERED" FORMAT)

The Middle School Student. . .	*The XYZ Middle School . . .*
□ Is enthusiastic	□ Has a team of specialists ready to challenge your child, to capitalize on and support his or her enthusiasm.
□ Must be motivated to learn	□ Encourages students to progress at their own rate, motivated by repeated success in an individualized program—*nothing succeeds like success!*
□ Has short-term objectives and attention span	□ Provides flexible scheduling, arranged around students' ability to maintain interest and complete tasks.
□ Differs widely in physical attributes and maturity. He or she is growing rapidly and is subject to overexertion.	□ Offers a wide range of activities designed for the developmental variations that mark this age group. Some activities will be instituted at student request.
□ Is activity-minded	□ Provides carefully planned physical education classes tailored for this age group. Intramural sports give an outlet for competitive feelings *without* serious injury to rapidly growing bodies.
□ Desires freedom, but fears loss of security	□ Allows students autonomy to create their own schedules and select areas of interest with counselor and teacher support and encouragement.
□ Needs communication with peers and adults outside the home	□ Affords opportunities for students to meet peers in small groups to foster social interaction with peers and adults.

HEALTH EDUCATION PROGRAM, LESSON TOPICS

6th Grade	7th Grade	8th Grade
Knowing About Health	Adolescence and Values	Introduction to Health, Values, and Decision Making
Making Decisions	Life Management Skills	
Self-Examination	Self-Concept	
Plan for Good Mental Health	Emotional and Social Changes during Adolescence	*Adolescence: Physical, Mental, and Social Changes
Belonging to a Family		Self-Concept
The Importance of Relationships	Responsibilities and Earned Privileges	Communication/Media
Abuse Prevention	Families and Characteristics	Parent Relationships and Characteristics
*Endocrine System	Dating, Purposes and Responsibilities	Dating Purposes
*Puberty, Male and Female		Dating Responsibilities
*Fetal Growth and Development	Dating Risks	Causes and Consequences of Inappropriate Sexual Activities
*Immune System	Abuse Prevention	
*AIDS	*Endocrine System	
Facts About Drugs	*Puberty, Male and Female	Teen Pregnancy Statistics
Types of Drugs	*Fetal Growth and Development	Abstinence and Return to Abstinence
Drugs in Your Life Now and in the Future	*STDs, Communicable Diseases	Abuse Prevention
Alcohol and Health	*AIDS	*Body Talk, Male and Female
Alcohol and Behavior	Drugs Affect People Differently	*Fetal Growth and Development
Tobacco and Health	Controlled Drugs	*STDs
Smoking and Behavior	Drugs That Promote Good Health	*AIDS
The Chew Story		Illegal Drugs
Weight and Energy	Preventing Drug Misuse and Abuse	The Innocent Victims
Eating Disorders	Illegal Drug Prevention	Facts About Alcohol
Physical Hygiene	The Effects of Alcohol	Alcoholism: A Chronic Disease
Dental Care	Dynamics of a Chemically Dependent Family	
Health Products		Treatment and Prevention
Health Services	Smokeless Tobacco	Understanding Chemical Dependency
Chronic Diseases	Diet Alert	
Nervous System Disorders	Consumer Decisions	Tobacco and Your Health
Common First Aid Procedures	Teeth and Disease	Issues Related to Smoking
Safety Around You	Cancer	Weight Watching
Safety From Disaster	Cardiovascular Disease	Diet Choices
	Health Care Providers	Good Dental Health
	Careers in Health	Effects of Physical Fitness
		Consumer Protection
		Choices about Time and Money
		Health Careers

*Will be taught by a trained nurse in separate classes for boys and girls.

TEAM NEWSLETTER

Dear Team F Parents,

Team F is a four-subject interdisciplinary team involving language arts, social studies, math, and science. In order to keep you informed as to what your child is doing in these areas, we will begin sending a newsletter home with your child at the end of each report period.

Following is a description of what has taken place these past six weeks.

1. *Social Studies* this past grading period was assigned the concept of exploration and discovery. We grouped the students in sections so that poor readers and those with above-average reading ability could move at their own speed.

    Using skill kits designed to help both groups, the average students were given task sheets to work from, designed to teach inquiry and concepts. We tried to have task sheets made up so that the student would use outside resources and the media center.

2. *Science* classes have been involved in a study of physiology. We have studied various body processes and also briefly reviewed various systems of the human body.

    Some students have been reading from a selected text, which covers various scientific topics from geology to biology. There are selected groups who are working in packets made from the Steck–Vaughn series, which includes various biological topics. Students have been allowed to proceed in their work on an individualized basis within a time framework. Extra-credit reports were submitted by those who desired to upgrade their work. Students are allowed to complete or submit extra-credit work on any scientific topic throughout the six-week period.

    Various students were assigned book reports on science-related books.

    The entire team was moved from a class-type situation to the lab. We will begin the new semester with various laboratory experiences.

3. In *Mathematics* students have been grouped according to their ability. The different topics being studied at this time include whole numbers, fractions, integers, rational numbers, and algebra. The groups are exposed to a variety of teaching techniques including skills kits, cassette tapes, worksheets, workbooks, textbooks, and lectures.

4. In *Language Arts* the students have been working on two skills kits and a six-week literature and creative writing unit. The skills kits covered usage, vocabulary, punctuation, and spelling. Each student worked at his own rate.

    The literature unit centered around a book called *Imagination, the World of Inner Space.* At the beginning of the unit students contracted for their grade, different amounts of work being required for each grade. The book contained short stories, poems, and plays. After reading the material students did creative writing assignments from a logbook. Students were also assigned a group project for completion of the contract. At the end of the six weeks the *Imagination* notebook and group project were handed in. I enjoyed reading them! Many students did good work.

SCHOOL NEWSLETTER

One of the highlights of the _____ Middle School program is the Humanities exposure. The students are encouraged to have encounters in art, music, and foreign language. Such experiences could be playing a musical instrument, singing songs, dancing, designing a leather disc, making a clay object, and learning to speak either Spanish or French. The general goal of the humanities program is to provide myriad opportunities for the student to gainfully use his or her leisure time. This knowledge could become invaluable later on when these people become involved in the world of work.

ATTENTION PARENTS—You must see to believe. Our agriculture program headed by Mr. _____ has developed faster than expected. His students are growing about anything you can name and have a hothouse second to none in the county. There are now 72 boys and girls learning to plant and grow things and appreciate the effort put forth by the farmers of America in growing what we eat. These kids are doing an outstanding job and enjoying what they are doing.

The academics are also being introduced to the vocational world. Many fine people from the local business and industrial community have come to the school to lecture and to show through slides how their particular business operates. We have recently had Mr. _____ from the _____ *Times* who had a slide presentation on "How to Make a Newspaper." This was a field trip which was brought to the school to give the students an insight into something most people take for granted, that is, our daily paper. Ms. _____ , a writer for the *Times,* also talked to many students about writing and the importance of getting as much as possible out of English.

Midshipman _____ also visited us. He is a second classman at the U.S. Naval Academy at Annapolis, Maryland. He is a math major, aspiring to be either a jet pilot or be stationed aboard nuclear subs. He told many of our students the importance of attaining as much proficiency in this area as possible and to be continually thinking about making a career choice. He emphasized that our students should explore a few career choices now and then make a final choice of one or two.

Including the people now attending, we have 18 boys and girls involved at the Work Evaluation Center in _____ . Here they are observed by several evaluators who assist them and test them in performance tasks. An example is taking a telephone apart and putting it back together by following directions. They are graded on time and quality of work. All tasks require a certain amount of reading and math to be able to perform. This nine-day series of work-related tests tells the students in which area they are proficient and a lot of times motivates them to stay in school and study harder. Several of our _____ students have also been given either the Ohio Vocational Interest Survey test or the Kudex Interest test. These tests are given on a voluntary basis and many times are a motivating factor in that they show the student where his or her interests lie.

We would at this time like to extend an open invitation to all parents to visit us at _____
Middle School and observe our students in action.

ADVISEMENT THEMES: MONTHLY SCHEDULE

CORONA–NORCO UNIFIED SCHOOL DISTRICT

Grade Seven

1. Orientation/Rationale/Rules
   Group Building/Get Acquainted/Goals   September
2. Study Skills/Time Management   October
3. Self-Esteem   November
4. Stress Management/Conflict Resolution   December
5. Interpersonal Relations (Peers/Adults/Family)   January
6. Accepting Responsibility/Decision Making   February
7. Communications (Peers/Adults/Family)   March
8. Community Involvement   April
9. Goal Setting, Career   May
10. Evaluation   June

Grade Eight

1. Orientation/Rationale/Rules
   Group Building/Goals   September
2. Study Skills/Time Management   October
3. Self-Esteem   November
4. Self-Awareness/Attitudes   December
5. Inter-/Intra-Personal Relations (Peers/Adults/Family)   January
6. Accepting Responsibility   February
7. Career Plannings/Future Communication (Peers/Adults/Family)   March
8. Problem Solving/Decision Making   April
9. Job Skills/Attitudes   May
10. High School Attitudes/Where Are You Going?   June

Resource J
Evaluation Instruments

EVALUATION BASELINE

1. *Discipline:* Number of referrals by school and grade—corporal punishment
2. *Achievement:* Stanford and SSAT Reading/Math Listening Range by school—Percentage of skill passage by school
3. *Grading:* Percentage of grade awarded by subject, grade, and school
4. *Attendance:* Quarterly ADA averages—baseline
5. *Student Mobility:* By school—internal and external
    Transportation report
6. *Low/High SES:* Lunch programs
    Migrant programs
    Chapter 1 eligibles
7. *Vandalism:* By school
8. *Age of Students:* By school, sex, race
9. *Teacher Experience:* Form
10. *Student–Teacher Attitudes:* Form
11. *10th Grade Follow-Up:* Form
12. *Instructional Practices:* School visits
13. *Facilities:* School visits
14. *Instructional Resources:* Supervisors

MIDDLE SCHOOL PROGRAM ANALYSIS

Directions:

Please check those items that are descriptive of the middle school program at your school.

Philosophy and Goals

_____ 1. A formal middle school-oriented philosophy exists and is accepted by principal and teachers.

_____ 2. The goals of the middle school program reflect a three-part thrust: personal development, skills for continued learning, and education for social competence.

_____ 3. Philosophy and goals are developed at my middle school based on an assessment of the needs of students attending the school.

Organization/Organization

_____ 4. The middle school day is flexibly scheduled using large blocks of time and "modular" time arrangements.

_____ 5. Teachers are organized into interdisciplinary planning/teaching teams that share a common group of students and planning period.

_____ 6. Teaching teams are located in physical proximity to one another.

_____ 7. Parent involvement/community involvement is built in to the school curriculum.

Curriculum/Organized Learning

8. The formal program of organized learning includes the following components:
   _____ Core academic learning consisting of language arts, mathematics, social studies, and science
   _____ Remedial and enrichment opportunities such as gifted programs
   _____ Exploring electives to expose new fields of knowledge and expand aesthetic and creative horizons
   _____ Career education components for all students
   _____ Physical development and health education for all students
   _____ Student-initiated elective choices in art, music, and other related areas
   _____ A required course in the area of computer literacy

9. General skill development is planned and included in major subject areas including:
   _____ Reading
   _____ Spelling
   _____ Writing
   _____ Library use skills
   _____ Problem solving
   _____ Finding and organizing information
   _____ Critical and creative thinking

10. A continuous progress approach to learning is present and does the following:
    _____ Assesses each student at entry level on a continuum of course objectives
    _____ Has ongoing monitoring to determine each student's readiness to progress in curriculum
    _____ Allows student to attain proficiency in skills and performance objectives at rate/level that matches the student's instructional needs
    _____ Assesses student performance based on progress through a skill-and-objective continuum

11. Schoolwide advisement programs are present and do the following:
    _____ Include a separate, planned nonacademic program
    _____ Include direction by guidance counselors
    _____ Have a regularly scheduled group activity
    _____ Involve all certificated personnel, staff, and support personnel
    _____ Provide ongoing personal interaction between staff (adviser) and students (advisee)
    _____ Maintain a teacher/pupil ratio of less than 1:20
    _____ Provide individual guidance opportunities when needed

12. A physical development/health program is present and is characterized by the following:
    _____ Experienced by all students
    _____ Students grouped on basis of development rather than grade level
    _____ Intramural program available to all students and organized around skill development
    _____ Formal health program to assist students in understanding and accepting physical and intellectual changes in themselves and others
    _____ Health screening and monitoring for all students
    _____ Graduated physical education program according to student development

Instructional Patterns

_____ 13. Students are grouped by intellectual, social, and/or physical characteristics in classes.
_____ 14. A variety of instructional methods are used in classes at any given time.
_____ 15. Instructional strategies other than lecture are used in most classrooms.
_____ 16. Varied instructional materials are regularly used in most classrooms.

17. There are interdisciplinary team planning/teaching approaches that provide for the following:
    _____ Teachers of different subjects meet during scheduled time to coordinate instruction for common groups of students.
    _____ Teachers of different subjects meet during scheduled time to monitor progress of common groups of students.

MIDDLE SCHOOL PROGRAM ANALYSIS *(continued)*

_____ Teachers of different subjects teach common group of students within a block of time and group/regroup students to meet varied instructional objectives.

_____ Teachers of different subjects participate in delivery of interdisciplinary units on periodic basis.

_____ Teachers of different subjects meet together with parents of individual students to discuss the student's program.

New Web Resources for Middle Schools

WEBSITES FOR TEACHERS

Public Broadcasting Service (PBS)

PBS's Teacher Resources Service is loaded with creative ideas for using video as a tool for classroom learning. Look for the Electronic Field Trips, Mathline, and Scienceline sections. A Teachers' Digest provides success stories from teachers based upon their classroom experiences.
WEBSITE: *www.pbs.org/learn/*

Smithsonian Education on the Web

An electronic version of our national museums, this site houses information about the Smithsonian's programs and collections, including an enormous photography database. Take note of the active-learning lesson plan and classroom activities geared especially for upper elementary and middle school students.
WEBSITE: *www.si.edu/*

Teacher Talk

Teacher Talk is an online publication for middle school educators with an extensive database of lesson plans. Articles range from the legal responsibilities of teachers to tips for maintaining a peaceful classroom. You'll discover practical advice and strategies for enhancing students' social and emotional growth and an Adolescent Directory Online.
WEBSITE: *education.indiana.edu/cas/tt*

Teachers Helping Teachers

Between 600 and 1,000 teachers visit this site daily. Why? Because it's full of lesson plans and links, activities for learning, and strategies for teaching. There's also a bulletin board and a teachers' chat room for exchanging ideas with others using Internet Relay Chat (IRC).
WEBSITE: *www.pacificnet.net~mandel*

WEBSITES FOR TEACHERS *(continued)*

Library of Congress

The Educator's Page and Learn More sections offer lesson plans, classroom ideas, and reading lists designed to help educators teach history, creative writing, and critical thinking. Roam through exhibitions, databases, or up-to-date legislative information. Or explore the American memory Collections of texts, photos, sound recordings, movies, and maps of historic events with corresponding lesson plans.
WEBSITE: *www.loc.gov*

National Geographic

You'll find lots of social studies resources, including lesson plans, units, maps, and activities searchable by grade level for K–12. A Map Machine lets you zero in on any place in the world for quick and easy access to statistics and information on individual countries.
WEBSITE: *www.nationalgeographic.com/resources/*

Eisenhower National Clearinghouse for Mathematics and Science Education

A comprehensive database of exemplary K–12 programs for teaching science and math, including tips on integrating math and science with literature. A professional development exchange lists workshops, internships, journal articles, classes, and grants for education.
WEBSITE: *www.enc.org*

Tools for Teachers Online

This enormous K–12 web site covers lesson plans in all subject areas. Tidbits include suggestions on classroom decor, five-minute learning activities, tips on dealing with tardiness, and classroom management techniques. There's a question-and-answer forum, too.
WEBSITE: *www.teacher.com*

Cable News Network

Help keep your students on top of current events with CNN's site. Get news summaries with the Quick News feature or top news stories from the past in the Archives. View news clips in the Video Vaults or listen to live news broadcasts. Available in Spanish, too.
WEBSITE: *www.cnn.com*

Busy Teachers' Web Site

This award-winning site was created to help K–12 teachers find direct source materials, lesson plans, and classroom activities. Information is divided into 19 categories, such as English, math, guidance/counseling, and even recess. To make things easier, there's background information on each category.
WEBSITE: *www.ceismc.gatech.edu/BusyT*

Discovery Channel School Online

Here's a monster site of information on resources related to science, social studies, language arts, and the humanities for K–12 teachers. Search its database of lesson plans by grade level and/or subject area and explore links to other educational sites.
WEBSITE: *www.school.discovery.com*

Education World

Offers lots of lesson-planning and curriculum resources. Information ranges from "outrageous women in history" to "Dr. Seuss celebrates reading." In addition to a huge education-oriented search engine, there's a message board and a searchable database of 50,000 web sites of interest to teachers.
WEBSITE: *www.education-world.com*

Educational Resources Information Center (ERIC)

Sponsored by the U.S. Department of Education, ERIC is the mother of all educational websites. It houses the largest database of educational materials in the world, including 850,000 abstracts of publications, lesson plans, a question-and-answer service, conference papers, and research.
WEBSITE: *www.askeric.org*

Learning Webs

A master site of sites. Focus on curriculum resources at all levels. Examples of Internet-assisted curriculum journeys.
WEBSITE: *www.learnweb.org*

WEBSITES FOR SPECIAL NEEDS STUDENTS

Following is a list of Special Needs sites that are useful to parents, students, and educators:

► Disabilities Sites to Explore:
  http://www.merrywing.com/newsites.htm

► Disability-related Sites on the World Wide Web:
  http://thearc.org/misc/dislnkin.html

► SERI—Special Education Resources on the Internet:
  http://www.hood.edu/seri/serihome.html

► NMSA Weblinks:
  http://www.nmsa.org/nhotlinks.htm

► Special Needs Resources
  http://www.roytoncr.demon.co.uk/spneed.htm

► NCIP (National Center to Improve Practice in Special Education) Links
  http://www.edu.org/FSC/NCIP/links.html

► Maddus List of Special Education and Disability Related Sites
  http://unr.edu/homepage/maddus/splinks.html

► Raising Special Needs Kids
  http://members.aol.com/wla1974/rsngspclkds.html

► Links to Other Online Resources
  http://www.cec.sped.org/ericec/links.htm

► Disability Information and Resources
  http://www.eskimo.com/~jlubin/disabled.html

► Disabilities (Health)
  http://galaxy.einet.net/GJ/disabilities.html

► Special Needs
  http://www.cksd.webnet.edu/janetslist/special.htm

► Learning Disability Resource
  http://curry.edschool.Virginia.EDU/curry/dept/cise/ose/categories/ld.html

The Council for Exceptional Children offers current information and resources at *http://www.cec.sped.org*. A list of some universities and colleges that have constructed home pages for their special education programs can be found at *http://curry.edschool.virginia.edu/curry/dept/cise/ose/resources/universities.html*

Special Needs Opportunity Window (SNOW) (*http://snow.utoronto.ca*) is a project aimed at supporting educators of students with special needs. This web site serves as a clearinghouse of practical resources and curriculum materials, as a place for educators to meet and share ideas, and a place for educators to develop their professional skills.

A nationwide directory of special education and learning disability resources, within the public school system and outside the public school system, is available at *http://www/.iser.com/ planning.html*.

A popular clearinghouse on disabilities is the ERIC Clearinghouse. ERIC is located at *http:// www.cec.sped.org/ericec.htm*. ERIC EC Digest #E521, titled, "Including Students with Disabilities in General Education Classrooms," is an excellent example of the material available through this clearinghouse.

WEBSITES FOR SCHOOL REFORM

SKILLS AND CONTENT BASED REFORM MODELS

► Breakthrough to Literacy
  www.wrightgroup.com
► Carbo Reading Styles
  wwwl.nrsi.com
► First Steps
  www.heinemann.com/firststeps
► Reading Recovery
  www.osu.edu/readingrecovery
► Comprehensive School Mathematics
  www.mcrel.org/products/csmp
► Math Connections
  www.mathconnections.com
► Galaxy Classroom Science
  www.galaxy.org

COMPREHENSIVE SCHOOL REFORM MODELS

► Accelerated Schools
  www.Ieland.stanford.edu/group/ASP
► ATLAS Communities
  www.edc.org/FSC/ATLAS
► Coalition of Essential Schools
  www.essentialschools.org
► CoNECT Schools
  www.co-nect.bbn.com

WEBSITES FOR SCHOOL REFORM (continued)

- Modern Reading Schoolhouse (K–12)
  www.mrsh.org
- Paideia
  www.unc.edu/paideia
- Success for All
  www.ssuccessforall.com
- Assessment and Evaluation
  http://www.middleweb.com/contntassess.html
- Teachers at Work
  http://www.middleweb.com/ContntsWork.html
- Teacher Professional Development
  http://www.middleweb.com/ContntTchDev.html
- Principal Professional Development
  http://www.middleweb.com/contntsPrin.html

WEBSITES FOR SAFE SCHOOLS

Web Guide to Safe Schools
www.air.org/cecp

Threats to Children
www.aacap.org

The Oregon School Safety Center
www.nsscl.org

The National School Safety Center
www.ncpc.org

The National Crime Prevention Council
www.ncpc.org

Safe Schools: A Handbook for Practitioners
www.nassp.org

Partnerships for a Drug-Free America
www.drugfreeamerica.org

TV Free America
www.tvfa.org

WEBSITES OF SUPPORT ORGANIZATIONS

Center for the Social Organization of Schools (CSOS)

http://scov.csos.jhu.edu/

Overview of CSOS, which maintains a staff of full-time sociologists, psychologists, social psychologists, and other scientists who conduct programmatic research to improve the education system, as well as full-time support staff engaged in developing curricula and providing technical assistance to help schools use the Center's research. Many links to useful sites, including promising school redesign programs, the Center for Research on the Education of Students Placed At-Risk (CRESPAR), and the Center for School, Family, and Community Partnership.

Center for Research on the Education of Students Placed At-Risk (CRESPAR)

http://scov.csos.jhu.edu/crespar/CReSaR.html

Site can also be accessed from the CSOS home page. CRESPAR is supported as a national educational research center by the Office of Educational Research and Improvement, U.S. Department of Education. Conducted through seven research and development programs and a program of institutional activities, the work of the Center is guided by three central themes: ensuring the success of all students at key development points, building on students' personal and cultural assets, and scaling up effective programs. Website includes information on CRESPAR programs, CRESPAR Research and Development reports, and newsletters.

U.S. Department of Education General Web Site

http://www.ed.gov/

Access information on Department of Education programs and services, publications and products, staff, and offices. Explore other sites through provided links, or search documents located on this site or elsewhere on the Internet.

U.S. Department of Education's National Institute on the Education of At-Risk Students

http://www.ed.gov/offices/OERI/At-Risk/

Supports a range of research and development activities designed to improve the education of students at risk of educational failure because of limited English proficiency, poverty, race, geographic locations, or economic disadvantage. Major components include: National Research and Development Centers, Field Initiated Studies, and Directed Research and Publications.

WEBSITES OF SUPPORT ORGANIZATIONS (continued)

Education Commission of the States Home Page (ECS)

http://www.ecs.org/

Explore this site for information on a series of "hot issues in education," including low-performance schools, school-to-work policies and programs, efforts to integrate technology into teaching and learning, school governance and finance issues, charter schools, and topics related to the cost and quality of higher education. Also supplies news releases, information on the New American School program, details on ECS publications and meetings, and links to other useful sites.

ERIC Clearinghouse on Urban Education

http://eric-web.tc.columbia.edu/

Monitors curriculum and instruction of students of diverse racial, ethnic, social class, and linguistic populations in urban (and suburban) schools by reviewing curricula and instruction of students from these populations, and by developing ways that public and private sector policies can improve conditions that place urban students at risk educationally. Site provides a wealth of resources including research, publications, handbooks, educational digests, parent guides, special reports, resource guides, and site links.

Education Week's Web Connection

http://www.edweek.org/ads/wedir.htm

Includes descriptions of and links to over 40 education web sites.

National Education Association

http://www.nea.org/

Presents union information, education news, reports, research, and statistics. Access NEA publications, parent guides, and educational resources. Read updates on education public policy and legislation, including congressional voting records. Also includes success stories from teachers and schools. Search the site for activities and updates on the NEA's National Center for Innovation (NCI).

NATIONAL ORGANIZATIONS ON STANDARDS

CONTENT STANDARDS CONTACTS

Arts

Music Educators National Conference
1806 Robert Fulton Drive
Reston, VA 20191
800–350–4223

Civics and Government

Center for Civic Education
5146 Douglas Fir Road
Calabasas, CA 91302–1467
800–350–4223

Economics

Economics America
National Council on Economics
  Education
1140 Avenue of the Americas
New York, NY 10036
212–730–7007

English Language Arts

National Council of Teachers of English
Book Order Department
1111 West Kenyon Road
Urbana, IL 61801
800–369–6283

International Reading Association
Order Department
800 Barksdale Road
P.O. Box 8139
Newark, DE 19714–8139
800–336–7323 ext. 266

Foreign Languages

American Council on the Teaching
  of Foreign Languages
6 Executive Plaza
Yonkers, NY 10701–6801
914–963–8830

Geography

National Council of Geographic
  Education
1145 17th Street, NW
Washington, DC 20036–4688
202–775–7832

History

University of California, Los Angeles
Associated Student
General Book Division
308 Westwood Plaza
Los Angeles, CA 90024–4108
310–206–0788

Mathematics

The National Council of Teachers
  of Mathematics
1906 Association Drive
Reston, VA 22091
703–620–9840

Physical Education

National Association for Sports
  and Physical Education
1900 Association Drive
Reston, VA 20191
703–476–3410

NATIONAL ORGANIZATIONS ON STANDARDS (continued)

CONTENT STANDARDS CONTACTS

Science

National Science Education Standards
2101 Constitution Ave., NW
HA 486
Washington, DC 20418
202–334–1368

Benchmarks for Science Literacy

American Association for the
   Advancement of Science
1333 H Street, NW
Washington, DC 20005
202–326–6660

Skill Standards

U.S. Department of Labor
Office of Policy and Research
2090 Constitution Ave., NW
Washington, DC 20210
202–208–7018

U.S. Department of Education
Office of Vocational and Adult
   Education
330 C Street, SW
Washington, DC 20202
202–260–9576

Social Studies

Expectations of Excellence: Curriculum
   Standards for Social Studies
National Council for the Social Studies
3501 Newark Street, NW
Washington, DC 20016–3167
800–638–0812

*General Information about Content
Standards*

Office of Educational Research and
   Improvement
National Institute on Student Achieve
   ment, Curriculum and Assessment
U.S. Department of Education
555 New Jersey Ave., NW
Washington, DC 20208
202–219–2179

RECOMMENDED RESOURCES ON MIDDLE SCHOOL RESEARCH

BLOCK SCHEDULING

The Nov/Dec 1996 issue of the Harvard Education Letter says the plunge into block scheduling is "just like starting over." "The first semester of managing 90-minute classes is like being a student teacher again, but many believe the payoff is worth it," says author Michael Sadowski, who includes WWW and non-Web resources for anyone who wants to explore block scheduling themselves. You can link to the Wasson High School site, where the school's successful switch to block scheduling is documented in detail.

If you'd like to see some real data, examine *the study on the effects of block scheduling on student performance in North Carolina high schools*. If all this weren't enough, you can find a few more chips off the block scheduling resource base here. The National Association of Secondary School Principals answers *some common questions* about blocking. And the September 1996 issue of School Administrator magazine is devoted to *block scheduling articles*. There's also a *teacher discussion about middle school block scheduling* here at Middle Web. And one middle school principal offers her plan to use a *new blocking strategy to increase student contact time*.

This ERIC article discusses ways to *schedule foreign languages on the block*. This article examines *blocking and music education*. And this $23 *book* collects some key articles on block scheduling under one cover. Also see next several entries.

The TERC Alliance offers these resources about block scheduling and teaming.

For Whom the Bell Tolls: Time Management and Block Scheduling

This cover story in *School Administrator's* issue on time management and block scheduling (March 1999) includes new research about adolescent sleep needs. Find the link on this page and a summary of other off-line stories about blocking, tri-semesters, and other teaching and time-management strategies. An article about *four-day school weeks* is also available on the Web.

Research: Block Scheduling in Junior High

This new study by a Colorado research team examines the effects of 4x4 scheduling in an unidentified middle school. The researchers used test data, grades, attendance rates, and enrollment rates in advanced high school courses to measure the block's effects. The researchers found the effects were "generally positive."

Block Schedule Strengthens Middle School

Longer instructional periods have helped this middle school on the island of St. Thomas address the achievement gap of many of its students who live in poverty. Expert mentor *comments* on changes. And a companion article offers some insights about schedule reforms.

RECOMMENDED RESOURCES ON MIDDLE
SCHOOL RESEARCH (continued)

The Copernican Plan

Education consultant Joseph M. Carroll, developer of the Copernican Plan, says the approach is not about block scheduling but the relationship between time and learning. Read his explanation in this article at the AASA website.

Intensive Scheduling

Corwin Press has published *Intensive Scheduling: Restructuring America's Secondary Schools Through Time Management* by David S. Hottenstein (1998). Order from Amazon.com.

Flexible Scheduling

NMSA's brief summary of research on flexible and block scheduling.

Looping

Links for teachers and schools interested in exploring "looping"—the practice of keeping kids and teachers together for more than one year. Also read the overview of looping in ASCD's Education Update (March 1998), *"Looping—Discovering the Benefits of Multiyear Teaching."*

Middle School Teaching That's "In the Loop"

Louisville math teacher Stacy Irvin relies on equal portions of standards-based instruction, backward lesson planning, and positive reinforcement to teach her "loopy" middle graders. A member of a team who will "loop" through three grades with the same group of students, Irvin says the looping concept holds teachers and students accountable. From "Changing Schools in Louisville" (Spring 1999).

Multiyear Teaching in Middle and High School

While multiyear teaching or looping crops up regularly at the elementary level, it is unusual at the secondary level because of added complexities. For instance, teams of teachers must work together closely over the course of two to four years, and it requires teachers to instruct complex new curriculum. But middle and high school teachers interviewed across the Expeditionary learning network said that the pros of staying with students for more than one year far outweigh the cons.

Multi-Age Grouping in the Middle School

http://www.nmsa.org/ressum15.htm
What is the rationale for multi-age grouping? How is it defined and what are its characteristics? Are there academic benefits from such an organizational configuration? The National Middle School Association explores these and other questions in this research summary.

Sixth Grade Schools

Some school systems are creating sixth-grade-only schools—for space or educational reasons, or both. Read *"Where Does Sixth Grade Belong?"* Also: a story about a *sixth-grade "center" start-up* in North Carolina and another in Wichita, Kansas.

Innovative Scheduling is Powerful

Alternative schedules may not add hours to the school day, but they can vastly improve the quality of the time students spend at school, say authors Robert Lynn Canady and Michael D. Rettig in the article, "The Power of Innovative Scheduling," published in November 1995 in *Educational Leadership*. If you're interested in nontraditional school scheduling, you may also want to read Canady and Rettig's related article in the September 1996 *School Administrator* magazine: *"All Around the Block: The Benefits and Challenges of a Non-Traditional School Schedule."*

Class Size Reduction

The WestEd regional educational laboratory publishes an e-mail newsletter about class size reduction issues, with a special focus on California, Arizona, Nevada, and Utah, "but it tries to keep a national focus." Contact Max McConkey at WestEd for more information. See our class size links for more information about the class size debate. Here's an update on California's class size initiative.

The Benefits of Small Schools

"The signals are growing stronger that a rejection of the depersonalization of schooling is under way," writes Phi Delta *Kappan* columnist Anne Lewis in this short article about recent research on small schools. "Anecdotal evidence about the benefits of smaller schools is now reinforced by quantitative data showing that student achievement, attendance, and graduation rates are higher in schools." (June 1999)

Substitute Teacher Sites

The collection of resources for long- and short-term subs will also be of interest to new and limited-experience teachers.

FAQ's about Middle Level Education

This page from the website of the National Association of Secondary School Principals answers questions about detracking, making the transition from junior high, characteristics of adolescents, the qualities of successful middle school teachers, and interdisciplinary teaming. Visit this page and find out how to join NASSP's National Alliance of *Middle Level Services.*

RECOMMENDED RESOURCES ON MIDDLE
SCHOOL RESEARCH (continued)

Innovative Block Scheduling at a Blue Ribbon Middle School

Fritsche Middle School in Milwaukee, Wisconsin is a national Blue Ribbon school dedicated to "continuous improvement." Read how Fritsche designed a block schedule to push student achievement even higher. You'll find links to their blocking scheduling discussion on this page. We've also prevailed upon Fritsche to share *their workshop notes* on MiddleWeb! *Preston Junior High* in Colorado has posted their block scheduling experiences on the web.

Making Detracking Work

Explore strategies for successful heterogeneous classrooms in this issue of the Harvard Education Letter. A text-only version is available. "Tracking and sorting practices rest on the old belief that 'some kids have it and some don't.' Schools that are detracking act out of a different system of beliefs." Also see the introduction to Anne Wheelock's book, *Crossing the Tracks* and her e-mail to *Linda,* a teacher with questions about tracking.

Grade Configurations

A research summary on various grade configurations by NMSA. Also see *"Grade Configuration: What Goes Where?"* (July 1997). This "hot topic" booklet produced by the Northwest Regional Educational laboratory explores the available research about the advantages and disadvantages of different grade configurations, including K–8, 5–8, 6–8, and 7–9. The booklet includes profiles of schools in the northwest United States that use different configurations. Very useful to anyone contemplating grade structure.

Smaller Middle Schools Could Raise Student Achievement

"Smaller Schools Create Communities with Results" concludes Sue Galletti, associate executive director of the National Association of Secondary School Principals, in this article from NASSP's "Schools in the Middle" magazine. Galleti summarizes recent research and trends. Also of interest is *this article* about the impact of smaller schools in *Catalyst* magazine.

Multi-Age Grouping in Middle School

What is the rationale for multi-age grouping? Are there academic benefits? Are there affective benefits for students? Are there problems and concerns? The National Middle School Association explores these questions in this research.

A Collection of Articles about Managing Time in School

The Spring 1999 issue of the Journal of Staff Development included these articles about time management and professional development: "Target Time Toward Teachers," by Linda Darling-Hammond; "Time Use Flows from School Culture," by Kent D. Peterson; "Apply Time with Wisdom," by Thomas R. Guskey; and "Making Time for _____."

Glossary

adviser/advisee program Daily or weekly period during which students interact with peers and teachers about personal and school-related concerns. Also called *advisement* or *advisory* program.

articulation Process by which the educational goals and curricular programs of a school system are coordinated among the various levels from preschool through high school. For example, a relationship with the elementary school is designed to make transition into the middle school easier; a relationship with the high school is designed to make transition there more comfortable and effective. Within a middle school, articulation is expected to facilitate movement between grade levels and learning levels and between continuous progress programs.

balanced/comprehensive curriculum Incorporates all three areas: essential learning skills, subject content, and personal development.

block schedule Organization of the school day into units of time that may be utilized in various ways by the school staff. A block of time allows a teacher or a team of teachers to teach a class in two or more subject areas, with the teacher or team determining the relative amount of time to be devoted to each subject, according to a daily estimate of needs. *See also* modular scheduling.

cognition Process of logical thinking.

cognitive learning Academic learning of subject matter.

common planning time Regularly scheduled time during the school day during which a given team of teachers is able to meet for joint planning, parent conferencing, or lesson preparation.

core (fused) curriculum Integration of two or more subjects; for example, English and social studies. Problem and theme orientations often serve as the integrating design. *See also* interdisciplinary program.

cooperative learning Two or more students working together on a learning task.

crisis intervention center A special center within or outside of the school designed to assist students with severe emotional problems. The center is staffed with psychologists, social workers, etc.

deductive learning Learning process that moves from larger generalizations and principles to illustrative examples and concepts.

departmentalization Students move from one classroom to another, with different teachers for each subject.

developmental physical education Instruction based on the physical development of the individual preadolescent learner, as opposed to a team sport approach.

developmental tasks Social, physical, maturational tasks regularly encountered by all individuals in our society as they progress from childhood to adolescence.

discovery learning A type of inquiry, emphasized especially in individualized instruction, in which a student moves through his or her own activities toward new learnings, usually expressed in generalizations and principles; typically involves inductive approaches. *See also* inductive learning.

early adolescence Stage of human development generally between age 10 and 14 when individuals begin to reach puberty.

essential learning skills Basic skills, such as reading, listening, and speaking, introduced in the elementary schools that must be reinforced and expanded within the middle school curriculum.

exploration Regularly scheduled curriculum experiences designed to help students discover and/or examine learnings related to their changing needs, aptitudes, and interests. Often referred to as the *wheel* or *miniclasses*. *See also* minicourses.

feedback Evidence from student responses and reactions that indicates the degree of success being encountered in lesson objectives. Teachers seek feedback by way of discussion, student questions, written exercises, and test returns.

formal operations Higher-level thinking skills; moving from concrete to abstract.

fundamental intermediate school Middle-grades school that emphasizes basic skills, dress codes, strict adherence to discipline, and parental involvement.

heterogeneous grouping Student grouping that does not divide learners on the basis of ability or academic achievement.

homogeneous grouping Student grouping that divides learners on the basis of specific levels of ability, achievement, or interest. Sometimes referred to as *tracking.*

house leader Educator who will act as a liaison between and among teams and other houses (units). This person reports directly to the principal.

house plan Type of organization in which the school is divided into units ("houses"), with each having an identity and containing the various grades and, in large part, its own faculty. The purpose of a house plan is to achieve decentralization (closer student–faculty relationships) and easier and more flexible team-teaching arrangements.

independent study Work performed by students without the direct supervision of the teacher so as to develop self-study skills and to expand and deepen interests.

inductive learning Learning that results when individual concepts in examples and illustrations lead to larger generalizations and principles.

innovations New instructional strategies, organizational designs, building rearrangements, equipment utilizations, or materials from which improved learning results are anticipated.

integrated curriculum Translation of the concepts of core subject areas into meaningful relationships for students.

interdisciplinary program Instruction that integrates and combines subject matter ordinarily taught separately into a single organizational structure.

interdisciplinary team Combination of teachers from different subject areas who plan and conduct coordinated lessons in those areas for particular groups of pupils. Common planning time, flexible scheduling, and cooperation and communication among team teachers is essential to interdisciplinary teaming.

interscholastic program Athletic activities or events whose primary purpose is to foster competition between school and school districts. Participation usually is limited to students with exceptional athletic ability.

intramural (intrascholastic) program Athletic activities or events held during the school day, or shortly thereafter, whose primary purpose is to encourage all students to participate regardless of athletic ability.

learning center Usually a large multimedia area designed to influence learning and teaching styles and to foster independent study. Also called a *learning station.*

magnet program A specialized school program usually designed to draw minority students to schools that historically have been racially segregated.

metacognition Process by which individuals examine their own thinking processes.

middle school A school in between elementary and high school, housed separately and, ideally, in a building designed for its purpose, and covering usually three of the middle school years, beginning with grade five or six.

minicourses Special-interest (enrichment) activities of short duration that provide learning opportunities based on student interest, faculty expertise, and community involvement. Also called *exploratory courses, short-interest-centered courses,* or *electives.*

modular scheduling The division of the school day into modules, typically 15 or 20 minutes long, with the number of modules used for various activities and experiences flexibly arranged.

nongraded organization System in which grade levels are abandoned and students move upward in continuous progress, associating in every subject field with other students who are at approximately the same point of development.

performance objectives Purposes pursued by the teacher expressed in terms of pupil behaviors, which in themselves act as evidences that the purposes have been achieved.

personal development Designed to foster intellectual, social, emotional, and moral growth of students through such programs as adviser/advisee, developmental physical education, and minicourses.

process-pattern learning Learning design that focuses on each student's experience rather than on a predetermined body of information.

programmed learning Materials built on a rational step-by-step development basis, usually presented in the form of a workbook or for use in a teaching machine, designed for independent study and learning. Emphasis is on subject-matter development.

scope The parameters of learning; for example, a subject-matter discipline sets its own scope, often by grade level.

self-contained classroom Students are housed in one classroom, with one teacher. Variations may occur in such subjects as music, art, shops, and physical education.

sequence The organization of an area of study. Frequently the organization is chronological, moving from simple to complex. Some sequences are spiraled, using structure, themes, or concept development as guidelines. A few schools use persistent life situations to shape sequence.

special learning center Instructional center that provides programs for special-needs students.

staff development Body of activities designed to improve the proficiencies of the educator–practitioner.

subject content A type of curriculum that stresses the mastery of subject matter, with all other outcomes considered subsidiary. The school may employ tracks, units within subjects, and ability grouping. Despite recent shifts from encyclopedic learning to structural recognition (e.g., from facts to understanding), the central focus at many traditional schools remains subject-matter mastery. Also called *subject-matter curriculum*. See also *homogeneous grouping*.

support personnel Ancillary personnel such as guidance, media, custodial, clerical, social services persons who help facilitate the instructional program.

systematic observation A method of observing teaching practices in a classroom using an observation instrument such as the Flanders System of Interaction Analysis.

team house Designated self-contained section or area of the school that contains a team of teachers and their assigned students to maximize feelings of team identity and minimize unproductive movement of students from class to class.

team-oriented course Emphasis is placed on the principles that hold the subject together. The micropedagogy of textbook teaching is changed to the macropedagogy of underlying principles.

team teaching Method of teaching that utilizes teacher strengths and allows teachers to work flexibly with individuals and with small or large groups. Also referred to as *teaming*.

time-out room Designated area in which disruptive students can receive specialized instruction under the guidance of a single teacher. Students sent to a time-out room are a step away from out-of-school suspension.

transescence The period in human development that begins in late childhood prior to the onset of puberty and extends through the early stages of adolescence.

TTT (Teachers Training Teachers) Inservice process by which teachers receive instruction from peers, usually at the school level.

unified arts Usually a grouping of subjects including art, music, industrial arts, drama, homemaking, and so forth, for which a time is scheduled with a team of teachers organizing the pupils into groups.

unified studies An approach to curriculum design in which a unifying theme is used to tie together many subjects; for example, the theme "conservation" could attract contributions from many fields. Often, team teaching is used for this type of organization. Also called *broad themes* or *broad-unit topics*.

unstructured time Time used for independent study, individual projects, and open laboratory activities. The student assumes responsibility for his or her own learning.

wing plan A number of classes at the same grade, housed in close proximity to each other, usually facilitating a horizontal interdisciplinary team-teaching arrangement. A wing plan can be part of a house plan.

work study Program that allows students to work outside the school during a portion of the school day.

About the Authors

Drs. Jon Wiles and Joseph Bondi have been active in the American middle school movement since the mid-1960s. Together, as Wiles, Bondi and Associates, Inc., they served middle schools in 40 states and seven foreign nations. Dr. Wiles serves as professor of education at the University of North Florida while Dr. Bondi holds a similar position at the University of South Florida.

Wiles and Bondi are the authors of a number of widely used texts in education, including *Curriculum Development: A Guide to Practice* (5th edition, 1998), and *Supervision: A Guide to Practice* (5th edition, 2000). They are the authors of another 12 books and approximately 30 monographs on educational leadership, teaching, and the process of change in education. Their monograph *Making Middle Schools Work* (ASCD, 1986) is the second most widely purchased book on middle school education after *The Essential Middle School,* the name carried by this book during the first two editions.

Name Index

Subject Index